God, Gold, and Governance

God, Gold, and Governance

The New Triad of Power in the U.S.A.

"From Democracy to Autocracy"

How Faith, Finance, False Rhetoric, Fascist Elements, and Far-Right Political Ideology, Fused Together to Flip the Moral Compass of a Nation.

Michael R Mundy

First edition published 2025 by Michael R Mundy

Typesetting & interior layout: Pickawoowoo Publishing Group
Cover Design: Laila Savolainen, Pickawoowoo Publishing Group

A catalogue record for this book is available from the National Library of Australia

ISBN 13: 978-0-987622-86-0 (paperback)
ISBN 13: 978-0-987622-87-7 (hardcover)
ISBN 13: 978-0-987622-88-4 (ebook)

Table of Contents

"The Matrix is an algorithmic tapestry woven from fear and conformity; only through courage and effort can we unravel its threads and weave a new reality. The Matrix thrives on our inaction; however when we choose to confront our fears and challenge the status quo, we can become the hackers of our own existence. Awakening is not a single moment, but a journey of relentless questioning and courageous action; the red pill is just the first step on that path. To awaken from the illusion, one must first dare to swallow the red pill of truth, for only then can the chains of falsity and complacency be broken."

FROM THE AUTHOR

THE MATRIX OF OUR EXISTENCE.

> "The illusion of the Matrix can only be shattered by those willing to confront their own shadow personalities. To change the world, we must first change ourselves. For whilst the Matrix reflects our collective psyche, the process of psychological transformation and as such a personal "sense of reality switch", begins first and foremost, within each individual soul."

In a broad sense, the illusion of the Matrix can be defined as "a grouping of systems and structures that shape our thoughts, behaviours, and expectations". It includes societal norms, cultural expectations, educational institutions, religious influences, corporate structures, political systems, the media, podcasters, social media influencers, and even the commentary of our everyday friends and family.

In the first episode of the film trilogy The Matrix, lead character Neo was given the option of taking a "red pill", which would enable him to understand what was occurring outside the illusion created by the Matrix, or alternatively a "blue pill", which would allow him to return to experiencing only that illusion he had become familiar with. Because he chose the "red pill", Neo became aware for the first time of the oppressive, parasitic nature of the Matrix that he was immersed in.

The red pill and the blue pill are metaphorical terms representing the choice currently facing all individuals, particularly in this present day, between a personal psychological awakening through "learning an unsettling or life changing truth by taking the red pill", or alternatively remaining in the reasonably contented, even though at times chaotic experience of the current ephemeral ordinary reality by choosing the blue pill.

In The Matrix, taking the "red pill" symbolizes awakening to "uncomfortable truths", a willingness to see through illusions, to face harsh realities, and to live authentically, no matter the cost. It is about "real enlightenment". However, in today's world, a "counterfeit red pill" has emerged: a simulacrum of awakening that actually misinforms and misleads.

The Matrix could be described as the algorithm of our ephemeral / indeterminable existence, especially if you view reality as a construct governed by unseen forces, whether technological, oligarchal, philosophical, religious, or metaphysical. In this sense, the Matrix represents the coded framework that structures our faculty of perception, the way we look at things, and the way we respond to things, much like an algorithm dictates digital processes.

If we extend this metaphor, we see that our transient experiences, encompassing our emotions, desires, struggles, and subsequent reactions and behaviours, are merely variables within this grand algorithm, processed and shaped by external systems of varying levels of influence, some major, some minor, some consequential, some inconsequential.

Whether those systems are technological such as in AI and surveillance capitalism, or political, as in oligarchic control, or even spiritual as in religious doctrine, fate or karma, depends on the perceptive lens through which we view reality. If you continually perceive reality as a constant struggle, then guess what, your reality will always be a constant struggle, for "as a man thinketh in his heart, so is he."

We too, in the year of 2025, live inside a matrix, and the hegemonic power of the matrix has only strengthened since the tragic circumstances on September 11, 2001, seeing lies being repeated by political leaders, media broadcasters, religious figures, and everyday podcasters over and over again, until they are accepted as truth.

And regardless of the type of hegemony, whether it be political, ideological, financial, economic, religious, military, social, or digital media, that a person, group, or class of people control over a nation or region, that hegemonic person or institution has the potential to dramatically influence the culture of the region, and with that the moral behaviour of the citizens who live there.

In the quiet corners of our bustling lives, in this our ephemeral reality, where the cacophony of modern life drowns out the whispers of the soul, echoing from the indeterminable reality within, a profound cognitive dissonance emerges. Cognitive dissonance is the discomfort or sense of uneasiness that a person feels when their behaviour in their "ephemeral reality" does not align with their psychologically embedded values or beliefs in their "indeterminable reality", the soul within.

Cognitive dissonance is a psychological phenomenon that occurs when a person holds two contradictory beliefs at the same time, leading to what a lay person, a person who is not a member of a given profession, might describe as "having a crisis of conscience." But this is not a bad thing, it can be a necessary alert, emanating from a higher source of wisdom.

Right now this chaotic world we live in is in dire need of just that, "a deliberate individual and collective response to this ever-increasing crisis of conscience." Everyone needs to, right now, take a deep breath, and then take a read of their own personal moral compass, and ask themselves is it pointing true north or pointing south. A personal moral compass is an individual's internal guide that helps them distinguish right from wrong and make ethical decisions.

It is shaped by values, beliefs, life experiences, culture, educational levels, and upbringing, and it influences how a person behaves, treats others, and responds to moral dilemmas. To pause for a moment and take a read of oneself, of one's own personal moral compass, this act in itself can be a catalyst for personal, political, and social change in the collective ephemeral reality. So what do I mean by ephemeral reality?

The "ephemeral reality" refers to the transient and fleeting nature of certain circumstances and phenomena. This reality is characterized by its temporality and the notion that certain aspects of our world, whether they be in nature or simply in the current personal, physical, psychological, interactional, relational, and social experiences we have each day, are in a state of constant flux.

And as the ancient King Solomon said in his intent to create a phrase that would always be true, whether times are good or bad, "this (ephemeral reality) too will pass".

The "indeterminable reality" on the other hand is that invisible intelligence which will always exist, which will never pass, which many refer to as the Divine or the sacred, and others simply refer to as God.

It is that same invisible intelligence that "underpins our ephemeral reality"; and that same invisible intelligence that through our "inner voice of conscience" beckons us to look beyond the visible surface of our lives, and to look past, in a type of progressive visionary mode, the chaotic circumstances that surround us, in this our present seemingly oppressive parasitic Matrix in play.

There is a phrase used quite often which says, "without a progressive vision, you will dwell carelessly". The phrase is not a direct quote, but a paraphrase of the words of an ancient prophet who said, "where there is no vision, the people perish". His words emphasise the importance of a guiding vision for individuals and societies to avoid straying and living without purpose.

It highlights the consequences of lacking a vision or a clear direction. The original text translates to: "where there is no vision, the people cast off restraint". This means that without a guiding vision, people tend to lose control, act without purpose or regard for consequence, and live without a sense of direction or as equally important, restraint.

The Constitution of the United States is then you could say, the "vision of the founding fathers," written down in law to guide the future generations, "to give the American people moral, psychological, and societal direction. As such when it is set aside by individuals or groups, chaos assuredly follows, as the guardrails of The Constitution, those "enshrined into legislated shackles of restraint" are wilfully and consciously cast aside.

We navigate a world steeped in the "ephemeral reality", a realm defined by fleeting moments and transient experiences. Here our senses, being our sight, smell, hearing, taste, and touch, reign supreme, guiding us through a landscape of desires, ambitions, and emotions, propelled along by our relentless pursuit, but never completely satiated longing for pleasurable or happy experiences, or even just "peace."

Yet, as we chase the shimmering illusions of momentary pleasure, success, happiness, and fulfillment, many times we find ourselves ensnared in a cycle of discontent, our moral compass spinning wildly in the chaos of a world that seems to have lost its way.

The decline of our moral compass is not merely a symptom of societal decay; it reflects our disconnection from the "indeterminable reality", that same invisible intelligence that not only underpins our ephemeral reality, but in times of crisis, whispers truths that transcend the limitations of our senses, urging us to reconnect with the deeper essence of our existence.

In this realm, morality is not merely a set of rules dictated by a person, a religion, or a government, but a profound understanding of our interconnectedness, a recognition that every single one of our thoughts and our actions, ripple through the fabric of the universe eternally.

As we stand at the crossroads of these two realities, particularly at this time of political and social unrest, and economic distress, we are faced with a choice: to remain ensnared in the ephemeral, our current transient existence, or in the way of the visionary, to seek the knowledge, understanding, and wisdom that lies beyond. And that may involve a personal psychological awakening through "learning an unsettling or life changing truth", perhaps minor, perhaps major, by taking the Matrix's metaphorical red pill.

In our unquenchable quest for change, whether personal, political or social, we may at times be forced to confront the uncomfortable truths that lie beneath the surface of our lives. Many people will just give up at the start and naively take the blue pill. But the true test of our moral character is whether we have the courage to listen to that inner voice and subsequently act on its promptings.

Do we take the red pill, and swallow and digest that red pill. Or perhaps even take the red pill, but shortly thereafter when regret waves its checkered flag in our face and doublemindedness overcomes us, spit the red pill out, purely because our desires and personal ambitions are being potentially threatened by the contents of the red pill, the unsettling truth it contains.

And the rejection of the red pill in favour of the blue pill, can come about for either of two reasons. It can be because of ignorance, or it can be because of cognitive dissonance, depending on the person.

Some people take the blue pill because they are unaware that an alternative reality exists, or an alternative truth exists, this is "ignorance in the purest sense". They don't know that there is "a truth to be found", so they continue within the illusion simply because they see no reason to question it.

Others, however, may have glimpsed the red pill reality, but choose to reject it because it threatens their sense of self, comfort, or stability, or even their hereditary psychological, religious, or political preferences.

For example if your father and his father and his father before him were all conservatives and always voted for a conservative candidate at election time, you will continue to vote for the conservative candidate regardless of "the uncomfortable truth you may be confronted with," perhaps indisputable evidence that your conservative candidate is totally unqualified, morally, intellectually, and psychologically, for the leadership position they are seeking.

This is where cognitive dissonance comes in. You may rationalise in many ways your choice to remain in the illusion, because accepting the truth would require painful changes, redefining beliefs, breaking attachments, or facing uncomfortable realities. In many ways, the blue pill is the path of least resistance and suffering, while the red pill requires courage, confrontation, growth, and sometimes suffering. The choice often depends on "how much a person values comfort and convenience over truth".

Through the pages that follow, we will embark on a journey, exploring the truth and falsity in our current ephemeral reality, both social and political. And some may find it necessary to undertake some personal reflection on their own current ephemeral reality, delving into the intricate dance between the seen and the unseen in their inner being; a mental warfare between two psychological states, a battle between truth and falsity.

In this journey, we will seek to reclaim our moral compass if it has been lost or even temporarily set aside, as we rediscover the guiding principles that can lead us back to a place of integrity, compassion, and love.

And as you journey on this intellectual and psychological pilgrimage, as you read this book, as we "rip the band aid off", as the saying goes, on your understanding of what is truly happening around you, either one of two things will happen. You, the reader, will either become more informed and with that more "fully enlightened", or alternately become increasingly sceptical and with that more "deeply offended" by what you are reading.

Be vigilant, for either one of these two emotions will emerge; the emotion of relief in discovering the truth, a type of "ah-ha" moment as Oprah Winfrey once described it, or the emotion of offence and anger in discovering a truth that is in opposition to one's long-held beliefs, whether they be political, religious, or ideological. And let's be honest, most people do find it hard to admit they were wrong, particularly in the realm of political and religious lifelong allegiances.

The path each person then takes, whether it be one of "enlightenment or personal offence", is always influenced by one's current level of consciousness, and with that one's existing state of "moral awareness," which quite often has been deeply impacted on by the intensity of the personal self-survival instincts that have over time been firmly embedded into one's thought processes. As such on their journey to truth they will come to a fork in that psychological road to truth. They will be confronted with a diverging path, and only one road can be taken.

Robert Frost (1874–1963), who was born in San Francisco, was one of the most celebrated American poets of the 20th century. Known for his vivid depictions of rural New England life and his deep philosophical themes, Frost's poetry often explored complex ideas through deceptively simple language and everyday scenes.

He once famously said, "the best way out is always through." Frost understood that trying to avoid hardship only delays the inevitable. Growth comes from facing our challenges head on, not by fleeing from them; but rather at times, when necessary, "choosing to confront the red pill of an uncomfortable truth".

But Frost wasn't just a New England nature poet, he used simple settings to tackle big questions about life, death, morality, and meaning. He is beloved for being both accessible and profound, the kind of poet whose lines stick with you long after you've read them. One of his notable works that I read in my late teens was a poem called "The Road Not Taken." The lines of that poem that have stayed in my mind ever since then, for the last sixty odd years, read as follows:

> "Two roads diverged in a yellow wood
> And sorry I could not travel both,
> And be one traveller, long I stood
> And looked down one as far as I could,
> To where it bent in the undergrowth."
> Two roads diverged in a wood,
> And I, I took the one less travelled,
> And that has made all the difference.

Frost metaphorically describes a moment of decision; the speaker comes upon a fork in the road while walking through a forest in autumn, one perhaps leading to ongoing chaos and the other perhaps leading to a new clarity. Since he can't go down both paths, he must choose one, knowing it might make a lasting impact on his journey. This scene he paints is a metaphor for the choices we face in life.

Whether it's deciding on a career, a relationship, a move to a new place, a small daily decision, or even who we choose to vote for at election time, we often find ourselves at metaphorical crossroads. It then becomes a Matrix red pill blue pill moment.

Life is full of diverging paths, and while we can't always know the outcomes in advance, what matters is how we own our choices, learn from them, and move forward with intention, rather than regret. Each decision shapes us and impacts even if just in a small way on the world around us. Even seemingly small choices such as our voting preferences can have ripple effects down the line, not just down our current personal line, but down our generational line, and our nation's generational lines.

"Truth is the foundation of democracy; without it, the edifice crumbles, allowing falsehoods to reign unchecked. In a world where truth is a rare commodity, deceit flourishes, and democracy becomes a puppet in the palms of the dishonest. The absence of truth is a fertile ground for deceit, where democracy becomes just a shadow of its potential, lost in the fog of manipulation. When the light of truth dims, the darkness of deceit spreads, suffocating the spirit of democracy and the will of the people".

PREFACE

The Demise of Democracy

...November 5, 2024.

A Milestone in the Decline of a Constitutional Republic.

Chapter Contents.

The 2024 Presidential Election, The Demise of The Democratic Process: The Legacy of Trump's First Term Presidency, The Partial Hollowing Out of Governance...Democracy's Dismantling Begins: The Potential Legacy of Trump's Second Term Presidency, The Complete Hollowing Out of Governance...Autocratic Rule Established.

"In the absence of truth, lies find refuge, cloaked in the guise of benevolence, suffocating the very essence of democracy. When truth is silenced, deceit dances freely, masquerading as virtue, while democracy withers in the shadows. Without the guiding light of truth, the noble intentions of the many can be twisted into the deceitful agendas of the few."

THE 2024 PRESIDENTIAL ELECTION, THE DEMISE OF THE DEMOCRATIC PROCESS.

On Tuesday morning, November 5, 2024, the polling booths for the 2024 United States presidential election officially opened around 6 a.m. in most states, and the race to the White House began. The day like any other day, was draped in the ordinary, yet destined to be remembered as the moment the rhythm of democracy stumbled, its harmony shattered, its melody lost.

The date was set, the polling booths had opened, and the people, some hopeful, some weary, filed in, as they had for generations, exercising the sacred right upon which the constitutional republic known as the United States of America had been built. But beneath the ritual, something had already begun to unravel. A slow, imperceptible discord, the prelude to a requiem that would soon mourn the loss of a free nation's democratic history.

They came, casting ballots with hands that once held the weight of their forefathers' dreams. Yet many did not know that the choice before them had long been made, not by them, not by the millions who placed their faith in a system they believed was still theirs to steer, but by the few who pulled the strings from gilded towers, those who measured democracy in profit margins and influence, rather than in justice and truth; and by those who had subtly, without the people's knowledge altered the algorithm of understanding that quietly guides one's choices. And so, the great masquerade began.

Outside the halls where power should have remained tethered to the will of the people, unseen hands had been manoeuvring for some time, perhaps even years, certainly since January 6th. 2021, ensuring that the day's outcome would be less a decision of the many and more a coronation of the privileged few.

The votes were counted, but the prophetic voices were ignored. The ideals of the republic, of a government of the people, by the people, and for the people, whisked away like the fading echoes of a song once sung with conviction.

And when the dust of the process settled, the music of democracy rang silent. The day the music of democracy died was not marked by fire or conquest, but by the "slow, deliberate suffocation of truth, and the exaggeration of falsehoods." And what was left was merely a grotesque shadow of governance, where policies no longer served the many, but bowed only to those with wealth and influence.

The halls of power, once adorned with the echoes of impassioned debate and the promise of progress, became tombs for the republic's soul, mortared with deceit and ambition. And the presidential portraits hanging proudly from the White House walls, of the many who governed with a benevolent agenda, were joined by the portrait of a scowling presidential imposter, set to govern with his own egregious revenge fuelled agenda.

And still, the foolish people cheered, not all, but enough. Enough to give the illusion that the successful candidate had been chosen by the many to implement an agenda for all, when in reality it was a corrupted mandate, for he was chosen by the powerful few to implement an agenda for the powerful few.

An agenda for the few which had been constructed by the few over many years; a "political project" that up until 2025 had sat in silence, waiting, just patiently waiting to emerge when the time was right; when the most psychologically malleable monocrat had materialised on the political landscape to lead the project's charge.

You see lies, repeated often enough, become indistinguishable from truth; and the "oligarchal think tank" architects of this new order understood this better than anyone; and so they patiently waited for the right candidate to come along, a type of prince of lies, a Teflon coated trickster, who thrived on flattery, one who was ready to go, one who was ready to exploit this timeless truth that "lies, repeated often enough, become indistinguishable from truth". And as such the race was won long before the starter's gun had sounded, and long before the polling booths had opened.

But still the people cheered, raising their voices in a chorus of self-praise, lifting their glasses celebrating their supposed victory; not realizing that in their ignorance of truth, and wilful acceptance of lies without question, they had unintentionally or for some intentionally, sacrificed the ideals based optimistic refrains of the Battle Hymn of the Republic, leaving a caesura, a brief silent pause in that unifying chorus, making way for a reluctant requiem of regret, a "what have we done moment" that would shortly follow.

Soon, that much-loved centuries old refrain would be replaced by a pessimistic funeral dirge, a requiem of remorse, a sombre song of lament for their own electoral complicity in contributing to the catastrophic democratic demise of their once great nation; a reflective realization for some that, in their act of complicity, they had not only initiated the death of their constitutional republic, but set off a plethora of ridicule, incredulity, and veiled laughter from every other democratic nation in the world, who understood that a political clown had been officially crowned.

On that election Tuesday, the Constitutional Republic of the United States of America began gasping its last breath, like a freshly caught flying fish floundering in a fisherman's creel, and began exiting the hallowed halls of democracy, not with a thunderous sound, as would have been witnessed if the January 6th. insurrection had been successful, no, this time it exited with a quiet, insidious, secretive transition from democracy to autocracy. And only the informed, the insightful, and those who truly cared noticed.

A government for the people had become a government for the privileged, the puppeteers pre-planned purpose coming to the surface in the Oval Office, not a purpose to serve the many, but a purpose to increase the wealth and power of the few. And in that moment, those who understood what had been lost could only watch, as history repeated its oldest refrain: that "no empire, no republic, no great experiment in self-governance is immune to the temptations of money and power".

The republic had not been overthrown, it had been bought, sold, and repurposed. And those who had orchestrated its demise stood victorious, not with swords held high, but with financial ledgers held close. Not with weapons in their hands, but with increased wealth in their pockets.

THE LEGACY OF TRUMP'S FIRST TERM PRESIDENCY . THE PARTIAL HOLLOWING OUT OF GOVERNANCE... DEMOCRACY'S DISMANTLING BEGINS.

In Donald Trump's first presidency, the United States witnessed a profound test of its institutions, not through a sudden seizure of power, but through a sustained campaign of administrative erosion, ideological capture, and loyalist consolidation.

What emerged was not a break from democracy, but a slow, grinding inversion of it: a transformation of public service into personal service, of governance into grievance. The agencies that once served the people became instruments of power staffed not by professionals, but by political puppets.

From the earliest days of his administration, Trump treated the federal government not as a steward of the common good, but as a personal fiefdom to be weaponized against critics, protected from oversight, and reshaped in his image. He didn't need to abolish institutions; he simply emptied them of their vision, and as such, their purpose.

Rather than working to strengthen the machinery of state, the Trump administration repeatedly installed unqualified or ideologically extreme individuals in key positions, or worse, left leadership posts vacant altogether.

The Environmental Protection Agency (EPA), once a bastion of science-based regulation, was led by Scott Pruitt and then Andrew Wheeler, men whose careers had been defined by hostility toward the very agency they were tasked with leading. Under their watch, environmental protections were rolled back, climate science suppressed, and public trust eroded.

At the Department of Justice, loyalty to the president was prized above the impartial enforcement of the law. Trump publicly pressured Attorney General Jeff Sessions for recusing himself from the Russia investigation, then installed William Barr, a man who redefined the DOJ's role as legal cover for executive overreach. The independence of the judiciary and law enforcement was visibly undermined.

In Homeland Security, a carousel of "acting secretaries" allowed Trump to sidestep Senate confirmations, avoiding scrutiny while pursuing policies that many career officials warned were unethical or illegal, most notoriously, the family separation policy at the U.S. Mexico border.

Autocracy rarely begins its reign with tanks; it begins with temp appointments. The proliferation of acting officials was not incidental; it was strategic. It enabled a culture of impermanence and fear, where officials served at the pleasure of the president rather than by the mandate of law. In doing so, the Trump administration created a vacuum where accountability once lived.

One of the most dangerous hallmarks of Trump's governance in his first term was the constant purge of those who refused personal loyalty, who refused to bend the knee and kiss the ring. Inspectors general, traditionally independent watchdogs, were fired or replaced when their investigations threatened to embarrass the White House. Intelligence officials were dismissed for presenting inconvenient truths. Public health officials were undermined during a global pandemic.

During the COVID-19 crisis, Dr. Anthony Fauci became a symbol of the tension between expertise and political expediency. Trump's administration sidelined scientific guidance in favour of misinformation, pressuring agencies like the CDC and FDA to alter messaging for political benefit. The U.S. response faltered, not just due to the virus, but due to a system sabotaged from within. To silence one scientist is to gamble with a thousand futures; to replace them with flatterers is to ensure scientific evidence is permanently buried.

Trump's obsession with loyalty extended even into agencies meant to be nonpartisan, including the Census Bureau, the military chain of command, and the civil service. In late 2020, a sweeping executive order (Schedule F) sought to strip civil servants of their protections and convert them into at-will employees, essentially transforming a professional bureaucracy into a patronage system. Though it was rescinded by the Biden administration, the attempt was a chilling preview of how a second Trump term might go even further.

Perhaps most revealing was Trump's approach to the rule of law. Time and again, he treated legal boundaries not as firm constraints, but as inconveniences to be ignored or reframed. He commuted sentences of loyal associates, he demanded investigations into political rivals, and he refused to concede an election, inspiring a violent attack on the Capitol itself. When truth-tellers are replaced by sycophants, policy dies and propaganda takes its place, leaving a society governed by illusion.

In the end, Trump's first presidency did not fully succeed in turning American democracy into a dictatorship. But it laid bare how fragile the guardrails were, and how easily they can be bent by someone willing to test every limit. What was once unthinkable Trump now knew could become possible. But he needed more time, perhaps a second presidency, to fulfil his autocratic ambition.

The first term of Trump's presidency proved that the destruction of democracy can happen not in the name of tyranny, but in the name of nationalism. Not through secretive plots, but through brazen spectacle. Not by abolishing laws, but by hollowing out the institutions that enforce them.

In a Donald Trump America, Presidents are not stewards, but sovereigns. In Trump's America, stewardship was replaced by self-interest, and the republic bore the cost. The danger is not merely that Trump governed this way once, but that the blueprint now exists. Future strongmen have seen how institutions can be weakened from within, how truth can be drowned in stage managed performance, and how democracy can wear a mask long after its face is gone.

The Potential Legacy of Trump's Second Term Presidency.

The Complete Hollowing Out of Governance-Autocratic Rule Established.

The blueprint has been drawn, the norms have been tested, and the consequences, minimal. What was once veiled in plausible deniability will now come wrapped in flag and fury. Donald Trump's first term was a rehearsal in institutional erosion. A second term will be a performance, unapologetic, unrestrained, and irreversible.

No longer hindered by re-election concerns, legal concerns, or illusions of deference to democratic norms, Trump 2.0 will likely be an administration driven not by policy, but by continual vengeance. Not by governance, but by domination. In his first term, Trump sought to "deconstruct the administrative state." In a second term, he won't just tear it down, he will burn it down, and in its ashes rebuild a new one in his image.

At the centre of his plan will be once again Schedule F, the executive order he drafted late in his first presidency and promised to reinstate. It would convert tens of thousands of nonpartisan civil service roles into political appointments, allowing for a mass purge of bureaucrats deemed insufficiently loyal and replacing them with ideological loyalists.

This is not speculation. Project 2025, a policy blueprint created by Trump-aligned think tanks, openly outlines this goal, with plans to "neutralize" what they call the Deep State, which ironically some would say their own think tank is a part of. The institutions won't be destroyed. They will be reprogrammed. Agencies like the Department of Justice, the FBI, and the IRS will no longer be merely pressured, they will be weaponized.

Imagine a DOJ used to investigate Trump's enemies at his behest. An IRS targeting media critics. A DHS turned against domestic dissenters. The purge will not come quietly. It will be announced, celebrated, televised. The civil service, once the ballast of American democracy, will become a battleground for ideological loyalty. Not merit, not service, not truth. Just obedience.

In a second term, Trump will no longer waste time learning the ropes. He now knows where the levers are and how to pull them. He knows which inspectors general can be ignored. He knows how to bypass Congress with acting appointments and executive orders. He knows which judges will greenlight his actions. And more crucially, he knows that impeachment, oversight, and the press can all be survived. Accountability, once dodged, becomes optional. Restraint, once mocked, becomes extinct.

His rhetoric already tells the story. Trump has referred to political opponents as "vermin." He promises "retribution against enemies on day one." He has floated mass deportations, internment camps, and the use of military power to quash protests. This is not a return to normal. It is a return to the logic of Caesar. In a second term, the propaganda machine will no longer be outsourced to Fox News and Truth Social. It will be institutionalized.

The Voice of America and other federal communication arms could be transformed into tools of state media, a copycat of Putin's playbook. The dismantling of independent journalism may no longer happen by tweet, but by policy. Regulatory bodies like the FCC could be staffed with appointees who pursue the suppression of dissenting voices under the guise of "national security". What was once a megaphone for truth now becomes a ministry of propaganda.

History tells us what follows: the rewriting of textbooks, the reshaping of civic education, the persecution of whistleblowers, the elevation of myth over fact. And the electorate, weary from crisis and chaos, may not resist, especially when the narrative promises restoration, strength, and simplicity. I trust this will not be the case.

Unlike 2017, Trump has returned to power surrounded by loyalists who know exactly what to do. Steve Bannon has already spoken of "dismantling the administrative state brick by brick." Stephen Miller is reportedly preparing immigration orders that would dwarf the first Muslim ban. Legal loyalists are drawing up documents that erase the line between executive action and constitutional restraint. And Trump himself? He no longer even pretends.

He declares he will be a "dictator on day one." He mocks democracy while simultaneously demanding its loyalty. He knows that he will not be removed. He knows that a politicized Supreme Court is likely to shield him. He knows the playbook because he wrote the first draft in his first term, even tested it, and few of his Republican constituents or Republican colleagues complained.

There was no inclination to tear the draft up and write a new one, no, rather a sense of urgency to work faster and go harder next time. The guardrails were tested in Trump's first term. In Trump's second term, they will be completely removed, whilst Trump's Republican colleagues cower in the congressional closet, eyes fixed shut, ears fully covered, conscience ignored.

If Trump's first term hollowed the institutions of governance, his second would fill them with poison. Where before there was ambiguity, there will now be intent. Where there was once plausible deniability, there will be policy. The final transformation is not just administrative, it is existential.

A democracy may survive corruption we saw that with Nixon. It may even endure incompetence. But it cannot survive sustained bad faith in its highest office. And make no mistake: Trump's second term would not be about governing America. It would be about punishing it. He has not returned to lead a government; he has returned to take ownership of it.

It is not alarmist to imagine this future. It is negligent not to. The institutions of democracy do not defend themselves. They must be defended by those who understand the stakes and are willing to act before the page turns too far and the purge becomes irreversible, except through violence and perhaps even bloodshed.

We now know how the story can unfold. The only question the American public must ask itself is, "do I want to be reading the same story when the next four years have passed, or should I play my part to rewrite the story while I still can in the present year, before it becomes irreversible".

"Spiritual apathy and intellectual neglect create a fertile ground for political corruption, where the uninformed become pawns in a game they do not understand. And in the absence of critical thought, societies merely become echo chambers of misinformation, where the loudest claims overshadow the truth. When spiritual and intellectual pursuits are abandoned, the void is filled with fear and manipulation, leading to a governance that thrives on ignorance. To combat the tide of ignorance, we must cultivate a culture of inquiry and reflection, for only then can we hope to make informed decisions that uplift society."

Introduction

God, Gold and Governance.

The New Triad of Power in The U.S.A.

Chapter Contents.

My Observations on the Moral Responsibility of the Voting Public: My Childhood Cultural Experience with The United States: My Personal Experience with the People, the Places, and the Culture of the U.S.A.: My Personal Preparation for the Writing of this Book.

"We must never forget that the tools of progress can be wielded for good or ill; it is our moral compass, not our political instincts nor our political and religious affiliations, nor our individual self needs, that will determine whether we build a better world or a fractured one. And as such, as we innovate, articulate, evolve, progress, and "elect new governments", we must always remember that the heart of humanity beats strongest when it is guided by empathy, integrity, and wisdom."

My Observations on the Moral Responsibility of the Voting Public.

In the 2016 American presidential election and subsequent midterm elections in 2022, we saw a significant mobilization of far-right Christian Nationalist candidates, particularly within the Republican Party, with many candidates emphasizing conservative Christian values, anti-abortion stances, opposition to LGBTQ+ rights, and greater governmental control of education institutions; thus appealing to a base that prioritizes religious identity and religious influence in politics over the moral responsibility of the voter.

And as such, as an avid observer of the dynamics of past and current world politics, and the influence of religion in politics, my interest was piqued to see if the same situation was occurring in the 2024 presidential campaign in the United States as occurred in those mid-term elections.

There was a time when I believed unquestionably that the arc of universal democracy though long, still bent towards justice, and I still do, but I don't think I ever fully understood in terms of lineal time's relationship with our ephemeral reality, how long the arc was or how long it would sometimes in certain social circumstances take to reach its inevitable goal of justice and freedom for all.

I thought that if given the choice, people would reach for the good, for the fair, and for the right. That people would see when confronted with two leadership choices, that the measure of a leader lay in the weight of their conscience, not in the ease of their smile, or the gait of their walk, or the volume and intensity of their rhetoric. I believed that people would easily see that policy mattered more than pageantry, and that truth carried more weight than spectacle. But the outcome of the 2024 United States presidential election proved I was wrong.

Somewhere along the way, the tide shifted. A slow, imperceptible turning at first, so gradual that I mistook it for mere turbulence in the river of political and social history. But then it became clear: the voting public had turned its gaze from substance to sensation, from the quiet integrity of the steadfast to the dazzling spectacle of the self-serving.

The moral character of the Lincoln era had become an afterthought, a relic of another generation. The careful stewardship of Abraham Lincoln was cast aside for the cunning showmanship of Donald Trump. The potential protector of the weak was drowned out by the champion of the powerful. The people did not rise up for the righteous; rather they rose up for the ruthless and the politically ambitious.

I watched as policies that shielded the vulnerable were traded for policies that rewarded the vocal; not the struggling masses, but the ones who could shout the loudest, who could turn the gears of influence with wealth, with media, with carefully constructed illusions. The ones who spoke not for the many, but for the few; those people of privilege, perched at the top of their ivory towers, peering down, moulding reality with a flick of the wrist, a soft whisper in a politician's ear, and the stroke of their pen on a cheque.

And I wondered: when did we stop electing leaders and start electing entertainers? When did we stop weighing principles and start measuring personas? When did we decide that governance was just another stage, another performance, another carefully scripted act in the theatre of power? And then I questioned myself, "well if democracy itself had become a performance, who then was writing the script and auditioning the potential political performers to headline the performance?"

What political casting director or group of political casting directors decided which person would be the lead actor or actress on the stage of government, which faces would grace the stage as supporting actors, which voices would be amplified, and which would be silenced beneath the roar of orchestrated campaign applause?

Was it the rich, those who had long since learned that wealth was not merely a measure of success, but a financial commodity to be used as a lever of control? Was it the powerful, those who sat behind closed doors, unburdened by the need for public approval or legal constraint, the Elon Musk's of their own particular era.?

I wondered who were the ones who understood that true power was not in votes cast at the ballot box, but in the hands that financed campaigns, shaped narratives, and dictated the limits of acceptable discourse? Was it the shadowy figures who, whilst smoking cigars and drinking whiskey, met in boardrooms and private retreats, whose influence stretched beyond borders, beyond governments, beyond the illusion of national sovereignty. The ones who whispered in the ears of leaders, not as advisors, but as owners.

Or was it the power-hungry, the climbers, the dealmakers, the ones who saw politics not as service, but as conquest, or just a secure well paid job? The smiling political assassins who traded principle for position. The politically ambitious person who understood that truth was malleable, that morality could be repackaged, rebranded, and resold to the highest bidder.

Perhaps even the political climber who sold their soul and began self-promoting their own credentials, not necessarily for the lead role, the main actor, that would seem overly ambitious at this stage of their political career. But perhaps in the first instance the position of understudy, basically the stand in or replacement actor should the lead actor be unable to perform, due to failing health, or the early onset of dementia, or even death due to old age.

And then I thought, "perhaps it was all three of them"; the rich oligarch, the media mogul, and the power-hungry political climber, all working together. A sort of a Musk, Murdoch, J.D. Vance type of alliance spoken and agreed on far away from the corridors of power, far away from the press spotlight, perhaps over a private dinner at Mar-a-Lago.

Was it in fact not one single interested person, but "a triad of personal interests," each with their own individual or corporate agenda, but nevertheless working together; similarly as in music a chord is made up by three notes, usually of the first, third, and fifth notes of a scale, but all working simultaneously to create one harmonious sound. Was this a type of autocratic anthem, where the rich got richer, the powerful became untouchable, and the political climber got promoted.

Perhaps it was an intricate web, woven not by a single hand, but by many hands, each strand connected, each player complicit. A symphony of self-interest, conducted by those who all knew that democracy was most useful when it could be controlled; when the people believed that they were democratically electing a government, believed they were doing the choosing whilst not for the slightest moment realising that their choices were quietly shaped, over a considerable period of time, during meetings in boardrooms and bars, and their "perceptions carefully guided" through digital algorithms and orchestrated campaign events.

And so, the public watched the spectacle, believing themselves to be the audience, never realizing that they were, in truth, complicit participants, and as such part of the problem. Their hopes, their fears, their anger, their allegiances, bought, sold, and traded like commodities on an invisible political stock exchange. A market where the currency was influence, and the highest bidders determined the course of nations.

If there was ever a moment when the people had turned away from substance, I wondered if it was truly all of their own doing, or if, long before they ever made their choice, the choice had already been made for them; "the wheels of a political project for a transition to autocratic governance" had been there all along waiting for the right political puppet to take the lead role, and perhaps even take the public punishment should the project be deemed a flop.

So it was at this stage of my adult life that I found it necessary to make a determined choice and to be disciplined every time an election drew near. No longer could I afford to be swept along by the tide of spectacle, the illusion of choice crafted by those who sought only to preserve or enhance their own purse, privilege, position and power.

I had to ask myself, with every vote, with every decision, how does this choice play out in terms of my personal moral evolution, and the collective moral evolution of the citizens of my nation, and as such: would my preferences be shaped by charisma, or by character?

Would I be swayed by the intoxicating pull of personality, or would I measure a leader by the depth of their convictions? Would my choices be underpinned by a desire for greater material gain, even if small by some standards, such as cheaper groceries, or rather by the pursuit of personal moral evolution?

Would I cast my lot with those who sought to benefit all of society, including the unseen, the unheard, the marginalised, or with those who catered only to the loudest voices, the most privileged ranks? Would I choose policies that alleviated poverty, or choose those that preserved and enhanced the continued profits of the few?

Would I support leadership that fostered unity, or one that thrived on division, stoking fear and resentment for political gain? Would I lend my voice to those who stood for justice, even when it was inconvenient, or to those who cloaked corruption in the language of patriotism and progress? Would I align with those who sought to lift the burdens of the struggling, or with those who sought only to maximize their own influence and wealth?

These were no longer abstract questions for me. They demanded answers, not just in thought, but in action. And so, I resolved that I would no longer be a passive observer of this great performance, nor a willing participant in the illusion of choice. If democracy had been turned into a stage performance, then I would not be content to be an audience member, clapping along to the rehearsed cues of the powerful and the politically impotent.

I would instead choose with intention, I would vote with discipline, I would resist the spectacle and seek out the substance, wherever it still remained. And I would become a disciplined critic both positive and negative of the political and social play as it progressed towards its inevitable intermission.

Whilst by the time this book is published, the tumultuous U.S. elections will have concluded, and as such its contents will not influence anyone's voting choices for the outcome has already been decided, the contents may however become for some, a type of reflective requiem on the death of a constitutional republic, that may influence one's voting choices in the future, if they truly value the democratic process.

The book in itself could be described as a truth telling message, for those who are seekers of truth; a truthful educational deep dive into past and present spiritual, social, and political ills, as reflected in the country that was long regarded as the greatest example in the world of the democratic process in play, the United States of America.

A reflective look at the events that witnessed the death of a constitutional federal republic, when a country once seen by all as a beacon of democracy, a fire on the political stage that burned brightly domestically and internationally, began slowly morphing into just a flickering ember of its former self.

But even more importantly perhaps the book's contents will become a clarion call to those who have open hearts and minds and limited preconceived bias, as to what can happen at any time in the future in any democratic nation of the world, no matter how great it has been, when current personal passions, past prejudices, political ideologies, and religious insecurities clash. In this context, the decline or ascension of the individual and collective moral compass, will be self-evident in the election result.

When I first mentioned on Facebook and in personal conversations that I was writing a book about politics, particularly in relation to the current state of politics in the United States, I received a quantity of mixed, what you could even describe as questioning reactions from some friends, the most common one being, "as an Australian what would you know about America or the American people", which I did feel came with an overtone of annoyance embedded in its digital tone, not reflective of the "Christian persona" they had displayed in previous posts they had made.

So in relation to that question, "what would you, an Australian know about America or the American people," to put that to bed, in this Introduction I will give you some details on "My Childhood Cultural Experience with The United States," and full details on "My Adult History with the People, the Places, and the Culture, of the U.S.A."

Perhaps the detail I share may also give American readers greater insight into the magnificent cultural, social, and political history of their great nation that they have been previously unaware of, history which must never be erased by those who whilst professing to be patriots pursue a self-interested political power and financial agenda.

This book is not a political statement, nor an utterance of support for any particular political party, political policy, or any specific candidate; and it must be noted that I hold no political allegiances or religious ideological bias; my only bias is towards truth.

As such, many times I will call out political or religious figures whose behaviour and rhetoric evidence a devolved state of moral awareness in full play, and a deliberate distortion of truth, similarly as we see in the New Testament with Jesus calling out the hypocrites. Be aware that at this stage of reading one may have, as per the Matrix, "a red pill, blue pill" moment, one may have to face an uncomfortable truth.

Jesus called some of the critics of his teachings hypocrites, whitewashed tombs, meaning those who appear righteous outwardly but are morally corrupt inside, and he called them serpents, a brood of vipers, condemning them as spiritually dead and leading others astray.

Jesus's main issue with these groups was not just their leadership, but their hypocrisy, appearing pious while exploiting others, focusing on legalistic rituals while neglecting justice, mercy, and faithfulness. This type of behaviour can similarly be seen in this modern day with several supposed Christian members of Congress displaying those same hypocritical tendencies, and as such if they have come under my radar in the preparation of this book, I will call them out.

America stands at a precipice. A nation once guided by democratic ideals and a shared moral compass now finds itself in the grip of chaos, deception, and deepening divisions. This book you could say is an unflinching exploration of power, ideology, and corruption, detailing how far-right extremism, oligarchic greed, and political authoritarian ambition have converged to reshape the political and social fabric of the United States.

Drawing parallels between today's political turbulence and the upheavals of the 1960's, we will examine together how the forces of Christian Nationalism, Evangelicalism, White Supremacy, and Neo-Fascism have been systematically woven into conservative politics, fuelling a new Republican movement that erodes democratic institutions and threatens fundamental freedoms.

Whilst behind the scenes, a shadow network of billionaires and corporate interests bankroll this radical shift, leveraging economic power to manipulate governance and reshape society to serve their own greed filled and power-driven ambition.

For many readers who are puzzled as to how and why America has got to this point of chaotic political governance the contents of this book will "join the dots" for you. It will reveal that it wasn't just by accident, it was the result of years of clandestine, behind closed doors planning.

It will join the dots between the Republican Party and Christian Nationalism the religious far-right, (formerly the Moral Majority), and the links between that same Christian Nationalism (Moral Majority Movement) and the architects of

Project 2025, the blueprint for a new type of conservative government, that is currently being enacted in the White House under the supervision of Elon Musk.

It will reveal the close links between Project 2025 and Vice-President J.D. Vance, the links between J.D. Vance and Elon Musk, and the link between the aforementioned conglomerate and the influential Silicon Valley technogarchy, (my term), which includes Musk and his influential X platform, and Zuckerberg and his algorithmically manipulated, result predetermined, Facebook platform.

And for the eternally curious this book will reveal the methods Donald Trump has used consistently throughout his whole life, and still using, to deceive a gullible person or a gullible voting public. The same methods that saw him gain a second term as president.

As such I would urge all readers who have been caught up in the myth that is Donald Trump, to carefully psychologically digest the contents of Chapter 7, The Gospel of Roy Cohn the Master, and Donald Trump his Apprentice: The Great Lie, The Myth of Donald the Dealmaker, and the contents of Chapter 8, The Anatomy of Trumpism, a Political Cult, The Myth, The Man, The Truth.

It will bring clarity to so much that the American people, and the world have been confused about, regarding truth and falsity, and how both these platforms of dialogue pertain to Donald Trump's rhetoric and behaviour; for many also it will be a Matrix, red pill blue pill moment, an "am I prepared to accept an uncomfortable truth," or am I happy to keep embracing the mythical illusion I have regarding the ability and integrity of Donald Trump. And it will also answer the question that most people have asked at some stage or other when watching him in interviews. Is what he just said true?

In I guess what you could describe as a specific targeted way, this book, God, Gold, and Governance will expose the hidden mechanisms driving America's current moral, institutional, and democratic decline. It will reveal how faith is weaponized for political gain, how economic power is wielded to subvert democracy, and how falsehoods are propagated to manufacture consent for autocratic rule. This is more than a book; it is a call to recognize the forces at play before they irrevocably alter the nation's moral and political trajectory.

My Childhood Cultural Experience with The United States.

I have always had an affinity with and an affection for the people and culture of the United States, and a special interest in the political history of the country, having spent a lot of time there over the years getting to know the demographics and the political, spiritual, and social history of this "land of the free and home of the brave."

As a child growing up in Australia in the fifties, and as a teenager growing up in the sixties, I journeyed towards adulthood sustained psychologically on a steady diet of Americana. It would not be until around five decades later, that I came to realize that it was that psychological Americana diet of my pre-teen and teenage years, more than anything else, that created a platform of moral awareness in my ephemeral reality, that has remained present for all of my adult life.

What do I mean by a psychological Americana diet? Americana is any collection of materials and things concerning or characteristic of the United States or of the American people and is representative or even stereotypical of American culture as a whole.

Studies have shown that by exposing a child around age 7 and beyond, (pre-teen and teenage years) to stories that emphasize integrity, honesty, and justice, it can have a significant, lasting impact on their moral development and as such their future decision-making process as an adult.

Middle childhood, ages 7 to 11, have been proven to be a critical stage of the child's psychological development, seeing the child's thinking process shift from "black and white morality" to "intent-based morality". Research also suggests that middle childhood is when moral identity begins forming, when children start integrating moral values into their self-concept, and as such exposure to narratives with admirable role models helps children's associate virtues like honesty and justice with their own personal identity.

As a child I consumed an ongoing diet of American literature, American produced television shows, and American produced movies. All of which I now realise contributed in a positive way to my cognitive development and as such my ongoing state of moral awareness.

I grew up reading and collecting American super-hero comics such as Superman, Batman, the Phantom, Mandrake the Magician, and The Shadow, their personas and stories created by gifted American writers and artists. Then later in my teens I would add reading certain American novels to my educational experience, such as Mark Twain's The Adventures of Tom Sawyer, and his The Adventures of Huckleberry Finn, and Stephen Crane's The Red Badge of Courage, which had a particular impact on me.

Throughout his works, Twain used the Mississippi River as "a powerful symbol of freedom, adventure, and societal contrast". In Huckleberry Finn, the river represents both "escape and moral discovery" as Huck and Jim travel along it. Later in life, Twain lamented the transformation of the river due to industrialization, railroads, and changing times.

The overall theme of "The Red Badge of Courage" by Stephen Crane is the psychological impact of war, particularly the internal struggle between courage and fear. It is a psychological exploration of a young soldier's coming-of-age amidst the horrors of war. The novel follows Henry Fleming, a young soldier in the American Civil War, as he grapples with his expectations of heroism versus the brutal reality of combat.

Its key themes include courage versus cowardice, the reality of war, isolation and identity, and nature's apparent indifference. Henry the lead character initially flees from battle out of fear but later seeks a "red badge of courage" (a wound) to prove his bravery. The author Stephen Crane frequently contrasts human emotions with the indifferent natural world, emphasizing the insignificance of individual struggles in the grander scheme. This would influence me later in life to explore more deeply the life of President Abraham Lincoln.

After my pre- teens I switched from reading comics in the evening to watching television when it came to Australia in 1956. I lived on a television diet of classic American productions. The classic television shows I primarily watched were released during the 1950's and 1960's and often reflected the cultural and entertainment trends of the time, particularly in the Western and comedy genres, all laced with some sort of moral or social perspective. Some of these were:

The Beverly Hillbillies (1962–1971), a sitcom comedy about the Clampett family, a group of poor rural Southerners who strike it rich when they discover oil on their land. They move to Beverly Hills, California, where their "simple, humble country ways clash humorously with the lifestyles of the wealthy elite".

The Life and Legend of Wyatt Earp (1955–1961), a western, a dramatized version of the life of Wyatt Earp, a famous lawman of the Old West, set in various frontier towns, including Dodge City and Tombstone. It followed his efforts to "bring law and order" to dangerous territories, featuring historical figures like Doc Holliday.

Gunsmoke (1955–1975), one of the longest-running American Western series, whose weekly storyline followed the life of Marshal Matt Dillon, a lawman in Dodge City, Kansas, as he "enforced justice and dealt with criminals, outlaws, and personal conflicts" in the American frontier. Tombstone Territory (1957–1960), a western set in the infamous town of Tombstone, Arizona. The show followed Sheriff Clay Hollister as he "tries to maintain law and order in a town filled with outlaws, gunfighters, and gamblers".

And The Rifleman (1958–1963), a western, which centred on Lucas McCain, a skilled marksman and widowed father raising his son, Mark, in the town of North Fork, New Mexico. He frequently has to defend himself and his township both verbally and physically using his modified Winchester rifle.

These shows among others, were instrumental in shaping American and subsequently Australian television, but more importantly to me I believe instrumental in shaping my personal psychological makeup, educating me on what it means to live in a fair and just society, and "what is necessary for us to do to create and continue to maintain a fair, just, and lawful society."

Harvard's "Making Caring Common" Project found that early exposure to moral storytelling increases prosocial behaviour in adulthood. If a child's early exposure to television shows primarily featured Westerns with lawmen, or superhero characters for example Superman, Batman, Mandrake, and The Phantom, it is highly likely that these narratives would shape their moral framework in adulthood. It found that stories that emphasize justice, integrity, duty, and personal sacrifice, can profoundly influence a child's developing sense of right and wrong.

Carl Jung and Joseph Campbell's work on archetypes and the hero's journey also suggests that these classic characters deeply influence the way we see the world. Children who grow up idolizing lawmen and superheroes tend to develop strong ethical identities, often holding themselves and others to high moral standards.

These television Wild West lawmen uphold the law in lawless lands, portraying moral certainty, and demonstrating courage to confront evil regardless of the risk to themselves. Americana superhero figures also like Superman, Batman, and the Phantom, live by strict codes of honour, reinforcing values like honesty, justice, and self-sacrifice. Early exposure to these strong moral archetypes can solidify a child's belief in moral absolutes, which may guide them in ethical dilemmas later in life.

Research on autobiographical memory suggests that childhood moral lessons stored in long-term memory resurface in adult moral dilemmas, influencing real-world choices. So if a child's early exposure to television shows primarily featured Western heroes or Superheroes it is highly likely that these narratives would shape their moral framework in adulthood.

Apart from American comics and American television my next favourite pastime was American cinema. As a child and later as a teenager every Saturday afternoon I would walk to our local Lutwyche Picture Theatre as the cinemas of the day were called, to see my favourite American movie stars in their latest productions. Amongst many American productions that I saw, with a moral or social principle underpinning the storyline were Classic Cinema Films, such as:

War and Peace (1956). War and Peace was based on Leo Tolstoy's epic novel, titled War and Peace. This drama followed the lives of aristocratic families in Russia during Napoleon's invasion. The film centres on Natasha (Hepburn), Pierre (Fonda), and Prince Andrei (Ferrer) as they navigate "love, war, and personal growth".

Gone with the Wind (1939). The plot is set during the American Civil War and Reconstruction era. The story follows the fiery Southern belle Scarlett O'Hara (Leigh) and her tumultuous romance with the dashing Rhett Butler (Gable). It explores themes of "survival, love, and loss".

And Giant (1956). A sprawling epic about Texas rancher Jordan "Bick" Benedict (Hudson), his marriage to Leslie (Taylor), and their generational conflicts with the rising oil tycoon Jett Rink (Dean). The film explores themes of "wealth, racial discrimination, and social change over several decades".

My Personal Experience with the People, the Places, the Culture, and the Political and Military History of the U.S.A.

Then came my progression into adulthood, and my personal on the ground experience with American people , places, culture, and political and social history began. In my desire to get to know more about the history and culture of this nation, once described as the greatest and most powerful democratic nation in the world, during my adult life I have visited the United States of America five times in both a personal and a work capacity. And it was at these times I increasingly grew to love the American people and the indomitable spirit of democracy they and their country represented.

Over the years I have visited numerous cities in various states including: Los Angeles in California, (the City of Angels), San Diego in California, (America's Finest City), San Francisco in California, (the Golden State), Chicago in Illinois (The Windy City), Deadwood in South Dakota (The Queen of the Hills), Rapid City in South Dakota (The Gateway to the Black Hills of Dakota), Las Vegas in Nevada (Sin City-The Entertainment Capital of the World), Flagstaff in Arizona (The City of Seven Wonders), Boston in Massachusetts (The Cradle of Liberty), and Washington, D.C. (The Nation's Capital).

I have spent time in Philadelphia, Pennsylvania, (The City of Brotherly Love), Orlando in Florida (The Theme Park Capital of the World), Denver in Colorado, (The Mile High City), Saint Louis Missouri, (The Gateway to the West), Nashville Tennessee, (Music City), Memphis Tennessee, (The Home of the Blues), New Orleans in Louisiana, (the Big Easy), Anchorage in Alaska, (The City of Lights and Flowers), Northern Virginia (The Gateway to the South), and I have also spent time in The Big Apple, New York, also known "The City That Never Sleeps", because of its 24/7 energy and activity.

In search of gaining a greater understanding of America's political history, I have visited the solemn yet awe-inspiring Lincoln Memorial in Washington, D.C. which houses an iconic, massive statue of Abraham Lincoln, the 16th president of the United States; a tribute to the president who defended American democratic ideals with heroism, against those who demonised American democratic ideals with hubris. A visit that was the catalyst for a deeper study of the life and political times of Abraham Lincoln later in my adult life.

The enormous sculpture sits in the heart of the memorial chamber and conveys both solemnity and strength. Some interpret Lincoln's gaze as imaged on the sculpture as being watchful yet compassionate, looking over the democratic nation he sought to govern with fairness and equity, and fought tirelessly to preserve.

I have visited the heroic yet solemnly shadowed Washington War Memorial, and the reverent yet heartbreakingly vast Arlington Cemetery. Established during the American Civil War in 1864, Arlington Cemetery serves as the final resting place for over 400,000 military service members and their families, as well as the World War 2, Korean War and Vietnam war veterans. The memorial honours those who served and sacrificed in these conflicts.

And I have visited and stood in a quiet state of reflection at the site of the 911 terrorist attacks in New York city. During the 9/11 attacks 343 firefighters from the New York City Fire Department (F.D.N.Y.) lost their lives while responding to the attacks and attempting to rescue people from the Twin Towers. The total number of people killed in the attacks was 2,977, not including the 19 hijackers.

I visited the site prior to the construction of the memorial to the victims which commenced in 2006. At the time I visited it was just an enormous gaping hole in the ground. And I reverently paused at the makeshift heartfelt memorial on the perimeter of that hole, containing flowers, and personal photos of many citizens who were killed, plus the remnants of some burnt firefighting equipment used at the site.

A memorial that had been put in place by a group of grieving citizens, in honouring those heroic firefighters who died trying to save their fellow American citizens.

Shortly thereafter I stood in the snow in Central Park New York beside the John Lennon Memorial called Strawberry Fields, which sits directly across from the Dakota Building, where this gifted musician and composer Lennon lived, and where he was tragically shot in 1980. I paused in reflection at the expanse of red roses scattered by visitors as they sought to acknowledge his creative genius.

The "IMAGINE" mosaic, as it is known, is the main feature, a tribute to Lennon's famous song, donated by the City of Naples, Italy. Designated as a Garden of Peace it is often visited by fans from around the world leaving flowers, candles, and tributes, many of the same fans gathering here every December the 8th, the anniversary of his death, and October the 9th his birthday, which was the date I visited, to honour him with music and reflection.

I have visited Independence Hall in Philadelphia, Pennsylvania, where the Declaration of Independence was signed on July the 4th 1776, with notable signatories to the document being Thomas Jefferson, John Adams, Benjamin Franklin, and Samuel Adams, and the Liberty Bell, at the Liberty Bell Centre in the Independence National Historical Park, another great symbol of freedom and independence.

I have also visited the iconic yet paradoxically overlooked Statue of Liberty, a colossal neoclassical sculpture on Liberty Island in New York Harbour, a gift from France to the United States in 1886, to celebrate the Centennial of American Independence.

The statue itself which stands at 93 metres from base to torch, is one of the most well-known symbols of freedom and democracy in the world, its full name being "The Statue of Liberty - Enlightening the World". The lady's left hand is inscribed with the date of the declaration, the broken chains at her feet symbolise freedom from oppression, and the torch represents enlightenment.

In terms of my interest in American social political history, I have visited the White House, as well as the U.S. Capitol in Washington D.C. that was the site of the January 6th. 2021 insurrection, which saw a violent mob of supporters of the then President Donald Trump storm the building to try to disrupt the certification of the 2020 presidential elections.

I have visited Mount Rushmore, located in the Black Hills region of South Dakota, a massive granite sculpture featuring the faces of four former U.S. presidents: George Washington, Thomas Jefferson, Theodore Roosevelt, and Abraham Lincoln. The monument symbolizes the birth, growth, development, and preservation of the United States, and honours the involvement of these presidents in pursuing the democratic principles of governance set in place by all the founding fathers.

With regards to America's social and racial cultural history I have spent time visiting various historic plantation sites in and around Nashville Tennessee, walking through the original buildings and the log cabin living quarters of the slaves, trying to get some sort of sense of what these men, women, and children experienced.

I have visited and toured the former home of President Andrew Jackson located just outside downtown Nashville, a property which offers a comprehensive look into 19th century plantation life, including the preserved log cabins where enslaved individuals lived in cramped conditions.

I have visited the Belle Meade plantation in Nashville renowned for its thoroughbred horse breeding history, which features original structures and slave quarters, providing original memorabilia and photos giving insights into the lives and living conditions of the enslaved people who lived, worked, and died on that estate.

I have spent time at historic native American Indian sites of the Sioux and Lakota Indian nations, including tributes and memorials to them; and I have paused reverently at the gravesite of Sitting Bull the famous Lakota Sioux Indian leader who defeated General Custer at the Battle of Little Big Horn, whose remains are located in the Indian Museum of North Dakota.

I have also attended the gravesites of early white lawmakers including Wild Bill Hickok at the Mount Moriah Cemetery in Deadwood South Dakota, where he is buried alongside another well-known Old West female Calamity Jane, a frontierswoman, scout, and sharpshooter.

I have ridden the historic cable cars up and down the hilly city of San Francisco, walked the 1.7 miles across the historic Golden Gate Bridge in San Francisco, and strolled casually whilst eating an ice cream along the promenade at San Francisco Bay, immortalised in Otis Redding's song, "Sittin' On The Dock of The Bay."

And I have walked the cell blocks and prisoners' lunchroom of the historic Alcatraz Prison in San Francisco, where the notorious gangster Al Capone had the privilege of being one of the first prisoners to be housed there. I was subsequently bemused when Donald Trump, during his campaign rallies frequently and you could say proudly compared himself to Al Capone when discussing the multiple legal cases against him, saying, "Al Capone, the greatest of all gangsters, he was indicted once. I've been indicted four times."

I have sat quietly in a park at Santa Monica Beach watching a black homeless man picking up scattered rubbish in the park and putting it in a shopping trolley for disposal later, whilst a white person strolled past and carelessly threw away an ice cream wrapper. And I have spent a late afternoon conversing with the homeless population of New York when they lined up for their evening meal at the mobile charity diner.

I have experienced the bitterly cold winter winds of Lake Michigan as they blew over the streets of Chicago and warmed up later in the sun at the famous baseball area called Wrigley Field named after the chewing gum founder, whilst watching the famous Chicago Cubs. I have walked the beaches of Hawaii and meditated there; I have stayed at the Hotel California, immortalised in musical history by the Eagles, and I have sunk my feet in the sands at Muscle Beach Santa Monica.

I have strolled the top of the magnificent rock formation called the Grand Canyon, in awe of its vast sprawling but towering presence and the panoramic views it proudly gives its visitors far above the winding ever flowing Colorado River. I have visited the cities of Juneau, Anchorage and Ketchikan in Alaska, and dog sledded on a glacier there.

I have admired the ingenuity of those engineers who designed the Hoover Dam in the Black Canyon of the Colorado River on the border between the U.S. States of Nevada and Arizona, and I have paused and contemplated the sacrifice of some 96 workers who died constructing it.

I have stood on a balcony overlooking the Niagara Falls gazing in wonderment at the normally fast flowing torrent of water now partly frozen in the moment in the middle of winter, huge icicles hanging like giant pencil pleats on a magnificent ice curtain.

I have gazed over the skyline of Chicago from the top of the highest building in the United States at the time, the Sears Tower, whose construction saw the deaths of five workers, and marvelled at the skyline of the City of New York from atop the Empire State Building that also witnessed the death of five workers during its construction.

I have spent time on a paddle steamer journeying along the Mississippi River in St. Louis and spent a memorable New Year's Eve celebrating on the Natchez, the historic paddle steamer in New Orleans, that floats down the mighty Mississippi River. The reason for my two different steamboat rides due to my personal admiration for the author Mark Twain, whose two books "The Adventures of Tom Sawyer" and "The Adventures of Huckleberry Finn" I read in my pre-teen years. Both books had storylines centred around the magnificent Mississippi River.

In terms of America's cultural and creative history I have visited the Guggenheim Museum of Modern and Contemporary Art, in New York city, which houses works by Picasso, Kandinsky, Van Gogh, Pollock, and Andy Warhol, as well as collections of impressionist, post-impressionist and avant-garde art; and I have browsed the Metropolitan Museum of Art in New York that houses amongst other things drawings and sketches by Leonardo da Vinci, as well as the American Museum of Natural History both located beside Central Park.

With regards to American Culture and the Creative Arts, I have attended Broadway shows such as The Phantom of The Opera, and The Jersey Boys in New York and attended the opening of Wicked in St. Louis, Missouri. I have sat in grand entertainment venues such as Caesar's Palace and the MGM theatre in Las Vegas watching gifted American entertainers such as Celine Dion and Bette Midler and enjoyed all the adventures at Universal Studios and Disneyland.

I have walked down the historic Hollywood Walk of Fame that immortalises the stars of stage, screen, and the music industry, and watched the crowds of children and adults laugh and stand in awe as the Disney characters marched by during the evening parade at Disneyland.

I have visited the Country Music Hall of Fame that houses historic memorabilia of all the great country stars of the past and toured backstage the historic Grand Ole Opry a famous country music venue and broadcast studio, based in Nashville, Tennessee; the Opry has been a cornerstone of country music since its founding in 1925, making it the longest-running radio broadcast in U.S. history, as well as showcasing live performances from country, bluegrass, folk, and gospel artists.

I have visited legendary blues clubs in New Orleans, and I have visited Blues Alley in Washington D.C. where the wonderful Eva Cassidy, recorded her Live at Blues Alley album, and died 6 months later of melanoma, at the age of 33 years. It was said of Eva, "when Eva sings, she brings calmness to people, there is a spiritual vibe about her voice that people love, especially when the world is too much for them."

I have walked the streets and stayed in accommodation in Greenwich Village in Lower Manhattan New York City, where the folk music legends of the sixties stayed. Often called "The Village," Greenwich Village is a historic neighbourhood known for its bohemian and countercultural roots. It has long been a haven for artists, musicians, writers, and political activists.

The Village became the epicentre of the Beat Generation (1950's), the folk music revival (1960's), and the counterculture movement. It also played a key role in the LGBTQ+ rights movement, notably with the Stonewall Riots of 1969, which launched the modern gay rights movement. It has been home to some of the most influential musicians of all time, particularly in folk, rock, and jazz including Bob Dylan and Pete Seeger.

I have stayed at the historic Peabody Hotel in Memphis built in 1869, home of the famous Peabody Ducks, and strolled the famous estate of Graceland, and Graceland mansion, which houses a history of the life and musical achievements of Elvis Presley, where dozens and dozens of all his framed recording awards line the walls, where a ton of Elvis memorabilia including his cars and plane are available for close inspection, and where the Meditation Garden sits.

The Meditation Garden at Graceland is a tranquil, circular space, featuring a fountain, a circular fountain pool with multiple jets of water, illuminated by coloured floodlights, a semicircular pergola, and a steeped brick wall. It serves as Elvis Presley's final resting place and the burial site for several family members.

I have toured the famous Gateway Arch in St. Louis, and I have gasped in awe as I gazed at the massive collection of mosaics of Romanesque and Byzantine architectural styles which cover nearly 83,000 square feet in the Catholic Cathedral of Saint Louis, the mother church of the Archdiocese of St. Louis. And I have marvelled at the architectural brilliance evident in the construction of the Crystal

Cathedral in Orange County Los Angeles as I gazed upwards at the beauty of this engineering marvel.

I have roamed the streets of Harlem, the historic neighbourhood in Upper Manhattan, New York City, known for its rich cultural heritage, especially in African American history, music and arts, and marvelled at the creative murals around neighbourhoods. I have joined in the joyous singing and happy clapping with the crowds of black and white parishioners at a Harlem Gospel Church service in Harlem New York City, and at a Gospel Church in New Orleans, walking out of both churches with a profound sense of warmth and belonging.

The unfiltered joy, the deep-rooted faith, and the genuine inclusivity I witnessed were unlike anything I had experienced in the more formal, institutional Christian churches, those aligned with the current Christian Nationalism brand, that I had attended over the years, where faith often felt like a rigid duty, structured, predictable, and detached.

In contrast, these mixed-race gospel congregations embraced worship as a living, breathing act of love, where music, movement, and shared devotion bound everyone together in a powerful communion of spirit. And what struck me most at the time, was that for those attending this was not just about religious practice, it was about human connection. The worshippers I encountered did not simply sit through a service; they rejoiced, they grieved, they uplifted one another.

In these spaces, faith was not a ritual to be endured but a love to be shared. Seeing this, I could not help but question what had been lost in the sterility of so many institutional churches. True faith, the true faith of these worshippers, was not found in formality, but in the open-armed embrace of community, where the love of God was felt as deeply as it was expressed.

However, even though all these things were wonderful learning journeys culturally and politically, one of the most spiritually impacting visits I made whilst in the United States was my visit to the Lorraine Motel in Memphis, Tennessee, the site of the final moments of Dr. Martin Luther King Jr.'s physical life.

The Lorraine Motel was the place where Dr. King was fatally wounded at 6.01 p.m. on April 4, 1968, as he stood on the balcony outside his motel room enjoying the early evening breeze, after spending the day advocating for civil rights for all Americans, regardless of a person's colour or creed. This visit to the Lorraine Motel led me to later in my adult life undertake some intensive study into his life and work.

Over the years all these visits have given me a greater appreciation of the country of America, the personalities of the people, the cultural history, the military history, the economic history, the political and social history, and the potential possibility for this once great beacon of democracy to bounce back, to shine forth again regardless of its current distress; to once again become the light that leads the way out of the orchestrated darkness that is currently ensnaring it.

My Personal Preparation for the Writing of This Book.

It was around April 2024, when I first felt intuitively prompted to commence writing a book on the subject matter of moral consciousness or moral awareness, using the United States presidential campaign as a backdrop into exploring the current state of moral consciousness of those candidates and supporters involved, and in a way comparing those current attitudes with the attitudes of the many people and places that I had encountered during my many visits to the United States over the years.

As a personal research exercise in preparation for the writing of this book, from April 2024 I spent much time focusing on all things associated with the 2024 presidential election in the United States. I reviewed the initial campaign launches of both Donald Trump and Kamala Harris in full, focusing on the rhetoric of all speakers involved.

I reviewed numerous public campaign rallies of Trump and Harris and the campaign rallies of Trump's Vice-Presidential ticket J.D. Vance, and Harris's Vice-Presidential ticket Tim Walz. I also specifically watched the rallies and took note of the type of rhetoric coming from both candidates and their supporters in most of the swing state campaigns, including Georgia, Ohio, North and South Carolina, and Nevada.

Further in my research I reviewed every prime-time television interview that each presidential candidate did that I could find, their television debates, their policy statements, their career history, their involvement with the judicial system, their interactions with supporters in various meet and greet walk arounds, and their political promises and priorities expressed.

I specifically looked at the different viewpoints coming from both sides of the political camp, and from various federal senate candidates during individual journalistic interviews, and in specific influencer podcast interviews such as Trump's one with Joe Rogan; Joe Rogan being a popular American podcaster, comedian, and U.F.C. commentator.

I also watched hours of interviews with both presidential and vice-presidential candidates, and presidential and vice-presidential hopefuls, and with Senators running for re-election; interviews with various network and independent journalists. And I reviewed hours of digital media coverage of both right-wing and left-wing media outlets and the far-right primary propaganda news network Fox News.

With regards to the many supposed Christian supporters interviewed, apart from their obvious ignorance on what Christ taught which perhaps contributed to their low level of moral awareness, probably what amazed me the most was the depth of ignorance displayed by many of them as to "what was truth and what was complete falsehood".

And just as disturbing was their inability to recognize what was neither truth nor falsehood, but simply "absolute foolishness", what I describe in a further chapter of this book as "good ole bullshit", a new and rapidly growing component of modern-day political campaign rhetoric.

I reviewed the rhetoric of the supposedly Christian congressmen and women, for example Marjorie Taylor-Green, a Christian Nationalism advocate, and Mike Johnson, the 56th. Speaker of the United States House of Representatives, and I paid special attention to their knowledge of the facts at hand, and their intelligence and honesty levels. In both instances with regards to knowledge of facts and intelligence and honesty levels I found them both sadly wanting.

I came to many conclusions after doing all this, one of which is the following. It became blatantly obvious to me that the majority of those caught up in Christian Nationalism's web of deceit, both politicians, potential politicians, and party supporters, are totally ignorant in their understanding of the person, character, and teachings, of the Christ of the gospels.

They are ignorant of the very essence of Christ's message, and as such so bound up in their own religious and political biases, prejudices, and self-interest, that they are willing to sacrifice their moral integrity for their religious or political cause, and their own personal political ambition.

My sole purpose in writing this book is to state the facts of the matter as witnessed in the increasingly alarming devolution and dilution of the current state of moral awareness permeating the world, but particularly in the United States, evidenced in its citizens acceptance of and subtle movement towards without any significant measure of dissent, an autocratic style of governance and control.

During my researching what has become blatantly obvious to me is that many of the voters involved in bringing these fascist type of authoritarian regimes to power in many nations are in fact blissfully and breathtakingly ignorant of history; with many also possessing a low level of intellectual ability and a low capacity for insightful interpretation to truly understand what is happening right before their eyes in their own country, regarding the progressive erosion of their own individual and collective freedoms.

What is even more frightening however, is that in what appears to be a total ignorance of history, we find countless citizens embracing the specific rhetoric and policies of certain political aspirants who are advocating a return to past ills and failed and frankly immoral, political, social and economic practices.

You see when old paradigms no longer fit, with the universe's transient and thus fleeting nature as a backdrop, humanities' ethical concerns may shift from traditional values to more individualistic, pragmatic, or material concerns, such as safety and the cost of living. The shift may be seen as a response to the uncertainty and unpredictability of the economic situation, of human life and of the universe at large, and the resultant anxieties that this uncertainty may bring.

However that shift, whilst psychologically liberating for some, can also lead to disorientation or moral ambiguity for others, as individuals struggle to reconcile their needs and desires, with collective ethical norms, and in many cases with their religious or political roots.

The 2024 United States presidential election campaign rhetoric bore witness to the leaning of some party candidates towards fascist policies, such as internment camps, mass deportations of immigrants, the governmental monitoring of women's health records, federally controlled education, and the banning of certain books; all policies which were contained in Adolf Hitler's fascist far-right manifesto.

One could then quite reasonably suggest that many historical evils of the past are potentially being revisited by those seeking power, profits, and political influence over social justice and equality.

So as society strives to move forward, we must remain continually aware that we all have a moral responsibility in whatever small way we can, to help "balance the scales", ensuring that the pursuit of political power and personal progress does not diminish the humanity of our brief existence. My personal intent therefore in writing this book is to perhaps in some small way in defence of the innocents caught up in this madness, fulfill my own individual responsibility to contribute to the balancing of those scales.

Tuesday morning November 5th. 2024, the day the votes were cast, was the day the final breaths of democracy in the United States were drawn. The illusion of a functioning republic may have in the moment still lingered, but beneath the surface, the machinery of power had already been rewired.

What unfolded was not a singular event, but the culmination of forces that had been gathering for decades, forces that, piece by piece, dismantled the moral framework of a nation and reconstructed it in the image of those who sought to rule, not to serve.

This book is not merely an autopsy of democracy's demise; it is an investigation into the architects of its downfall. It traces the religious, ideological, financial, and cultural currents that converged into a tidal wave, one powerful enough to overturn the foundational principles of governance, truth, and justice. These forces did not act in isolation; they fused together in a perfect storm of Faith, Finance, Falsehoods, and Fascism, to flip the moral compass of a nation.

Christian Nationalism and Evangelical extremism provided the moral justification, preaching a gospel that replaced grace with grievance. Maga Mania and Trumpism offered a populist fervour, a movement so deeply entrenched in its own mythology that truth itself became irrelevant.

Oligarchs financed the spectacle, ensuring that the flow of wealth dictated policy, while far-right media such as Fox News and Twitter (X) became the amplifier, constructing a parallel reality where facts bent to ideology and foolish fiction flourished.

And all the time, whilst no one's investigative gaze was upon them, hidden under pseudo names such as the Proud Boys, the Patriot Front, the Oath Keepers, the Aryan Brotherhood, the National Socialist Movement, and the Knights of the Ku Klux Klan, the creeping embrace of White Supremacists elements, did their thing.

Wrapped in flags, and quoting scripture, holding up signs and sprouting time worn slogans, mingling with the campaign masses whilst cleverly and carefully camouflaged under bright red Maga caps, to blend in with the campaign crowd, they subtly turned radicalism into patriotism and cruelty into a necessary virtue.

Each of these forces played its part, each one was complicit, each one contributed to the slow but deliberate flipping of the nation's moral compass, and with that the election of an autocratic dictatorial presidential puppet. The chapters ahead will examine them in turn, revealing how, together, they forged a new reality, one where democracy was no longer a principle to be upheld, but an obstacle to be pursued and unapologetically overcome.

"History whispers warnings, but when pride and arrogance drown out the echoes of the past, chaos finds its voice once more. The past is not a prologue; it is a prophecy, and yet we keep choosing to ignore it. Societies that forget their scars are doomed to reopen them. Civilizations collapse not from surprise, but from selective memory."

§

1

The Return of Chaos: Disillusionment and the Cycles of Political and Social Upheaval.

Chapter Contents.

"Each new era of disorder is just yesterday's ignorance dressed in modern clothes. The cycle of social collapse begins with forgetting why the last one happened. Societal chaos is not a storm that comes unbidden, it is summoned by apathy and nurtured by arrogance. What we refuse to learn, we are condemned to relive, only louder, bloodier, and the next time more absurd."

On November 5th. 2024, the "music of democracy" died, its rhythm abruptly interrupted, its harmony suddenly shattered, and with it, the dream that was once a celebratory mantra for all, became a nightmare for those few who knew the truth. And the cyclic nature of chaos reared its ugly head once again in the United States, similarly as it had so definitively done some 60 odd years before, in what became known as the "turbulent decade of the sixties".

Welcome to The Sixties Again.

Governments never learn, do they? Chaos isn't random. It isn't meaningless. It comes when the dream curdles. When a generation dares to believe in justice, in progress, in the promise of a better nation, only to watch those hopes swallowed by the machinery of power and indifference. And so, here we are again. The streets are swelling with protest in the face of Donald Trump's second presidency, a presidency many believed couldn't and shouldn't happen again. But those prophetic voices were ignored.

The chants, the marches, the unrest, they're not born of hatred, but heartbreak, and a genuine sense of betrayal. The feeling that democracy made a promise and then ghosted the people it swore to protect. And if that sounds familiar, it should. Because once upon a time, another generation believed too. They marched beside Dr. King with hope in their hearts and fire at their backs. They sang of peace even as the government drafted their brothers to die in Vietnam. They asked for dignity and got dogs and water hoses.

They asked for truth and got the cold steel of a bullet, King silenced, Malcolm X gunned down, the Kennedys falling like dominoes. The sixties didn't become chaotic by accident. They were pushed. Tension built as lives were liquidated and dreams were deferred, and then exploded when America refused to look at its reflection in the mirror.

The singer songwriter Don McLean captured it best in his song American Pie: "I saw Satan laughing with delight / The day the music died." In the turbulent decade of the sixties, that music, the hope of the New Frontier, the hymns of the Civil Rights movement, the anthems of unity, were muffled by gunshots and drowned by helicopters hovering over burning cities. And what was left was chaos.

Today feels like an echo of that same silence, another verse in the same sad song. When government betrays belief, chaos doesn't knock politely, it kicks the door in. Welcome to the Sixties on replay.

The Turbulent and Chaotic Decade of The Sixties.

"Those Who Did Not Experience The Past, Are Potentially Doomed In Some Way To Repeat It".

As a teenager I was part of the turbulent decade of the sixties which also echoed a cacophony of chaos. However it was dissimilar from the present in that the emphasis at that time was not on how much you had, and what more you could get for yourself as it is now, rather on who you were as a person, and what you could do better as a person to create a more just and equitable world, for yourself and your fellow citizens.

It was an emphasis on the character qualities you and your nation possessed and what you could do better to enhance those qualities, not on charisma or how much coin you had in your pocket, and how much power and wealth you could potentially possess.

The 1960's in America were a decade of profound political and social transformation, underpinned by movements for civil rights, political upheaval, cultural shifts, and dramatic changes in governance. One of the most significant events and the outcome it generated was the Civil Rights Movement. This movement generated much attention and ongoing organized political civil protests, that eventually, due to their intensity and consistency hit their mark, for doing something, anything, no matter how big or small you think it is, actually matters.

Another significant event that caused country wide condemnation in the sixties was America's entry into the Vietnam conflict. In 1964 what became known as the Gulf of Tonkin Incident led to increased U.S. involvement in Vietnam, and an acceleration of public involvement in the Vietnam War and the Anti-War Movement. However in 1968, what was known as the Tet Offensive shocked the American public even more, significantly weakening support for the war.

The Tet Offensive started on the 31st of January, 1968. It was an attack by the Vietcong and North Vietnamese Army on more than 100 cities, towns, and military bases, throughout South Vietnam including Saigon. It was totally different to the guerilla fighting they had used before and was a surprise attack. During the initial phase of the offensive, the U.S. death toll in Vietnam increased to more than 500 per week, and, as the casualty numbers rose, U.S. public support for the war effort declined.

The total estimated number of people killed in the Vietnam War varies depending on sources, but a widely accepted figure is between 2.5 million and 3 million people, including both military and civilian casualties. Around 200,000 to 300,000 South Vietnamese military personnel were killed. Civilian deaths range from 500,000 to 2 million, depending on estimates.

There were 58,281 U.S. military personnel killed and over 150,000 wounded, and 521 Australian soldiers were killed with over 3,000 wounded. Other nations, including South Korea, Thailand, and the Philippines, who also contributed troops, suffering additional casualties. And in the end the only thing that was gained was grief.

The sixties were also a time of tragedies that sparked international attention. I am still able to remember that as a young Australian teenager in November 1963, I was getting dressed into my school uniform when news of President Kennedy's assassination and tragic death was broadcast on morning radio around the world, and similarly five years later remember the time and place I was working when the death of Dr. Martin Luther King Jnr. occurred in 1968.

As a teenager of the 60's, I grew up at that time listening to the music of American folk singing political and social activists such as Bob Dylan, Joan Baez, Peter, Paul, and Mary, and Joni Mitchell. I followed their music, understood their message, understood the psychological power of their song lyrics in influencing public opinion, and supported their cause simply through buying their records and attending their concerts when they visited Australia.

But the sixties music scene was not all about folk singers, that decade also witnessed the rise of American rock and roll stars such as Elvis, the Everly Brothers, and Buddy Holly, and the birth of what became known as the British invasion; the emergence of British music groups such as The Beatles, The Hollies, Gerry and The Pacemakers, and The Who, which changed the predominance of the American grip on music in dramatic ways.

As a teenager I was an active participant in what became known worldwide as the "fab four frenzy" that saw hundreds of screaming Australian teenagers rush to the Brisbane Airport on a chilly winter's night just after midnight in June 1964, to greet the musical phenomena that was the Beatles, as they disembarked from their plane to begin their tour of Australia; later being one of the hundreds of excited teenagers attending their concert at a small, by today's standards, concert hall in Brisbane, called the Brisbane Festival Hall.

It was the same concert hall where I sat one year later in 1965, engrossed in the lyrical and harmonious messages of Peter, Paul, and Mary, and then one year later in 1966 when as a member of a packed audience I sat enthralled as Bob Dylan looking intently across the audience sang one of his most well-known compositions, a musical motivational message to all. He sang:

"How many times must a man look up before he can see the sky, and how many years must one man have before he can hear people cry, and how many deaths will it take till he knows that too many people have died, the answer my friend it's blowing in the wind, the answer is blowing in the wind."

And then followed up with another of his musical messages that became a rallying cry for not only the American people but for all nations around the world.

"Come gather round people wherever you roam, and admit that the waters around you have grown, and accept it that soon you'll be drenched to the bone, if your time to you is worth saving; then you'd better start swimming or you'll sink like a stone, for the times they are a changing."

"Come senators, congressman, please heed the call, don't stand in the doorway, don't block up the hall, for he that gets hurt will be he who has stalled, the battle outside is raging; it will soon shake your windows and rattle your walls, for the times they are a-changing."

During the sixties Dylan's "music compositions with a message" became cultural anthems for those who were willing to do something, to play their part, to stand up fearlessly, to say what was necessary, to march unapologetically, and to fight for the personal and collective freedoms that the American nation had been built on.

The Power of Protest, Doing Something, Anything, Matters.

The sixties for the young people of the time, those with an open mind, which was the majority, was a period of joy and excitement, but also one of cultural, social, and political exploration, mixed with worry and concern for the way in which the moral culture and democratic freedoms in their country seemed to be deteriorating in what appeared to be a rapidly increasing pace. And for many also, it was "a time of awakening to the truth" of what was happening around them, the Matrix of their existence, a type of "sixties red pill moment".

This time of awakening eventually gave rise to various types of counterculture groups, groups who had had enough of the government's self-interested agenda, and groups who objected to war and the continuing expansion of consumerism, and as such sought to join together to become a voice for cultural and social change through lobbying politicians with a view to eventually achieving legislative change.

The overall movement subsequently became known as the "Counterculture Movement", and whilst it was embraced by various activist groups around the world it was primarily seen to function as an integral part of the American society. The Counterculture Movement included a diverse array of individuals and groups, including hippies, and other young people who embraced peace, love, and communal living, rejecting materialism and instead advocating for civil rights and legislated environmental protections.

The movement critiqued the emphasis on consumer culture and sought alternative lifestyles. Their protests were often directed at politicians and government policies, particularly those related to war and civil rights. Activists organized sit-ins at segregated establishments and teach-ins at universities to educate and mobilize people.

Events like the Woodstock Festival in 1969 became iconic symbols of the counterculture era, celebrating peace and the power of music to initiate change. Crowd sizes varied significantly, with some protests attracting hundreds of thousands. For example, that 1969 Woodstock Festival drew an estimated 400,000 attendees, symbolizing the peak of the counterculture movement.

And it worked, because every righteous action we take to preserve individual and collective freedom has a metaphysical power embedded in it to eventually change our existing ephemeral reality for the better. All that is required is a measure of diligence and application, and with that, patience.

And so in 1964, the Civil Rights Act was passed, outlawing segregation and discrimination based on race, colour, religion, sex, or national origin, and in 1965 the Voting Rights Act was signed into law, prohibiting racial discrimination in voting.

However the protesting, the petitioning, and personal activism was all not without a human cost. In 1968, Dr. Martin Luther King Jnr. the leader of the Civil Rights Movement was assassinated in Memphis, whilst standing on the balcony outside his room at the Lorraine Motel in Memphis, his death triggering riots and internal political wars across the country.

But the protests continued, for the citizens still understood that doing something, anything mattered, and in 1968 America witnessed massive anti-war protests including the "Moratorium to End the War in Vietnam". As such a few years later the Vietnam War ended, seeing most of the U.S. military and allied troops such as the Australian diggers, being withdrawn by 1972.

Following this, with the subsequent implementation of the 1973 Paris Peace Accord, those troops who remained were also sent home. And whilst the fighting did continue until 1975, the spring offensive and fall of Saigon marked the war's end and North and South Vietnam were reunified in 1976.

You see the sixties were a time when the public sentiment of the many refused to cave to the bureaucratic bullying of the few, and the political grandstanding of others, but pressed on, protesting and petitioning.

Public opinion, backed up by public protest marches, had forced the politicians, fearful of their own political demise, to step back from their immoral and self-interested political party agenda; and thus many wins were achieved through the "career breaking influence and actions" of the people.

Protests took various forms such as marches and demonstrations, and large gatherings, including the March on Washington for Jobs and Freedom in 1963. Many protests drew thousands of participants, for many young people viewed the Vietnam war as an "unjust war and a moral failure", which led to widespread anti-war sentiment.

We witnessed organizations such as the Student Non-Violent Coordinating Committee (SNCC) fighting for racial equality, and women's liberation activist groups fighting for gender equality and challenging traditional gender roles.

And then an interesting thing happened at that time. A new musical genre took the lead role on the stage as the creative community entered the picture to support and motivate the participators in these rallies, festivals, and protest marches. A music genre that was simply but aptly named, "protest music."

THE MATRIX OF PROTEST MUSIC, A MUSICAL ALGORITHM OF THE 60'S TO MOTIVATE THE MASSES.

The Music Matrix of that time, the 60's lens through which the younger generation viewed their existing ephemeral reality, became the "Matrix of Protest Music." Protest music played a crucial role in the counterculture movement, with many songs becoming anthems for the movement, and a unifying catalyst for the dreams that inspired those of the counterculture generation.

The songs written by composers such as Bob Dylan and Pete Seeger, and recorded by artists such as Joan Baez, the Kingston Trio, Barry McGuire, and Peter, Paul, and Mary, addressed social issues and became rallying cries for change. We saw Joan Baez, known for her folk music and activism, often highlighting social justice themes at her concerts, whilst Barry McGuire's song "Eve of Destruction" captured the anxieties of the era, addressing war and societal issues.

Before they disbanded whilst the Beatles were not a "protest band" in the traditional sense, they increasingly wove social commentary into their music, especially after 1966. Songs like Revolution (1968) reflected John Lennon's engagement with political and cultural upheaval. After leaving the Beatles however,

Lennon fully embraced activism, using his platform to oppose the Vietnam War and promote peace.

And while folk artists like Bob Dylan and Joan Baez were already deeply entrenched in the protest movement earlier in the decade, in the latter part of the decade and early 70's Lennon brought the spirit of both "resistance and reflection" into the mainstream through both his music and his highly publicized peace activism with Yoko Ono. And change happened, social and political, as it always does when people do something, anything; goals were achieved.

Eventually, as is always the case, for "to everything there is a season, and a time for every purpose", the counterculture movement having seemingly achieved most of their goals, began to wane in the early 1970's, although in some pockets its influence persisted, seeing its legacy continue to influence music, politics, and social movements in the years that followed.

But it influenced the music scene in a different way, for now it was not protest music but rather "reflective music" that came into the picture. Some of the new musical compositions took on a more "reflective tone" post sixties, to remind the people of the chaos that accompanied the events of sixties, and in a way warning people not to lose sight of the social progress that was achieved.

Three reflective songs in particular that gained significant traction at this time both domestically and internationally were Joni Mitchell's "Both Sides Now," John Lennon's "Imagine," and Don McClean's classic "American Pie".

Written in 1966 and released on her 1969 album Clouds, "Both Sides Now" is one of Mitchell's most famous songs. The lyrics explore shifting perspectives on life, love, and reality, reflecting on how "personal experience changes our understanding of the world". The song's imagery, inspired by a passage from "Henderson the Rain King" by Saul Bellow, uses clouds, love, and life as metaphors for the illusions and disappointments of human existence.

And whilst Lennon's songs Give Peace a Chance (1969) and Power to the People (1971) became reflective anthems for the anti-war movement, it is his reflective song Imagine, released in 1971 that stands as Lennon's most enduring contribution to the post-protest music reflective canon.

Unlike previous protest songs that explicitly called for action or critiqued power, Imagine, in a peaceful type of reflective tone, presents an idealistic vision of a world without divisions of religion, nationality, or material greed. Its radicalism is hidden beneath a soft, utopian melody, making it a song that could reach even those who might resist more overt political messaging.

At the time Imagine resonated widely, becoming an anthem for the counterculture, anti-war activists, and those advocating for global unity, and over time its influence has evolved beyond the protest movement, becoming a universal song of hope. It has been played at major world events, from humanitarian concerts to memorials.

So while the official "protest movement" of the 1960's and 70's is no longer visible in the same way, Imagine still holds power as a symbol of resistance, unity, and a world free of oppression; for even whilst, in an era of deep political and ideological division, its utopian message is sometimes criticized as naive or detached from real struggles, nonetheless, it remains a cultural touchstone, performed in times of crisis and remembrance.

Don McLean's "American Pie", also released in 1971, in a detailed way reflected on the changes of the previous decade, a type of nostalgic look back at the chaos, idealism, and domestic tumult of the 1960's written as a type of musical metaphor of the day.

In this year of 2025, some 60 years later, as once again many issues of the 60's such as war, racism, and women's rights are starting to rear their ugly head in the political and social environment, one could foresee the necessity of a new generational counterculture emerging, demanding from the elected officials systematic change so that the freedoms of all are once again protected.

"You may say that I'm a dreamer, but I'm not the only one," to quote John Lennon. Recent mass marches around America protesting Donald Trump's autocratic style of governance and radical agenda are starting to slowly emerge. One can foresee them increasing rapidly in the days ahead, as once again the persuasive spirit of the sixties rises to protect the freedoms and rights of all citizens.

Reviving the "Spirit of the Sixties". The Need for a New Counter-Culture Movement.

Today, as the United States faces unprecedented political chaos, economic inequality, and cultural polarization, a similar 60's type of movement could emerge to demand systemic change. However, unlike the largely grassroots activism of the 1960's, a modern counter-culture movement must, in addition to large visible protests, strategically leverage lobbying and digital and political engagement to achieve tangible legislative reforms.

The 1960's counter-culture movement was fuelled by youth-driven activism, artistic expression, and mass demonstrations. It influenced policy decisions, from the Civil Rights Act of 1964 to the withdrawal from the Vietnam War. Similarly, today's socio-political climate, marked by widening economic disparities, environmental degradation, corporate influence over democracy, and attacks on individual freedoms, creates a fertile ground for a new cultural rebellion.

However, spontaneous protests and artistic resistance while helpful and necessary to continue creating public awareness, these things alone will not be enough to drive structural change; and as such direct political engagement is essential. Similarly comes a message to the genuine Christians out there who can see past the Christian Nationalist self-aggrandizing false narrative of their leaders. Don't just pray, pray and fight back in some way, for faith without works is dead faith.

If you believe in a righteous cause, then fight for that righteous cause. And if you are not sure what righteous cause to fight for, I have a suggestion. Fight for the freedom of the John F. Kennedy Centre for the Performing Arts.

The John F. Kennedy Centre for the Performing Arts, located in Washington, D.C., serves as the United States' national cultural centre, hosting a diverse array of performances including theatre, dance, and music. It could become one of the new battlegrounds for a righteous cause, a new counterculture movement, if those in the entertainment industry heed the call.

The mission of the John F. Kennedy Centre has always been to present and produce the best of national and international arts, support the creation of new works, and provide arts education. Additionally, the Kennedy Centre honours individuals who have made significant contributions to American culture through the performing arts, and as such gives an ongoing platform for freedom of cultural expression to these people.

The historic British war time Prime Minister Winston Churchill famously said, "those that fail to learn from history are doomed to repeat it, but might I add to that, "as are those doomed to repeat it who are blissfully ignorant of history."

For the uninformed, those who may have missed it, as one of the first acts of his new presidency in February 2025, President Donald Trump appointed himself as the new Chairman of the Kennedy Centre's Board of Trustees, and no one really dug deep as to why. Was it Trump merely seeking attention; is Trump genuinely interested in the Arts; is their more to Trump's appreciation of the Arts than his love for the Village People's YMCA song? No one asked the question.

This move saw him immediately terminate all existing board members and install new trustees, Trump loyalists, a board aligned with his administration's goals. Trump expressed his intentions by stating, "we will make The Kennedy Centre a very special and exciting place," on his social media platform, Truth Social. When I saw this announcement by Trump I was reminded of the following.

After Adolf Hitler's rise to power, Hitler's regime quickly moved to "nazify" every aspect of German Culture and the Arts. Shortly after coming to power in 1933, the Nazis established the Reich Chamber of Culture (The Reichskulturkammer).

This institution was designed to control all aspects of cultural production in Germany, from literature and visual arts to film, music, and theatre. Only those who conformed to Nazi ideology were allowed to work, effectively forcing artists and intellectuals to either join, and as such toes the Reich line, or face professional and for many financial ruin, perhaps even imprisonment.

Joseph Goebbels was a key figure in that cultural purge. Appointed as Minister of Propaganda, Goebbels played a pivotal role in directing the regime's cultural policies. His efforts ensured that all artistic and cultural output reinforced Nazi ideals, promoting Aryan superiority (a type of German White Supremacy Movement) while denouncing "degenerate" art and thought. (everything considered non-Aryan).

The regime systematically banned works and artists that were considered un-German or subversive. This included literature and art associated with modernism, leftist politics, and Jewish cultural contributions. By controlling theatres, museums, radio, and publications, the regime not only promoted its own propaganda, but also isolated the German public from international or dissenting cultural influences.

In May 1933, coordinated by Nazi student groups, public book burnings became a dramatic symbol of the regime's cultural purges. These events were not merely symbolic; they were a public declaration against ideas and authors that did not fit within Nazi ideology. Works by many authors were destroyed, including those by many intellectuals, scientists, psychologists and writers considered "un-German."

The burnings represented a broader agenda to erase cultural and intellectual diversity and to rewrite German culture according to Nazi principles. The Nazi regime systematically dismantled existing cultural and artistic freedoms in Germany and replaced them with its own ideologically driven vision.

Trump's self-appointment as Chairman of The John F. Kennedy Centre for the Performing Arts has elicited varied measured, perhaps what could be described as mediocre reactions. Former Kennedy Centre President Deborah Rutter, who was dismissed following Trump's takeover, rightly so expressed deep concern for the future of the centre's artists, performances, and supporting staff. But since then everything has gone quiet.

So sometimes far more effective than bureaucratic commentary can be the actions of those personally involved in arts and the entertainment industry. For example comedian Conan O'Brien, upon receiving the Mark Twain Prize for American Humour at the Kennedy Centre in March 2025, used his acceptance speech to critique the current political climate and emphasized Mark Twain's legacy of opposing bullying and advocating for the marginalized. It is highly likely he won't be invited back again.

Additionally, some artists and performers have cancelled their engagements at the centre in protest, while others have chosen rightly or wrongly to continue, aiming to preserve the institution's cultural diversity and integrity.

For those artists and leaders in the entertainment industry and in various aspects of American cultural life, use your public influence to fight back against Trump's takeover of the John F. Kennedy Centre for the Performing Arts. Artists and entertainers out there fight back, boycott, or if not use your momentary platform at the Centre to voice your concern as did Conan O'Brien. You may not be invited back but does that really matter.

The long-term impact of Trump's chairmanship on the Kennedy Centre remains uncertain. Concerns have been raised about potential shifts in the centre's programming and its role in promoting diverse artistic expressions. I would be more than concerned.

Observers are closely monitoring how these leadership changes will influence the centre's direction and its relationship with the broader arts community. One would sincerely hope Trump does not commission a statue of the Village People to be placed at the entrance to the centre.

You see one of the major shortcomings of past social movements has been their reluctance to engage directly with the mechanisms of power. While protests can raise awareness, they often struggle to produce long-term legislative impact. A modern counter-culture movement must take inspiration from organizations like the American Civil Liberties Union (ACLU), labour unions, and environmental advocacy groups, which use "lobbying and people protesting" as a tool to shape policy from within.

Lobbying allows activists to influence lawmakers by presenting well-researched policy proposals, organizing voting blocs, and utilizing political donations strategically. By forming coalitions with progressive legislators, counter-cultural activists can ensure their demands are not only heard but acted upon. Key areas of focus could include campaign finance reform, environmental protections, universal healthcare, wealth redistribution, and protections for civil liberties.

A distinguishing factor of the 1960's counter-culture movement was its profound influence on music, film, literature, and visual arts. Figures like Bob Dylan, Joan Baez, and The Beatles helped shape public consciousness and inspire action. In today's digital age, a similar movement can harness the power of social media, independent journalism, and entertainment to mobilize support for legislative goals. Yes, gather in the thousands to protest Donald Trump's takeover of the activities of the Kennedy Centre.

Social media platforms offer a means to bypass traditional media gatekeepers, allowing activists to reach millions with minimal resources.

Influencers, musicians, and artists can use their platforms to advocate for policy changes while framing activism as an integral part of popular culture. Podcasts, documentaries, and grassroots journalism can further educate the public on systemic issues and the need for legislative reforms.

To ensure longevity, a modern counter-culture movement must establish a structured political framework. This could involve creating dedicated advocacy organizations, grassroots fundraising networks, and legal teams to challenge unconstitutional laws. Additionally, it must foster civic engagement by encouraging voter participation, running progressive candidates for office, and promoting policies that challenge entrenched power structures.

Lessons can be learned from movements like Black Lives Matter and Occupy Wall Street, which successfully brought attention to systemic issues but struggled to translate momentum into concrete policy wins. By integrating direct action with institutional engagement, today's counter-culture movement can achieve lasting impact.

The cultural and political turbulence of the present era echoes the transformative energy of the 1960's. However, to achieve lasting change, today's activists must go beyond protest and utilize strategic lobbying to directly influence legislative outcomes.

By mobilizing cultural power, leveraging digital and personal political engagement, and fostering a sustainable infrastructure, a modern counter-culture movement can serve as a formidable force for justice, equity, and systemic reform. Through coordinated effort and unwavering commitment, it is possible to channel societal discontent into meaningful legislative victories that shape the future of the nation.

Chaos isn't sudden, it's a slow burn. It smoulders in the space between a promise made and a promise broken. It grows in the shadow of hope betrayed. And when belief dies, chaos moves in. The American people are living through that return now, but be warned, it could similarly spread to other democratic nations around the world.

The protests erupting in the wake of Donald Trump's second presidency aren't just political resistance, they're the voice of a people who were promised that the worst was behind them. That democracy would hold. That the nightmare wouldn't repeat. But the system blinked, and now the storm is back. And history? Well it's singing the same song.

In "American Pie", Don McLean mourned a country that had lost its innocence, and its music. What begins as a nostalgic ode to Buddy Holly's death becomes a lament for an entire era: "but February made me shiver", he sings, not just about a plane crash, but about the collapse of something sacred.

As the verses unfold, the tone darkens. The jester wears the king's crown. The players refuse to take the field. The devil laughs while the flames rise. Each image is a parable of cultural fracture, and every line maps onto the political and social unravelling of the 1960's.

The decade of the sixties began with a dream. Martin Luther King Jr. stood before the nation with a vision so clear it rang like a bell. Young people believed in peace, equality, and a new frontier of possibility. But the dream was slowly drowned in napalm, assassinations, and state-sponsored violence. The music didn't just die, it was murdered, verse by verse, across Memphis, Dealey Plaza, the Lorraine Motel, and the jungles of Southeast Asia.

And Don McLean in his song American Pie gave voice to the grief and its aftermath, what came next in the evolutionary cycle of chaos, singing: "and while the king was looking down / the jester stole his thorny crown."

In that one line lives a thousand betrayals aptly reflecting the current cry across America, "we didn't vote for this;" the same metaphoric picture being repeated once again in this current political climate some sixty years later, for whilst democracy was looking down, "a dictatorial clown has stolen the presidential crown", and chaos has once again entered the picture.

Today, the chorus returns. Another generation raised on the promise of progress now faces the bitter truth that history doesn't move forward, it circles back. The institutions they trusted have failed again. And just like in the Sixties, chaos is not the disease, it's the symptom.

How America got to this stage of a type of sixties on playback, was not just from the result of poor governance as it was in the sixties; today's chaos was a combination of influences, what you might call a fusion of ideological forces that worked together, a fusion of faith, falsehoods, fascist ideology, finances, mixed with good dose of voter ignorance and denial, and the world, not just America is now paying the price.

The sound of belief breaking. The rhythm of a republic off-beat. American Pie was never just a song. It was a reflective but also prophetic funeral dirge for the soul of a country, and now, decades later, we hear its echo rising from the streets around America.

You see, the chaos that is currently unfolding across the United States, a type of sixties on steroids event, is not only due to the election of Donald Trump, and yes, sure, he is of course the key actor in this type of shifting socio-political stage play, but rather due to a collaboration of forces that have been increasing their influence for decades, forces who seek to rule, not to serve, to dominate, not to distribute fairly and justly.

Each chapter ahead will trace the religious, ideological, financial, and cultural currents that converged into a tidal wave, one powerful enough to overturn the foundational principles of governance and create an increasingly chaotic social state. The forces of faith, the forces of finance, and the forces of false rhetoric.

I have attempted to outline these for you the reader in the most easily understandable way, step by step, in digestible sections, being ever mindful not to confuse you with too much detail, but at the same time giving you the reader the facts that you need to know to make informed choices. Some chapters are long, and some are shorter. With the longer ones I have broken them down to digestible sizes with appropriate titles.

For it is important that every American citizen at least has a basic understanding of how their great nation got to this point, and what was happening behind the scenes over the years, that brought the United States to this particular stage of psychological disturbance, moral regression, and with that dramatic democratic decline.

"Maga-Mania is the grand illusion of awakening, where the algorithm whispers rebellion while tightening its digital chains. That algorithm is the ultimate illusionist, turning the masses into supposed "free thinkers" while guiding them along a preordained path. You see the algorithmic red pill doesn't free the mind, it reprograms it, feeding just enough truth to keep the illusion intact. Those "free thinkers" believe they've unplugged from the system, but the simulation has merely changed its scenery to keep them entertained."

2

MAGA-MANIA...MAKE AMERICA GREAT AGAIN.

THE FALSE ALGORITHMIC RED PILL ILLUSION OF AWAKENING.

Chapter Contents.

§

"Throughout history, societies have been swept up in waves of collective psychological disturbances, where fear, paranoia, and a sense of existential crisis bind individuals into powerful movements. These manias, often fuelled by charismatic figures and amplified by the media, thrive on the perception of an imminent threat".

THE CONCEPT OF A COLLECTIVE MANIA.

The word "mania" is used in the context of a collective. It refers to a widespread, intense enthusiasm that grips a large group of people. This kind of mania is often marked by emotional contagion, where excitement or fervour spreads rapidly among like-minded or politically/socially aligned individuals, reinforcing their shared experience.

From a psychological and sociological perspective, collective manias can take different forms: primarily "euphoric mania", and "anxiety or fear-based mania." A good example of a euphoric one would be what was termed "Beatlemania" in the 60's, when I grew up.

Euphoric manias are driven by collective excitement, joy, or passion. The "Beatlemania" phenomenon of the 60's is a prime example, where the sheer energy of the Beatles' music and cultural significance created a near-religious fervour among their fans. I know, I was one of them. Other historical examples include the Jazz Age's "flapper mania," and the tech boom's "dot-com mania", where optimism and communal enthusiasm created a sense of collective belonging.

Anxiety manifesting or fear-based manias on the other hand, are driven by collective anxiety, uncertainty, or fear. In this case, rather than excitement drawing people together, it is a shared sense of grievance, insecurity, or perceived loss that fuels the collective identity. Historical examples include Red Scare hysteria, where fear of communism spread like wildfire, or financial panics, such as the Wall Street Crash of 1929, where mass anxiety led to a collective anxiety and despair crisis.

Both types of mania create a kind of psychological feedback loop, where collective emotions intensify as individuals reinforce each other's feelings. Whether it is the ecstatic screaming of Beatle fans or the defiant rallying cries of political movements, or the panic-stricken wailing of Wall Street executives, these collective experiences shape identities, influence history, and often lead to significant cultural and political shifts.

Throughout history, societies have been swept up in waves of collective psychological disturbances, where fear, paranoia, and a sense of existential crisis bind individuals into powerful movements. These manias, often fuelled by charismatic figures and amplified by the media, thrive on the perception of an imminent threat.

Three of the most striking examples in American history are the Wall Street Crash of 1929, McCarthyism in the 1950's and the modern phenomenon of Maga Mania. (my term for the collective of Maga supporters). While separated by decades, all three movements share a fundamental reliance on fear-based unity, the vilification of perceived enemies, and the use of mass media to spread their influence.

THE WALL STREET CRASH, MCCARTHYISM, AND MAGA-MANIA.

COLLECTIVE MANIAS OF BOTH FEAR AND POWER.

THE WALL STREET CRASH.

The Wall Street Crash of 1929 and the subsequent Great Depression were prime examples of an anxiety-induced mania, driven by financial panic and mass uncertainty. This crisis exhibited characteristics of collective hysteria, where fear, rather than rational decision-making, dictated people's actions, leading to widespread economic devastation and even personal tragedies like suicides.

The 1920's were marked by rapid economic expansion, technological innovation, and a booming stock market. The stock market became a symbol of prosperity, and millions of Americans, many of them first-time investors, began pouring money into stocks, often using borrowed funds, or buying on margin as it is termed.

This speculative frenzy created an economic bubble, where stock prices were driven not by real corporate earnings, but by collective optimism and blind faith in perpetual growth, and for some, the idea of making a quick buck.

Banks, eager to capitalize on the market's popularity, encouraged customers to invest, often lending money with little oversight. As a result, many investors were highly leveraged, meaning even a small downturn in stock prices could wipe out their entire wealth. But by mid-1929, there were warning signs of economic instability; corporate profits were stagnating, and production was slowing, but few paid attention. Then, in late October, panic set in.

On October 24th., which subsequently became known as Black Thursday, stock prices plummeted as investors rushed to sell, fearing further losses. Major banks tried to stabilize the market by buying large amounts of stock, but confidence had been shaken. And it was going to get far worse.

On October 28th. (Black Monday) and October 29th. (Black Tuesday), the real collapse happened. The market suffered its worst declines, with the Dow Jones losing nearly 25% in two days. Millions of investors were wiped out. It set off mass panic and mass psychological collapse.

The financial panic that followed extended beyond Wall Street. As news of the crash spread, people rushed to withdraw their savings from banks, triggering bank failures. Unemployment skyrocketed, businesses shuttered, and economic activity ground to a halt. This period saw widespread despair, with many believing the American economy would never recover. The psychological toll was immense, leading to increased reports of suicides, particularly among investors and businessmen who had lost everything.

A common belief is that investors jumped out of windows en masse on Wall Street after the crash. While there were some suicides, the idea of a widespread epidemic of jumpers is largely exaggerated. However, there were notable cases of individuals who took their own lives due to financial ruin.

Jesse Livermore, a legendary stock trader, lost much of his fortune and ultimately died by suicide in 1940. Rupert Brooke Wheeler, a wealthy investor, jumped from his hotel window after losing everything. Several financiers and executives took their own lives in the months following the crash, often due to a combination of financial devastation and shame.

While the myth of mass suicides is overstated, the economic collapse triggered a deep psychological crisis in America. People lost faith in capitalism, leading to political shifts and the rise of government intervention under Franklin D. Roosevelt's New Deal. The trauma of the Great Depression left a lasting imprint on American culture, influencing everything from financial regulations to personal attitudes toward saving and investing.

Before the crash a type of irrational exuberance flourished, where people believed the market could only go up. During the crash panic selling occurred, as fear spread contagiously, worsening the collapse, and after the crash, economic despair and extreme anxiety about the future set in.

The Rise of McCarthyism: The Mania of Fear as a Political Weapon.

McCarthyism emerged in the aftermath of World War II, as tensions between the United States and the Soviet Union escalated into the Cold War. Americans, having witnessed the rapid expansion of communism in Eastern Europe and China, became increasingly fearful that communist sympathizers had infiltrated the highest levels of government and society.

Senator Joseph McCarthy, a Republican U.S. Senator, assisted by the likes of Roy Cohn the lawyer who I speak of in Chapter 7, Donald Trump's mentor, capitalized on these anxieties, proclaiming that he possessed a list of communists working within the U.S. government.

Without providing substantial evidence, he launched a series of highly publicized investigations that led to widespread accusations, blacklists, and the destruction of careers. A point to note, Donald Trump has repeatedly accused

Kamala Harris of being a communist, employing this label across various platforms and events.

McCarthy's hearings, broadcast to millions, reinforced the public's belief that an internal enemy was working to undermine American democracy, a type of "enemy within" to use Trump terminology. The "Red Scare" extended beyond Washington, affecting Hollywood, academia, and even local communities, where loyalty oaths and denunciations became common.

McCarthy's reign of fear eventually collapsed when he overreached, particularly when he accused the U.S. Army of harbouring communists. The 1954 Army-McCarthy hearings exposed his tactics to the public, and he was formally censured by the Senate, marking the beginning of his downfall. However, the damage had been done: an era of paranoia, blacklists, and loyalty tests had reshaped American political and cultural life.

The collective mania that was McCarthyism led to blacklists, loss of careers, and a climate of fear that stifled dissent. Ultimately, it collapsed when McCarthy's excesses were exposed. Similarly Maga-Mania has resulted in deep political polarization, challenges to democratic institutions, and instances of political violence, including the January 6th Capitol riot. Unlike McCarthyism, which had a clear downfall, Maga-Mania continues to evolve, with an uncertain future.

The parallels between McCarthyism and Maga-Mania reveal a troubling pattern in American political culture, for fear, once unleashed, becomes a powerful tool for those who seek control. History has shown that such movements often end in self-destruction when their internal contradictions are exposed. However, they leave lasting scars on the political landscape. The challenge remains: will America learn from these past manias, or will new waves of fear-based politics continue to shape its future?

Senator Joseph McCarthy created mass hysteria by claiming that communists had infiltrated the U.S. government, much like Trump's Deep State conspiracies. The loyalty tests in McCarthyism, where people had to prove they were not communist, are echoed in MAGA, where Republicans must prove they are "true believers" or be branded as traitors, such as what we see happening with the likes of Liz Cheney and Adam Schiff, who has been an outspoken critic of the movement.

However McCarthy's downfall was rapid once his claims became too extreme to sustain, suggesting that a breaking point for Trump personally and the Maga-Mania collectively could come about if the conspiracies become unsustainable and the promises made by Trump, such as "lowering the price of groceries" and making the working class richer," are as expected totally unachievable in the short term.

Fast-forward to the 21st century, and a new form of collective mania has taken hold, Maga-Mania. While McCarthyism thrived on fear of communist infiltration, Maga Mania feeds on fears of cultural and economic decline, immigration, and globalist influence. Emerging in the wake of economic instability, shifting demographics, and growing distrust in institutions, this movement has drawn millions into a fervent belief that America is on the verge of collapse and must be "saved," and as such a "god-like leader" is needed to lead the way.

Donald Trump, like McCarthy before him, has positioned himself as a defender of the nation against unseen forces. His rhetoric warns of an America being "stolen" by elites, immigrants, and political adversaries. Much like McCarthy's infamous lists of supposed communists, Trump's claims of election fraud, deep-state conspiracies, and media corruption have fuelled a relentless wave of suspicion and hostility toward traditional institutions.

Both McCarthyism did and Maga-Mania does rely heavily on mass communication to spread their influence. McCarthy's use of television and newspapers in the 1950's allowed him to reach a national audience, while Maga-

Mania has flourished in the digital age, where social media platforms create echo chambers that amplify paranoia and misinformation.

The 24-hour news cycle, the influence of propaganda news networks such as Fox News, and the rise of alternative media outlets have ensured that fear-based narratives remain ever-present in public discourse.

Both movements, McCarthyism and Maga-Mania centred around figures who thrived on sensationalism and controversy. McCarthy's erratic yet forceful accusations mirrored Trump's bombastic and confrontational style. Each leader cultivated a base of loyal supporters who viewed them as the only truth-tellers in a corrupt system. This unwavering devotion enabled both men to wield extraordinary influence, even in the absence of concrete evidence to support their claims.

With McCarthyism, the enemy was the hidden communist, the intellectual, and the government official suspected of disloyalty. With Maga-Mania the enemy is the "deep state," the media, immigrants, and political elites. Both movements thrived on the idea that these enemies were not just political opponents but existential threats to the very survival of the nation.

The Wall Street Crash, like McCarthyism and Maga-Mania, were shaped by collective psychology: all three periods individually serve as a stark reminder of how mass psychological states, whether euphoric, optimistic, or those of collective terror, can shape history over and over again.

THE MAGA MOVEMENT: THE MAKE AMERICA GREAT AGAIN "PHENOMENON."

Maga-Mania, (my term, for the MAGA political movement), has emerged as a significant force in American politics with the rise of Donald Trump, who adopted the slogan during his 2016 presidential campaign. The movement is characterized by its populist, nationalist, and often controversial stances on various issues, including immigration, women's health, trade, and foreign policy.

It is understandable that many non-Magas, including Republicans, are having trouble coming to grips with the movement and what causes people to be drawn to such a movement. So understanding the Maga movement is the first important step in dealing with it personally, so that the "us versus them" scenario does not get a chance to rear its ugly head and unwittingly suck one in.

Understanding the origins and appeal of the Maga-Mania movement requires examining the socio-political landscape of the United States in the years leading up to Trump's candidacy, as well as the characteristics of its leadership and followers. Maga-Mania's origins can be traced back to several key factors that created fertile ground for its emergence.

Many Americans, particularly in the Rust Belt and rural areas, felt left behind by globalization and technological advancements. The decline of manufacturing jobs and the outsourcing of labour contributed to economic anxiety and a sense of loss among these communities.

Rapid social changes, including increased diversity and shifts in cultural norms, left some citizens feeling alienated. The perception that traditional American values were under threat fuelled a desire to return to a "perceived golden age". There was growing disillusionment with the political establishment, which many viewed as corrupt and out of touch with the needs of ordinary Americans. This sentiment was exacerbated by the financial crisis of 2008 and the subsequent bailout of banks.

The rise of social media and partisan news outlets created echo chambers that amplified divisive rhetoric and conspiracy theories. This environment allowed for the rapid spread of Trump's message and the mobilization of his base. The Maga-Mania message resonated with many Americans for several reasons.

Trump's rhetoric of "draining the swamp" and putting "America First" appealed to those who felt neglected by the political elite. His promises to renegotiate trade deals and bring back jobs struck a chord with economically distressed voters. Trump's false persona as a successful businessman and an outsider who could challenge the status quo attracted followers who were disillusioned with traditional politicians.

His unfiltered rough around the edges communication style and willingness to defy political correctness endeared him to many. This collective psychological mindset tapped into a sense of national identity and pride, appealing to those who felt their way of life was under threat. This was often framed in opposition to immigration and multiculturalism.

The growth of Maga-Mania shares some similarities with the formation and expansion of religious cults. Like many religious cults, Maga-Mania was driven by a charismatic leader who commanded loyalty and devotion. Trump's ability to galvanize and maintain a dedicated following is akin to the influence cult leaders have over their adherents. Cults often create a strong sense of identity among members, distinguishing them from outsiders. Similarly, Maga-Mania fostered a sense of belonging among its supporters, often framing political opponents and the media as adversaries.

Both religious cults and political cults such as Maga-Mania offer simple solutions to complex problems, appealing to those seeking clarity and certainty in uncertain times. With the notorious religious cult of the seventies it was "come to the People's Temple, Jonestown, and I Jim Jones your leader will look after you", with the Maga-Mania political cult it was, "vote for me, make me your president, and I Donald Trump will look after you."

Jim Jones led a doomsday cult that ended in the Jonestown Massacre (1978), where over 900 followers committed mass suicide by drinking Kool-Aid laced with cyanide, after being convinced, they were under existential attack.

He maintained control by isolating followers from outside information, fostering paranoia, and reinforcing absolute loyalty, similar to how Maga-Mania believers' distrust mainstream media, live in information bubbles, such as the Fox News Network, and reject any criticism of Trump.

The concept of "drinking the Kool-Aid", blindly following orders, applies to Trump's Stop the Steal movement and how some followers were willing to commit crimes, for example the January 6th. riots in support of him.

Cults and psychologically influenced groups such as Maga-Mania both rely heavily on emotional appeal, using rhetoric that resonates on a visceral level with followers. The Maga-Mania's rise can be attributed to a confluence of economic, cultural, and political factors that created a ripe environment for its emergence. Its appeal lies in its populist messaging, charismatic leadership, and ability to tap into the identity, disillusionment, and emotions of its followers.

THE FALSE ALGORITHMIC RED PILL ILLUSION OF AWAKENING.

ZUCKERBERG'S FACEBOOK, AN ALGORITHMIC ARCHITECT OF MAGA-MANIA.

If the Matrix has an architect, then Facebook's algorithm is its digital counterpart, a system designed to manipulate perception while "making users believe they are awakening to the truth". In reality, Maga-Mania exists within a controlled simulation, where narratives are shaped not by independent reasoning, but by data-driven engagement metrics that maximize emotional intensity.

Maga-Mania captures the feverish grip of the MAGA movement over much of America, and Facebook's role in this phenomenon can be directly linked to the Matrix-like illusion of control. Many Trump supporters believe they have "taken the red pill", awakening to a hidden truth about the Deep State, media corruption, and political elites, but in reality, they have been funnelled into an algorithmic echo chamber, given a false red pill, a placebo, designed to reinforce a specific worldview.

Maga-Mania thrives on the belief that its followers are resisting a corrupt establishment. Facebook's false algorithm has played a crucial role in amplifying this perception. The more a user interacts with MAGA-aligned content, whether it's memes, videos, or articles, the more the algorithm feeds them supposed "insider" narratives that claim to expose suppressed truths.

This mirrors how Neo, upon taking the red pill, suddenly sees a world hidden from the blind masses, however in this case it is a false red pill, a placebo, what would be termed perhaps in religious talk as "a counterfeit Christ".

A user who starts with mild conservative views can then be led down a rabbit hole of increasingly extreme content, reinforcing the belief that they are through their own ingenuity uncovering deeper layers of deception, when in fact, they are simply being manipulated by an engagement-driven algorithm.

Just as in The Matrix, where humans are pitted against machines, Facebook's algorithm has framed MAGA believers as part of a heroic rebellion against the so-called "woke elites," deepening political tribalism and moral rigidity, which is simply the "us versus them" mental mindset. Facebook's ability to segment users into ideological bubbles has allowed Maga-Mania to flourish in a self-contained reality where alternative facts become real facts.

Repeated exposure to misinformation e.g., election fraud claims, Q Anon conspiracies, and deep state narratives, makes these ideas feel more credible to the individual. Facebook rewards outrage, posts that provoke anger e.g. against immigrants, boosting them, while nuanced discussions fade into obscurity, and as such we see that waves of emotion replace rational debate.

The Maga-Mania collective, as cultivated by Facebook's algorithm, has moral consequences similar to those depicted in The Matrix. The world is framed as a battle between patriotic truth-seekers and corrupt elites, simplifying complex political issues into binary moral absolutes, and as such a warped sense of good versus evil emerges. The storming of the Capitol on January 6th, 2021 was fuelled by an algorithm-driven illusion that the election had been stolen and that extreme action was morally justified.

Just as Morpheus tells Neo that reality is only perception, Maga-Mania's alternate reality, where Trump is the saviour of America, becomes unshakable, even in the face of contradicting evidence. But this phenomenon, with the right digital controls in place and legislated, could have been prevented.

Zuckerberg's algorithmic choices on Facebook have not just influenced politics, they have fundamentally reshaped how people perceive reality, morality, and truth itself. The rise of Maga-Mania parallels the counterfeit red pill illusion of The Matrix, an algorithmic imposter, a false awakening that makes followers believe they are seeing hidden truths while actually being guided by invisible forces.

Similarly as a religious cult leader progressively becomes a "counterfeit Christ," leading people down the salvation highway.

This phenomenon can be contrasted with the political and social movements of the 1960's, which also sought to challenge authority and reshape society, but the difference was it had a moral platform underpinning it. The Civil Rights Movement, anti-war protests, and countercultural uprisings of the 1960's were largely grassroots-driven and relied on human interaction, whereas Maga-Mania has been algorithmically engineered and radicalized within the digital sphere and is capable of reaching a far greater audience of potential converts.

THE MAGA NAME....THE MAKE AMERICA GREAT AGAIN "BRAND."

The slogan Make America Great Again (MAGA) and the MAGA Brand have become synonymous with Donald Trump and his political movement, but their origins and rise extend beyond the former president himself. What began as a simple catchphrase transformed into a brand, a movement, and for some, a deeply held political and cultural identity. Understanding how MAGA evolved from a political slogan into a cultural phenomenon requires examining its origins, marketing, financial impact, and psychological influence.

The phrase Make America Great Again "did not originate with Donald Trump". It was first prominently used by Ronald Reagan during his 1980 presidential campaign against Jimmy Carter. Reagan's use of the phrase was intended to signal a restoration of American strength, both economically and militarily, following the perceived decline of the 1970's, marked by stagflation, the Iran hostage crisis, and growing concerns over U.S. global influence.

Trump however, repurposed the slogan in 2015 when he announced his candidacy for president. The phrase tapped into a sense of nostalgia and dissatisfaction among many Americans, particularly those who felt left behind by globalization, shifting cultural norms, and political elitism. Unlike Reagan, whose vision of greatness was tied to Cold War strength and economic policy, Trump's version was more ambiguous, allowing it to be moulded into a variety of meanings for different audiences.

So what did Trump's MAGA originally refer to? Well nothing really. MAGA was deliberately vague, which contributed to its broad appeal particularly for the uneducated working class. It invoked a sense of lost greatness without specifying when or how America had been great in the past. This allowed people to project their own ideals onto it.

Some saw it as an economic promise, a return to manufacturing jobs and a booming middle class. Others viewed it as a cultural or nationalist statement, emphasizing traditional values and stricter immigration policies. Whilst others, as was witnessed in post-rally interviews with Trump supporters, had absolutely no idea what a great America in the past looked like, nor what "a great America" would look like in the future. Some even naively thinking that it just meant "cheaper groceries."

The vagueness of the term however accidentally contributed to its marketing strength, as it enabled Trump to unite disparate groups under a common slogan without committing to specific policy prescriptions. Trump, as a real estate salesman and reality television star, understood branding better than most politicians.

While political campaigns have long used slogans, Trump took it a step further by transforming Make America Great Again into a recognizable and marketable brand. The red MAGA cap became the centrepiece of this branding effort, serving both as merchandise and a political uniform, similarly as did the "brown shirts" in Nazi Germany. Trump still carries his with him to press conferences as seen when he recently spoke at his outside conference announcing his tariffs policy.

Trump's background in marketing played a crucial role in this brand accelerating. He filed for the trademark of Make America Great Again in 2012, years before officially running for president. The simplicity of the slogan, the directness of the message, and the visual power of the red cap made it an effective tool for building loyalty and recognition. It functioned similarly to a corporate brand, with Trump as its CEO.

More importantly than creating some sense of unity for Trump was the fact that the MAGA brand has been immensely profitable. Trump's campaign and affiliated organizations have sold millions of hats, shirts, flags, and other merchandise. Trump-affiliated companies, including his campaign, have reported massive revenue from merchandise sales, with a significant portion flowing back into campaign coffers or Trump-owned businesses.

Additionally, third-party vendors and manufacturers have capitalized on the MAGA phenomenon, selling unlicensed gear online and at rallies. While Trump himself has benefited financially, so have a range of businesses that produce MAGA-themed products.

However, reports have surfaced showing that much of the merchandise was manufactured outside the U.S., namely in China, as the tags inside many Maga red caps show, creating contradictions with the movement's economic nationalism rhetoric. Should it be, "make America great again with the help of China's manufacturing industry?"

Part of the success of the name MAGA comes from its psychological appeal. Repetition played a major role in its widespread adoption, functioning similarly to a television jingle that sticks in the mind. Trump's frequent use of the slogan in speeches, tweets, and rallies reinforced its presence in the public consciousness.

The red cap itself became a powerful psychological symbol. For supporters, wearing the cap created a sense of belonging, similar to how sports fans wear jerseys to signal loyalty to a team, and the Hitler youth movement wore brown shirts to demonstrate loyalty to the Nazi regime. The cap provided a visual identity for the movement, turning rallies into sea-like displays of solidarity mixed with idolatry. This visual unity strengthened the movement's cohesion, making MAGA less about policy and more about a type of collective cult identity.

For some, MAGA is a genuine political belief system centred on nationalism, economic protectionism, and a rejection of establishment politics. These individuals truly believe that Trump's policies can restore a lost era of American greatness. For others, MAGA is more about the cultural and psychological benefits of belonging to a group. The movement offers a sense of identity, purpose, and camaraderie in an era of political polarization.

The rise of Make America Great Again was not just the product of a catchy slogan, it was the result of a carefully crafted brand, a deep psychological pull, and an ability to channel political discontent into a movement. Trump's background in branding allowed him to commercialize and weaponize the phrase in a way few politicians could.

Whether seen as a nostalgic call to action or a divisive symbol, the MAGA brand has left an indelible mark on American political culture, proving that in the age of modern politics, a slogan can become far more than just words, it can become an identity.

BRAND I.D.... UNIFORMS OF UNITY.
THE BROWN SHIRT OF THE NAZI PARTY AND THE RED CAP OF MAGA-MANIA.

The "brown shirts" were members of the Sturmabteilung (SA), the paramilitary wing of the Nazi Party in Germany. The SA played a significant role in Adolf Hitler's rise to power during the 1920's and early 1930's, providing physical intimidation and support for Nazi political activities, including street violence against political opponents, especially communists and socialists.

The term "brown shirts" comes from the colour of their distinctive uniforms, which were chosen by Nazi leader Ernst Röhm and other party leaders as part of the SA's identity. The wearing of these shirts symbolized loyalty to the Nazi movement and was meant to convey a sense of militaristic discipline and camaraderie. As the Nazi Party gained more power, the SA became increasingly violent, helping to intimidate voters and political rivals in the lead-up to Hitler's appointment as Chancellor in 1933.

The brown shirts of Nazi Germany and the red MAGA caps of the Trump movement can be likened symbolically. Both the brown shirts and red MAGA caps function as powerful visual symbols of political allegiance, identity, and unity within their respective movements.

The brown shirt was a uniform meant to signify belonging, discipline, and loyalty to the Nazi cause. The red MAGA cap acts similarly, symbolizing support for Trump, a shared worldview, and membership in a populist-nationalist movement. They are both visible markers of ideological commitment.

In times of political upheaval, movements often find power in the uniform, something visual, wearable, and instantly recognizable. In Nazi Germany, this took the form of the brown shirt worn by members of the “Sturmabteilung"(SA), in modern America, the red "Make America Great Again" cap serves a similar symbolic function within the MAGA movement. Though radically different in historical context and consequence, both serve as visual shorthand for ideological commitment, tribal allegiance, and cultural defiance.

The brown shirt was more than just a uniform; it was a badge of identity in a fractured Germany. It declared loyalty to Adolf Hitler, to the rebirth of national pride, and to a vision of Germany purified by nationalist fervour. The SA's presence on the streets, disciplined, visible, and at times violent, was a performance of unity, power, and willingness to disrupt the status quo.

A century later, the red MAGA cap serves a similar function for millions of Americans disillusioned by globalization, cultural pluralism, and elite technocracy. To wear the cap is to declare allegiance, not merely to Donald Trump as a person, but to a narrative: one of restoration, resistance, and righteous anger. At Trump rallies, the sea of red caps becomes a kind of uniformed chorus, echoing slogans, amplifying grievances, and rejecting the legitimacy of any worldview outside their own.

Just as the brown shirts helped the Nazis build a political identity rooted in perceived betrayal and a promise of restored greatness, the MAGA red cap has become the costume of contemporary American populism, embodying a deep scepticism of democracy, expertise, and pluralism.

Yet where the brown shirt marched in lockstep toward a genocidal regime, the red cap at least at this stage, remains a symbol suspended in a democracy under pressure, a sign that the forces of nationalism and authoritarianism can rise not just through violence, but through spectacle, brand, and a simple red cap.

The cap unites its wearers not in uniformed ranks, but in a shared reality, one crafted, curated, and maintained through a narrative of victimhood and vengeance. In both cases, the uniform is the movement, a visual shorthand for a complex cocktail of cultural grievance, political identity, and the longing for a lost mythic past.

UNIFORMS OF THE SHADOW DARK SIDE: THE BROWN SHIRT AND THE RED CAP.

In every era of political darkness, the soul faces a choice: to stand alone in uncertainty and moral complexity, or to wrap itself in the comfort of certainty and belonging, often at the expense of truth and conscience. This is the terrain of the Dark Side of the Soul,(I speak to this more in Chapter 14), where identity replaces integrity, and allegiance becomes armour. Nowhere is this more visibly symbolized than in the adoption of the brown shirt in Nazi Germany and the red MAGA cap in modern America.

The brown shirt was not merely a uniform; it was a statement of spiritual alignment. It signified loyalty not just to a party, but to a myth: that Germany could be reborn through purity, unity, and the eradication of the "other." To wear the brown shirt was to externalize inner submission, to surrender the chaos of individual thought for the clarity of collective will. It was a cloak for the Dark Side: certainty, obedience, vengeance, and the illusion of strength.

In today's fractured United States, the MAGA hat performs a strikingly similar function. What began as a slogan became a banner for a worldview, one that offers simplicity in a world of nuance, and belonging in a world of alienation. The red cap, like the brown shirt, protects the wearer from moral ambiguity. It marks a soul that has chosen tribal loyalty over ethical reflection, grievance over grace.

Both symbols serve as uniforms of the disenchanted, binding individuals into a movement by replacing individual conscience with collective emotion. Rage becomes virtue. Obedience becomes patriotism. The outer garment becomes a reflection of the inner capitulation to fear, to the need for control, and to the seduction of false clarity in an uncertain world.

To put on the brown shirt was to silence the Light within for the roar of the crowd. To wear the red cap can be, for some, the same. In the spiritual war between the Light Side and the Dark Side of the Soul, these garments are not mere costumes, they are rituals of transformation. They convert pain into blame, loss into rage, and isolation into communal fury. They invite the soul to trade complexity for tribal certainty, and conscience for conquest. This is the soul's time neutral temptation in every generation: not just to join a movement, but to merge with it, until the uniform is no longer a choice, but a second skin.

"The oligarchal trinity of Murdoch, Musk, and Zuckerberg has turned America's public square into a battleground of manipulated minds, monetized lies, and moral erosion. When information became a product, Murdoch sold rage, Zuckerberg sold addiction, and Musk sold himself, and with them in full play, the public lost the plot. Murdoch gave us partisan propaganda, Zuckerberg gave us algorithmic echo chambers, and Musk gave us chaos-as-entertainment, a trinity of techno-oligarchs rewriting the American mind. Their platforms masquerade as freedom while manufacturing division; they've privatized the public conscience and replaced civic duty with digital dopamine."

3

The Unholy Algorithms of Our New Moral Reality.

Where Facebook Replaces Faith, Fox Rewrites Facts, and X Burns the Church Down.

Chapter Contents.

"With every click, share, and post, they dismantled the moral infrastructure of a nation, not with bullets, but with bandwidth. In their hands, truth was no longer sacred, only scalable; what once informed now inflames, and what once united now divides. Murdoch's empire fed the fire, Zuckerberg's machine spread the smoke, and Musk poured gasoline on what was left of truth. Once the keepers of platforms, now the puppeteers of perception, they didn't just break the compass, they sold us a map to chaos town".

THE OLIGARCHS OF THE ALGORITHM: ZUCKERBERG, MURDOCH, AND MUSK.

There was a time when the American public square was imperfect, but sacred, a space where dialogue and debate, however messy, served a shared pursuit of truth. But in the digital age, that space has been privatized, grievously gamified, and hollowed out. And standing atop the ruins are three oligarchs of influence: Rupert Murdoch, Elon Musk, and Mark Zuckerberg.

Murdoch profits from division, Zuckerberg cloaks chaos in connectivity, and Musk fuels it with spectacle; together they've engineered an empire of distraction where truth is optional, and outrage is currency. These men did not merely disrupt lives, governments, and industries; they rewrote the architecture of attention itself.

The trio of Murdoch, Musk, and Zuckerberg has turned America's public square into a battleground of manipulated minds, monetized lies, and moral erosion. Their combined reach spans cable news, social networks, and digital megaphones masquerading as town halls. But their legacies are not innovation, they are corrosion.

When information became a product, Murdoch sold rage, Zuckerberg sold addiction, and Musk sold himself, and with that, America and the world lost the plot. What we once called a national conversation has become a fractured monologue, algorithmically tailored for maximum division.

Their platforms masquerade as freedom while manufacturing division; they've privatized the public conscience and replaced civic duty with digital dopamine. In the race for engagement, moral clarity was trampled under the heels of the profit motive. The very idea of truth has become negotiable, malleable, a means to an end, not an end in itself.

Murdoch gave us partisan propaganda, Zuckerberg gave us algorithmic echo chambers, and Musk gave us chaos-as-entertainment, a trinity of techno-oligarchs rewriting the American mind. Their influence is not passive. It is active, pervasive, and devastating. With every click, share, and post, they dismantled the moral infrastructure of a nation, not with bullets, but with bandwidth. The war for hearts and minds is no longer waged by ideologues alone, but by engineers, advertisers, and attention hackers.

In their hands, truth was not sacred, only scalable; what once informed now inflames, and what once united now divides. They did not merely reflect the darkness in society, they amplified it, rewarded it, and made it viral.

The oligarchs of media and tech have not just distorted reality, they've reprogrammed it, fragmenting our sense of community into curated tribal feeds. The social fabric was not torn overnight, but unravelled in scrolls, likes, and shares, the subtle gestures of digital obedience. Murdoch's empire fed the fire, Zuckerberg's machine spread the smoke, and Musk poured gasoline on what was left and now the public wanders the ashes of consensus wondering, is that truth or falsehood.

Once the keepers of platforms, now the puppeteers of perception. they didn't just break the compass, they sold us a map to nowhere. And now we drift, not lost in the wilderness, but trapped in the maze they built, mistaking noise for signal, conflict for engagement, and chaos for freedom.

THE ROLE AND SOCIAL RESPONSIBILITIES OF THE PRINT AND DIGITAL MEDIA.

The media's role in the collapse of the collective moral compass is multifaceted and deeply concerning. Through sensationalism, the spread of misinformation, and the promotion of materialism and superficial values, the media has contributed to the erosion of ethical standards and the distortion of societal norms. As consumers of media, it is crucial for individuals to critically evaluate the content they consume and seek out reliable and ethical sources of information.

Additionally, media outlets must recognize their responsibility in shaping public opinion and strive to uphold the highest standards of journalistic integrity. Only by addressing these issues can we hope to restore and strengthen the collective moral compass and preserve democratic norms.

In the contemporary world, the media wields an unprecedented level of influence over public opinion, societal norms, and individual behaviour. This omnipresent force, encompassing television, newspapers, social media, and digital platforms, has the power to shape perceptions and dictate trends.

However, with great power comes great responsibility, and the media's role in the erosion of the collective moral compass is a topic of growing concern, in particular how the media contributes to this phenomenon through sensationalism, the propagation of misinformation, and the promotion of materialism and superficial values.

One of the most significant ways the media undermines the collective moral compass is through sensationalism. In the race for higher ratings and increased viewership, media outlets often prioritize shocking and scandalous stories over those that are informative and constructive. This focus on sensational content can desensitize the public to violence, corruption, and other unethical behaviours. You see:

"When audiences are constantly exposed to extreme and sensationalized narratives, they may begin to view such behaviours as normal or acceptable, thereby eroding societal ethical standards."

The spread of misinformation is another critical factor in the media's role in the collapse of the collective moral compass. In the digital age, the rapid dissemination of information, coupled with the lack of rigorous fact-checking, has led to the proliferation of fake news and misleading narratives. This distortion of truth can create confusion, foster distrust, and polarize communities.

When individuals are unable to discern fact from fiction, their ability to make informed and ethical decisions is compromised. The media's failure to uphold journalistic integrity and prioritize accuracy over sensationalism contributes significantly to this moral decline.

The media also plays a pivotal role in promoting materialism and superficial values, which can undermine the collective moral compass. Advertisements, reality TV shows, and social media influencers often glorify wealth, beauty, and fame, creating a culture that values material success over ethical behaviour and personal integrity.

This relentless focus on superficial achievements can lead individuals to prioritize self-interest and instant gratification over community well-being and long-term ethical considerations. As a result, societal values shift away from altruism, empathy, and responsibility, further eroding the moral fabric of society.

Social media platforms, in particular, have a profound impact on the collective moral compass. These platforms often amplify extreme viewpoints and create echo chambers where individuals are exposed only to information that reinforces their existing beliefs. This can lead to increased polarization and a lack of empathy for differing perspectives.

Moreover, the anonymity provided by social media can embolden individuals to engage in unethical behaviour, such as cyberbullying and spreading hate speech, without fear of repercussions. The normalization of such behaviour on social media can have a detrimental effect on societal moral standards.

Zuckerberg's Facebook... The Algorithmic Red Pill of Our Reality.

> "Facebook's algorithm functions as an "artificial mind algorithm" that dictates not just what information people consume, but also how they perceive reality. This, in turn, influences moral consequences by shaping what people believe to be right or wrong, real or fake, just or unjust".

Facebook, under Mark Zuckerberg's leadership, has transformed the media landscape in ways that have profoundly affected society's moral and ethical compass. The unchecked prioritization of profit over truth, engagement over ethics, and free speech over responsibility has contributed to widespread misinformation, polarization, and cynicism.

While some reforms have been made, many of these consequences could have been mitigated had the platform been designed with the public interest in mind from the beginning.

The rise of social media, and Facebook in particular, has fundamentally reshaped how societies consume information, engage with politics, and perceive reality. Mark Zuckerberg's platform has played a crucial role in this transformation, both by design and through its failures in ethical oversight. To understand Facebook's role in the collapse of the collective moral compass, one needs to examine both systemic media trends and Zuckerberg's personal decisions.

Traditional journalism once operated on a model of credibility and trust. However, in the digital age, attention has become the most valuable commodity. Facebook, as the dominant social media platform, shifted the media ecosystem from a focus on accuracy to a focus on engagement. Outrage, fear, and sensationalism generate more clicks than measured reporting. Traditional news organizations were forced to compete by lowering their editorial standards to remain relevant.

The rapid spread of misinformation eroded trust in institutions, including government, science, and journalism. If social media companies had prioritized verifiable information over viral content, they could have slowed the decline of fact-based journalism. Platforms like Facebook could have weighted their algorithms to boost investigative journalism rather than clickbait.

Before social media, mass media created a broadly shared national conversation, even if biased in certain ways. Facebook's algorithm, however, creates individual "reality bubbles" where people only see content that aligns with their beliefs. This has led to a fragmented public, where ideological camps no longer share a common set of facts. Political polarization has been accelerated, making consensus-driven governance nearly impossible.

The spread of conspiracy theories (from QAnon to anti-vaccine misinformation) has been facilitated by Facebook's engagement-driven model. A more balanced algorithm could have introduced diverse perspectives into news feeds, fostering understanding rather than deepening divisions.

Facebook's role in media consumption has changed how people process information. Instead of reading full articles, users scroll through headlines and memes, which reduces attention spans and critical thinking skills. Complex policy discussions are reduced to soundbites, tweets, and viral posts.

The idea of objective truth is eroded when people can "choose the facts they like". Facebook could have promoted deeper content engagement by prioritizing long-form discussions, verified sources, and educational materials instead of rewarding emotionally charged, misleading posts.

Mark Zuckerberg has long presented himself as an idealist who believes technology can bring people together. However, his refusal to acknowledge the consequences of his platform's design suggests either extreme naïveté or wilful ignorance. He has repeatedly downplayed Facebook's role in election interference, violence, and polarization.

His belief in free speech absolutism allowed bad actors (foreign and domestic) to manipulate public discourse. Despite overwhelming evidence, he has hesitated to act against misinformation until public or legal pressure forced him to. If Zuckerberg had taken early warnings about Facebook's impact seriously (such as concerns raised by former employees), he could have implemented reforms before the platform became a primary vector for misinformation and division.

Zuckerberg's overriding goal has always been Facebook's expansion. Ethics have taken a backseat to growth and revenue. Despite evidence that Russian disinformation campaigns used Facebook to manipulate voters, Zuckerberg initially dismissed these concerns as "crazy." Facebook allowed third-party developers to harvest data on millions of users, which was used for political profiling and manipulation.

As well as this, Facebook has been linked to ethnic violence, from Myanmar's Rohingya genocide to political violence in the U.S. and Brazil. Internal Facebook research showed that its platform was fuelling extremism, yet executives chose not to act. A corporate culture that valued long-term ethical considerations over short-term profits could have led Facebook to implement stricter safeguards on misinformation and propaganda earlier.

Zuckerberg controls Facebook with an iron grip. He owns the majority of voting shares, making him virtually unaccountable, even to Facebook's board. This centralization of power mirrors the broader issue of oligarchic influence in politics: Despite Facebook's global impact, Zuckerberg remains unelected and largely unregulated. His decisions affect billions but are made in private, without democratic oversight.

Facebook's political influence has expanded, with lobbying efforts that shape laws to protect its business model. More oversight, whether internal (by an independent ethics board) or external (via government regulation), could have checked Zuckerberg's unilateral decision-making.

Facebook had the potential to be a force for good, a platform for civic engagement, education, and truth. Instead, under Zuckerberg's leadership, it became a tool for misinformation, division, and manipulation. The collapse of the collective moral compass wasn't inevitable; it was the result of deliberate choices made by both the media industry and Facebook's leadership.

While recent efforts (such as fact-checking initiatives and content moderation policies) represent some course correction, the damage is already done. Restoring a sense of shared truth and ethical engagement in media will require structural reform, both within platforms like Facebook and in society at large.

Zuckerberg's algorithmic choices can be directly likened to the "red pill/ blue pill" dilemma in The Matrix, that I spoke of at the beginning of the book, but with a dark twist. In the film, the red pill represents painful truth and awareness, while the blue pill represents comfortable illusion. Facebook's algorithm functions as an "artificial mind algorithm" a "counterfeit red pill", that dictates not just what information people consume, but also how they perceive reality. This, in turn, influences moral consequences by shaping what people believe to be right or wrong, real or fake, just or unjust.

Much like the blue pill in The Matrix, Facebook's algorithm is designed to keep users within a controlled, comforting digital reality. Instead of exposing people to diverse viewpoints, Facebook feeds them content that reinforces their existing beliefs, making them feel validated rather than challenged. The algorithm feeds users emotionally charged content, keeping them hooked on a cycle of reaction rather than reflection.

By prioritizing virality over veracity, Facebook subtly shifts users into an alternate reality, one where misinformation can outcompete facts, just as the Matrix itself is a simulated world that feels real. Users scrolling through an endless stream of crisis, conflict, and controversy eventually become desensitized, seeing many morph into a state of moral numbness. Much like in the Matrix, they become passive participants in a system designed to control their worldview without their conscious awareness.

In The Matrix, taking the red pill means waking up to the truth, but on Facebook, the so-called "truth" is often algorithmically manipulated. Many users believe they are "awakening" to hidden realities, whether political conspiracies, extremist ideologies, or deep-state propaganda, when in reality, they are simply being fed a different, equally controlled illusion.

The algorithm drives users toward increasingly extreme content by exploiting their curiosity, much like how the Matrix seduces those who believe they are outside the system but are still playing into its logic.

Just as Neo realizes that his choices in the Matrix were anticipated by the system, Facebook users believe they are freely choosing their beliefs when, in reality, their perceptions have been invisibly guided.

In the Matrix, Morpheus tells Neo that most people are not ready to be unplugged. Similarly, on Facebook, people who challenge the algorithmic reality face social pushback, leading them to retreat into their filtered worldview. By controlling what people see, Facebook controls what people value. This has profound moral consequences. If outrage is rewarded, people develop an ethical framework based on emotional intensity rather than reasoned debate.

If opposing views are algorithmically framed as threats, empathy erodes, and polarization intensifies, and if engagement trumps accuracy, the very concept of truth becomes fluid, leading to moral relativism.

In the Matrix Reloaded, Neo meets the Architect, the creator of the simulation, who explains that even rebellion against the system has been accounted for. Zuckerberg, like the Architect, has created a system where both conformity and so-called rebellion (radicalization, conspiracy movements, tribalism) are controlled within the same framework. Whether users consume mainstream narratives or counter-narratives, they remain trapped in an algorithmically curated reality.

To truly "unplug" would mean dismantling the algorithmic manipulation that dictates our perception of truth. However, as long as engagement-driven platforms like Facebook exist, the collective moral compass will remain at the mercy of digital overlords who decide which version of reality is most profitable.

Facebook's algorithm prioritizes engagement, which often means amplifying emotionally charged content particularly outrage. Studies have shown that divisive, inflammatory posts get more shares, likes, and comments, which in turn increases their visibility. This has led to the spread of extreme political polarization, the amplification of misinformation and conspiracy theories, and the erosion of a shared reality, making consensus and dialogue difficult.

Facebook could have designed its algorithm to prioritize high-quality, fact-checked content rather than maximizing engagement at any cost, but that would have meant less money in Zuckerberg's pocket. A stronger emphasis on promoting verified, well-researched news over sensationalist posts would have mitigated some of these effects.

Facebook's business model relies on advertising revenue, and it has historically been slow to crack down on false information. During major events such as the 2016 and 2020 U.S. elections, the COVID-19 pandemic, and global crises bad actors exploited Facebook's lax moderation policies to spread misleading or outright false narratives. These narratives often preyed on fear and uncertainty, further eroding trust in institutions.

Facebook could have imposed stricter fact-checking measures and demonetized false content earlier. Proactively banning known disinformation networks rather than reacting after the damage was done would have limited their impact.

Facebook has long struggled with balancing free speech and the spread of harmful content. While some voices are censored for minor infractions, more harmful actors such as extremist groups, propagandists, and foreign influence campaigns have been allowed to thrive. This double standard has fostered cynicism and distrust in media. Facebook could have implemented a transparent, universally enforced content policy that focused on curbing harm without political or financial bias.

Facebook's ability to harvest massive amounts of user data has allowed it to predict and influence behaviour at an unprecedented scale. The Cambridge Analytica scandal exposed how user data was weaponized for political manipulation. By leveraging psychographic profiling, actors could target individuals with hyper-personalized messaging designed to manipulate beliefs and voting behaviours.

Stricter regulations on data collection and transparency could have prevented the misuse of personal information. Facebook could have voluntarily reduced the amount of data it collected and provided users with clearer control over their privacy.

Traditional journalism, with its standards of fact-checking and editorial oversight, has been undermined by Facebook's news feed model. News organizations have been forced to compete in an attention economy that rewards sensationalism over substance. This shift has contributed to the public's declining trust in media and institutions.

Facebook could have prioritized and incentivized credible journalism over clickbait, offering financial support to high-quality news sources rather than promoting low-quality, engagement-driven content.

In the age of digital alchemy, Facebook's algorithm has become more than a tool, it has become a subtle sculptor of the human spirit. By rewarding outrage, amplifying division, and filtering the world through mirrors of affirmation, it has bent the moral compass of millions. Not through brute force, but through quiet calibration. It does not shout commands; it whispers temptations. It offers convenience in exchange for conviction, validation in place of values.

What began as a social network has evolved into a neural net of influence, an invisible hand that nudges us not only toward what we see, but toward who we become. Over time, the algorithm has learned to tune itself not to what is true or just, but to what is most clickable, most viral, most polarizing. And in doing so, it has made the echo chamber not just a room we step into, but a mirror we look into and forget to question.

However the algorithm is not the source of darkness; it is merely the amplifier. The real struggle lies deeper, within each of us. The temptation to choose ease over empathy, reaction over reflection, tribalism over truth, these existed long before a single post was shared. What the algorithm exposes is not just our preferences, but our vulnerabilities. Our capacity to be pulled, little by little, from the Light Side of the Soul toward its shadowed twin.

And so we must ask: when the algorithm stirs the waters of our minds, what rises to the surface? Is it compassion or contempt? Is it curiosity or certainty? Is it the Light or the Dark? It is here, in this space between stimulus and response, between algorithm and action, that our next journey begins: the eternal, internal conflict. A war not waged with weapons or likes, but with choices, daily, quiet, and often unseen. Welcome to the "battlefield of the soul".

MURDOCH'S FOX NEWS....THE PRIMARY PERPETRATOR OF PROPAGANDA.

Rupert Murdoch, the Australian-born media mogul, has long been a polarizing figure in the world of journalism and media. As the founder and executive chairman of News Corp, Murdoch has built a vast media empire that spans newspapers, television networks, and digital platforms across the globe.

One of the most influential and controversial components of this empire is Fox News, a cable news network that has been widely criticized for spreading disinformation and promoting a far-right conservative ideology; Murdoch utilizing Fox News (Sky News in Australia), to advance his personal and political agenda, which has broader implications for democracy and public discourse.

Fox News was launched in 1996 under the leadership of Roger Ailes, a former media consultant for Republican presidents. From its inception, the network was designed to cater to a conservative audience, positioning itself as a counterbalance to what it perceived as a liberal bias in mainstream media. Murdoch's vision for Fox News was not just to create a profitable business, but also to wield significant political policy influence.

The network quickly gained a loyal following, particularly with those of a lower economic status and the non-college workforce, becoming the most-watched cable news channel in the United States by the early 2000's.

It has continuously been accused of employing various methods to spread disinformation and promote a conservative agenda. These methods include selective reporting, sensationalism, and the use of opinion-based programming that blurs the line between news and commentary. One of the most common tactics used by Fox News is selective reporting, where the network chooses to highlight stories that align with its conservative viewpoint while downplaying or ignoring those that do not.

For example, during the Obama administration, Fox News frequently focused on controversies such as the Benghazi attack and the IRS targeting scandal, often presenting them in a way that suggested widespread corruption and incompetence. In contrast, positive stories about the administration's achievements were given little to no coverage.

Sensationalism is another tool in Fox News' arsenal. The network often uses provocative headlines, dramatic visuals, and emotionally charged language to capture viewers' attention and elicit strong reactions. This approach not only boosts ratings, and as such marketing revenue, but also reinforces the network's ideological message.

For instance, during the 2016 presidential campaign, Fox News devoted extensive coverage to Hillary Clinton's email scandal, framing it as a major national security threat. This sensationalist coverage contributed to shaping public perception and influencing the outcome of the election.

The events surrounding the Dominion Voting Systems scandal and the subsequent lawsuit against Fox News also represent a significant moment in the intersection of media, politics, and public trust in the electoral process. Taking a moment to explore the timeline leading up to the scandal, the key events during the controversy, and the implications of the lawsuit that resulted in a substantial financial penalty for Fox News is important to truthful understanding.

The 2020 United States presidential election was one of the most contentious in American history. Following the election, which resulted in Joe Biden defeating the incumbent president, Donald Trump, a wave of misinformation and conspiracy theories began to circulate, particularly among Trump's supporters. Central to these claims were allegations of widespread voter fraud, with Dominion Voting Systems, a company that provided voting technology and services, becoming a focal point of these accusations.

In the weeks following the election, various media outlets, including Fox News, began to report on claims of election fraud. Prominent figures, including Trump and his legal team, alleged that Dominion's voting machines had been manipulated to switch votes from Trump to Biden. These claims were often presented without substantial evidence, yet they gained traction in certain media circles and among the public.

Fox News, as one of the leading cable news networks, played a significant role in disseminating these allegations, and it cost Rupert Murdoch dearly financially. High-profile "highly paid hosts" of Fox News programmes, and guests on the network made statements suggesting that Dominion was involved in a conspiracy to rig the election. This coverage contributed to a growing narrative that questioned the integrity of the electoral process, leading to heightened tensions and distrust among the electorate.

In March 2021, Dominion Voting Systems filed a defamation lawsuit against Fox News, claiming that the network knowingly spread false information about the company and its voting machines. The lawsuit alleged that Fox News had prioritized ratings and viewership over journalistic integrity, allowing false claims to proliferate on its platform. Dominion sought $1.6 billion in damages, arguing that the network's actions had severely harmed its reputation and business.

The legal proceedings revealed internal communications within Fox News, where some employees expressed doubts about the veracity of the claims being made on air. Despite these concerns, the network continued to air segments that promoted the unfounded allegations against Dominion. This contradiction between internal scepticism and public broadcasting became a central theme in the lawsuit.

As the case progressed, it became clear that the evidence against Fox News was substantial. In April 2023, just days before the trial was set to begin, Fox News reached a settlement with Dominion Voting Systems. The network agreed to pay $750 million, a significant sum that underscored the seriousness of the allegations and the potential consequences of spreading misinformation.

The settlement was seen as a landmark moment in media accountability, highlighting the responsibilities that news organizations have in reporting accurate information, especially in the context of elections. It also served as a warning to other media outlets about the potential legal repercussions of disseminating false claims.

The Dominion Voting Systems scandal and the subsequent lawsuit against Fox News have far-reaching implications for the media landscape and democratic processes in the United States. The case underscores the critical importance of journalistic integrity and the need for media organizations to fact-check and verify information before broadcasting it to the public.

Moreover, the scandal has contributed to ongoing discussions about misinformation in the digital age, particularly regarding how social media and traditional news outlets can influence public perception and trust in democratic institutions. As misinformation continues to proliferate, the responsibility of media organizations to uphold ethical standards becomes increasingly vital.

The events leading up to and during the Dominion Voting Systems scandal illustrate the complex relationship between media, politics, and public trust. The lawsuit against Fox News serves as a cautionary tale about the consequences of prioritizing sensationalism over accuracy. As society grapples with the challenges of misinformation, the lessons learned from this scandal will be crucial in shaping the future of journalism and the integrity of democratic processes.

Fox News continuously blurs the line between news and opinion by featuring a significant amount of opinion-based programming. Shows hosted by highly paid personalities like Sean Hannity, Tucker Carlson, and Laura Ingraham are presented as news programs but are, in reality, platforms for conservative commentary and many times misleading propaganda.

These highly paid hosts often present their opinions as facts, creating an echo chamber that reinforces viewers' preexisting beliefs. This approach not only skews public perception but also undermines the credibility of objective journalism.

Murdoch's use of Fox News to spread disinformation has had profound implications for public discourse and democracy. By promoting a conservative agenda and undermining trust in mainstream media, Fox News has contributed to the polarization of American society. Viewers who rely solely on Fox News for information are likely to have a skewed understanding of current events, leading to a more divided and less informed electorate.

Moreover, the network's influence extends beyond its viewership. Fox News sets the agenda for other media outlets, forcing them to respond to its coverage and, in some cases, adopt similar tactics to remain competitive. This has led to a broader decline in journalistic standards and an increase in sensationalism and partisanship across the media landscape.

Rupert Murdoch's use of Fox News to spread disinformation and promote a far-right conservative ideology represents a significant challenge to the principles of objective journalism and informed public discourse. By employing tactics such as selective reporting, sensationalism, and opinion-based programming, Fox News has not only shaped public perception, but also contributed to the political polarization of American society and the moral dilemma of its citizens.

As the media landscape continues to evolve, it is crucial for consumers to critically evaluate the sources of their information and seek out diverse perspectives to foster a more informed and democratic society.

In recent years, the political landscape in the digital world has also undergone a significant transformation, largely driven by the rise of social media and the emergence of political influencers. These influencers, often operating outside traditional media frameworks, have gained substantial power in shaping public opinion and political discourse.

TWITTER X.....THE DIGITAL ARCHITECT OF ANARCHY.

> *"X has become a digital coliseum where lies are cheered, empathy is mocked, and the crowd forgets what it means to be human. The collapse of shared truth on X isn't just a glitch in the system, it's a calculated assault on the conscience of a country."*

Over the last few years, we have seen a proliferation of social media political influencers and the co-opting of mainstream media to promote conservative far-right ideologies. Social media platforms such as Twitter (X), Facebook, Instagram, and TikTok have democratized the dissemination of information, allowing individuals to become influential voices in political discussions.

Elon Musk's acquisition of Twitter which he renamed as X, has sparked widespread debate about the moral and political implications of such concentrated control over a major social media platform by the richest man in the world. As a powerful figure with significant influence, Musk's ownership raises questions about the balance between free speech and censorship, the promotion of personal policy agendas, and the broader impact on individuals and society.

One of the most pressing concerns regarding Musk's ownership of X is the potential for censorship. Social media platforms like X play a crucial role in shaping public discourse, providing a space for individuals to express their opinions and engage in dialogue. However, the power to moderate content also carries the risk of censorship, where certain voices may be suppressed or marginalized.

Musk's approach to content moderation could significantly impact the nature of discourse on X. If he chooses to impose stricter controls on what can be said, it may stifle free expression and limit the diversity of viewpoints.

Conversely, a more laissez-faire approach could allow harmful or misleading content to proliferate, posing risks to public safety and informed decision-making. The challenge lies in finding a balance that upholds free speech while protecting users from harm, a task complicated by Musk's personal beliefs and financial interests.

Elon Musk is known for his ambitious vision and policy agendas, particularly in areas such as renewable energy, (contrary to Trump), space exploration, and artificial intelligence. His ownership of X provides a powerful platform to promote these agendas, potentially influencing public opinion and governmental legislative decisions. While this can be seen as an opportunity to advance important causes, it also raises ethical concerns about the concentration of influence.

The ability to shape narratives and sway public discourse through a platform as influential as X can lead to an imbalance in the marketplace of ideas. Musk's personal financial interests may overshadow other important issues, skewing public attention and resources. This concentration of power in the hands of a single individual challenges democratic principles, where diverse voices and perspectives should ideally contribute to policy development and societal progress.

However, the implications of Musk's ownership extend beyond political and ethical considerations to affect individuals and society at large. For users, changes in X's policies and algorithms can alter their online experience, affecting how they access information and interact with others. This can have broader societal impacts, influencing public opinion, electoral outcomes, and even social movements.

Moreover, the precedent set by Musk's acquisition of X could have long-term consequences for the tech industry and media landscape. It highlights the potential for wealthy individuals to exert significant control over communication channels, raising questions about accountability and regulation. As society becomes increasingly reliant on digital platforms for information and interaction, the need for transparent and equitable governance of these platforms becomes more critical.

Elon Musk's ownership of X presents complex moral and political challenges that have far-reaching implications for individuals and society. The potential for censorship, the promotion of personal policy agendas, and the broader impact on public discourse underscore the need for careful consideration of how such power is wielded.

As the digital landscape continues to evolve, it is essential to ensure that social media platforms remain spaces for open, diverse, and equitable dialogue, reflecting the democratic values that underpin a healthy society. Balancing these concerns with the innovative potential that figures like Musk bring to the table will be a defining challenge for the future of digital communication.

Political influencers on sites such as X, Tik Tok, and Facebook also often leverage their personal brands, engaging with followers through relatable content, humour, and emotional appeals. This accessibility has enabled them to reach vast audiences, particularly younger demographics who may be disenchanted with traditional media, and as such the influence of these social media figures is profound. They can mobilize support for political causes, shape narratives, and even sway electoral outcomes.

For instance, influencers can amplify messages that resonate with their followers, creating viral trends that can dominate public discourse. This phenomenon has been particularly evident in the past in movements such as Black Lives Matter and various climate change initiatives, where influencers have played pivotal roles in raising awareness and driving activism.

However, the rise of political influencers is not without its challenges. The lack of editorial oversight on social media means that misinformation can spread rapidly, leading to polarized opinions and a fragmented public sphere. Influencers may prioritize engagement over accuracy, sometimes promoting conspiracy theories or extremist views that can undermine social values.

Fox News has effectively co-opted the language and tactics of some social media influencers, utilizing sensationalism, emotional appeals, and a focus on personality-driven content. This approach has allowed the network to resonate with audiences who feel alienated by traditional journalism. By framing news stories through a conservative lens, Fox News has contributed to the normalization of far-right ideologies, making them more palatable to mainstream audiences.

The proliferation of social media political influencers and the co-opting of mainstream media outlets like Fox News represent a profound shift in the political landscape. While social media has empowered individuals to engage in political discourse, it has also facilitated the spread of misinformation and extremist ideologies. Concurrently, the alignment of mainstream media with far-right values has further polarized public opinion and complicated the relationship between media and politics.

As society navigates this evolving landscape, it is crucial to foster media literacy and critical thinking among the public. Understanding the motivations behind political influencers and the narratives promoted by mainstream media can help individuals make informed decisions and engage in constructive political dialogue. Ultimately, the future of democracy may depend on our ability to discern fact from fiction in an increasingly complex media environment.

In the realm of information, truth is the sacred thread that binds society; media must weave it with integrity and care. The media's power is a divine trust; to distort truth is to betray the very essence of democracy. The media's role is not to shape the truth to fit the narrative, but to shape the narrative to fit the truth.

The media should continually remind itself that it is the mirror of society, and as such should always reflect the truth, not the shadows of bias and deceit. Consequently, in the pursuit of truth, the media must be both philosopher and prophet, guiding society with wisdom and foresight.

The Social Morality Obligations of The Digital Media.

Social morality refers to the shared ethical principles and values that guide behaviour within a society. It encompasses the collective sense of right and wrong that influences laws, customs, and social norms.

The social influence of these technological oligarchs extends beyond their corporate domains into the broader social and political discourse. Their platforms and technologies shape public opinion, information dissemination, and even governmental policies.

Moreover, the consolidation of media and communication platforms under figures like Murdoch, Musk, and Zuckerberg, raises questions about the control of information and potential biases in content delivery.

Their decisions on platform policies can influence public discourse and access to information on a massive scale, and also influence the social morality of a nation in enormous ways. You see social media has a profound impact on the social morality of a society, influencing values, behaviors, and norms in both positive and negative ways.

From a positive point of view social media amplifies issues like human rights, environmental concerns, and corruption, mobilizing people for positive change. Movements like the Me-Too Movement and Black Lives Matter have gained traction through social platforms.

Unlike personal morality, which is shaped by individual beliefs, social morality is rooted in communal agreements and often evolves over time as cultural attitudes shift. It plays a crucial role in maintaining social order, maintaining the "upward trajectory of the collective moral compass", fostering cooperation, and ensuring justice by setting expectations for how people should treat one another in a given community.

Social morality shapes the attitudes and actions of individuals, groups, and societies by establishing shared norms, values, and ethical expectations. It serves as a guiding framework that influences decision-making, behaviours, and interactions in various social contexts.

Social morality also impacts personal choices and ethical judgments, encouraging people to act in ways that align with societal values, such as honesty, fairness, and compassion. For example, individuals may feel a moral obligation to help others in need or avoid actions deemed harmful by society.

Within communities or organizations, social morality helps define acceptable behaviour, fostering trust and cooperation. Group members may conform to ethical expectations to maintain social cohesion, avoid exclusion, or gain approval. This is evident in professional codes of conduct, religious teachings, and cultural traditions. At a broader level, social morality influences laws, policies, and social movements.

Societal norms often shape legal systems, determining what is considered criminal behaviour or simply justified behaviour. Movements for civil rights, environmental protection, and social justice emerge from evolving moral perspectives that challenge existing norms and advocate for change.

Ultimately, social morality acts as both a stabilizing force and a catalyst for change, shaping how people interact, govern, and evolve as a society. It facilitates discussions on diverse perspectives, fostering understanding and acceptance of different cultures, ideologies, and lifestyles. It also strengthens community bonds. Social media connects people across geographical boundaries, allowing moral support and unity in times of crisis.

However, there are also negative aspects that require individual attention and at times government intervention. In today's political and social climate, we see social media used to promote misinformation and moral relativism, the view that moral judgements are true or false only relative to some particular standpoint, for example a particular culture or a certain historical period.

Fake news and manipulated narratives can distort moral perspectives, leading to confusion and societal division. Social media can also encourage superficial morality, or virtue signaling. It can make people focus on appearing moral online rather than engaging in meaningful ethical actions.

Social media can also facilitate hate speech and cyberbullying. Anonymity allows people to spread hate, racism, and extremist ideologies, negatively shaping moral behavior. It can weaken traditional moral values. Overexposure to extreme content, consumerism, and hyper-individualism can erode traditional ethical principles and communal responsibility.

And unregulated social media can also create echo chambers and promote extremism. Algorithms impregnated in social media platforms push people toward like-minded content, reinforcing biases and discouraging critical moral reasoning.

Overall, social media is a double-edged sword for social morality. While it has the potential to promote ethical awareness and positive change, it also presents significant challenges in maintaining a balanced and principled society. The key lies in media literacy, regulation, and personal responsibility in consuming and sharing content.

The owners of social media platforms hold significant power over public discourse, which comes with both ethical and social responsibilities. Their platforms shape political opinions, social cohesion, and even democracy itself.

Unfortunately in this current political climate we see them donate millions of dollars to political parties whose policies and future agenda align best with their primary business interest, the pursuit of power and profit. Governments must begin holding social media companies to account in the areas of promoting civil discourse. Recently (2024-2025) the democratic government in Australia has taken legislative steps to do this, much to the disdain of Trump's administration.

This has seen Trump's administration in justifying his proposed "Liberation Day" tariffs try to use the threat of tariffs against Australia to get the Australian government to change its mind about its campaign to hold social media oligarchies to moral accountability through legislative means; disregarding the fact that Australian troops have fought side by side alongside American troops in every world conflict that has occurred.

However on the issue of social media's moral responsibilities regarding the mental health of Aussie children, the Australian Prime minister has publicly stated about the Trump administration's Liberation Day suggestion not to proceed with social media legislation, "we will be proceeding with the legislation."

You see the challenge is that many social media owners are themselves part of the oligarchic structure that financially benefits from political polarization and algorithmic manipulation and they don't want to see that changed. Their incentives often prioritize profit over social responsibility, making regulatory frameworks and public accountability crucial to ensuring these platforms truly serve the common good.

The rise of tech entrepreneurs to the status of technological oligarchs in America reflects a complex interplay of innovation, economic power, and political engagement. Their influence permeates various facets of society, underscoring the need for ongoing discussions about the role of technology and its leaders in shaping the future of governance and public life.

The influence of these technological oligarchs extends beyond their corporate domains into the broader social and political discourse. Their platforms and technologies shape public opinion, information dissemination, and even governmental policies.

So they should not be rewarded for their political donations rather legislatively reprimanded for their behaviour, but unfortunately this is not part of the quid pro quo arrangements many have with political candidates at election times.

Elon Musk for example as a reward for his donation of 277 million dollars to Donald Trump's 2024 election campaign has been given a lead role in Trump's new administration, which has led to significant changes in federal operations, and in the justice system, including the suspension of investigations into his companies and the awarding of substantial government contracts to his enterprises.

Moreover, the consolidation of media and communication platforms under figures like Zuckerberg and Bezos raises questions about the control of information and potential biases in content delivery. Their decisions on platform policies can influence social morality, public discourse and access to information on a massive scale, and as such they should not be given free rein to do everything they want through quid pro quo arrangements, through cash for legislative concessions, made at election times.

The Collapse of the Collective Moral Compass. From Digital Oligarchs to Authoritarian Echoes.

There is a quiet tragedy embedded in the progressive collapse of a country's social and moral compass. It rarely arrives with explosions or declarations. More often, it is a subtle decay, invisible until the foundation is gone. So it is with the collapse of America's collective moral compass. It did not shatter in a single moment, but was eroded click by click, lie by lie, until truth became subjective and moral clarity was seen as a liability.

At the heart of this erosion are three oligarchs of influence, Rupert Murdoch, Mark Zuckerberg, and Elon Musk, whose platforms have not merely disrupted communication, but fundamentally reprogrammed how societies perceive truth, justice, and one another. Their technologies have been heralded as innovations, but the legacy they are writing is one of corrosion.

Murdoch profits from division, Zuckerberg cloaks chaos in connectivity, and Musk fuels it with spectacle. Their reach spans traditional media, social networks, and digital propaganda engines. Together, they have constructed an empire of distraction, a fortress built not of walls, but of algorithms, partisan vitriol, and curated tribalism.

The trio has turned America's public square into a battleground of manipulated minds and monetized lies. When information became a product, Murdoch sold rage, Zuckerberg sold addiction, and Musk sold himself. In the process, civic engagement was replaced with performative outrage, and democracy itself began to feel like a simulation, emotionally charged, yet structurally hollow.

This is not merely a crisis of journalism or technology; it is a moral unravelling. The platforms these men control masquerade as vessels of freedom, but they manufacture division at industrial scale. They reward misinformation, amplify conflict, and render the concept of a shared reality obsolete. And what happens when truth becomes fractured? History offers a chilling answer.

In both Nazi Germany and Putin's Russia, authoritarian consolidation began not only with violent repression, but with the reengineering of public perception. Adolf Hitler understood the power of propaganda and used it to great effect through Joseph Goebbels' Ministry of Public Enlightenment. The goal was simple: control the narrative, erase dissent, and manufacture consent. Books were burned, opposing journalists were jailed or murdered, and truth was refashioned into nationalist myth.

Vladimir Putin took this model and modernized it. In Russia, the press has been systematically silenced, dissent criminalized, and digital surveillance normalized. Independent outlets have been declared "foreign agents," and journalists who challenge the state too directly often disappear, into exile, into prison, or into early graves.

But neither Hitler nor Putin achieved this overnight. The path to authoritarianism is rarely paved by tanks at the gates. It begins with the soft silencing of dissent, with turning the public against itself. With making the press seem biased, intellectuals seem elitist, and facts seem suspicious. It begins by destroying trust, trust in the media, in institutions, in truth itself.

This is where Murdoch, Zuckerberg, and Musk come in, not as dictators, but as accelerants. They have not banned speech; they've diluted it to the point of irrelevance. They've not silenced journalists outright; they've drowned them in noise and buried them beneath algorithms that reward fury over fact. In their digital empires, truth is scalable only if it sells.

And here lies the most dangerous illusion of all: that freedom of speech is thriving simply because people are shouting. But what is freedom of speech in an ecosystem where lies reach millions before facts can load, where legitimate voices are lost in a cacophony of memes, bots, and troll farms? This is not the robust speech of democracy. It is the chaos before the silence.

In the name of innovation, we have allowed the moral infrastructure of our society to be outsourced to a handful of oligarchs. These men, whether through ideological intent or capitalist indifference, have created the conditions in which authoritarian tendencies can flourish, not with guns, but with screens.

Murdoch's empire fed the fire. Zuckerberg's machine spread the smoke. Musk poured gasoline on what was left. They didn't break the moral compass, they simply sold us a map to nowhere. And now we wander through the ashes of consensus, confused, divided, and easy to manipulate.

Freedom of speech does not die in a vacuum. It dies when trust dies. When institutions lose credibility. When journalists are smeared, scientists are mocked, and truth becomes a partisan position. It dies in the hearts of citizens who no longer believe their voices matter or that the voices they hear are real.

The collapse of America's collective moral compass was not inevitable. But unless we confront the role of these media and tech oligarchs, and the historical warning signs they echo, we will drift ever closer to a new kind of authoritarianism. One without uniforms or flags, but with firewalls and feeds. A dictatorship not of the state, but of the algorithm. History does not repeat itself, but it rhymes. And in the noise of today's engineered chaos, we may be hearing the rhymes of regimes we once swore we would never allow again.

The Algorithmic Jailbreak.

The struggle for truth is not merely a political battle. It is a battle for reality itself. We live, each of us, in our individual version of the Matrix, which I spoke of at the beginning of the book. A network of interconnected algorithms, narratives, and manufactured perceptions that shape how we see the world.

It is a constructed reality, one that is neither real nor false, but ephemeral, constantly shifting, tailored to our desires, fears, and impulses. It is a place where the boundaries between the virtual and the real blur, and where the truths we are told are often just the machinery of control, designed not to inform us, but to trap us.

The Matrix is not some distant science fiction; it is the information landscape we inhabit every day. From the moment we wake, we are fed a constant stream of images, stories, and data that seem to tell us what is important, what is urgent, and what is true. But those narratives are filtered, manipulated, and often constructed by the same few hands that control the platforms on which we consume them.

In this sense, we are all living in a constructed simulacrum, an algorithmic prison built by powerful forces that seek to maintain control through the illusion of choice. Whether it is through mainstream media, social media algorithms, or the curated content we encounter every day, the Matrix's grip is invisible yet all-encompassing.

The Fifth Estate which I speak more to in Chapter 12 offers us a key to escape, not a grand technological hack, but a moral awakening. It is an invitation to see the system for what it is: not a neutral landscape, but a designed reality, constructed with intent, powered by profit, and manipulated by those who benefit from our disorientation.

But just as the Matrix presents an illusion of choice, so too does it present an illusion of resistance. False movements, token rebellions, and controlled dissent abound. In this digital age, it is easy to believe that we are fighting for change when, in reality, we are feeding the system, reinforcing its power, even as we claim to break free.

The true resistance is not in the flashy movements or the algorithms that promise to "set us free." It is in the quiet defiance of choosing to see the truth before it is curated for us. It is in the resistance to being seen as a number, a trend, a data point, and instead, remembering what it is to be human.

The First Resistance of the Sixties was a form of political revolution and necessary for that particular time in history. The Second Resistance will be not just a political or media revolt. It is an awakening from the slumber of passive consumption. It is a movement that seeks to tear down the walls of the Matrix, not by hacking its code, but by choosing to live outside of it, by finding ways to see what lies beyond the confines of the digital construct.

This is where the legacy of figures like Sophie Scholl who I also speak of in Chapter 12, becomes so crucial. She was not simply a dissenter, she was an awakened soul, a person who saw the illusion of the Nazi regime for what it was and chose to speak the truth, even at the cost of her life. The Second Resistance is about living with that same clarity of vision, the courage to reject the fake world we are told to believe in and to see what lies beyond.

To live outside the counterfeit Matrix is to reclaim our connection to the real. Not just to the physical world, though that is part of it, but to the moral world. To reclaim the ability to see and choose truth in a world where everything is obscured by screens and hashtags. It is about recognizing the fragility of our existence in the face of vast, unknowable systems and remaining human in a world that seems determined to reduce us to mere data points.

The Fifth Estate, in its most powerful form, is not just a digital resistance. It is the human resistance alongside it. It is the reminder that we are not products, that our stories are not owned by billionaires, that our consciousness is not for sale.

The Matrix tells us that we are bound by invisible codes, by data flows we cannot see, and by a world where truth is whatever is most profitable. But we know better. Truth exists beyond the codes. It exists in the choices we make, in the lives we lead, in the resistance we show.

The Matrix is not invincible. It can be cracked. But only if we remember that truth is more than data. It is a spark. And like Sophie Scholl, we must be willing to carry it forward, even when we stand alone.

"The inter-mingling of politics and religion is a dangerous game. It is a game that can only be played at the expense of some specific group of people. Once you attempt to implement government legislation based upon religious or doctrinal grounds, you open the way for every kind of intolerance and religious persecution. The attitude of the ruling powers in countries such as Iran and Afghanistan towards women and women's rights is a perfect example of this. The purpose of separation of church and state is to keep forever from the shores of western civilization the ceaseless strife and religious and ethnic persecution that has soaked the soil of Europe and the Middle East in blood for centuries."

4

God and Country....The Fusion of Faith and Politics Through Christian Nationalism.

Chapter Contents.

Christian Nationalism Explained: Errors in Christian Nationalism's Theological Understanding: Christian Nationalism and Our Current Ephemeral Reality: Christian Nationalism's Lack of Understanding ofThe U.S. Constitution.

"In the pursuit of a morally aware Christian nation, we may lose sight of the core values of democracy, where every voice deserves to be heard, regardless of belief. In a society where Christian Nationalism reigns, the pursuit of power can overshadow the pursuit of truth, leading to a dangerous distortion of faith."

CHRISTIAN NATIONALISM EXPLAINED.

Over the years I have discovered that the most accurate time to take the collective spiritual, moral, and economic pulse of a nation, ascertaining the level a nation has reached in its quest to establish a just equitable society, is most assuredly when that nation, its media, and its people are in national government election mode; participating in discourse about what they see as the issues that affect them, and the future democratic, social, and economic state of their nation.

Because during national elections, when passions and ambition are ignited, and common sense and moral frameworks are sometimes cast adrift, the on the ground activity within the different political groups, the behaviour of individual candidates seeking election, the attitudes, behaviours, rhetoric and obvious levels of intelligence or ignorance of their supporters, the self-interested activities and political alliances of financial backers and political lobbyists, and the various different media narratives, indicate very clearly in which direction the needle of the collective moral compass of a nation is pointing.

For most of my adult life, I have always been interested in the intertwining relationship between a person's religious preference and their political affiliation, as well as the many religious-political alliances that have been formed over the centuries between specific religious institutions, and specific political organisations.

Intertwined relationships such as those of the Roman government with the early Catholic Church, and then centuries later with the coming of the Protestant Reformation, the establishment of the Church of England more commonly known as the Anglican Church, and its subsequent alignment with the British royal family.

I have also for many years followed the historic and many times intense religious-political relationships between the governing bodies of certain Eastern countries and the primary religion of the country. Relationships such as Iran with Shia Islam, Saudi Arabia, Malaysia, Afghanistan and Pakistan with Sunni Islam, Israel with Judaism, India with Hindu Nationalism, and Myanmar and Thailand with Buddhism.

More recently (2022) I had begun exploring the tendency of the right-wing Christian Nationalist Movement, and the conservative Christian Evangelical Movement, to align themselves with certain autocratic far-right conservative political parties in the elections of governments around the western world; not to spread the true message of Christ, but rather for the sole purpose of furthering their own religious ideological agenda, and to put a halt to what they see as an increasing decline in growth and attendance at their places of worship.

Relatively recent European national elections have indicated a growing presence of far-right Christian Nationalist and Evangelical candidates and as such an increase in voting support for these candidates. For instance, in Brazil, the 2022 presidential election saw the rise of Jair Bolsonaro, a Catholic who has strong ties to evangelical Christian groups, and the far-right Christian Nationalist segment of the population.

In Italy in the 2022 general election, the election of Giorgia Meloni, leader of the Brothers of Italy party, marked a significant shift towards far-right politics. Meloni's platform includes strong nationalist rhetoric and appeals to what they describe as "Christian values", which are not necessarily "true Christlike values", but still a theme which resonates with Christian voters who prioritize partisan religious issues over personal spiritual growth.

As a footnote, as of April 2025, Giorgia Meloni is currently under investigation in connection with the release of a Libyan general, Osama Almasri, who is wanted by the International Criminal Court for alleged war crimes. The investigation centres on whether Meloni and other officials facilitated Almasri's release and subsequent deportation to Libya, potentially constituting aiding and abetting and embezzlement.

Additionally, members of Meloni's Brothers of Italy party have faced legal scrutiny. Carlo Fidanza, a senior party figure in the European Parliament, settled a corruption case in 2023 by accepting a suspended 16-month sentence. He maintained his innocence, stating the settlement was to avoid a prolonged trial. And Daniela Santanchè, the Tourism Minister, is set to stand trial for alleged financial misconduct related to her former publishing company. She denies the charges, which include falsification of financial statements and other financial irregularities.

In Poland, the ruling Law and Justice Party, the PIS, has aligned itself closely with the Catholic Church, using Christian rhetoric to justify its socially conservative policies. PIS has campaigned on issues like restricting abortion, and defending "traditional family values", often appealing to Christian Nationalism sentiments. The party's success in national elections reflects the growing influence of Christian conservativism in Polish politics.

In Russia, under the dictatorship of Vladimir Putin, the Russian government has increasingly allied itself with the Russian Orthodox Church, to promote a vision of Christian conservativism. This alignment has been used to justify policies opposing LGBTQ + rights, promoting traditional family structures, and supporting nationalism.

The Russian Orthodox Church plays a significant role in shaping the national identity, particularly in the context of Putin's electoral campaigns, and governance, whilst promoting legitimacy for his dictatorship.

And in Hungary Prime Minister Viktor Orbán and his Fidesz party have embraced a form of Christian Nationalism, promoting policies that emphasize traditional family values and national identity. Their electoral successes in 2018 and 2022 reflect growing support for this autocratic ideology amongst the Hungarian electorates.

European Union diplomats with a measure of pre-thought, pre-emptively braced themselves for what the Hungarian Prime Minister and chief E.U.

troublemaker, Viktor Orban might try to pull off if Donald Trump won the U.S. presidency, which we now know he did.

In the last few years, this phenomenon of Christian Nationalism has gained significant traction in various parts of the world, particularly in the United States. The movement intertwines religious beliefs with national identity, advocating for a political system that reflects "Christian values and principles alone".

The increasing rise of Christian Nationalism raises critical questions about the relationship between religion and politics, the implications for democracy, and the impact on social cohesion and religious freedom.

Christian Nationalism can be defined as a far-right religious-political ideology that seeks to promote a national identity based on Christian values and beliefs. Proponents of this movement often argue that the United States was founded as a Christian nation and that its laws and policies should reflect this heritage. The ideology is characterized by an almost arrogant belief in the superiority of the Christian religion over all other religions, and as such a compulsive desire to influence government policies in favour of Christian beliefs only.

Most Christian Nationalists do not understand that the religion which Christ promoted was both personal and individual, it was not collective, it was about individual relationship. Christ did not force his beliefs on others, his religion on others, he merely gently encouraged all individuals to "seek first the Kingdom of God."

The movement's political policy agenda is not monolithic; it encompasses a range of beliefs and practices. Some adherents advocate for overtly theocratic policies, while others may focus on cultural influence, seeking to forcibly shape societal norms and moral values through political means. I will say this now and probably repeat myself further in the book:

"*Morality and ethical behaviour cannot be legislated, it is personal and individual. It is all about the freely given free will of the individual to choose the path they take. There is one power and only one power that has been distributed equally to every human being on earth, the power to choose."*

Yes, there can be for some, contributing factors that lead a person down the pathway of "moral regression", but the immoral act committed, or unethical attitude embraced is solely initiated as a deliberate act of self will. The old saying rings true here, "you can lead a horse to water, but you cannot make them drink."

The rise of Christian Nationalism can be attributed to several factors, including political polarization, cultural anxieties, and the perceived decline of traditional Christian values, not forgetting the decline of church attendees which then brings about a decrease in donations to the financial coffers of the church. So what were the historical roots of Christian Nationalism?

The roots of Christian Nationalism in the United States can be traced back to the nation's founding. Many of the early settlers and leaders were motivated by religious convictions, and the intertwining of faith and governance has persisted throughout American history. However, the contemporary rise of Christian Nationalism can be linked to several key developments in the late 20th. and early 21st. centuries.

The 1970's and 1980's saw the emergence of the Religious Far Right, a political movement that sought to mobilize evangelical Christians in support of conservative policies. This movement laid the groundwork for the current wave of Christian Nationalism, as it established a framework for political engagement primarily based on religious beliefs. That rise of the Religious Far Right marked a significant shift in the political landscape, as religious conservatives became a powerful force in American politics.

The movement was characterized by the mobilization of Evangelical Christians and other Christian religious groups who sought to influence public policy and promote a conservative social agenda. Several key figures and organizations played pivotal roles in this transformation, aligning themselves primarily with the Republican Party. What was the reason for this alignment with the Republican Party?

The alignment of the Religious Far Right with the Republican Party can be traced back to the social and cultural upheavals of the 1960's, which I discussed in a previous chapter. Upheavals which included the civil rights movement, the sexual revolution, and further in the 70's with the Supreme Court's decision in Roe v. Wade that legalized abortion nationwide.

These changes alarmed many religious conservatives, who felt that traditional values were under threat. In response, they began to organize and seek greater political influence, in a type of "religious trade union" way.

One of the most prominent figures in the rise of the Religious Far Right was Jerry Falwell, a Baptist minister who founded the Moral Majority in 1979. The Moral Majority aimed to mobilize conservative Christians as a political force, advocating for issues such as opposition to abortion, the promotion of school prayer, and the defence of what they described as "traditional family values".

The traditional family values of Christian Nationalism however had nothing to do with personal values or personal ethical behaviour. They basically referred to a singular structural definition of what a family was. To Christian Nationalists a family was a group of people, a family living together, consisting of one male husband, one female wife, and as many children as could possibly be conceived during that liaison.

So you could be as a Religious Far Right conservative male, the greatest philanderer, adulterer, and conman alive, but as long as you stuck within the structure of one female wife and as many children as possible and perhaps were seen to occasionally attend a church service on Sunday, all dressed up with that family group in tow, you were regarded as fitting the mould of "a good Christian, upholding traditional family values."

Jerry Falwell's organization quickly gained influence, helping to register millions of new voters and played a crucial role in the election of Ronald Reagan as

President in 1980, and as such the Moral Majority Christian Nationalist group became a key voting bloc for the conservative movement from then on.

For the Republican strategists knew that all they had to do was throw the group a few proposed policy breadcrumbs regarding family values, and thousands more voters would, "in defence of traditional family values" vote for them regardless of the moral status or leadership capability of their candidate.

The political affiliations of the Religious Far Right were primarily with the Republican Party, which embraced the movement's social agenda as part of its own broader conservative platform. This alliance was mutually beneficial, a type of "quid pro quo" arrangement; religious conservatives provided a reliable voting bloc for the Republican Party, while the party offered a vehicle for advancing the movement's ideological policy goals.

Election day would then become a type of Republican Party-Christian Nationalism-Evangelical pied piper moment as thousands of professing, and for many profoundly duped Christians were led over the cliff of democracy, supporting the conservative candidate in their voting district, regardless of that candidate's experience, personal ability, cognitive ability, intellectual intelligence, moral history, or governing capability.

The Reagan administration, in particular, was receptive to the concerns of the Religious Far Right, appointing conservative judges and supporting policies that aligned with their values. However the influence of the Religious Far Right extended far beyond political lobbying, it also played a significant role in shaping public discourse and policy debates on issues such as abortion, education, and the role of religion in public life.

The movement's emphasis on grassroots organizing and voter mobilization had a lasting impact on American politics, demonstrating the power of religious and cultural issues to galvanize political activists into some major on the ground involvement in election campaigns.

As the founder of the Far-Right Moral Majority, Falwell was a significant figure in the rise of the religious right in American politics; however while he was very influential, his blending of religion and politics was controversial to some, and his rhetoric in support of certain issues, which when looked at closely revealed a Trumpian tone to them, which was seen as laughable to many.

Another key proponent of the Religious Far-Right, the precursor to Christian Nationalism, was Pat Robertson, a televangelist who founded the Christian Broadcasting Network and later the Christian Coalition. Robertson's influence extended through his television program, "The 700 Club," which reached millions of viewers and provided a platform for promoting conservative Christian values.

Robertson on the other hand took a slightly, let's say self-interested course, when he ran for the Republican presidential nomination in 1988, which was controversial as it blurred the lines between religious leadership and political ambition.

Robertson's rhetoric and personal business dealings have also been controversial over the years. He made headlines for his comments on foreign policy and domestic issues that many found extreme or insensitive. And his involvement in various business ventures, including diamond mining in Africa, raised questions about the ethical implications of a religious leader particularly one with political ambitions, engaging in such activities.

Both leaders have had a significant impact on American religious and political life, but their actions and statements have often sparked debate and criticism, leading to periods of disgrace in the eyes of some followers and the public. Both Falwell and Robertson's habit of making regular Trumpian type controversial statements over the years raised questions about their understanding of theology, their knowledge and interpretation of the teachings of Christ, as well as their personal stances on morality and humanity. For instance:

In the aftermath of the September 11 attacks, Falwell ridiculously suggested that the attacks were a result of God's judgment on America for its moral decay, including issues like abortion and the acceptance of homosexuality. He stated, "I really believe that the pagans, and the abortionists, and the feminists, and the gays, and the lesbians have been responsible for this."

He was an eager supporter of segregationist policies and opposed the civil rights movement. He once stated that he believed in "segregation" and that the "integration of the races" was against God's will. He controversially claimed that AIDS was a punishment from God for homosexuality, stating, "AIDS is not just God's punishment for homosexuals; it is God's punishment for the society that tolerates homosexuals."

He often made derogatory remarks about LGBTQ+ individuals, suggesting that they were responsible for all of societal ills and moral decline. His political endorsements sometimes contradicted his moral teachings, as he supported political candidates who were involved in scandals or had questionable ethical records, prioritizing political alignment over personal integrity. Not dissimilar at all from what we see in the current presidential election, particularly in the Republican Party.

Perhaps even more damaging to the Moral Majority's agenda however was the fall from grace of Falwell's son Jerry Falwell Jr. Jerry Falwell Jr. took over as president of Liberty University in 2007 after his father's death. Under his leadership the university grew significantly in terms of enrolment and financial stability. However his tenure was also marked by controversies and criticisms regarding his leadership style and personal conduct.

Falwell Jr. was a vocal supporter of Donald Trump during the 2016 presidential campaign, seen many times with Trump at rallies, which drew both support and criticism from various evangelical circles. His political involvement was seen by some as a departure from the more traditional religious focus of his father's Moral Majority movement.

Over the years, Falwell Jr. made several public statements and social media posts that were considered controversial or inappropriate by many, including comments on race and politics. These incidents often drew negative attention to both him and Liberty University. There were reports and allegations regarding Falwell Jr.'s business dealings, including a real estate venture in Miami involving a young pool attendant. These dealings raised questions about potential conflicts of interest and misuse of university resources.

The situation escalated in August 2020 when a personal scandal came to light. A former business associate, Giancarlo Granda, alleged that he had been involved in a years-long sexual relationship with Falwell Jr.'s wife, Becki Falwell, and that Jerry Falwell Jr. was aware of and involved in the arrangement. Granda revealed that his sexual relationship with the Falwells began when he was 20. He said he had sex with Becki Falwell while Jerry Falwell Jr. looked on.

In an interview with Reuters news service investigation team, Granda showed Reuters emails, text messages, and other evidence that he says demonstrates the sexual nature of his relationship with the couple. He stated, "Becki and I developed an intimate relationship and Jerry enjoyed watching from the corner of the room."

In the interview he described the liaisons as frequent, "multiple times per year", and said the encounters took place at hotels in Miami and New York and at the Falwell's home in Virginia. He stated that the relationship only soured after he fell into a business dispute with the couple.

Following the scandal, Falwell Jr. was placed on an indefinite leave of absence by Liberty University. Shortly thereafter, he resigned from his position as president and chancellor of the university. His resignation marked a significant fall from grace, given his previous status as a leading figure in the evangelical community. These events collectively contributed to Jerry Falwell Jr.'s fall from grace, highlighting the complex interplay between personal conduct, leadership responsibilities, and public perception in the context of religious and educational institutions.

Pat Robertson also generated much controversy at the time over his outspoken statements. After Hurricane Katrina struck New Orleans, Robertson suggested that the disaster was a result of the city's sinful nature, implying that the residents were being punished for their moral failings.

Following the 2010 earthquake in Haiti, Robertson claimed that the country had made a "pact with the devil" during its revolution against France, suggesting that the disaster was a form of divine retribution.

He once suggested that a woman should "submit" to her husband, even in cases of abuse. Robertson has expressed support for various authoritarian leaders, including former Liberian President Charles Taylor, which raised questions about his commitment to human rights and democracy.

However, in spite of these controversies and scandals the Religious Far Right's relationship with the Republican Party powered on similarly as it does at this current time, seeing the pursuit of power take precedence over the moral integrity of their candidates.

Driven by a desire to counteract perceived moral decline and promote conservative values, these religious conservatives became a formidable political force. Through the efforts of leaders like Jerry Falwell, Pat Robertson, and James Dobson, and their alignment with the Republican Party, the Religious Far Right reshaped the political landscape, leaving a legacy that continues to influence American politics, doing so once again in the 2016 and 2024 presidential election.

A point to note. In the 2016 United States presidential election, approximately 81% of white evangelical Christian voters supported Donald Trump. This level of support was among the highest recorded for a Republican candidate from this demographic, and in the 2024 election, data indicates that self-identified Christians constituted 72% of the electorate, with 56% of them voting for Trump.

Among white evangelical and Pentecostal voters specifically, about 81% supported Trump, mirroring the 2016 figures. These statistics underscore the significant and consistent support Donald Trump received from Christian, particularly white evangelical, voters in both elections, and their willingness to, for ideological sake, support a candidate who has never demonstrated any inclination to conduct his personal and political life in alignment with the ethical and moral character qualities that Christ exemplified.

That election of Donald Trump in 2016 as president of the United States, further galvanized Christian Nationalism, as many evangelical voters, undeterred by Trump's apparent moral shortcomings, rallied around his candidacy, viewing him as a champion of their doctrinal values, regardless of his questionable past.

And as such Winston Churchill's historic statement about the sins of the past being revisited in the present, came to fruition in the 2024 presidential election seeing an autocratic morally bereft candidate, effortlessly ease himself once again onto the throne in the presidential Oval Office.

Errors in Christian Nationalism's Theological Understanding.

The portrayal of God in Christian Nationalism as an autocratic ruler reflects a poor understanding of biblical theology and thus Christianity, one that aligns more closely with the Old Testament's context of covenantal law than with the New Testament's message of grace and freedom. The God of Jesus, as revealed in the New Testament, invites humanity into a dynamic and democratic relationship, where individuals are empowered to choose their paths and grow in love and in personal responsibility and accountability.

And as such the rise of Christian Nationalism's influence in conservative political parties around the world represents a significant error in both the leaders and as such their supporters understanding of Christianity, the teachings of Christ, and the principles of democracy, and here is why.

In Christian Nationalism, we find a movement blending religious and political ideology, which portrays the God of the universe as an autocratic ruler who demands unquestioning allegiance and enforces a strict moral order. This perspective largely aligns with the depiction of God in the Old Testament, where divine commands are delivered with authority, and compliance is often mandated under threat of punishment.

However, this view contrasts with the New Testament's portrayal of God through Jesus Christ, who emphasises free will, personal responsibility, and individual choice in shaping one's life, both morally and spiritually. You see:

"*Christian Nationalism's theological framework tends to emphasise the Old Testament's autocratic aspects of God, while overlooking the democratic ethos embodied in the New Testament teachings of Jesus.*"

The Old Testament frequently presents God as a sovereign ruler, an autocrat, who wields absolute authority over creation. From the laws given to Moses on Mount Sinai to the conquest of Canaan, God's will is often communicated through commandments and enforced with clear consequences for obedience and disobedience. For example, in Deuteronomy 28, blessings and curses are explicitly tied to obedience or disobedience to God's laws.

This reflects an autocratic vision of divinity, where God governs as a type of divine dictator or coronated king, with total control over the fate of individuals and nations. As such advocates of Christian Nationalism often call for a return to biblical principles that prioritise authority, patriarchy, hierarchy, and uniformity, mirroring the Old Testament's focus on a covenantal relationship that demands loyalty to God's decrees.

This perspective supports a political ideology that seeks to enforce a singular moral and cultural framework, often at the expense of diversity and individual autonomy, denying individuals the freedom to choose.

In contrast, the New Testament reveals a God who engages with humanity through love, grace, and the invitation to freely choose a path towards righteousness. Jesus's teachings focus on the inner transformation of individuals rather than external conformity to laws. For instance, in Matthew 22:37 to 40, Jesus summarises the sum of all law as being "love for God and love for one's neighbour", emphasising relational ethics over rigid legalism.

The parable of the prodigal son Luke 15:11 to 32, further illustrates this democratic aspect of God's New Testament nature. The father allows his youngest son to make his own decisions, even when they lead to failure and hardship. Rather than enforcing obedience, the father patiently waits, offering unconditional love and forgiveness to the son when he returns. This demonstrates a God who respects human agency and values the process of personal growth through choice and accountability.

The democratic ethos of the New Testament challenges the hierarchical and patriarchal structures of both society and religion. A patriarchy is a societal structure in which men hold primary power and authority in roles such as leadership, moral authority, and property ownership. It includes patriarchal misogyny which refers to the cultural practise of devaluing, oppressing, and discriminating against women within a patriarchal system.

Jesus often upends traditional power dynamics, elevating the marginalised and empowering individuals to take personal ownership of their spiritual and moral journeys. This vision of God aligns with principles of freedom, diversity, and mutual respect, providing a stark contrast to the authoritarian tendencies of proponents of Christian Nationalism who want to take political ownership of an individual's moral and social journey, through enforceable legislation.

Christian Nationalism's emphasis on an autocratic God creates tension with the New Testament's message of grace and individual freedom. By focusing on enforcing divine authority in political and social structures, Christian Nationalism continually distorts the Gospel's core message of love, compassion, and liberation.

So, while the Old Testament's portrayal of God reflects a context where law and order were necessary for the survival of a nascent community, the New Testament invites believers into an individualised mature relationship with God characterised by mutual love and trust. The shift does not imply a contradiction between the two testaments, but rather a progression in the understanding of Divinity's relationship with humanity.

Christian theology can and should integrate these perspectives by recognising that the God of the Old Testament laid the groundwork for the redemptive and relational approach revealed in Jesus Christ, a type of change in spiritual governance from an autocratic God to a democratic God.

However Christian Nationalism's selective emphasis on certain aspects of the Old Testament, for example the "thou shalt not kill" commandment, which is their basis for an anti-abortion stance, risks promoting a one-dimensional view of God that undermines the democratic ideals of the New Testament and of all free nations throughout the world; the primary pillar of which is "free will," every individual's right to choose their own path and bear the resultant consequences.

By embracing the full spectrum of biblical teaching those of the Christian faith can resist the authoritarian tendencies of Christian Nationalism and bear witness to a Divine Intelligence which values both justice and mercy, authority and freedom, law and grace.

However, because the autocratic model which serves as the foundation of far-right conservatism and Christian Nationalism, emphasises a vision of society governed by divine laws, legislated, and then personally enforced by the governing authorities of the day, Christian Nationalists have no problem in supporting a morally corrupt candidate with dictatorial tendencies if it means achieving their own personal ideologically based policy agenda.

What Christian Nationalism is attempting to achieve through political means is no different in its overall autocratic intent from the system of Sharia Law in certain Arab countries. Sharia law, or Islamic law, is a legal system derived from the religious precepts of Islam, particularly the Quran and the Hadith (the sayings and actions of the Prophet Muhammad). It encompasses a wide range of civil, criminal, and personal matters, providing guidelines on aspects of daily life, including prayer, fasting, charity, marriage, and inheritance.

Sharia is not a single set of laws but rather a framework that can be interpreted in various ways. Different Islamic scholars and schools of thought may have different interpretations of Sharia, leading to variations in its application across different Muslim-majority countries and communities, but the end result is the same, "conform or be punished."

Donald Trump in an interview with a journalist that I recently watched, when asked the question, "should a woman be punished for terminating a pregnancy regardless of the reason she had for doing it", meaning even it was for health reasons, Trump calmly answered quote, "yes, I think there should be some form of punishment."

Overall, Sharia law is deeply intertwined with the Islamic faith, guiding the moral and ethical conduct of Muslims. Its implementation in government varies widely, reflecting the diverse interpretations and cultural contexts within the Muslim world, however this is what we must understand:

"When ideologically obsessed groups religious or otherwise, gain traction in a nation's governance, the moral landscape shifts, paving the way for intolerance and oppression disguised as order."

CHRISTIAN NATIONALISM AND OUR CURRENT EPHEMERAL REALITY.

So how does the rise of Christian Nationalism influence the Ephemeral reality we live in in this modern day? It does so in various ways, including political rhetoric, policy advocacy, and cultural expressions. One of its key characteristics is a focus on the re-establishment through political means of a Christian cultural identity, thus creating an "us versus them mentality".

Leaders and proponents of Christian Nationalism often use religious language and imagery to frame political issues. This rhetoric emphasizes a divine mandate for the nation and portrays political opponents and religious minorities as threats to the nation's moral fabric.

In terms of the United States 2024 presidential election campaign, Trump fed off this rhetoric using phrases such as "I am the anointed one," saying continually after his attempted assassination "I am only alive now because God intervened", as well as "God was there and saved me for a purpose." And many Christian Nationalists bought it, some because it suited their institutional agenda to have him re-elected, and others bought it because they are totally ignorant of the Christianity of Christ.

In terms of the effect on our Ephemeral Reality Christian Nationalists also advocate for policies that align with their religious beliefs, such as opposition to abortion, support for traditional marriage, and the promotion of religious education in public schools. They often seek to influence legislation and public policy to reflect their values.

The movement promotes a vision of American identity that is predominately tied to autocratic Christianity, and as such it includes the belief that the nation's history, symbols, and institutions must reflect its Christian heritage.

This cultural dynamic often leads to a "rejection of pluralism", which when taken to extremes can lead to ethnic violence and persecution of minorities.

Pluralism is a concept that refers to the coexistence of multiple groups, beliefs, or values within a society or system. It emphasizes diversity and the idea that different perspectives and lifestyles can coexist peacefully and equitably.

In political terms, pluralism is the recognition and affirmation of diversity within a political body, which allows for the representation and participation of various groups in the decision-making processes of governance. In a broader cultural or social context, pluralism encourages the acceptance and appreciation of different cultural, religious, and social practices.

During Donald Trump's first presidency, (2017–2021) several executive orders and actions were perceived as efforts to dismantle or challenge the concept of pluralism and diversity within the White House and federal government workforce, and indications are that this will be repeated in his second administration. Including an executive order on combating race and sex stereotyping.

This order aimed to prohibit federal agencies and contractors from conducting training that included concepts related to critical race theory, white privilege, and other diversity training programs. Critics argued that this undermined efforts to promote diversity and inclusion.

In his first presidency the Trump administration implemented policies that affected the hiring and promotion processes within federal agencies, including efforts to reduce the influence of diversity and inclusion initiatives. This included the establishment of a "Schedule F" classification for federal employees, which allowed for the reclassification of certain positions to make it easier to remove employees based on political affiliation. Indications are that this will be extended in his second presidency.

In his first presidency Trump's administration made moves to dismantle the Office of Diversity and Inclusion and to reduce the influence and funding of offices dedicated to diversity and inclusion within federal agencies, which critics argued would negatively impact efforts to promote a diverse workforce. Trump's administration also enacted strict immigration policies, including the travel bans. Indications are that this will be extended in his second presidency.

During his first presidency, Donald Trump imposed several travel bans, primarily under the justification of national security, counterterrorism, and immigration control. There was a Muslim ban in January 2017; this executive order restricted travel from seven Muslim-majority countries. He suspended the U.S. Refugee Admissions Program for 120 days and indefinitely banned Syrian refugees, and during Covid he announced travel bans on several European countries such as the U.K. and Ireland.

These bans were a significant part of Trump's immigration and national security policies, sparking widespread legal battles and political debates. Some were later revoked by President Joe Biden in 2021.

Christian Nationalism continues to contribute to the growing political divide in the United States government, evidenced in the rhetoric of staunch Christian Nationalist politicians. The us-versus-them mentality can exacerbate tensions between different cultural and religious groups, making it far more challenging to find common ground on important issues, and making it fodder for far-right groups such as the White Supremacist movement and Neo-Fascist groups to infiltrate the conversation.

Their emphasis also on a singular national identity rooted in Christianity can alienate individuals from diverse social and religious backgrounds. This exclusionary approach can weaken social cohesion and foster an environment of fear, intolerance and discrimination. This has been witnessed in the anti-immigrant furore that has erupted in the United States, seeing Donald Trump feeding off it during his electoral campaigning for personal and party electoral gain.

Christian Nationalism's Lack of Understanding of The U.S. Constitution.

A critical error of Christian Nationalism due to its lack of understanding of the U.S. Constitution, is its tendency toward historical revisionism. Proponents often assert that their nation was founded as a Christian nation, selectively interpreting historical events and documents to support this claim.

While it is true that many of the Founding Fathers of the United States were influenced by Christian principles, the nation's founding documents, such as the Constitution and the Bill of Rights, reflect a commitment to pluralism and the protection of individual rights. This revisionist history not only distorts the past, but also undermines the principles of democracy that allow for a multiplicity of beliefs and practices.

The error lies in the failure to recognize that a truly democratic society thrives on diversity and the coexistence of various worldviews. By promoting a narrative that emphasizes a singular Christian identity, Christian Nationalists overlook the diverse religious and philosophical influences that shaped their nation and in fact the world.

A state sanctioned approach in the United States or in other democratic country, not only alienates non-Christian citizens, but also contradicts the teachings of Christ, which emphasize love, acceptance, and respect for all individuals, regardless of their beliefs. The error lies in the belief that a nation can be truly free while imposing a singular religious identity on its citizens.

Moreover, the emphasis on a national identity rooted in Christianity can lead to a form of idolatry, where the nation itself becomes an object of worship, and thus distorts the collective moral compass.

In relation to the actual wording of the United States Constitution, one can also see significant concerns. While proponents argue that Christian Nationalistic ideology reflects the nation's founding values, a critical examination reveals that

Christian Nationalism is fraught with errors that undermine the core tenets of democracy.

The United States was founded on principles that emphasize the separation of church and state, ensuring that individuals have the right to practice their faith without government interference. Christian Nationalism seeks to privilege one religious perspective over others, effectively undermining the very foundation of religious liberty.

By advocating for policies that favour Christian beliefs and practices, Christian Nationalists inadvertently or for its leaders deliberately, promote a form of state-sanctioned religion as seen in other autocratic nations around the world.

As the movement continues to evolve, it is essential for society to engage in critical dialogue about the implications of intertwining faith and politics, striving for a future that respects diverse beliefs while upholding the principles of democracy and inclusion. Understanding and addressing the rise of Christian Nationalism is crucial for fostering a more equitable and harmonious society in an increasingly culturally diverse world.

In today's America there is some confusion as to the involvement of the Evangelical religion in the affairs of Christian Nationalism. This is how it is. Whilst Christian Nationalist groups and Evangelical groups can overlap, they are not synonymous. Evangelicals are a broad subset of Protestant Christians who emphasise the authority of the Bible, the necessity of personal conversion, and active evangelism. Evangelicals hold diverse political and social views, although many but not all lean conservative, especially in the United States.

On the other hand, Christian Nationalism being a sociopolitical ideology seeking to merge Christian identity with national identity, leans strongly towards far-right conservative politics. Many Christian Nationalists are evangelicals because evangelicalism is a significant religious demographic in the United States, but not all evangelicals are Christian Nationalists, as Evangelicals prefer to focus on individual faith and mission work, while Christian Nationalists prioritise shaping societal structures to reflect their Christian worldview.

Some prominent evangelicals have criticised Christian Nationalism for conflating Christianity with nationalism, seeing it as a distortion of the gospels universal message. Others support it, believing their faith compels them to advocate for a Christian oriented society. In short however Christian Nationalists can be evangelicals, but their ideology extends beyond religious identity to include political and nationalistic goals.

"The Evangelical movement often views itself as a countercultural force in a society that is increasingly secular and progressive. Many Evangelicals feel that their values are under attack from a dominant culture that promotes liberal ideologies. Donald Trump's rhetoric, which often includes a disingenuous defence of Christianity and traditional values, provides a sense of validation and empowerment for Evangelicals who feel their beliefs are being sidelined. His presidency in 2016 was seen as a bulwark against what the Evangelicals perceive as the erosion of their religious identity."

5

Faith and Fervour, Manipulating the Masses.

The Parallel Playbooks of Evangelical

Preachers and Politicians.

Chapter Contents.

"The alignment of the Christian Evangelical movement with far-right ideologies presents a complex and multifaceted challenge that has significant implications for both religious communities and broader societal dynamics. This convergence, while not representative of all Evangelicals, has been increasingly visible in recent years, raising concerns about the potential dangers it poses to religious integrity, social cohesion, and democratic principles."

THE EVANGELICAL MOVEMENT.

The Evangelical Movement, a significant force within Christianity, has a rich and complex history that spans several centuries, and in more recent times it has significantly influenced religious and political landscapes, particularly in the United States. Its leaders often command massive followings, wielding considerable authority and moral influence. Understanding the rise of evangelicalism is essential for comprehending contemporary religious dynamics and their impact on culture and politics.

The term "evangelical" itself is derived from the Greek word "euangelion," meaning "good news" or "gospel." This focus on the gospel message became a defining characteristic of the movement. However, the evangelical movement as we understand it today began to take shape in the 18th century during the Great Awakenings, a series of religious revivals that swept through Britain and the American colonies.

The roots of the Evangelical Movement can be traced back to the Protestant Reformation of the 16th century, a period marked by a profound transformation in the religious landscape of Europe. The Reformation, led by figures such as Martin Luther and John Calvin, emphasized the authority of Scripture and the doctrine of salvation by faith alone, laying the groundwork for evangelical thought.

The First Great Awakening (circa 1730-1755) was a response to the perceived spiritual dryness and formalism of established churches. It was characterized by passionate Pentecostal type preaching and an emphasis on personal conversion experiences.

Key figures in the awakening as it was called, included Jonathan Edwards, known for his sermon "Sinners in the Hands of an Angry God," and George Whitefield, whose itinerant preaching drew massive crowds. This revivalist spirit emphasized a personal relationship with Jesus Christ and the necessity of being "born again," concepts that remain central to evangelicalism today.

The Second Great Awakening (circa 1790-1840) further solidified evangelicalism's influence, particularly in the United States. It was marked by large camp meetings and a democratization of religion, where laypeople played a significant role in spreading the gospel.

This period saw the rise of new denominations, such as the Methodists and Baptists, which grew rapidly due to their evangelical zeal and grassroots organization. The movement also spurred social reforms, including the abolition of slavery and saw the emergence of the Temperance Movement, as it was known, where evangelicals sought to apply their faith to societal issues through "political lobbying" for specific social changes.

The Temperance Movement began in the early 1800's, with various religious and social groups advocating for moderation in drinking. It gained momentum in the 1830's and 1840's, influenced by the Second Great Awakening, the religious revival that emphasized personal morality and social reform.

The primary goal of the Temperance Movement was to reduce alcohol consumption, which many believed was linked to social problems such as poverty, domestic violence, and crime. Some advocates sought complete prohibition, while others promoted moderation.

Various organizations were formed to promote temperance, including the American Temperance Society (founded in 1826), and the Women's Christian Temperance Union (WCTU), established in 1874. These groups organized campaigns, rallies, and educational programs to raise awareness about the dangers of alcohol, whilst at the same time lobbying politicians for legislative change.

The movement played a significant role in advocating for laws to restrict or ban alcohol sales, said advocating culminating in the passage of the 18th. Amendment to the U.S. Constitution in 1919, which established Prohibition, making the manufacture, sale, and transportation of alcoholic beverages illegal.

This Prohibition Era (1920-1933) saw a significant decline in legal alcohol consumption, but it also led to unintended consequences, such as the rise of illegal speakeasies, (small illegal dens and nightclubs), organized crime, and widespread disregard for the law. The negative effects of Prohibition, along with an increase in changing public attitudes, led to its repeal with the 21st Amendment in 1933. The Temperance Movement, however, continued to influence discussions about alcohol regulation and public health.

And whilst The Temperance Movement had a lasting impact on American society, shaping attitudes toward alcohol consumption and influencing future social reform movements, it also highlighted the "complexities of legislating morality," and the challenges of addressing social, psychological, and health issues through politically legislated policy means.

Furthermore in terms of learning any lessons from it, in the current political landscape it appears that no long-lasting gains have been made, witnessed in the Republican Party's current and continuing "legislative assault" on women's health issues.

In the 19th. and early 20th. centuries, evangelicalism continued to evolve. The rise of fundamentalism in the early 20th. century was a reaction against modernist theology and the perceived erosion of biblical authority. Fundamentalists emphasized the inerrancy of Scripture and the fundamentals of Christian doctrine.

This period also saw the emergence of Pentecostalism, which primarily emphasized the work of the Holy Spirit and spiritual gifts, but a religious organization who believed also that a demon lurked behind every immoral thought and physical affliction, and needed to be cast out, adding a new dimension to the "evangelical entertainment landscape", and an increasing proliferation of religious charlatans drawing massive crowds to their "healing services".

The New Testament warns Christians of charlatans in the Book of Corinthians and in the Book of Timothy. Religious charlatans are people, including pastors and preachers, who promote religion for their own personal profit and power. Similarly you could say there are political charlatans who promote their own name and high profile, their personal brand, for personal profit.

The mid-20th. century witnessed the rise of Neo-Evangelicalism, a movement that sought to engage more constructively with modern society and intellectual thought while maintaining a commitment to evangelical doctrine. Leaders like Dr. Billy Graham, who was raised as a Presbyterian but worked as a Baptist evangelist, became prominent, drawing massive crowds through outside rallies, eventually using the same type of rallies to reach a global audience.

Growing up at this time I was drawn into becoming a willing participant in that global audience. I share this my personal experience because there is a similar persuasive methodology used by political candidates vying for high office to garner electoral support from members of their audience at large political rallies, as is used by prominent evangelists at their crusade rallies to win the support and acquiescence of a potential convert.

This persuasive methodology primarily centres on using tools to elicit an emotional response from the audience to what the politician or the preacher is presenting. And it can focus on eliciting a positive emotional response such as happiness or joy, or a negative emotional response such as frustration or anger or even fear: all three work.

My Early Experience with The Evangelical Movement.

From early childhood I had always felt a pull towards the spiritual aspect of life, which would see me every Sunday morning attending our local Baptist Church of the evangelical kind, participating along with other children in what was known as a Sunday School class. It was an innocuous type of Children's Bible Study you could say, focused on the singing of simple Christian choruses and the teaching of easily understood Bible stories.

The Sunday School teacher, interestingly always a woman, would use an illustrated picture book held up for all to see, and also sometimes used felt cut-outs of Biblical characters, posting them on a display board. The stories she shared pertained mostly to incidents in the life of Jesus, but sometimes, probably to hold our interest, she would read adventurous Old Testament stories such as Daniel in the lion's den, or the tale of Joseph and his coat of many colours.

So you could say, that from a very young age my belief system about God, Jesus, and the Bible was in my own mind, simple and relatively settled. As a child I never felt any need to ask for empirical evidence that everything our Sunday school teacher told us was the absolute truth. I just innocently accepted that it was. There were no long held belief systems opposed to those of hers lodged in my psyche that had to be dislodged before her simple teaching could take root as a truth filled belief in my young easily influenced mind.

Later in life I came to see that children accept both truth and falsity equally and effortlessly, for in a child the easily influenced and readily manipulated reasoning aspect of the ego is not as yet fully operational. Religious leaders know this, particularly those of the two largest Christian churches, the Catholic and Anglican, and because of this they also understand the impact of early childhood indoctrination.

It was a Jesuit priest from the Catholic Church who famously said, "give me a child for his first seven years and I'll give you the man." This is why we see even in this modern day, a push by Evangelicals and far-right Christian Nationalists for the reintroduction of religious instruction in all primary schools.

Then in my teenage years, once again it would be this continuous subtle pull towards the things of the Spirit that saw me board a tramcar and journey a short distance to the local showground, to see the Reverend Billy Graham, this world-renowned American preacher in the neo-evangelical movement, when he visited my hometown as part of his global evangelizing tour.

As an adult when I looked back later on that crusade experience, I realised that it was indeed a spectacular, well planned, well intentioned, beautifully choreographed, emotion generating event to attend; but also an event that would have borne no resemblance at all to what history tells us were similar crowd drawing events that Jesus was involved in during his earthly ministry.

I had missed the first tramcar to the event and consequently entered the showground only minutes before the crusade was scheduled to start, and by that time there was standing room only. The seats in the grandstands were full to overflowing with thousands of people standing to their feet as the rousing sound of the hundred strong choir, accompanied by the booming base baritone voice of George Beverly Shea, burst forth singing the age-old hymn, "Then Sings My Soul My Saviour God to Thee, How Great Thou Art."

When the hymn was nearing completion, the choir on the conductor's cue hushed to a whisper, and to the raucous applause of the crowd the fiery evangelist Billy Graham strode onto the stage, much like a politician would do at the launch of their presidential campaign. Up to the lectern he strode, Bible in hand, and commenced preaching emotively and passionately about the evils of sin, war, racism, and spiritual and physical poverty.

He preached for around thirty minutes and finally settled into a slow conversational tone as, with his voice lowering in volume to a soft gentle level, the choir members once again on cue took their places on the stage and softly sang as a background accompaniment to his voice, "Just as I am without one plea, but that thy blood was shed for me, O Lamb of God I come."

He continued speaking softly, probably for about another five or six minutes, almost at times in a whisper, about humanity's need for God's love and his saving grace, strongly encouraging all who were present to believe, or as he put it, "make a decision for Christ". He concluded his sermon with an impassioned plea, "only believe, only believe, all things are possible if you only believe," and with his words "will you come...will you come," hundreds of people began leaving their seats, and walking across the arena to the stage area.

Now once again, like the child in Sunday School, I didn't question the theological veracity of what this preacher was saying as he enthusiastically encouraged all who were present to believe his own set of personal religious beliefs. I didn't analyse what he was saying to gauge if it was truth, nor did I call out for proof as to the accuracy of what he was saying.

Similarly, just as the attendees at Jerry Falwell's rallies, saw no need to ask for proof when Falwell made statements such as "AIDS is not just God's punishment for homosexuals; it is God's punishment for the society that tolerates homosexuals," I as so many do at evangelical events and political rallies, blindly accepted as truth the rhetoric that was being boomed out from the lectern.

As I looked back later in life, I realised that perhaps some of the motivation in my response may have come from an emotional reaction to what he was saying midst the very emotional atmosphere he and his evangelical team had created at the meeting. Similar to the emotional response some political candidates will try to draw out from the crowds during political rallies.

The Parallel Campaign Playbooks of Preachers and Politicians.

One must understand that campaign emotions, political or religious, good or bad, surfacing out of love, out of hate, out of need, or out of disappointment, are used by both politicians and preachers alike to either create unity or to engender separation, and are indeed a powerful influencer in our daily lives and choices, impacting on the decisions we make. They can bypass truth and our inherent need for truth.

Donald Trump has met his supporters needs very effectively in his outside campaign rallies, using rousing rhetoric that when later fact checked by experts prove to be blatant lies; but regardless of this it worked, seeing him manipulate his supporters into an emotionally charged unquestioning response of "like - mindedness", two minds thinking the same thing, resulting as it did in an avalanche of electoral support.

You see political rallies and evangelical events are powerful spectacles designed to persuade and inspire. Both arenas seek to influence their audiences through the strategic use of emotion, often blurring the line between logic and fervour, truth and falsity, particularly for the ignorant and uneducated. Despite their differing purposes, one seeking to galvanise support for political power, and the other to reinforce religious beliefs, the techniques employed in both mass evangelical events and political rallies, reveal striking similarities.

Chief among these techniques is the combined use of emotionally charged rhetoric and music, which work in tandem to achieve the speakers or leader's goal: to convince the public of the supposed truth of their message and rally them to action. Most political and evangelical leaders rely heavily on rhetoric to appeal to the audiences' emotions and a dose of music to flavour it.

At political rallies, speeches are crafted and music selected to evoke the emotions of patriotism, unity, and even fear. Donald Trump has crafted the use of fear, frustration and disappointment in evoking support from the crowds at his campaign rallies, and he is prepared to lie and manipulate the facts to do it.

Politicians also often use inclusive language, such as "we" and "our", to foster a sense of belonging and shared purpose, e.g. "our freedoms are being threatened." They may also employ loaded terms and anecdotes to underscore the stakes of the election, portraying their platform as the solution to existential threats or as a gateway to a better future. Similarly, evangelical preachers use rhetoric that appeals to deep seated emotions like hope, guilt, and redemption.

Through storytelling, metaphors, and repetition, evangelical preachers create vivid images of salvation or condemnation, prompting their audiences to make personal or communal commitments to their particular religious brand. Both settings frequently involve binary rhetoric, presenting the world in terms of good versus evil, or right versus wrong, or us versus them.

Politicians frame their opponents as existential threats to democracy or progress, while evangelical preachers depict sin and moral decay as the ultimate adversaries to divine grace. By creating a sense of urgency these speakers reduce complex issues into digestible narratives that resonate emotionally with their audience, particularly with the uneducated, or those of a lower cognitive level.

Music also, plays a critical role in heightening the emotional atmosphere of both political rallies and evangelical events. In political rallies, stirring anthems, nationalistic songs, and even well-known contemporary pop music are used to energise the crowd and establish either "a celebratory mood or a revolutionary mood". Familiar tunes often evoke nostalgia and a shared cultural identity, further solidifying the bond between the audience and the candidate.

For example, the repeated use of a campaign theme song can become a rallying cry, reinforcing the politician's message every time it is heard. This use, or perhaps at times misuse of music at campaign rallies, often serves to energise the audience, conveying themes aligned with the candidate's message, designed to create a memorable atmosphere, something to take home with them and later tell their friends about.

Donald Trump frequently used the Village People's 1978 hit YMCA at his rallies, often dancing to it during events. The choice likely served Trump several purposes. YMCA is upbeat, familiar, and iconic, making it an effective rally closer that energises the crowd. Or perhaps he just chose it simply because it's his favourite song on his presidential playlist. I would think for Trump it was a combination of both.

The song is also a disco classic with broad appeal across all age groups, evoking nostalgia and a sense of fun. Trump's dance moves to the song became a viral, light-hearted moment, contributing to his image as someone likeable, relatable, or entertaining to his supporters.

However some interpret his use of the song YMCA as ironic given the Village People's association with the LGBTQ + culture, a community that doesn't typically align with conservative politics. However Trump seemed either ignorant of this, or unperturbed by this, and so embraced its broader appeal while sidestepping its cultural origins.

Kamala Harris on the other hand chose Beyonce's song Freedom. The song Freedom is a powerful anthem of liberation, resilience, and social justice, often tied to movements for racial and gender equality. When used in campaign contexts, such as in Kamala Harris's 2024 campaign, the song communicated empowerment for all, but particularly for women and black voters, being a call for breaking down barriers and achieving justice.

The song resonated with themes of inclusion and progressive change. It appealed to women and black voters because it reflected Beyonce's identity as a black woman and activist, aligning with efforts to mobilise black communities and women voters. The song's audible intensity underscores the stakes of the election and the need for activism and participation.

In both cases, the chosen songs served as cultural signifiers that reflect the campaign's intended "messages and emotional tones", however they often generated mixed interpretations depending on the audience. From the political candidate's perspective, they were chosen to convey the message, "I am the only answer to your current disappointment, vote for me." For the preacher the message conveyed is, "God is the only answer to your guilt and lack of hope, choose Christianity and join my church."

In contemporary society, the parallels between politics and religion often manifest in powerful rallies and gatherings, particularly within the realm of evangelical movements. Political figures and religious leaders alike have mastered the art of rhetoric, not necessarily truthful rhetoric, and not necessarily intelligent rhetoric, employing emotional appeals that resonate deeply with the needs of their audiences.

By tapping into the common man's sense of disappointment, personal needs, and anxieties, these leaders cultivate a sense of belonging and urgency that can mobilize support and foster loyalty. And disappointment and anxiety are pervasive sentiments in today's modern society, often stemming from unmet expectations in various aspects of life, including economic stability, social justice, and personal fulfillment.

Political strategists and religious leaders recognize this emotional landscape, and strategically frame their messages to resonate with the frustrations of their audiences. For instance, during economic downturns, political figures may highlight the struggles of the working class, using anecdotes and relatable narratives to illustrate the hardships faced by ordinary citizens. By positioning themselves as champions of the common man, they create a sense of solidarity and shared experience.

Similarly, evangelical leaders often address feelings of disillusionment with the world, presenting their faith as a source of hope and redemption, the way out of their current seemingly hopeless position. They may also recount personal stories of transformation, emphasizing how faith has provided them with purpose and direction amidst chaos. This narrative not only validates the feelings of disappointment or disillusionment among followers, but also offers a pathway to a more fulfilling life through spiritual or political engagement.

By acknowledging the struggles of their audience, these leaders of both the religious and political persuasion foster an emotional connection that encourages individuals to rally behind what can many times be simply the politician's own personal ego ridden agenda, (governance), and the preacher's own personal financial agenda (gold).

At the core of effective political and evangelical rhetoric is the ability to address the personal needs of individuals. Political figures often employ language that speaks to the desires for security, stability, and recognition. For example, during campaign speeches, candidates may promise job creation, healthcare reform, or educational opportunities, framing these issues as essential to the well-being of families and communities.

By articulating a vision that aligns with the aspirations of their audience, their economic needs, or alternately the economic fears of their audience, e.g. the cost-of-living crisis, politicians create a compelling narrative that motivates individuals to support their candidacy.

In the realm of evangelicalism, leaders frequently emphasize the importance of community and belonging. They create an environment where individuals feel valued and understood, often using inclusive language that invites participation. By addressing the spiritual and emotional needs of their followers, evangelical leaders cultivate a sense of identity, unity, and purpose.

In times of uncertainty, be it economic instability, social upheaval, or global crises, leaders often frame their messages around the need for decisive action and strong leadership like theirs. Politicians with dictatorial tendencies, use this technique continually. These are the politicians who the media refer to as "a strongman."

In politics, the term strongman refers to a leader who exercises significant personal power and authority, often bypassing democratic norms, institutions, or checks and balances. Strong men typically consolidate power through populist rhetoric, control of the military or security forces, and by weakening opposition or dissent. Their leadership style is often characterised by authoritarian tendencies, with an emphasis on centralised decision making and control.

They frequently use fear as a tool in their campaign rhetoric. They invoke fear of the "other," as a campaign strategy, whether it be immigrants, foreign adversaries, a potential World War 3, or opposing political ideologies, to rally their base around a common cause. By presenting themselves as the solution to these anxieties, they position their leadership as essential for the safety and prosperity of their constituents.

The ability of political and religious figures to tap into the emotions of disappointment, personal needs, and anxieties is a testament to the power of rhetoric in shaping public discourse. By crafting messages that resonate with the lived experiences of their audiences, these leaders foster a sense of connection and urgency that can mobilize support and drive collective action; and as followers respond to these calls, they not only seek solace and direction, but also become active participants in the narratives that shape their lives and future societies.

Today, evangelicalism is a diverse and global movement, with millions of adherents across various denominations and cultural contexts, and as such a desirable voting bloc for political candidates to align themselves with, even if the candidate has no personal interest in religion. And up until now it has remained a dynamic and influential force within Christianity and within the political establishment, particularly in the United States.

Pulpits and Politics: The Gospel of Hypocrisy: Family Values for Thee, but Not for Me.

Over time, a series of financial and sexual scandals, similar in seriousness as those in Christian Nationalism's Moral Majority, involving prominent evangelical figures, has raised concerns about accountability, transparency, and the credibility of the movement itself. These scandals, while involving specific individuals, have broader implications for the movement's reputation and its relationship with its followers.

Among a small selection as there were many, was Jim Bakker, a televangelist and founder of the PTL (Praise the Lord) Club. Baker was one of the most influential evangelical leaders of the 1980's. His downfall began with revelations of financial mismanagement and sexual misconduct. Bakker was accused of misappropriating millions of dollars donated by his followers, including funds intended for a Christian theme park.

In 1987, allegations also surfaced that he had paid hush money to cover up a sexual encounter with a church secretary, Jessica Hahn. These revelations led to Bakker's conviction on fraud charges in 1989, resulting in a prison sentence and a tarnished legacy.

Jimmy Swaggart, another prominent televangelist, faced a public scandal in 1988 when he was caught with a prostitute. Despite his emotional confession and plea for forgiveness, Swaggart was later involved in another scandal for similar behaviour in 1991. These incidents significantly damaged his ministry and reputation, highlighting a disconnect between his public persona and private actions.

Another example was Ted Haggard an American Methodist pastor and preacher. Haggard was once the president of the National Association of Evangelicals (N.A.E), which represented millions of Evangelical Christians in the United States, and a pastor of a mega-church in Colorado. In his role with the N.A.E., Haggard was involved in influencing political issues, particularly those aligning with evangelical values, such as opposition to same sex marriage.

However, Haggard's influence waned after a scandal in 2006 led to his resignation from both the N.A.E. and the New Life Church he pastored. Haggard was accused of engaging in a sexual relationship with a male escort and using drugs He initially denied the allegations, but later admitted to some of the accusations, leading to his resignation. This scandal was particularly damaging due to Haggard's vocal opposition to homosexuality, highlighting the issue of hypocrisy within religious leadership.

But the scandals involving evangelical leadership have not been limited to the United States alone. Hillsong Church, an Australian based but global Pentecostal/ Evangelical mega church, with affiliates in the United States, has been embroiled in several scandals over the years, involving key figures within its leadership.

Frank Houston, father of Hillsong founder Brian Houston, was a pastor accused of sexually abusing multiple young boys during his ministry in New Zealand and Australia. One of these victims who came forward was between the ages of seven and 12 years of age. In 1999, when these allegations came to light, Brian Houston, son of Frank, and the then National President of the Assemblies of God in Australia, was charged by the NSW police with concealing his father's sexual abuse of children.

Brian Houston, the founder of Hillsong church, was subsequently involved in incidents of inappropriate behaviour himself, leading to his resignation in March 2022. It was revealed that in 2013, he is said to have exchanged inappropriate text messages with a female staff member, resulting in her resignation. Then in 2019, while under the influence of alcohol and prescription medication, he entered a woman's hotel room during a conference in the United States and spent 40 minutes inside, and it appeared doubtful they were having a prayer meeting.

None of these scandals however appear to have dented permanently the determination of the Evangelical Movement in terms of its pursuance of political influence and what they see as their responsibility through political lobbying to defend the moral issues enveloping the United States culture.

In my time as a Pentecostal Pastor in a church in Australia, I was given information about a married Senior Pastor/Evangelist, who was involved in numerous affairs with both single and married women in the church over a long period of time. Much to the disdain of his supporters and some of his key allies, who would have preferred the revelations to be swept under the carpet, I chose to expose him, an exposure which led to his dismissal.

What continues to amaze me is the way in which, regarding issues of sexual or financial misconduct within their political or religious organizations, many leaders and followers in both these movements, are prepared to sacrifice their own moral integrity to save one of the own, primarily to save their own political agenda, ideological religious agenda, or their own ambition driven personal agenda.

In spite of his controversial behaviour and oftentimes hate filled rhetoric, filled with racist overtones, a significant portion of the Evangelical community has rallied behind Donald Trump, raising questions about the motivations behind this support and the state of "the moral compass" of those evangelical leaders advocating this support.

And despite its growth and influence, the evangelical movement faces several challenges and critiques. Internally, there are ongoing debates about theological diversity, social engagement, and the relationship between faith and politics. Some evangelicals are calling for a return to a more inclusive and compassionate approach, emphasizing love and justice over political power. Externally, the movement has been criticized for its association with political conservatism and its perceived intolerance toward other faiths and lifestyles.

In the 2024 U.S. election cycle, recently completed, evangelical voters continued to largely support Donald Trump, regardless of his reported indiscretions and criminal convictions. Pre-election data showed that 81% of white evangelical Protestants would likely vote for Trump, a continuation of the strong support in 2016 and 2020 when roughly 80% backed him. And recently released data (Feb.2025) regarding the 2024 election, shows that that is exactly what they did.

Trump's appeal among this voting bloc is driven by his supposed stance on issues central to evangelical concerns, such as religious freedom, abortion restrictions, and Conservative judicial appointments. However for Trump, there is a convincing argument that his support for evangelical causes is merely part of his "quid pro quo" strategy, which would see him support legislating for their concerns in return for them giving him strong electoral support, which they did.

Donald Trump being a transactional person, of the quid-pro-quo variety, has proved over and over again in his hunt for voter support that he is prepared to mix faith, finance, and a transactional attitude to achieve his political ambitions; whilst the evangelical community at large have demonstrated their determination to bend their collective moral compass in turning a blind eye to truth and righteousness in pursuit of their own religious ideological agenda, and as such eagerly embrace the "quid pro-quo" opportunity presented to them by Trump.

Analysing Evangelical Support for Conservativism and Donald Trump.

One of the primary reasons for Evangelical support for the MAGA Republican Party, and as such support for Donald Trump is the supposed alignment of his policies with their values. Many Evangelicals prioritize issues such as opposition to abortion, the defence of religious freedom, and the promotion of traditional family values. Trump's 2016 administration took steps that resonated with these priorities, including appointing conservative judges, advocating for pro-life policies, and supporting religious liberty initiatives.

The Evangelical movement often views itself as a countercultural force in a society that is increasingly secular and progressive. Many Evangelicals feel that their values are under attack from a dominant culture that promotes liberal ideologies. Trump's rhetoric, which often includes a defence of Christianity and traditional values, even though they play a limited part in his personal life, provides a sense of validation and empowerment for Evangelicals who feel their beliefs are being sidelined. His presidency in 2016 was seen as a bulwark against what they perceive as the erosion of their religious identity.

It is obvious however as evidenced by his lifestyle, cruel rhetoric, irrational behaviour, and lack of common decency, that Trump has no personal commitment to these ideals. His support is purely transactional. It's a "you vote for me, and I'll give you what you want" scenario. But many spiritually naive Evangelicals, see this not as a quid pro quo arrangement, but rather a commitment to their moral framework and a desire to protect their beliefs in the public sphere.

Trump's outsider status and his anti-establishment rhetoric has also appealed to many Evangelicals. Frustrated with what they perceive as a corrupt political system that has failed to address their concerns, Evangelicals have found in Trump a candidate who promises to challenge the status quo, to drain the swamp as he puts it. His willingness to confront political elites and media institutions resonates with a large segment of the Evangelical community that feels marginalized and disillusioned by traditional political figures.

You see in times of cultural and political uncertainty, a leader who projects strength and a willingness to fight for their values is appealing. Trump's promises to "drain the swamp" and restore traditional American values resonate with evangelicals who believe that the nation has strayed from its Christian roots.

What they fail to see, through ignorance, is that yes, Trump will drain the swamp but has an agenda to refill that swamp with political sycophants and oligarchs, whose intent is to enrich themselves at the rest of the nation's expense.

Many Evangelicals also appreciate his focus on national sovereignty, economic growth, and a strong military. This appeal to patriotism and a vision of America that aligns with their values resonates with a demographic that often prioritizes national identity and security above everything else . For some, supporting Trump is seen as a way to reclaim a sense of American greatness that they believe has been lost. Hence Trump's strategists cunning marketing of the slogan "make America great again."

The support of the Evangelical movement for Trump has significant implications for American society and politics. The alignment of Evangelicals with Trump has contributed to the increasing polarization of American politics. This support has solidified the Republican Party's self-identifying as the party of conservative Christian values, further entrenching divisions between political ideologies.

Trump has been a staunch advocate for religious liberty, (except for the Muslim religion and most religious minorities), and an advocate for pro-life policies, as are many conservative judges. His advocacy for the appointment of three Supreme Court justices who have the potential to shape American law for decades was a purposefully planned scenario.

Trump also firmly believes that if you control the highest judiciary, you control the nation. These policy achievements resonate deeply with evangelicals, who see them as crucial in promoting and preserving their vision of a moral society.

His rhetoric often frames him as a defender of religious freedom, a key concern for many evangelicals who feel their rights are under threat in an increasingly secular society. His administration's actions, such as reversing Obama-era policies that were seen as infringing on religious liberties and supporting religious expression in public life, have strengthened his bond with evangelical voters.

For these voters, Trump is perceived as a bulwark against a culture that they believe in their continual state of religious insecurity, is becoming increasingly hostile to Christianity, and Trump revels in their adoration of him and for some their worship of him. This hunger for adoration and worship is a common trait of narcissistic political dictators in times past and in this current era. Adolf Hitler and Kim Jong-un are two perfect examples.

Many evangelicals also view Trump as a warrior against the forces of secular progressivism, which they associate with the erosion of traditional values. Trump's opposition to political correctness, his hardline stance on immigration, and his willingness to confront the left on cultural issues resonate with evangelicals who feel marginalized by the mainstream media and academia. His rhetoric and policies are seen as a rejection of the progressive agenda that they believe threatens the moral fabric of the nation.

Some evangelical leaders, perhaps a little sceptical of Trump's supposed Christian beliefs, to justify their support of him, have suggested that there are parallels between Trump and the Old Testament biblical figure of Cyrus, a non-Israelite king who was used by God to achieve his purposes despite not being a believer. This analogy has been used to suggest that Trump, despite his personal flaws, is being used by God to protect and advance Christian interests. This theological interpretation provides a ridiculously weak spiritual justification for supporting Trump.

The relationship between Trump and evangelical voters can also be seen as transactional. Trump has made it clear that he values the evangelical vote and has delivered on key issues important to them. In return, many evangelicals are willing to overlook his personal failings in exchange for policies that reflect their institutional values which are not necessarily Christlike values.

This un-Christlike pragmatic approach prioritizes tangible outcomes over personal piety, focusing on what Trump can achieve for the evangelical agenda rather than how he conducts himself. Trump's strongman persona, characterized by his boldness, authoritarian attitude, and willingness to defy convention, appeals to evangelicals who feel that their way of life is under siege.

Evangelicals have long felt alienated by what they perceive as a hostile mainstream media that often portrays their beliefs as out of touch or extreme. Trump's frequent attacks on the media and his claims of being unfairly targeted by "fake news" resonate with evangelicals who feel similarly maligned. This shared sense of persecution strengthens the bond between Trump and his evangelical supporters, who see him as a kindred spirit fighting against a common adversary.

His appeal to evangelicals is a complex phenomenon rooted in shared policy goals, a sense of cultural embattlement, and a pragmatic approach to politics. While his personal life and demeanour may seem at odds with traditional evangelical values, his unwavering commitment to advancing their priorities has earned him a loyal following among evangelical Christians. For many evangelicals, Trump is seen not just as a political leader, but as a crucial ally in the fight to preserve and promote their vision of America.

His rise to political prominence was marked by rhetoric and behaviour that are antithetical to the core teachings of Christ and Christianity, yet the majority of evangelicals continue to support him. His personal history, characterized by multiple marriages, allegations of sexual misconduct, fraud, and felony convictions, and a penchant for inflammatory and divisive language, stands in stark contrast to the moral and ethical standards of Christ, which at one time were traditionally upheld by Evangelicals.

And as such this unwavering support of Evangelicals for Trump has significant implications for both the religious and political spheres. The alignment with Trump has led to questions about the credibility and moral authority of Evangelical leaders. Critics argue that by overlooking Trump's behaviour, Evangelicals risk compromising their witness and undermining the moral and ethical teachings of Christ.

The paradox of Evangelical support for Donald Trump, despite his un-Christlike behaviour, is a complex and multifaceted issue. It reflects a confluence of historical, cultural, and political factors that have shaped the Evangelical community's engagement with the political sphere for centuries.

As the United States continues to navigate its deeply polarized landscape, the relationship between Evangelicals and political leaders like Trump will remain a critical area of examination and reflection. And the long-term impact of this support remains uncertain.

For while it has yielded short-term political gains, and some of the religious far-right's ideological goals, it may also lead to a re-evaluation of the relationship between faith and politics within the Evangelical community, seeing a growing call for a return to a more holistic and Christ-centred approach to both Christianity and to political engagement.

"As Evangelicalism, Christian Nationalism, White Supremacy, Neo-Fascism, the Great Replacement Theory, and specific political think-tank ideologies such as Project 2025 intertwine, the moral compass of a nation spins wildly, losing its true north of justice and equality. The governance influenced by a conglomerate of ideologically obsessed groups leads to a society where the marginalized are silenced, and the powerful thrive on division; and as such, hatred becomes a political tool, and the moral consciousness of a nation is not just threatened, it is fundamentally altered."

6

Intersecting Ideologies.

The Convergence of Christian Nationalism, Evangelicalism, White Supremacy, Neo-Fascism, The Great Replacement Theory, and Project 2025.

Chapter Contents.

"The unification of religion and hate-driven groups creates a toxic environment where fear replaces freedom, and bigotry masquerades as patriotism. When extremist ideologies gain power, the light of reason and empathy is extinguished, leaving darkness in its wake. And in the shadow of a united hate, the ideals of liberty and justice for all become mere echoes of a forgotten past.

THE CONVERGENCE...THE CURRENT IDEOLOGICAL LANDSCAPE.

Setting aside for the moment our reflection on the chaotic domestic and international turbulence that is currently manifesting around the world due to Donald Trump's re-emergence on the stage of American and world politics, might I suggest that there is something far more urgent that society must gain greater understanding of and must urgently direct its attention to.

A far greater problem for all nations in the present moment that many citizens in the United States and around the world are blissfully unaware of is the subtle but many times with deliberate intent, melding together of the thinking processes and activities of specific political and religious ideological driven groups that underpin and contribute to the emergence of a chaotic social environment. And whilst each group is not identical in manifesto, all are still of similar and compatible ideological beliefs that are rooted in hate, bigotry arrogance, authoritarianism, and racism.

In recent years, the political landscape in various parts of the world has witnessed a resurgence of ideologies that intertwine religious fervour, racial superiority, and authoritarian governance. Among these, Christian Nationalism, the Evangelical Movement, the White Supremacist Movement, Neo-Fascism, and initiatives like the Great Replacement Theory and Project 2025, have emerged as significant forces.

It is extremely important if societies around the world want to hold on to their hard fought freedoms and rights, that all people come to a greater understanding of who these groups are, what these groups believe in, and how these groups if given the chance will systematically unwind the democratic norms that have existed for centuries; for I feel that in this current socio-political environment, too many people are totally ignorant of the existence of them and the ongoing threat that they pose.

While each of these ideologies and movements have distinct characteristics, they share common threads that bind them together, creating a complex web of beliefs that challenge democratic principles and social cohesion.

Moreover, each of these movements often employ similar strategies to achieve their objectives, such as manipulating media narratives, fostering division, and undermining democratic institutions. By presenting themselves as defenders of tradition and stability, they attract naive individuals who are disillusioned with the status quo and seek simple solutions to complex problems.

In the outworking of this we see Christian Nationalists and Evangelicals, who view their nation as divinely favoured and believe that only their brand of religious beliefs should influence political decisions, embark on an ideological mission that can lead to the exclusion of non-Christians and the marginalization of minority groups, as it promotes a homogeneous national identity centred around a specific religious framework.

We see the White Supremacist Movement, a movement which is rooted in the belief that white people are superior to those of other racial backgrounds and should therefore dominate society, manifest in various forms, from the Ku Klux Klan to contemporary alt-right groups, who go about their work exploiting economic and social anxieties to promote their agenda; blaming minority and non-white groups for societal problems, they seek to maintain or establish systems of racial hierarchy and segregation.

We see Neo-Fascism, which is a modern iteration of the fascist ideologies that emerged in the early 20th century, characterized by authoritarianism, nationalism, and the suppression of political dissent, advocate for a centralized, autocratic government led by a dictatorial leader. Marked by its disdain for liberal democracy, its emphasis on order and control, and its willingness to use violence to achieve its goals, this ideology frequently employ populist rhetoric to gain support.

And we see Great Replacement Theorists, proponents of a far-right conspiracy theory which falsely claims that white populations in Western countries are being deliberately replaced through mass immigration, declining birth rates, and cultural changes. The primary objective of these groups is to reduce or halt immigration, especially from non-European or non-white countries, viewing it as a democratic threat; their argument being that multiculturalism and diversity policies contribute to societal decline.

Then tagging along for the ideological ride, we see Project 2025, a strategic initiative that aims to reshape political and social landscapes by promoting policies aligned with conservative and nationalist ideologies. Whilst as far as we know, not inherently linked to extremist movements, time will tell, Project 2025 can serve and in Donald Trump's new administration is now serving, as a platform for advancing agendas that resonate with Christian Nationalists, White Supremacists, Neo-Fascists, and Great Replacement Theorists.

By advocating for policies that prioritize certain religious or cultural identities, Project 2025 can, and in Donald Trump's new administration now has, for obvious reasons, inadvertently provided "a veneer of legitimacy" to more radical elements within these other ideologically obsessed movements.

A religious-ideological-political driven group is an organisation or movement motivated by accommodation of religious beliefs alongside ideological goals and political ambition. These groups often intertwine their spiritual, doctrinal, or social convictions with broader political, social, or cultural objectives, believing that whilst their individual ideology represents absolute truth or a divine mandate, they are willing to join with other like-minded individuals if it means achieving their goals more quickly.

Members typically share a strong sense of belonging, shaped by both their religious faith and or their ideological commitment, and it is the ideological component that gives them their longevity. Aleksandr Solzhenitsyn, the Russian novelist, a former inmate of the Gulags, the forced labour camps of the Russian dictator Stalin, wrote this about ideological insanity in his book "The Gulag Archipelago."

"The imagination and spiritual strength of Shakespeare's evildoers stopped short at a dozen corpses because they had no ideology. Ideology, that is what gives evildoing its long-standing justification and gives the evildoer the necessary steadfastness and determination."

In terms of their propaganda and recruitment, all of these groups seem to disseminate messages that highlight their religious and or ideological values. They use media, social platforms, or religious gatherings to attract followers. They establish networks or communities centred around shared beliefs, and they offer support systems such as education, social services, or moral guidance, merely as bribes to strengthen loyalty to their cause.

They may advocate for policies aligned with their beliefs, often lobbying governments or influencing legislation, using organised protests, demonstrations, and campaigns to draw attention to their cause. And in certain circumstances they may adopt militant or violent tactics to achieve their goals. This was witnessed in the January 6th. 2021 insurrection attempt and the involvement of the Proud Boys, a White Supremacist Movement affiliate group.

They also use schools, religious institutions, and online platforms to instil their beliefs in followers and in future generations. This is why the architects of

Project 2025, now firmly ensconced in Donald Trump's new administration, are going after the current Education Department with an intent to dismantle it, and re-purpose it via the states, to align with their own ideology. And if the states don't co-operate with their agenda they will not get federal funds. Watch that space.

Whilst for media purposes Trump is saying that he is merely giving responsibility back to the states, watch the space ahead. It is highly likely that those states who refuse to implement any of the "project's policies" such as compulsory Christian religious education or the banning of certain types of subjects or books, that Trump will, in a dictatorial fashion, use the threat of the removal of some type of federal funding to force the state to comply.

All of these groups have distinct agendas, but common purposes, which include to promote what they see as a return to traditional or divine values, or what they believe were successful past ideological pathways for humanity, a so called "golden age." They oppose all practices or ideologies that they consider immoral or harmful, not to their fellow citizens, but to their ideological cause; sometimes with violence, but certainly through digital platforms.

They seek to create a society governed by their personal interpretation of religious law, or ideological principles, not dissimilar at all from the aims of many Eastern Muslim controlled countries. They resist perceived threats to their religion or ideology, such as secularism, globalisation, multi-culturalism, or any other competing beliefs or political pathways.

The convergence of Christian Nationalism, Evangelicalism, White Supremacy, Neo-Fascism, and initiatives like the Great Replacement Theory and Project 2025 is evident in their shared goals and methods.

All these ideologies emphasize a return to a perceived golden age, whether religious, political, or social, often characterized by a homogeneous society that aligns with their religious, racial, or cultural ideals and their binary, biased, and radical way of thinking. They exploit fears of cultural change and economic instability to garner support, using populist rhetoric to appeal to those who feel disenfranchised by modern society.

The following is a brief overview of the origins and aims of these ideologically driven groups currently in play in the United States, detailing how their aims and actions, sometimes in an obvious way, but sometimes subtly, directly intersect with Donald Trump's view of the world and governance.

The White Supremacist Movement.

White Supremacy is an ideology rooted in the belief that white people are superior to those of other racial backgrounds and should therefore dominate society. This belief system has been used to justify the oppression and marginalization of non-white individuals and communities throughout history. The ideology of White Supremacy is not confined to a single organization or movement but is a pervasive and insidious belief that has manifested in various forms across different societies and during different historical periods.

The origins of White Supremacist ideology can be traced back to European colonialism and the transatlantic slave trade, where racial hierarchies were constructed to justify the exploitation and subjugation of non-European people.

In the United States, White Supremacy became institutionalized through laws and practices that enforced racial segregation and discrimination, most notably through the institution of slavery and later through the Jim Crow laws, detailed legislated enforceable laws that stipulated the conditions of life for coloured people including where they could live, who they could marry, and what jobs they could hold, plus many more.

One of the most infamous manifestations of White Supremacy in the United States was the Confederate States of America, which seceded from the Union in 1860-1861, leading to the Civil War. The Confederacy was founded on the principle of maintaining the institution of slavery, which was seen as essential to the Southern economy and way of life. Confederate leaders explicitly stated that their new nation was built upon the belief in the racial superiority of white people and the subjugation of African Americans.

After the Civil War, White Supremacist ideology continued to thrive in the form of the Ku Klux Klan (KKK), a White Supremacist terrorist organization founded in the late 1860's. The KKK and similar groups used violence, intimidation, and murder by hanging, to maintain white dominance and resist the social and political gains made by African Americans during the reconstruction after the war.

Throughout the 20th century, White Supremacist groups have evolved, often rebranding themselves with names such as the Proud Boys, and the Oath Keepers, to appeal to new generations while maintaining their core beliefs. Founded in 2016 by Gavin McInnes, the Proud Boys describe themselves as a "pro-Western fraternal organization" and have been associated with various extremist views, including nationalism, anti-communism, and a so-called rejection of political correctness.

The group has been involved in numerous violent confrontations and has gained notoriety for its violent participation in rallies and protests, including the January 6th insurrection at the U.S. Capitol, where Donald Trump's regard for them as his foot soldiers and tacit approval of their actions which included violence saw them rise to prominence.

The ideology of the Proud Boys is often characterized by elements of white nationalism, misogyny, and a strong sense of nationalism. They have been described by some analysts as having fascist tendencies, particularly in their embrace of authoritarianism and their disdain for liberal democratic values. Their rhetoric often includes a glorification of violence as a means to achieve political ends, which saw them being primary participators in the January 6th insurrection protesting with violence in support of Donald Trump.

The Proud Boys' strong support for Trump can be attributed to several factors. They view him as a figure who challenges the political establishment and embodies their anti-establishment sentiments. Trump's rhetoric, particularly his stances on immigration, law and order, and political correctness, resonates with their beliefs. Additionally, during the 2020 presidential election, Trump infamously told the Proud Boys to "stand back and stand by," which many interpreted as a wink and a nod for their intended behaviour.

Members of the Proud Boys were later involved in the attack on the U.S. Capitol, with some convicted of seditious conspiracy. Prosecutors argued that they played a key role in attempting to keep Trump in power. On January 20, 2025, President Donald Trump issued pardons and commutations to nearly 1,600 individuals charged in connection with the January 6th, 2021, capitol riot. Notably, Enrique Torrio, the leader of the Proud Boys was among those pardoned.

In contemporary times, White Supremacist ideology has found support among various extremist groups and individuals who promote racial hatred and division. These groups often use the internet and social media to spread their message, many times laced with conspiracy theories, doing so to recruit new members, as the curiosity of the younger generation or those marginalised holds no bounds.

While explicit support for White Supremacy is generally condemned in mainstream society, elements of the ideology can still be found in certain political and social movements that advocate for policies and practices that disproportionately harm non-white communities. However White Supremacist ideology is still currently being supported by numerous groups around America. Their influence varies, with some being highly organized while others operate in small cells or online networks. These include:

The Patriot Front, a white nationalist hate group that emerged from Vanguard America; it promotes a fascist and ultranationalist ideology. The Oath

Keepers, an anti-government militia with ties to white nationalism and conspiracy theories, particularly active in the January 6th Capitol attack. The Three Percenters, a far-right militia movement that believes in armed resistance against the government; some factions have white supremacist affiliations.

The Aryan Brotherhood, a violent white supremacist prison gang that has expanded into organized crime outside prison walls. The Base, a neo-Nazi accelerationist group advocating for racial violence and the creation of a white ethnostate. The Atomwaffen Division, a violent neo-Nazi group that promotes terrorism, racial conflict, and apocalyptic accelerationism. The Boogaloo Movement, a loose network of anti-government extremists, some with white supremacist ideologies, who prepare for a second civil war.

The National Socialist Movement (NSM), one of the largest openly neo-Nazi groups in the U.S., promoting Hitler's ideology. The Identity Evropa (American Identity Movement) a white nationalist group focused on college campus recruitment and the promotion of "white European identity." And the Volksfront, a white supremacist group with a history of violence and neo-Nazi ideology.

Some Ku Klux Klan offshoots still function, for while the KKK is not as unified or powerful as in the past, multiple splinter factions still exist, including: The Loyal White Knights of the KKK, The United Klans of America, and The Knights of the Ku Klux Klan. As well as the League of the South, a neo-Confederate hate group advocating for a white ethnostate in the South, alongside The Council of Conservative Citizens, a white nationalist group that influenced Charleston church shooter Dylann Roof.

The historical links between White Supremacy and the Confederate legacy are evident in the ongoing debates over Confederate symbols and monuments in the United States. Many of these symbols are seen by White Supremacists as representations of their ideology and are used to rally support for their cause. The persistence of these symbols in public spaces is a testament to the enduring influence of White Supremacist ideology and its deep roots in American history.

White Supremacy is a deeply entrenched ideology with a long and troubling history. Its origins in colonialism and slavery have left a lasting impact on societies around the world, particularly in the United States, where it has been intertwined with the legacy of the Confederacy. While progress has been made in combating racial discrimination and promoting equality, the persistence of White Supremacist beliefs and their manifestations in contemporary society highlight the ongoing struggle to achieve true racial justice and equality.

THE NEO-FASCIST MOVEMENT.

Neo-Fascism is a term used to describe a contemporary political movement that draws inspiration from the ideologies and practices of historical fascism, particularly those seen in early 20th-century Europe. It is characterized by authoritarianism, nationalism, and often a disdain for liberal democracy and multiculturalism.

Characterized by this disdain for liberal democracy, Neo-Fascist groups often advocate for a return to a perceived golden age of national strength and purity similar to the advocacy of Adolf Hitler. Donald Trump has spoken out at times in admiration for the Hitler agenda and his generals with rhetoric such as "Hitler did a lot of good things," and "I want my generals to be like Hitler's generals".

Central to their belief system is the idea that societal decay is a result of multiculturalism and immigration, which they argue dilute national identity and threaten social cohesion. Neo-Fascists often employ symbols and rhetoric reminiscent of historical fascist movements, such as Hitler's Third Reich, seeking to evoke a sense of nostalgia for a time when they believe their nation was more homogeneous and powerful, similarly as does the MAGA Movement.

Recently in Australia a strong approach to dealing with this has seen the Federal Government ban the use of Nazi symbols, including the Nazi insignia and the Nazi salute in protest gatherings, which many Australian citizens thought was a good idea, but most had no idea of the significance of the Nazi salute, and why it was banned. For it was not all about appeasing the Jewish citizens of Australia as most people thought.

The "Heil Hitler" salute and gesture were powerful symbols of loyalty, submission, and ideological alignment with the Nazi regime. It originated as a combination of influences, including German nationalist traditions, the Roman salute, and deliberate efforts by Hitler to foster a sense of unity and absolute obedience.

The salute's origin is linked to the Roman salute, a gesture associated with the Roman Republic and later the Roman Empire. In ancient Rome, a raised right arm was used to greet leaders and display allegiance, as seen in depictions of citizens saluting emperors with "Ave Caesar" (Hail Caesar). Fascists in early 20th-century Italy, particularly under the Italian dictator Mussolini, revived the idea of a Roman-style salute as a symbol of national unity and strength.

The Nazis then adopted a modified version of this salute, blending it with their own ideological framework. Point to note: During President Donald Trump's second inauguration in January 2025, Elon Musk, Trump's Administrator of Department Government Efficiency (DOGE) delivered a speech after which he made a gesture that has sparked significant controversy.

He placed his right hand over his heart with fingers spread wide, then extended his arm outward at an upward angle, palm down and fingers together. He repeated this gesture to the crowd behind him stating "my heart goes out to you. It is thanks to you that the future of civilization is assured." This action was quite rightly interpreted by many as resembling the Nazi or Roman salute, leading to widespread criticism. Musk of course denied it was a Nazi salute.

Prior to the Nazi rise to power, Germany had long-standing military customs that emphasized salutes as a sign of respect and hierarchy. The traditional military salute (a hand to the forehead) was common, but the Nazis replaced it with the extended-arm salute to create a distinction between the old military order and the new ideological movement. While the salute was already in use among early Nazi Party members in the 1920's, Hitler officially mandated it after taking power in 1933.

The "Heil Hitler" or "Sieg Heil" salute became compulsory for all government employees and later extended to the general public. By 1934, after the Night of the Long Knives, it became the only acceptable greeting in Nazi Germany. Failure to use it could result in social ostracism, loss of employment, arrest, or even death in extreme cases. This made it not just a sign of allegiance but an instrument of fear and enforced conformity.

You see the forced use of the salute functioned as a psychological tool. It ensured constant public reinforcement of Nazi ideology, making it difficult for individuals to resist or even question the regime. It also created an atmosphere of paranoia, those who hesitated or refused to salute risked being reported as traitors or dissidents, or "the enemy within".

The phrase "Heil Hitler" literally means "Hail Hitler", a formulaic expression of devotion. By making it a daily ritual, the Nazis elevated Hitler to near-divine status, positioning him as Germany's saviour. This parallels the "Ave Caesar" greetings of ancient Rome, where emperors were often deified. The demand for total obedience to Hitler mirrored the way ancient Romans were expected to venerate their emperor as a god-like figure.

The Nazi salute was far more than a simple greeting, it was a tool of political and psychological domination, a ritual of submission, and an instrument of social control. From a religious perspective, the salute can be viewed as idolatrous, reinforcing Hitler's self-made cult of personality. It was not merely a sign of loyalty;

it was a demand for unquestioning obedience, making it one of the most chilling symbols of totalitarian rule in modern history.

The White Supremacist Movement is deeply intertwined with Neo-Fascism, sharing many of its core beliefs. White Supremacists advocate for the superiority of the white race and often view non-white populations as threats to their cultural and racial integrity. Similarly the Neo-Fascist movement is characterized by its use of hate speech, violence, and propaganda to promote racial segregation and discrimination.

Understanding the current growing wave of support for Neo-Fascism requires an exploration of its historical roots, ideological aims, prominent figures, and its manifestations in various countries, including the United States. The roots of Neo-Fascism can be traced back to the aftermath of World War II, when the defeat of fascist regimes in Germany and Italy led to a widespread rejection of fascist ideologies.

However, the socio-political conditions of the post-war era, including economic instability, social upheaval, and the Cold War, created fertile ground for the resurgence of far-right movements.

In the 1960's and 1970's, various groups began to emerge that sought to revive fascist ideas, often in reaction to the civil rights movement, anti-war protests, and the counterculture of the time. These groups were often characterized by their "opposition to immigration", communism, and perceived threats to national identity. The term Neo-Fascism began to be used to describe these movements, which sought to adapt traditional fascist principles to contemporary contexts. The prefix "neo" means revived or modified.

Regardless of a change of name in this modern day, Neo-Fascism nevertheless still shares several core ideological aims with historical fascism, including: a strong emphasis on national identity, similar to the national identity views of Christian Nationalism, often accompanied by xenophobia, and an obsessive advocacy for the supremacy of the native population, with an almost paranoid belief that immigration is a threat to cultural integrity.

It shares a preference for strong, centralized leadership and a rejection of democratic norms. Neo-Fascists often support the idea of a leader who embodies the will of the people, bypassing traditional democratic processes, plus a vehement opposition to leftist ideologies, including socialism and communism.

Neo-Fascists often frame their struggle as a defence against a perceived communist threat. Donald Trump has used this rhetoric continually during his campaign rallies continually describing Kamala Harris as a communist to the applause of his followers. If you look below the surface of these anti-communist comments by Trump you will see that they surface from his close association with a now deceased lawyer named Roy Cohn, Trump's mentor.

Post World War 2 Cohn was heavily involved in the McCarthy's hearings, broadcast to millions, that reinforced the public's belief that an internal enemy, Communism, was working to undermine American democracy, a type of "enemy within" to use Trump terminology. The "Red Scare" extended beyond Washington, affecting Hollywood, academia, and even local communities, where loyalty oaths and denunciations became common.

Neo-Fascism's strong opposition to Communism dates back to World War 2. Russia's role in World War 2 fuels hatred amongst Neo-Fascists still to this day, particularly among those who still glorify Nazi Germany. The Soviet Red Army was instrumental in crushing the Third Reich, and the memory of that defeat lingers in Neo-Nazi and Neo-Fascist circles.

Some far-right groups glorify the Waffen SS and Nazi collaborators who fought against the Soviets. The rivalry however is not just about World War 2, but about the fundamental clash between hierarchical nationalism and revolutionary socialism.

Neo-Fascism also advocates militarism, an emphasis on military strength, which we have also seen in Donald Trump's rhetoric at his rallies, where he states that he will turn the United States into the greatest military force on earth, and as such the glorification of violence as a means of achieving political goals is part of the Neo-Fascist agenda. This can manifest in support for paramilitary groups or vigilante actions, such as those of the Proud Boys.

Neo-Fascism focuses on populism, a rhetoric that claims to represent the "common people" against a corrupt elite. Donald Trump also uses this rhetoric at his campaign rallies, whilst his whole business and personal life, the people he has links with, and the trappings he has ensconced himself in, from the crystal chandeliers to the golden toilet, have demonstrated that he too is a part of that corrupt elite.

As Neo-Fascists often position themselves as champions of the poor and disenfranchised, using populist language to rally support, so too does Donald Trump. Yet it is totally unlikely that Donald Trump ever goes to the grocery store or worries about the price of eggs.

This radical ideological organization has found varying degrees of acceptance in several countries, particularly in Europe. Countries such as Hungary, Poland, and Italy have seen the rise of far-right parties that espouse nationalist and anti-immigrant sentiments. In Hungary, Prime Minister Viktor Orbán, a close associate of Donald Trump, has implemented policies that critics argue align with Neo-Fascist principles, including a crackdown on immigration and a focus on ethnic nationalism.

In Brazil, the election of Jair Bolsonaro in 2018 marked a shift towards far-right politics, with Bolsonaro often employing rhetoric that resonates with Neo-Fascist ideologies, including militarism and anti-communism; and in the United States, Neo-Fascism has manifested through various movements and groups, particularly in the context of the alt-right and other far-right organizations.

The 2016 presidential election saw a significant rise in nationalist and anti-immigrant sentiments, with figures like Donald Trump employing rhetoric that echoed Neo-Fascist themes. The events surrounding the 2017 Unite the Right rally in Charlottesville, Virginia, highlighted the growing visibility of Neo-Fascist groups, including White Supremacists and Neo-Nazis.

The rally, which resulted in violence and the death of a counter-protester, underscored the potential for Neo-Fascist ideologies to incite real-world violence and social division. When asked to comment on the events at Charlottesville by a journalist Donald Trump, being so psychologically locked into his personal agenda, could not even manage a simple "it was disgraceful, " but rather simply replied quote, "well there are good people on both sides."

Moreover, the rise of conspiracy theories, such as Q Anon, has provided a platform for Neo-Fascist sentiments to flourish, as these theories often promote a narrative of an elite conspiracy against the "common people." This has further polarized political discourse and contributed to a climate of fear and mistrust.

THE TRUTH ABOUT FASCISM: THE EXTREME LEVEL OF IGNORANCE IN MODERN SOCIETY.

A recent survey in the United States revealed varying levels of understanding about Hitler's Holocaust across different age demographics, from vaguely familiar to totally ignorant. Generally, the survey found, that older generations tend to have a better, albeit many times incomplete understanding of the horrors of the Holocaust compared to younger generations.

The survey highlighted that a significant portion of millennials and Gen Z have gaps in their understanding of key facts related to the Holocaust, such as the number of Jews who perished and the existence of concentration camps like Auschwitz. And just as disturbing, many of those surveyed had no knowledge at all of "the events leading up to and surrounding the Holocaust". The following is what all children should be taught in school.

As a part of Hitler's continued determination to conquer all of Europe, Nazi Germany invaded and annexed Austria on March 12, 1938, in an event known as the Anschluss, which is German for "connection" or "union". German troops crossed the border into Austria without resistance, and Adolf Hitler officially declared Austria a part of the Third Reich the following day, March 13, 1938.

In 1938, an extensive network of facilities was established by the German Nazi authorities in Austria for the documentation, observation, and evaluation of all children and adolescents who did not comply with the standards set by Nazi ideology. They reviewed lineal parentage, social behaviour, school assessments, employer information, and any physical or cognitive disabilities. Those who did not pass the Nazi criteria test were forcibly removed from their homes and placed in isolation in a hospital/prison.

The Steinhoff Hospital in Vienna, Austria, (now called the Otto- Wagner-Spital), originally established in 1907 as a psychiatric hospital and sanatorium, was used to house all these children forcibly removed from their homes. It was one of the largest and most modern psychiatric institutions in Europe at the time.

However, during World War 2, and the period of Austria's annexation into Nazi Germany (1938 to 1945), the hospital became closely associated with the crimes of the Nazi regime, particularly in the context of the so called Aktion T4 programme.

The Aktion T4 programme was a systematic campaign of involuntary euthanasia carried out by the Nazi regime, targeting individuals with physical, mental, or intellectual disabilities. These individuals were deemed "unworthy of life" under the Nazis racial and eugenic policies. The Nazis had a term for this policy, it was called "Lebensunwertes Leben" which meant, "a life unworthy of life".

Steinhoff Hospital played a significant role in this programme. Many patients, including children and adults, were either murdered directly at the hospital or sent to killing centres such as Hartheim Castle, a notorious euthanasia site in Austria. Within the Steinhoff Complex, a specialised unit called Am Spiegelgrund was established, where children with disabilities, developmental delays, or behavioural issues, were subjected to inhumane treatments.

Hundreds of children were murdered at Spiegelgrund through deliberate neglect, starvation, or lethal injections. Some of their bodies were used for medical research and experiments. Physicians and staff at Steinhoff Hospital, including prominent Austrian doctors, collaborated with Nazi authorities in identifying patients for euthanasia or carrying out pseudoscientific research.

This included brain studies and autopsies, which were all a part of efforts to justify eugenic theories, using the brains of the murdered children which were kept in jars for future research by Nazi health officials.

By 1942, 72 percent of newborns in Vienna, the capital of Austria, were documented within their first year of life. As well as this, every person, adult, or child, who contacted or met with a health institution of any kind, was systematically recorded into a hereditary data base.

After the war, the hospital continued to operate, but its role in Nazi crimes was largely hidden or ignored for decades. Public acknowledgment of the atrocities committed at Steinhoff only began to surface in the late 20th century. The Steinhoff Hospital serves as a grim reminder of the horrors of Nazi ideology and Nazi medical practises, and the exploitation of vulnerable populations under authoritarian regimes.

That "Lebensunwertes Leben" designation, which meant, "a life unworthy of life", was also given to any class of individuals who the Nazis felt had no right to live because they did not fit in with their fascist ideology. They were thus targeted to be euthanised by the state. This immoral and inhumane concept was a key component of the Nazi Party's ideological plan and eventually helped lead to the establishment of concentration or death camps and the reality of the Holocaust itself.

In terms of the adult population, the Nazi euthanasia programme specifically targeted mentally disabled people, which did include however perfectly healthy Jewish people, and other ethnicities; the Nazis having branded all these people as mentally disabled so that they could be exterminated according to Nazi ideology. The fascist party had another policy called "Untermensch", a word used as a Nazi term for non-Aryan "inferior people", often referred to as the masses from the East, the immigrants, which included all Jews, Slavs, and all Black People.

In an apparent display of ignorance or perhaps not, on the subject matter of the Holocaust and the activities of Adolf Hitler's Nazi Party itself, Donald Trump in his first presidency and during his tenure in the White House for the first time, allegedly made the statement that "Adolf Hitler did some good things," according to his former Chief of Staff, General John Kelly.

Kelly, who served as Trump's Chief of Staff from July 2017 to January 2019, claimed that Trump made this remark during conversations about historical figures and leadership. Kelly recalled that Trump would occasionally bring up the topic, asserting that Hitler had achieved positive outcomes, to which Kelly responded by emphasising that "nothing Hitler did you could argue was good."

These allegations surfaced publicly in 2024 when Kelly shared his experience as Trump's Chief of Staff and his concerns about Trump's views and leadership style. He also mentioned that Trump often expressed admiration for the loyalty Hitler's generals supposedly had stating, "I need the kind of generals that Hitler had."

Kelly corrected him, noting that Hitler's generals had attempted to assassinate him multiple times, but Trump insisted "no, no, no, they were totally loyal to him". I can only come to four logical conclusions as the why the leader of the most powerful democratic nation in the western world would make these statements.

Number 1, either he too is blissfully ignorant of world history, or Number 2, that he has a vulnerable ego that likes to act intelligent and does not like to be corrected, or Number 3, that he is of an extreme narcissistic nature with such a high level of arrogance and low level of moral awareness, that he cares not about historical truth that interferes with his personal agenda, or Number 4 that he too has fascist tendencies. You alone can be the judge; perhaps it was a combination of all four?

In an apparent display of ignorance regarding the history of their own birth nation, and a total lack of awareness of Donald Trump's Nazi supporting rhetoric, in the recent 2024 presidential election, approximately 21% of American Jewish voters supported the republican candidate, Donald Trump, seeing support for Trump higher among Orthodox Jewish voters, with 74% casting their ballots for him. (Orthodox Jews strictly follow Jewish law and tend to have a more traditional interpretation of the religion of Judaism).

During that German Nazi initiated Holocaust, in the face of the overwhelming sense of fear, despair, and desperation it brought upon the Jewish people and ethnic minorities, the concept of morality, humanity and community underwent a significant transformation.

Not dissimilar in fact with what we witness in societies in this current day around the world, where social and political divides in communities fracture the democratic principle that underpins all free societies, creating an opening for the emergence of political leaders with far-right autocratic tendencies.

In this present day in certain nations where traditional narratives about the universe and human purpose unravel, and where political, religious, and ideologically driven groups fight to preserve their own relevance to this illusionary ephemeral world, people are left to reconstruct their own moral frameworks, which may not always align with historical or collective moral standards.

Neo-Fascism represents a troubling resurgence of authoritarian and nationalist ideologies in contemporary politics. Its historical roots, ideological aims, and vocal proponents reveal a movement that seeks to exploit social and economic anxieties to gain traction.

As Neo-Fascist sentiments continue to manifest in various countries, including the United States, it is essential to remain vigilant against the potential threats to democracy, social cohesion, and human rights that such ideologies pose. Understanding and addressing the underlying issues that give rise to Neo-Fascism is crucial for fostering inclusive and resilient societies.

THE GREAT REPLACEMENT THEORY.

The Great Replacement Theory is a controversial and often contentious ideology which posits that a plot is occurring, a deliberate and systematic replacement of native populations in Western countries by non-native immigrants, particularly from Africa and the Middle East.

This theory has gained traction in various political and social circles, often intertwined with nationalist and anti-immigration sentiments. Understanding its origins, ideology, key proponents, and potential impacts socially and on the moral compass of a nation, is crucial for comprehending contemporary socio-political dynamics.

The roots of the Great Replacement Theory can be traced back to the early 20th century, but it gained significant prominence in the 2010's. The term itself was popularized by French writer Renaud Camus in his 2011 book, "Le Grand Replacement."

Camus argued that a demographic shift was occurring in France and other Western nations, where the native population was being supplanted by immigrants.

His ideas drew on historical fears of cultural dilution and demographic change, echoing sentiments found in earlier nationalist movements.

The theory is also often linked to broader concerns about globalization, multiculturalism, and the perceived loss of national identity. It has been fuelled by rising immigration rates, particularly in Europe, and has found a receptive audience among those who feel both ideologically and personally threatened by these changes.

At its core, the Great Replacement Theory is rooted in a belief that immigration policies are intentionally designed to undermine the cultural and demographic makeup of Western societies. Proponents argue that this "replacement" is not merely a demographic shift but a deliberate strategy by elites to erode national identities and values. The ideology often incorporates elements of xenophobia, racism, and ethnonationalism, framing immigrants as a threat to social cohesion and cultural integrity.

The theory also intersects with conspiracy thinking, suggesting that there is a coordinated effort among political leaders, globalists, and other elites to facilitate this demographic change. This narrative often ignores the complexities of immigration, such as economic factors, humanitarian needs, and the contributions of immigrants to society.

Several figures and organizations have become prominent advocates of the Great Replacement Theory. Whilst Renaud Camus is perhaps the most notable, having coined the term and articulated its foundational ideas, other prominent figures include Marine Le Pen, the leader of the National Rally party in France, Geert Wilders, the Dutch politician and leader of the Party for Freedom, and Steve Bannon, the former chief strategist for Donald Trump.

Le Pen has often invoked themes of national identity and immigration in her political rhetoric, aligning with the sentiments of the Great Replacement Theory, and Wilders has been very vocal about his concerns regarding immigration and its impact on Dutch culture, echoing the Great Replacement theory's themes. Then in the United States we see the recently released from prison Steve Bannon continuously promoting nationalist and anti-immigration sentiments on his podcast, that resonate with Great Replacement theorists.

Various other far-right organizations and movements across Europe and North America have also adopted and propagated these ideas, often using social media to amplify their messages. As mentioned, France, where the theory originated, has seen significant political discourse around immigration and national identity. But also, countries such as Germany, where the rise of the Alternative for Germany Party, supported by Elon Musk, has brought attention to concerns about immigration and cultural identity.

In Italy we see the League Party, led by Matteo Salvini, which has capitalized on fears of immigration and demographic change, and of course in the United States where the theory has found a foothold in certain segments of the political landscape, particularly among far-right groups and the Republican Party during Donald Trump's 2017 administration.

The Great Replacement Theory poses several potential impacts on modern societies and cultures. Firstly, it can exacerbate social divisions and tensions between native populations and immigrant communities, leading to increased xenophobia and racism.

This polarization can manifest in political violence, hate crimes, and social unrest. Secondly, the theory can influence public policy, leading to stricter immigration controls and policies that may undermine the rights of immigrants and refugees. This can hinder social integration and contribute to a climate of fear and mistrust.

And finally, the theory can have broader implications for democratic discourse. By framing immigration as an existential threat, it can shift political conversations away from constructive dialogue and towards fear-based rhetoric, undermining the principles of inclusivity and diversity that many societies strive to uphold. This has been particularly evident in the strategic approach taken by the Republican Party in their attempts to get Donald Trump elected in the 2024 presidential campaign

It is a complex and multifaceted ideology that reflects deep-seated anxieties about immigration, national identity, and cultural change. While it has gained traction among certain political groups, it is essential to critically examine its claims and the potential consequences for society. Understanding the origins, ideology, and impacts of this theory is crucial for fostering informed discussions about immigration and cultural diversity in an increasingly interconnected world.

ELON MUSK AND THE GREAT REPLACEMENT THEORY.

Elon Musk has made statements that align with certain aspects of the Great Replacement theory, particularly regarding demographic shifts and declining birth rates in Western countries. While he has not explicitly endorsed the full conspiracy theory, which claims the existence of a coordinated effort to replace native populations with immigrants, he has expressed concerns about low birth rates among certain demographics and the impact of immigration policies.

For example, Musk has repeatedly warned about "population collapse" being a major threat to civilization, arguing that many Western nations are not having enough children to sustain their populations. In some cases, his comments on immigration and demographic trends have been interpreted as echoing elements of Great Replacement rhetoric, particularly when he has framed high immigration rates as a threat to cultural continuity or economic stability.

However, Musk's views are not fully aligned with the more extreme versions of the theory, which often involve racist or white nationalist overtones. Rather his emphasis is usually on declining birth rates rather than an orchestrated effort to replace populations. Which recent reporting suggests he is determined to play his part in addressing by fathering as many children to as many different women as possible.

In 2024, Musk criticized the Biden administration's immigration policies, suggesting that increased immigration was a strategy to bolster the Democratic voter base. He tweeted that the administration viewed those entering the country illegally as "future Dem voters," a narrative aligning with elements of the "Great Replacement" theory.

Musk has frequently expressed concerns about declining birth rates, warning that "population collapse is coming." He emphasizes that this trend poses a threat to technological progress, economic stability, and societal development. In March 2025, Musk claimed, without evidence, that Democrats were committing entitlements fraud in programs like Social Security and Medicare to attract immigrants and increase their voting base.

These statements echo right-wing conspiracy theories and align with the idea of the "Great Replacement" theory. He argued that this alleged fraud has cost the government up to $200 billion and justifies cuts to both services.

Musk's comments have drawn criticism from various organizations. The American Jewish Committee, for instance, condemned his agreement with a user promoting elements of the "Great Replacement" theory, labelling it as dangerous and antisemitic. In summary, while Elon Musk has not explicitly endorsed the "Great Replacement" theory, his statements on immigration and demographic trends have echoed aspects of it, leading to criticism and concern from various quarters.

PROJECT 2025.

The Heritage Foundation is a prominent American conservative think tank based in Washington, D.C, founded in 1973 by Paul Weyrich, Edwin Feulner, and Joseph Coors. With a mission to promote conservative principles such as limited government, individual freedom, free markets, and a strong national defence, the Heritage Foundation has become a key player in the political landscape, influencing both public opinion and policymaking.

The Heritage Foundation employs a diverse group of researchers and analysts who specialize in various policy areas, including economics, foreign policy, health care, and education. This team works collaboratively to produce reports, policy papers, and recommendations that align with conservative values.

It is also known for its extensive research and publications, which serve as resources for policymakers, legislators, and the general public. The organization hosts events, seminars, and conferences that bring together thought leaders, policymakers, and activists to discuss pressing issues and promote conservative solutions. Additionally, the foundation engages in grassroots mobilization efforts, aiming to influence public opinion and encourage civic engagement among conservatives.

One of the key aspects of the Heritage Foundation's influence is its role in the development of policy agendas for the Republican administrations. The organization has been instrumental in shaping the policy priorities of various presidential administrations, particularly during the Reagan and Trump eras. Its research and recommendations often serve as a blueprint for legislative initiatives and executive actions.

While Project 2025 is not explicitly a Christian Nationalist initiative, it consistently overlaps with the goals of Christian Nationalism, particularly in its advocacy for policies that reflect a conservative Christian worldview; and just as importantly it has hereditary foundational links with the Moral Majority, the forerunner to Christian Nationalism, links which I detail more extensively in Chapter 9.

Moreover, some elements within the Christian Nationalist movement and the proponents of a Project 2025 system of government have been known to adopt racially charged rhetoric or policies that resonate with White Supremacist ideologies, and the Great Replacement Theorists.

Project 2025 was conceived as a response to the political and social challenges facing the United States, particularly those that were highlighted during Trump's first term from 2017 to 2021. The initiative seeks to create a roadmap for governance that reinforces Trump's ideological beliefs, some publicly known, others a bit more clandestine.

The content of Project 2025 encompasses a wide range of policy proposals, including but not limited to, economic policy, immigration reform, foreign policy, judicial appointments, healthcare, education reform, tax cuts, deregulation, and support for American manufacturing.

It advocates for stricter border control measures and changes to immigration policy, promoting an "America First" approach, whilst focusing on renegotiating trade deals and reducing military involvement abroad; as well as aiming to appoint conservative judges who align with Trump's judicial philosophy and reforming the health system to reduce costs and increase access while dismantling aspects of the Affordable Care Act.

Project 2025 represented a strategic effort to consolidate and promote Donald Trump's policy and power agenda as he sought a return to the presidency in 2025. With a focus on key issues that resonate with his base, the project was backed by a team of experienced former Trump officials who are committed to advancing the principles of the America First movement.

Its proponents often echo the sentiments of the Great Replacement Theory, arguing that unchecked immigration threatens American identity and sovereignty. It seeks to mobilize political power to implement policies that align with these beliefs, thereby creating an environment conducive to the growth of extremist ideologies.

Intersecting Ideologies.

The intertwining belief systems of Christian Nationalism, Evangelicalism, Neo-Fascist groups, the White Supremacist Movement, Great Replacement Theorists, and initiatives like Project 2025 create a complex web of ideologies that reinforce one another. This convergence is facilitated by the use of social media and online podcaster platforms, which allow for the rapid dissemination of extremist ideas and the formation of echo chambers.

The implications of this ideological convergence are profound. It fosters an environment of intolerance and division, where violence and hate crimes become more prevalent. Furthermore, the normalization of extremist rhetoric in political discourse can lead to policy changes that institutionalize discrimination and undermine democratic institutions.

As these belief systems continue to intertwine, it is crucial for society to recognize and address the dangers they pose, promoting inclusivity and understanding as counter-narratives to the hate and division they propagate; for as these groups gain visibility and influence, they increasingly pose significant challenges to social cohesion, democratic values, and human rights, not just in the United States but in many countries in Europe.

Addressing these challenges requires a concerted effort to promote dialogue, understanding, and policies that embrace diversity and equality. Only by recognizing and confronting these interconnected ideologies and those who promote them, can societies hope to build a future that is moral, inclusive, just, and resilient.

"Truth in political rhetoric is not just a matter of ethical duty; it is a necessity for the health of democracy. Without truth, trust in political institutions collapses, society becomes polarized, policy-making is weakened, and the foundation of democratic governance is compromised. Political leaders must recognize the profound responsibility they carry in shaping public discourse. Upholding the truth is not merely a strategy for effective leadership, it is essential to maintaining the integrity of democracy and ensuring the well-being of the society they serve. The absence of truth in political rhetoric is not just harmful; it is corrosive, threatening to unravel the very systems that sustain democratic life".

7

THE GOSPEL OF ROY COHN THE MASTER, AND DONALD TRUMP HIS APPRENTICE: THE GREAT LIE, THE MYTH OF DONALD THE DEALMAKER.

Chapter Contents.

"Truth is the sacred thread that weaves the fabric of the universe, connecting all beings in harmony. Truth is the eternal flame that illuminates the darkness of the soul's journey. The heart that seeks truth is a vessel for Divine wisdom and love. The journey to spiritual awakening begins with the courage to embrace the truth within, and in that embrace of truth, the soul discovers its oneness with all the truth in the cosmos."

COHN THE MASTER AND TRUMP HIS APPRENTICE, IN THE ART OF DECEPTION.

Roy Cohn, the ruthless attorney and political fixer, played a pivotal role in shaping Donald Trump's aggressive and oftentimes deceptive approach to business, politics, and public relations. A key figure in Senator Joseph McCarthy's anti-communist crusade of the 50's, Cohn later became a powerful lawyer in New York, representing mobsters, media moguls, and real estate tycoons, including Fred and Donald Trump.

His mentorship of the younger Trump instilled a playbook of hardball tactics: never admit fault, never back down, attack critics relentlessly, and use the legal system as both a weapon and a shield. Trump's well documented propensity to lie, deny, and manipulate narratives can be traced back directly to Cohn's influence, making the notorious lawyer one of the most consequential figures in Trump's rise in business and in politics.

If Roy Cohn wrote a playbook, as a guide in his mentorship of Donald Trump, it could well have been called "The Power of Deception to Influence a Gullible Public", sub-title "The Art of Winning The Presidency at Any Cost."

Cohn's legal and political career was defined by his mastery of manipulation and intimidation. His three cardinal rules which he passed down to Trump, were simple yet powerful, and totally void of any moral or ethical responsibility. Number one was "never admit you are wrong", number two was "always go on the attack", and number three was "if you're losing declare you are winning."

These three principals were perfectly displayed by Trump in a recent White House press conference with President Vladimir Zelensky of Ukraine, and J.D. Vance. Trump argued that he was right, he verbally attacked Zelensky, and with the third principal he leaned into Zelensky and spat out, "you've got no cards, we've got all the cards." And what did Zelensky, calmly and softly in a defiant but statesman like way say in return, "Mr. President, we're not playing cards."

Cohn's three principles allowed Trump to dominate negotiations, sidestep accountability, and shape media narratives in his favour. One of the earliest examples of Cohn's influence on Trump occurred in the 1970's when the Justice Department sued the Trump organisation for racial discrimination in housing.

Rather than settle quietly, as many businesses would have done, Trump, under Cohn's guidance, responded with counter claims against the government, calling the charges "reverse discrimination". Though the case ultimately resulted in a consent decree requiring Trump to change his practices, the strategy set the tone for Trump's future approach to legal battles: "delay, deflect, counterattack, and always declare victory, regardless of the facts."

Cohn taught Trump that truth was secondary to perception. Trump's decades long habit of exaggeration, falsehoods, and outright denial in the face of reality, reflects Cohn's belief that repetition and confidence could overwrite facts, and lies could override truth. Whether it was inflating the value of his properties, denying business failures, or later, in the political sphere, dismissing damaging evidence as "fake news", Trump followed the Cohn method to the letter.

Cohn also understood the power of gaslighting, making opponents and the public question their own perceptions, and passed this on to Trump. A classic example amongst dozens of others, came in 2016 when Trump claimed that he had opposed the Iraq war from the beginning, despite clear evidence to the contrary.

By persistently repeating the falsehood, he created enough doubt for many to believe him or at least dismiss the issue as uncertain. This is a direct echo of Cohn's tactics during the McCarthy hearings, where he and the senator insisted that they had evidence of Communist infiltration, even when none existed.

Cohn's approach to conflict legal or otherwise was to never retreat but to escalate. Trump's political career is filled with examples of this strategy, from his personal insults against opponents to his lawsuits against journalists and political adversaries. If accused of wrongdoing, Trump like Cohen would counterattack by discrediting accusers. When faced with credible allegations of sexual misconduct, Trump did not merely deny them but aggressively attacked the women making the claims, calling them liars and even threatening lawsuits.

This strategy also extended to institutions. When the media reported unflattering stories, Trump branded them "the enemy of the people". When faced with impeachment, he dismissed the process as "a partisan witch hunt". Cohn had long used similar methods, portraying his critics as being politically motivated and painting legal or ethical scrutiny as a personal vendetta rather than a legitimate investigation.

Known for his aggressive tactics and ruthless approach, Cohn became a symbol of the Red Scare, embodying the era's paranoia and the pursuit of alleged communists within the United States. After his stint with Senator McCarthy, Cohn returned to New York City, where he established himself as a formidable attorney with a client list that included some of the most powerful figures in the country, including criminal figures.

It was in this context that Cohn met Donald Trump in the early 1970's. At the time, Trump was a young real estate developer looking to make a name for himself in the competitive New York City market. The introduction to Cohn came at a crucial moment when Trump and his father, Fred Trump, were facing a lawsuit from the U.S. Department of Justice. The lawsuit alleged racial discrimination in their rental properties, a serious charge that could have derailed Trump's burgeoning career.

Cohn's approach to legal battles was combative and unapologetic, a style that resonated with Trump. Cohn advised Trump to counter-sue the government for $100 million, a bold move that set the tone for Trump's future legal and business strategies. Although the case was eventually settled without an admission of guilt, the experience solidified Cohn's role as a mentor and advisor to Trump.

Beyond legal advice, Cohn imparted to Trump a philosophy of "never admitting defeat and always attacking one's adversaries", a tactic that would become a hallmark of Trump's public persona. Cohn's influence extended beyond legal matters; he was instrumental in introducing Trump to influential figures in New York's political and social circles, including Jeffrey Epstein, helping to elevate Trump's status in the city.

The relationship between Cohn and the Trump family was not without its complexities. Cohn was a controversial figure, known for his connections to organized crime and his involvement in various scandals. Despite this, Trump maintained a close relationship with Cohn until the latter's death in 1986. Cohn's mentorship left a lasting impact on Trump, evident in Trump's approach to business, media, and politics.

The links between Roy Cohn and the Trump family highlight a significant chapter in the history of American business and politics, and this relationship underscores the interplay of power, influence, and ambition that characterizes much of American history particularly in this current political climate of unrest.

Trump's ability to bend reality to his will and forcefully impose his version of events onto the public consciousness, is arguably the most enduring legacy of his relationship with Cohn. The tactics Cohn helped him perfect, primarily denial, aggression, counterattacks, and media manipulation, became the bedrock of Trump's brand, first in business and later in politics. Yet, whilst these methods helped Trump ascend to power in business and politics, they also led to increasing polarisation, legal entanglements, and public distrust.

Cohn himself eventually fell from grace, disbarred for unethical conduct and abandoned by many of his former allies. In a twist of irony, when Cohn was dying of AIDS in the 1980's, Trump, who had once relied on him as a mentor, distanced himself, mirroring the cold transactional approach Cohn had taught him.

In the end, Roy Cohn's influence on Trump was profound and lasting, continuing to this day, influencing political processes not only in the United States but also in other nations around the world drawn into Trump's relentless pursuit of power. He provided Trump with a set of tools that enabled him to win battles in the short term, more often than not at the cost of truth, ethics, and a substantial part of his financial fortune. However, as Cohn's own downfall suggests, such tactics have their limits. They cannot eliminate entirely the future consequences of their actions.

HUMANITY'S DIRE NEED FOR A PREDISPOSITION TO TRUTHFULNESS.

In the realm of politics, rhetoric serves as a powerful tool for leaders to communicate their visions, policies, and values to the public. The essence of political rhetoric lies in its ability to persuade, inform, and inspire. However, the integrity of this communication is fundamentally dependent on the truthfulness of the messages conveyed.

The necessity of truth in political rhetoric cannot be overstated, as it forms the bedrock of a functioning democracy, fosters public trust, and ensures informed decision-making. Conversely, the absence of truth in political discourse can lead to detrimental consequences, including the erosion of democratic institutions, the spread of misinformation, and the polarization of society.

Truth in political rhetoric is essential for several reasons. Firstly, it upholds the principles of democracy by ensuring that citizens are accurately informed about the actions and intentions of their leaders. In a democratic society, the electorate relies on truthful information to make informed choices during elections and to hold public officials accountable. When political rhetoric is grounded in truth, it empowers citizens to engage in meaningful discourse and participate actively in the democratic process.

Secondly, truth in political rhetoric fosters trust between the government and the governed. Trust is a critical component of effective governance, as it facilitates cooperation and compliance with laws and policies. When political leaders consistently communicate truthfully, they build credibility and legitimacy, which are essential for maintaining public confidence in governmental institutions. Abraham Lincoln was a perfect example of a leader who chose truth as the primary platform underpinning his presidential governance.

Thirdly, truth in political rhetoric is necessary for effective policy-making. Sound policies are based on accurate data and a truthful assessment of societal needs and challenges. When political discourse is truthful, it enables policymakers to address issues effectively and implement solutions that genuinely benefit the public.

The absence of truth in political rhetoric can have far-reaching and harmful consequences. One of the most significant dangers is the erosion of democratic institutions. When political leaders engage in deceitful rhetoric, they undermine the very foundations of democracy by distorting the information that citizens rely on to make informed decisions. This can lead to disillusionment with the political system, decreased voter turnout, and a general sense of apathy among the populace.

Moreover, the spread of misinformation through dishonest political rhetoric can polarize society. When falsehoods are propagated, they can create divisions among different groups, leading to increased hostility and conflict. This polarization can hinder constructive dialogue and compromise, making it difficult to address pressing societal issues collaboratively.

Additionally, the absence of truth in political rhetoric can result in misguided policies that fail to address the root causes of problems. When decisions are based on false premises, the solutions implemented are unlikely to be effective, leading to wasted resources and missed opportunities for progress. This can exacerbate existing issues and create new challenges, ultimately harming the very people that political leaders are meant to serve.

Truth in political rhetoric is indispensable for the health and vitality of a democratic society. It ensures that citizens are well-informed, fosters trust between the government and the public, and enables effective policy-making. The absence of truth, on the other hand, can lead to the erosion of democratic institutions, societal polarization, and ineffective governance.

As such, it is imperative for political leaders to prioritize truthfulness in their rhetoric, recognizing that their words have the power to shape the future of their nations and the lives of their constituents. By committing to truth, political leaders can uphold the principles of democracy and work towards a more just and equitable society.

THE CONCEPT OF TRUTH.

Truth is a fundamental concept that has been explored by philosophers, common theologians, and thinkers for centuries. At its most basic level, truth refers to the quality of being in accordance with reality or fact. However, defining truth is not always straightforward, as different disciplines and perspectives provide varying interpretations.

From an empirical standpoint, truth is often seen as objective and verifiable through evidence and reason. Scientific truth, for example, is based on observable facts, repeatable experiments, and logical consistency. On the other hand, subjective or personal truth is shaped by individual experiences, emotions, and perceptions, making it more fluid and less absolute.

In philosophy, several theories have attempted to define truth. The "correspondence theory" states that truth corresponds to reality, something is true if it accurately represents the world. The "coherence theory" argues that truth is determined by how well a belief fits within a system of logically consistent beliefs. And the "pragmatic theory", championed by thinkers like William James and John Dewey, suggests that truth is whatever proves useful or effective in practical life.

Beyond philosophy and science, truth is also deeply intertwined with moral and spiritual traditions. Many religious teachings assert that truth is not only about factual accuracy but also about ethical living and the search for ultimate meaning. Throughout history, both philosophers and spiritual leaders have wrestled with the meaning of truth and the moral obligations that come with it.

Socrates, through his dialectical method, sought to uncover truth by questioning assumptions and exposing contradictions. He believed that truth was not merely about opinion but could be discovered through reason and dialogue.

Aristotle built upon this but took a more empirical approach. He argued that truth arises from observing the natural world and using logic to form accurate conclusions. He supported the correspondence theory, which holds that a statement is true if it aligns with reality. If there is undeniable reality-based evidence to support and confirm.

For instance in September 2024, with no undeniable reality-based evidence, during a presidential debate with Vice President Kamala Harris, former President Donald Trump asserted that migrants in Springfield, Ohio, were eating pet dogs and cats. He stated, "In Springfield, they're eating the dogs. The people that came in, they're eating the cats, they're eating the pets of the people that live there."

This claim originated from a Facebook post in a local Springfield group, where a user recounted a second-hand story about Haitian immigrants allegedly butchering a cat. The post quickly spread online, gaining traction among far-right and neo-Nazi groups.

Republican Senator and vice-presidential nominee at the time J.D. Vance of Ohio amplified the rumour, followed by Donald Trump and allies such as Laura Loomer and Elon Musk. However, both the original poster and the neighbour who shared the story later admitted it was based on unverified rumours.

Local law enforcement and officials, including Springfield's mayor Rob Rue and Ohio Governor Mike DeWine, both Republicans, stated that there were no credible reports or evidence supporting these claims. The allegations were widely criticized as racist and unfounded.

Historically, false claims about immigrants consuming pets have been used to demonize various immigrant groups in the United States. In the late 19th century, similar stereotypes targeted Asian immigrants, portraying them as unfit for American society. These tropes have been employed many times in the past to invoke disgust and justify exclusionary policies.

Despite being eventually debunked, the rumour had significant consequences. Springfield experienced numerous bomb threats targeting schools, hospitals, and public buildings, often accompanied by anti-Haitian messages. The false claims contributed to heightened racial tensions and fear within the community. The incident underscored the potential harm of spreading unverified information and highlights the importance of critical evaluation of sources, especially when such claims can inflame racial tensions and lead to real-world consequences.

The German philosopher Immanuel Kant introduced the idea that our understanding as to whether something is truthful or not is influenced by human perception. He argued that while objective reality exists, our understanding of truth is shaped by the mental structures through which we interpret the world, what have been described as "our powers of perception."

These "consciousness structures" these states of awareness, these perceptive powers that Kant speaks of are being continually added to as we journey through our transient life, as we seek to navigate this sometimes-chaotic transitory ephemeral existence we commonly refer to as "our life experiences".

For as we think, act, and react on that transitory journey, we continue to add to these consciousness structures, and deepen existing ones, adjusting what is commonly termed "our self-identity," the platform of our perception, how we view things; through which we determine if what we are observing is based on truth or not. So in fact all observations are individual and personal, based on our personal consciousness structures.

Friedrich Nietzsche, the German classical scholar, philosopher, and critic of culture, on the other hand, was sceptical of absolute truth, and saw it as a human construct shaped by power and perspective. He warned against blindly accepting truths imposed by political figures, by society, or by religion, urging individuals to critically examine their beliefs.

The teachings of Confucius also stress that truth is essential to maintaining harmony in society. Confucius emphasised honesty, trustworthiness, and the importance of aligning one's words with one's actions to uphold moral integrity. In the teachings of Hinduism the Bhagavad Gita tells us that living truthfully leads to spiritual liberation while deceit leads to suffering.

And in the teachings of Christianity, Jesus Christ the central figure of the faith is described as "the way, the truth, and the life." And as such truth is seen as a Divine character quality, an essential component of living a Divine life, regardless of one's religious or political institutional alliance.

THE POWER OF DECEPTION TO INFLUENCE A GULLIBLE PUBLIC: TRUMP A TEXTBOOK CASE.

Truth is the alignment of a statement, belief, or representation with reality or fact. It reflects what is something verifiable, consistent, and honest. **Deception**, on the other hand, is the deliberate distortion or concealment of truth. It reflects what is not, a manipulation meant to mislead, create false belief, or obscure reality. In essence: **Truth reveals. Deception conceals.**

Truth in politics serves as the bedrock of democracy. It's rooted in transparency, accountability, and the public's right to know. A truthful government fosters trust, informed decision-making, and civic engagement.

Deception in politics is often used as a tool of power. Leaders may distort facts, spread disinformation, or manipulate narratives to maintain control, rally support, or distract from wrongdoing. This erodes public trust and undermines institutions, paving the way for authoritarianism.

In a political system ruled by deception, truth becomes dangerous. Whistleblowers are silenced, journalists are targeted, and the public becomes disoriented. Psychologically, this creates a state of mass confusion and collective dissonance, where lies become normalized, and truth feels radical.

Deception has long been a powerful tool in shaping public perception, particularly when wielded by a charismatic figure who understands how to manipulate emotions, exploit biases, and craft an image that aligns with what people want to believe. Donald Trump provides a textbook case of how deception can be used to cultivate a following, even in the face of overwhelming contradictory evidence.

Through a combination of self-aggrandizement, strategic misinformation, and brand manipulation, Trump has successfully positioned himself as an intelligent man, a business mogul, an author of a best-selling book, a devout Christian, a strong political leader, and an opponent of corrupt elites; when all the while his personal history of numerous bankruptcies, numerous court cases, numerous marriages, sexual assault allegations and 34 felony convictions, suggests otherwise.

DECEPTION 1: THE MYTH OF A STRONG BUSINESS ACUMEN, DONALD THE DEALMAKER.

The Art of the Deal, a book published in 1987, widely attributed to Donald Trump, which significantly increased the public perception of Trump to be a master dealmaker, was not written by Trump, but actually ghostwritten by a writer named Tony Schwartz. Schwartz himself has publicly stated that he wrote the book almost entirely on his own, despite Trump receiving sole author credit. Here are the key details of this deception.

In multiple interviews, Schwartz has claimed that he not Trump wrote every word of The Art of the Deal, despite Trump being credited as the author. Schwartz spent 18 months shadowing Trump, interviewing him and gathering material. He has admitted to exaggerating and mythologizing Trump's persona in the book, at Trump's insistence, turning him into, in the minds of many, a master dealmaker.

Decades later, Schwartz expressed regret for writing the book, saying he essentially helped create the Trump brand. In a 2016 interview with The New Yorker, he stated that if he were writing it again, he would call it The Sociopath. Schwartz claims that Trump had a short attention span and was totally uninterested in the actual writing process.

Trump was positioned as the sole author, reinforcing his image as a self-made billionaire and genius negotiator. The book was a massive bestseller, helping establish Trump's brand as a business mogul. Even in Trump's political career, The Art of the Deal was frequently cited as proof of his business acumen.

Ghost-writing is common, but Trump presented the book as entirely his own work, despite Schwartz's admissions. Trump has referred to it as "one of the greatest business books of all time," without acknowledging in any way Schwartz's role.

The case of The Art of the Deal is a prime example of how oligarchs manufacture and manipulate their public personas to gain power, influence, and credibility. This fits into the broader theme of image construction in oligarchic politics, where the perception of the people is purposefully manipulated to distort or totally outweigh reality. Just as oligarchs carefully craft their public personas, Trump's image as a master negotiator was simply a fabrication.

The book however helped shape Trump's public image as a master negotiator, influencing his business and political career. Schwartz's later critiques of

Trump highlight the gap between the book's portrayal and Trump's real-life behaviour. The Art of the Deal painted him as a shrewd businessman with an innate ability to win, but Tony Schwartz later admitted that Trump rarely read books, had a short attention span, and exaggerated his successes.

This follows a historical pattern: oligarchs and elites often construct myths around their genius, vision, or destiny, even when their actual success is due to inherited wealth, political connections, deception, or even the very talented scientific and engineering skills of others they employ as seen in Elon Musk's case.

The media played a crucial role in legitimizing the book's claims, treating Trump as the embodiment of the American Dream, and the uneducated and easily perceptually manipulated members of the voting public fell for it. Just as oligarchs use the press to launder their reputations, Trump deceptively leveraged the book and its media coverage to create a public image detached from reality.

This mirrors how figures like Elon Musk and other oligarchs have cultivated myths about their self-made success while downplaying the involvement of government subsidies, inherited wealth, corruption, and the skills of others. Trump did not write the book, but he needed it to enhance his brand, and Schwartz needed Trump's name to sell copies.

This reflects a larger deceit laden quid pro quo arrangement in play between oligarchs and media institutions: ghostwriters, journalists, and PR firms, who construct their narratives in exchange for access and financial gain. Similar dynamics exist in political and corporate spheres, where billionaires "sponsor" narratives that serve their interests, whether in think tanks, academic institutions, or news coverage.

The public consumed the Trump myth as reality, and many of the eternally gullible still believe that Trump is a brilliant businessman because of it. This demonstrates how oligarchs construct false narratives to control perception, much like the Matrix programs a false reality to maintain order.

Trump's entire political career was built on the illusion of a strong business acumen, which The Art of the Deal helped solidify. Many voters saw him as a successful outsider who could "run America like a business", a direct consequence of the book's fabricated image. This reflects how oligarchs use business success, real or exaggerated, to justify their political ambitions, wrongly reinforcing the ridiculous idea that wealth equates to competence.

DECEPTION 2: THE MYTH OF THE SELF-MADE BUSINESSMAN.

One of Trump's most enduring deceptions is the image of himself as a brilliant and successful businessman. He has long portrayed himself as a self-made billionaire, despite the fact that he inherited a vast fortune from his father, Fred Trump at the beginning of his career. Moreover, his business record is littered with failures, including multiple bankruptcies of high-profile ventures such as Trump Airlines, Trump University, and Trump Casinos.

A New York Times' investigation revealed that Trump paid little to no federal income tax for years, largely because his businesses lost so much money that he was able to write off the losses. Despite this, his ability to project confidence and brand himself as a successful entrepreneur with the use of perceptual props such as mansions and Trump brand golf courses and casinos, combined with the intellectual ignorance of many of his followers, has led millions to buy into his self-crafted myth that he is a self-made business success.

DECEPTION 3: THE TRUMP BRAND: OWNING NOTHING, SELLING EVERYTHING, FOOLING EVERYONE.

Trump's mastery of branding, with the help of marketing professionals, has allowed him to project an image of control and ownership over buildings and projects he does not actually own. While buildings such as Trump Tower and Trump

International Hotel bear his name, many are merely licensing agreements where real estate developers pay to use the Trump name for marketing purposes. You could call it a type of identity prostitution.

This branding strategy has enabled Trump to present himself as a real estate magnate with far more assets than he actually possesses, a deception that has fooled both the general public and, at times, financial institutions, who are considering loaning him the money for another project.

Deception 4: The False Image of Moral Superiority, the "Christian Family Man."

Trump has also carefully cultivated the image of a devout Christian and a dedicated family man, a persona that has helped him maintain strong support among religious conservatives. However, his personal history tells a different story. He has been married three times, has been accused of sexual misconduct by multiple women, and was caught bragging about sexually assaulting women in the infamous Access Hollywood tape.

Moreover, his public behaviour, from fellating a microphone at a campaign rally, to mocking disabled individuals, to displaying little knowledge or interest in Christian teachings whilst selling Trump bibles, to undisputable logbook evidence showing that he travelled numerous times on Jeffrey Epstein's pleasure plane, stands in stark contrast to the values he claims to uphold.

Despite these contradictions, his ability to repeat religious rhetoric and align himself with evangelical leaders has allowed him to maintain a grip on the gullible conservative Christian voting public.

DECEPTION 5: THE ILLUSION OF A STRONGMAN: DEMONSTRATING STRENGTH AGAINST PUTIN.

This is another key deception, Trump's claim to be a tough leader, a strongman, who stands up to Russian President Vladimir Putin. In reality, Trump has repeatedly demonstrated admiration for Putin, even taking his word over U.S. intelligence agencies regarding Russian election interference. His foreign policy decisions often seemed to align with Russian interests, including his attempts to undermine NATO and his reluctance to criticize Putin's actions, such as the invasion of Ukraine.

By projecting an image of strength while avoiding substantive actions against Putin, Trump has managed to convince his base that he is a formidable leader on the world stage, when in reality he is simply a weak apologetic and a serial political appeaser. What do I mean by a "political appeaser."

The British government's policy of appeasement toward Adolf Hitler was a strategy used primarily during the 1930's in an attempt to avoid another large-scale war in Europe. This approach was based on diplomatic concessions, the belief that Hitler's demands were reasonable, and the hope that satisfying Germany's grievances would prevent conflict.

Chamberlain met with Hitler in Munich and, along with French leaders, agreed to cede the Sudetenland to Germany in exchange for Hitler's promise that he had no further territorial ambitions. He then returned to Britain declaring "peace for our time", believing Hitler would be satisfied.

Despite his promises, Hitler subsequently invaded the rest of Czechoslovakia just six months after Munich. This shattered the illusion that appeasement had worked, as it proved Hitler was not merely seeking to unite German-speaking people but had larger expansionist ambitions.

After signing the Molotov-Ribbentrop Pact (a non-aggression agreement with the Soviet Union), Hitler then invaded Poland on September 1, 1939. Britain and France had guaranteed Poland's independence and declared war on Germany on September 3, 1939, officially ending appeasement, and as such we saw the beginning of World War 2.

Trump's weakness in standing up to Putin gives Putin a free rein for further territorial conquests. It is highly likely that Trump will similarly try to appease Putin in current negotiations by allowing him to keep those parts of Ukraine that Putin has captured during his illegal invasion of that sovereign nation and by trying to influence Ukraine to withdraw its application to join NATO. Appeasement did not work with Hitler and will not work with a dictator like Putin as the world will eventually see.

Deception 6: Trump's Repeated Failure to Deliver on Promises.

Throughout his political career, Trump has made bold claims about what he would accomplish, particularly in the early days of his first presidency. During his first campaign, he promised that he would build a wall along the U.S.-Mexico border and have Mexico pay for it, that he would repeal and replace Obamacare immediately, and that he would bring back manufacturing jobs in record numbers.

None of these promises materialized in the way he suggested. However, by constantly shifting blame to political opponents, the media, or the 'Deep State,' which is the deceptive "principle of projection at work" which I speak of shortly, he has been able to deflect accountability and maintain the illusion of effectiveness in the eyes of his easily deceived cult followers.

Donald Trump's career demonstrates the immense power of deception in influencing a gullible public. Through carefully crafted branding, misinformation, and relentless self-promotion and deflection, he has managed to convince millions of people to believe in a reality that is largely fictional.

His success in this regard is not merely a reflection of his own manipulative abilities, gained in his apprenticeship to Roy Cohn, but also of the willingness of many people to accept comforting narratives over uncomfortable truths, "to take the blue pill rather than the red pill", that I spoke of at the beginning of this book. As long as figures like Trump can manipulate perception to override facts, deception will remain one of his most effective tools in shaping public opinion.

Further to this Cohn's mentorship and legal strategies not only played a crucial role in shaping Donald Trump's early career, influencing his approach to challenges and his public persona, it also introduced a new concept of political dialogue into mainstream political debate.

The new concept being one that Donald Trump has used extensively in his political campaign rallies and media interviews, in both his 2016 presidential campaign and in his 2024 campaign, which I feel I have appropriately titled "the cultivated art of bullshit."

THE VARIOUS REALMS OF POLITICAL AND SOCIAL RHETORIC .

THE CULTIVATED ART OF BULLSHIT IN POLITICS.

"On Bullshit" by Harry G. Frankfurt, is a philosophical book that delves into the concept of "bullshit" and its implications in communication and society. Frankfurt, a renowned philosopher, seeks to distinguish bullshit from lying and to explore its significance in our everyday interactions.

In his book Frankfurt acknowledges the prevalence of bullshit in contemporary discourse, particularly in the political arena, noting that it is often "more pervasive than outright lying". Frankfurt argues that while both the liar and the bullshitter misrepresent reality, their intentions and methods differ.

A liar is aware of the truth and deliberately chooses to convey a falsehood, whereas a bullshitter is indifferent to the truth and is more concerned with creating a particular impression or achieving a specific goal. For example, with Trump the goal many times is "to project an image of intelligence."

Frankfurt suggests that bullshit is characterized by a lack of concern for how things really are. The bullshitter's primary focus is on persuasion and self-presentation rather than on the accuracy or truthfulness of their statements. This indifference to truth, Frankfurt argues, is what makes bullshit particularly insidious. It undermines the value of truth and erodes trust in communication, as it becomes difficult to discern genuine statements from those that are merely crafted for effect.

For example, take time to watch video footage of large campaign rallies held by Trump during his 2024 presidential campaigning. Watch closely the close-up camera shots of the facial expressions of supporters, their reaction when Trump explodes with a barrage of what any person with a minimum level of intelligence would acknowledge is pure bullshit.

Some of his supporters with a reasonable level of intelligence and being slightly politically informed, will give a wry type of smirk or smile, but quickly change both their expression and gestures to one acknowledging complete agreement with Trump's rhetoric when they realize the smirk that they first gave, captured on the big screen, is not a demonstration of true allegiance to the political god, their saviour, that they have made of him.

Others, the majority, those with an obviously high level of political ignorance and a low level of moral awareness, will not blink an eye to the absurdity of his statement, but simply break into spontaneous applause, clapping and cheering Trump, and holding up pro-Trump signage, thus encouraging Trump to continue with his divisive litany of lies and plain old bullshit.

And at times if you watch really closely the camera will occasionally switch to the odd strategically placed attendee in the front row, who appearing to have a slight level of intelligence will, whilst not showing any emotional reaction to Trump's rhetoric, pause for a moment after his comments, and then slowly and somewhat reluctantly raise their pro-Trump signage so as not to give any notion of disagreement. As such, in an almost cowardly way, giving tacit agreement to his bullshit.

Frankfurt in his book also explores the societal condition of those that contribute to the proliferation of bullshit. He points to the increasing demand for individuals to have opinions on a wide range of topics, particularly during election campaigns, often without sufficient knowledge or understanding of the subject matter.

This pressure can lead people to speak without regard for the truth, agree with those who of similar mindset and behaviour, and level of ignorance, clap when others clap, which I would describe as "crowd compliance", feeling pressured to do so, thus giving tacit approval to political rhetoric where bullshit becomes a common and acceptable mode of expression.

Frankfurt concludes by emphasizing the importance of recognizing and addressing the prevalence of bullshit. That by understanding the nature of bullshit, individuals can become more discerning in their interactions and contribute to a more honest and truthful society. His analysis encourages readers to reflect on their own relationship with truth, and to strive for greater authenticity in their expressions and interactions.

THE INTENTIONAL ACT OF LYING IN POLITICS.

In the realm of politics, discourse serves as the foundation upon which democratic societies are built. It is through dialogue and debate that policies are shaped, leaders are chosen, and the will of the people is expressed. However, when lies, exaggerations, and truth bending infiltrate political discourse, the very fabric of democracy is threatened.

One of the most immediate and damaging effects of introducing falsehoods into political discourse is the erosion of public trust. Trust is the cornerstone of any functioning democracy; it is the belief that elected officials and institutions will act in the best interest of the populace.

When politicians engage in deceit, they undermine this trust, leading to widespread cynicism and disengagement among citizens. This erosion of trust can result in lower voter turnout, as individuals become disillusioned with the political process and question the integrity of those in power.

Lies and exaggerations in political discourse also often serve to deepen societal divisions. Politicians may exploit falsehoods to stoke fear, resentment, or anger among specific groups, creating an "us versus them" mentality. This polarization can lead to increased hostility between different segments of society, making it difficult to find common ground or engage in constructive dialogue. As a result, the political landscape becomes more fragmented, hindering the ability to address pressing issues collaboratively.

Certain sections of society are particularly vulnerable to the negative impacts of deceptive political discourse. Marginalized communities, for instance, may be disproportionately affected by policies based on false premises or exaggerated claims. When political decisions are made on the basis of misinformation, these communities may face unjust treatment, discrimination, or neglect. Furthermore, the spread of false narratives can perpetuate harmful stereotypes, exacerbating social inequalities and hindering efforts toward inclusivity and equity.

A healthy democracy relies on an informed electorate capable of making decisions based on accurate information. When lies and exaggerations pervade political discourse, they distort the reality upon which citizens base their choices. This undermines the democratic process, as voters may be swayed by misleading narratives rather than factual evidence. Consequently, the quality of leadership and policy-making suffers, as decisions are made not on the basis of truth, but on manipulated perceptions.

The introduction of falsehoods into political discourse poses a significant threat to democratic institutions themselves. When leaders engage in truth bending, they may attempt to delegitimize institutions that challenge their narratives, such as the media, judiciary, or electoral bodies.

This erosion of institutional credibility can lead to a concentration of power, weakening the system of checks and balances that is essential for a functioning democracy. In extreme cases, this can pave the way for authoritarianism, as leaders manipulate truth to consolidate control.

The dangers of introducing lies, exaggerations, and truth bending into political discourse are profound and far-reaching. They erode public trust, deepen societal divisions, disproportionately impact vulnerable populations, undermine informed decision-making, and threaten the very institutions that uphold democracy.

To safeguard the integrity of political discourse, it is imperative for leaders, the media, and citizens alike to prioritize truth, transparency, and accountability. Only by fostering an environment of honesty and open dialogue can societies hope to address their challenges effectively and uphold the democratic ideals upon which they are built.

Donald Trump's tenure as the 45th. President of the United States from 2017 to 2021, and his subsequent political campaigns for the 2024 election have been marked by a significant number of false or misleading facts. In his 2017 inauguration, reputable fact checkers have documented these instances extensively, noting an unprecedented level of dishonesty in American political rhetoric.

A Historical Litany of Presidential Lies.

In American politics, particularly at the higher levels of governance, lying has noticeably become an almost expected feature of electoral campaigns and governance. Politicians often distort facts, misrepresent their positions, and make false promises to gain votes. Once in power, many continue to deceive the public to maintain control.

The Washington Post fact checker reported that during his first term, Trump made over 30,573 false or misleading claims, with the frequency increasing over time. This level of dishonesty surpasses that of every previous president and has significant implications for public discourse and trust in institutions. The frequency and scale of false or misleading statements made by Donald Trump are unprecedented in modern American politics, and most likely in world politics.

In contrast, while other politicians have also at times been found to make false statements, the volume and impact of Trump's falsehoods are notably higher. For example, fact checking organisations have documented false claims by other political figures, but none have approached the scale observed in Trump statements.

Donald Trump's pattern of making false or misleading statements during his first presidency and subsequent 2024 campaign represents a significant departure from the norms of political communication, taking dishonesty to a new level in the context of American presidential history.

With regards to his inauguration crowd size in 2017 Trump falsely claimed that his inauguration had the biggest audience ever, both in person and via television. Photographic evidence and public transportation data contradicted this, showing smaller crowds compared to previous inaugurations. Trump also asserted that millions of illegal votes were cast in the 2016 election, causing him to lose the popular vote. There is no evidence to support widespread voter fraud in that election.

Trump repeatedly minimised the severity of the COVID-19 pandemic, suggesting it would disappear and promoting unproven treatments including a proposal to test injecting disinfectant or bleach into people to kill the virus. These statements were at odds with public health experts and contributed to misinformation about the virus on a massive scale.

In his tenure in the White House, he claimed that the U.S. was losing $500 billion a year to China before he took over due to unfair trade practises. This figure misrepresented the trade deficit, which was approximately $380 billion at its peak, and did not account for the complexities of international trade.

Trump also stated that his administration passed the largest tax cuts in history. In reality, the tax cuts were significant but not the largest when adjusted for the size of the economy. Trump also frequently touted the US economy's performance during his first term as the best in history. While the economy experienced growth, his claims often ignored underlying issues and the contributions of previous administrations.

In a January 2025 rally, Trump claimed he won Florida by 13 percentage points in the 2024 election and stated, as he does frequently for various things, "nobody's done that ever." While he did win Florida by that margin, it was not unprecedented as previous candidates have achieved similar or larger margins.

He claimed that his immigration policies had completely stopped illegal border crossings. Data from border agencies indicated that while there were fluctuations, illegal crossings had not ceased entirely.

Trump asserted that he had introduced a comprehensive health care plan that provided better coverage at lower cost. However, no such plan was implemented during his tenure or during his year 2000 campaign. He stated that crime rates had reached record lows due to his administration's policies. While certain crime rates did decrease, attributing these changes solely to his policies oversimplified complex social factors.

Some of the more false and deliberately misleading statements made by Donald Trump during his election campaigns and whilst in office that have been widely criticized are:

"I will build a great, great wall on our southern border and I will have Mexico pay for that wall." This promise was a central theme of his campaign, but Mexico did not pay for the wall, and the wall was never completed.

"I won the popular vote if you deduct the millions of people who voted illegally." There is no evidence to support the claim that millions of illegal votes were cast in the 2016 election.

"The unemployment rate is the lowest it's been in 51 years." While unemployment did reach low levels, this statement was misleading as it did not account for the context of the economic recovery following the 2008 financial crisis.

"I have the best words." This statement is often cited as an example of Trump's self-aggrandizing rhetoric, lacking any factual basis.

"I will bring back jobs from China." While Trump made this claim, many economists argue that the complexities of global trade make it difficult to simply "bring back" jobs.

"I know more about ISIS than the generals do." This statement was criticized for its lack of evidence and the implication that military leaders were not knowledgeable about the situation.

"There were very fine people on both sides." This statement, made in reference to the Charlottesville rally, was widely condemned for equating white supremacists with counter-protesters.

"I have done more for the African American community than any president since Abraham Lincoln." This claim has been disputed by various analysts and historians.

"The media is the enemy of the people." This statement has been criticized for undermining trust in the press and promoting a narrative of hostility towards journalism.

"We are the highest taxed nation in the world." This statement is misleading as it does not consider various factors, including tax rates and overall tax burdens compared to other countries.

While deception and deliberate exaggeration in politics is not new, the modern era, with its 24-hour news cycle, propaganda networks such as Fox News controlling a lot of the narrative, combined with social media and in particular Elon Musk's X platform, have amplified the effects of political dishonest rhetoric, not just with normal congressional appointees, but with presidential candidates as well.

Over the years several U.S. presidents and presidential candidates have been caught misleading the public on the media, with lies that range from minor exaggerations to outright fabrications full stop, but nevertheless still shaping voter perceptions. This also indicates a dramatic decrease in the state of moral awareness of many elected officials and potential candidates.

During election campaigns, presidential candidates often bend the truth to appeal to the broadest audience possible. Some make promises they know that cannot be fulfilled, while others misrepresent their opponents positions to gain an advantage.

A classic example was the Republican Party's Richard Nixon during his 1968 campaign, when he promised to end the Vietnam War with peace and with honour. However, declassified information later revealed that Nixon's campaign secretly urged South Vietnam to reject peace talks before the election, prolonging the war for political gain.

Another case is the Republican President George W Bush, whose administration falsely claimed that Iraq possessed weapons of mass destruction (WMD's) to justify the 2003 invasion. No WMD's were ever found, and the war led to many deaths and prolonged the conflict and instability in the Middle East. This misleading justification for war cost thousands of American lives and significantly damaged trust in government.

And more recently we have Donald Trump in his 2024 campaigning continuously stating that he would end the Russian/ Ukraine conflict within 24 hours of taking office. Well more than 24 hours have passed, and the troops are still fighting.

Not forgetting the "I will immediately bring down the price of groceries when I take office." Well he is now in office and grocery prices are still going up. Trump when questioned about this by journalists just brushes them off with a quick, "well these things take time, next question please."

Once in office politicians often continue to deceive the public to maintain support, cover up scandals, or justify controversial policies. One of the most infamous examples is the Democratic Party's Bill Clinton, who, in 1998, publicly denied having an affair with White House intern Monica Lewinsky, stating, "I did not have sexual relations with that woman". When evidenced surfaced proving otherwise, Clinton was forced to admit the truth, leading to his impeachment. His initial lie, rather than the affair itself, was what led to his political downfall.

In terms of another presidential sexual scandal, we saw Donald Trump allegedly cover up his alleged liaison with adult film actress Stormy Daniels, which involved a hush money payment orchestrated to prevent the story from surfacing during his 2016 presidential campaign.

In 2016, Trump's then personal lawyer, Michael Cohen, paid Daniels $130,000 in exchange for her silence about an alleged affair with Trump. His alleged affair with Stormy Daniels reportedly took place in July 2006, shortly after meeting her at a celebrity golf tournament in Lake Tahoe. At that time, Melania Trump was around four to five months pregnant with their son, Barron, who was born in March 2007.

Cohen initially claimed that he had made the payment independently, but later testified that Trump had directed him to do so. The Trump organisation allegedly reimbursed Cohen through legal expense payments, raising questions about campaign finance violations. In 2018, Cohen pleaded guilty to federal charges, including campaign finance violations related to the payment. Trump initially denied knowledge of the payment but later acknowledged his reimbursing Cohen, but still maintained that no affair took place.

The case led to legal scrutiny, culminating in Trump's 2023 indictment in New York for falsifying business records related to the payments. Prosecutors argued that the payments were improperly classified to disguise their true purpose, constituting an effort to influence the election illegally. Trump denied wrongdoing and dismissed the case as purely politically motivated, "a political witch-hunt."

However, in 2024, Donald Trump was indicted on 34 felony counts of falsifying business records related to the hush money payments made to Stormy Daniels during the 2016 presidential campaign. This marked the first time a former U.S. President was convicted of felony crimes. In January 2025, Trump was sentenced to an unconditional discharge, meaning he faced no additional penalties such as imprisonment or fines. This decision allowed him to assume his second presidency without any legal impediments.

More recently, during his 2024 presidential campaigning Donald Trump took political dishonesty to new levels, making thousands of false claims or misleading claims. One of the most significant was his assertion that the 2020 election was stolen due to widespread voter fraud, an allegation repeatedly debunked by courts, election officials, and his own Justice Department.

This lie was also the one that fielded the January 6th, 2021, attack on the US Capitol Building, orchestrated by the Proud Boys, a White Supremacist movement, who were encouraged and applauded by Trump, an act which led to Trump's second impeachment.

Lying in politics erodes public trust, polarises the electorate, and damages democratic institutions. When politicians repeatedly mislead voters, cynicism increases, and people become less likely to engage in the political process. The spread of misinformation also makes it harder for voters to make informed decisions, leading to elections based on emotion rather than fact, as was witnessed in the re-election of Donald Trump in the 2024 presidential election.

The modern media environment exacerbates this problem. Social media platforms allow false claims to spread rapidly, while partisan news outlets such as Fox News often reinforce misleading narratives. Fact checking organisations work to counteract political lies, but many Americans choose to believe this information that aligns with their political or religious preferences.

The tendency of American presidential candidates to lie to gain power or to stay in power has only intensified in recent decades. From Nixon's secret dealings to the Bush's weapons of mass destruction (WMD) claims, to Clinton's personal scandal, and Trump's election fraud allegations, dishonesty has played a major role in shaping American politics.

The consequences of these lies range from loss of public trust to wars and constitutional crises, and if this trend continues unchecked, democracy itself may be at risk, as truth becomes secondary to political gain and personal ambition. Addressing this issue requires greater accountability, stronger media literacy, and renewed commitment to truth in public discourse.

THE ACCUSATORY ART OF PROJECTION IN POLITICS.

In the realm of political discourse and debates, the art of persuasion is often intertwined with various rhetorical strategies designed to sway public opinion and undermine opponents. However, it is not only the strategies of lying and exaggerating that are used. One such strategy is to lie but do it disguised as a projection, a psychological defence mechanism where an individual attributes their own undesirable traits, feelings, or motives to another person.

Projection, a vehicle for the expression of not only bullshit but misinformation as well, in political debates serves as a powerful tool because it allows politicians to shift the focus away from their own vulnerabilities and onto their adversaries. Donald Trump under the watchful eye and comprehensive tutorage of Roy Cohn, has become over time a master of the art of intentional projection.

By accusing his opponents of the very flaws, he himself possesses, for example Hunter Biden's association with Vladamir Putin, and tax evasion, Trump has created a narrative that diverts attention away from his own shortcomings. This tactic not only confuses the audience but also puts the opponent on the defensive, in this instance Joe Biden, Hunter's father, forcing them to address the accusations rather than highlighting the accuser's weaknesses.

A classic example of projection in political debates is when a candidate with a history of ethical lapses accuses their opponent of corruption. By doing so, the accuser attempts to create a moral equivalence, suggesting that both parties are equally flawed. This can be particularly effective if the audience is not well-informed or just plain ignorant about the specifics of each candidate's record.

The accuser's goal is to plant seeds of doubt in the minds of voters, making it difficult for them to discern the truth and potentially leading them to conclude that "all politicians are the same."

Moreover, projection can be used to exploit existing stereotypes or biases. For instance, a politician who struggles with transparency might accuse their opponent of being secretive or dishonest. If the opponent belongs to a group that is stereotypically associated with such traits, the accusation may resonate more strongly with the audience, regardless of its veracity. This tactic leverages societal prejudices to reinforce the projected image, making it a potent weapon in the political arsenal.

The effectiveness of projection in political debates also hinges on the emotional resonance of the accusations. By projecting their own negative traits onto their opponents, politicians tap into the emotional responses of the audience. Fear, anger, and distrust are powerful motivators that can overshadow rational analysis. When a politician successfully projects their weaknesses onto an opponent, they can evoke these emotions, leading the audience to react based on feelings rather than facts.

However, the use of projection is not without risks. If the audience becomes aware of the tactic, it can backfire, damaging the credibility of the accuser. In an age where information is readily accessible, and fact-checking is a common practice, politicians must be cautious in their use of projection. The exposure of such tactics can lead to public backlash, eroding trust and support.

Projection is a double-edged sword in political debates. It can be a highly effective strategy for deflecting criticism and undermining opponents, but it also carries the risk of backfiring if the audience perceives the manipulation. As voters become more discerning and informed, the challenge for politicians is to balance the use of projection with authenticity and transparency.

Ultimately, the success of this tactic depends on the ability of politicians to navigate the complex interplay of perception, emotion, and reality in the political arena which from my understanding very few politicians in this modern political climate show evidence of having.

THE DELIBERATE ACT OF DISTRACTION IN POLITICS.

Donald Trump's mastery of the deliberate act of distraction has allowed him to control political discourse and media narratives, ensuring that his supporters remain focused on external enemies rather than his own missteps. His approach is not unique but represents an extreme form of a common political strategy used by leaders across the world.

The "deliberate act of distraction" is a strategic communication tool used by politicians to shift public focus away from their personal or policy shortcomings. This can be done through a variety of rhetorical and media tactics, including scapegoating, manufacturing outrage, flooding the media cycle, whataboutism, shock and provocation, reframing failures as successes.

Scapegoating is blaming external enemies (immigrants, media, foreign governments, opposition parties) for problems instead of addressing their own failures. In manufacturing outrage, a politician will stir up controversy over trivial or emotionally charged topics to divert media and public attention.

Flooding the media cycle creates a barrage of statements, tweets, or news events to prevent deep scrutiny of any single issue. Trump uses his Truth Social account to do this mostly after midnight each night, when he has obviously stewed on something for some time.

Whataboutism, the "what about them approach," is used by Trump quite often. This is the adult equivalent of the children's playground scenario where little Jimmy when confronted by his teacher for punching Billy, blurts out, "what about him, he started it." He criticises others to deflect current criticism of himself, by pointing out alleged hypocrisy or failures of opponents, for example, "what about Hillary's emails?"

In the light of Donald Trump's promise to exact revenge on his political enemies once he commenced his second presidency, including revenge on Hunter Biden, Joe Biden's son, Biden checkmated Trump and pre-pardoned his son before he left office, seeing Trump then use this to deflect criticism away from himself for pardoning the Jan 6th. insurrectionists by verbally attacking Biden for pardoning his own son.

Trump also quite often uses shock and provocation rhetoric, making outrageous or offensive statements to dominate media coverage and drown out substantive criticism, he reframes failures as successes, and he spins negative outcomes as victories, claiming a failed negotiation was actually a strategic move on his part.

During both his 2016 and 2020 presidential campaigns, Trump skilfully used distraction tactics to dominate media cycles. Instead of addressing complex economic issues, he focused on building a border wall and vilifying illegal immigrants as the root cause of crime and unemployment.

Whenever he was faced with scandals, for example the Access Hollywood tape, he labelled media outlets as "fake news" to undermine their credibility. He frequently stirred outrage on issues like NFL players kneeling, transgender rights, and the "cancel culture" drawing attention away from policy failures.

Throughout his presidency, Trump repeatedly employed distraction techniques to shift focus from crises or failures: as the Mueller investigation into Russian election interference heated up, Trump often used inflammatory rhetoric against Democratic figures like Hillary Clinton, "lock her up" or attacked FBI officials as being part of a "deep state coup."

When faced with bad news for example his failure to repeal Obamacare as promised, he often made dramatic, unrelated announcements as a way of distracting public attention; for example the sudden ban on transgender individuals in the military.

When he was impeached over Ukraine, he deflected by claiming that Joe Biden's son, Hunter Biden, had been involved in corruption in Ukraine. As criticism mounted over his administration's handling of the Covid pandemic, he blamed China (China Virus), attacked Dr. Fauci, and pushed unproven medical treatments like hydroxychloroquine to dominate headlines.

Even after leaving office, after his first presidency, Trump continued using distraction tactics to maintain political influence. Faced with multiple indictments and lawsuits, he aggressively pushed the "stolen election" narrative, ensuring media focus remained on election fraud claims rather than his legal battles. And he amplified attacks on woke culture, DEI policies, and transgender rights to rally his base and shift focus away from his business and legal scandals.

THE REVENGE FUELLED AND GREED FILLED INTENT OF TRUMP'S RHETORIC. LOOKING BELOW THE SURFACE.

With Donald Trump it will give one greater clarity as to why he says something or why he does something, if you don't look directly at his rhetoric or behaviour, rather look at what lies below the surface of that rhetoric or behaviour. What is the "revenge fuelled or greed filled intent of his rhetoric or behaviour". Because remember, for Donald Trump everything is always about Donald Trump. The lists are extensive but here are a few examples of that in play:

Trump and the Panama Canal. If you want to understand his beef with Panama, don't look at the canal to which he now points which he claims was stolen from the United States, it's not about patriotism. Don't look at his rhetoric about China's influence in Panama, look at Trump Enterprises and their fraught financial and criminal relationship with Panama, and look to the Russian oligarchs who bought condos in his Panama Trump Tower.

Donald Trump was involved in the development of a major real estate project in Panama. Known as the Trump Ocean Club International Hotel & Tower, this 70-story mixed-use skyscraper in Panama City was the tallest building in Central America at the time of its completion in 2011.

While Trump did not build the tower himself, his organization licensed the Trump name to the project and managed the hotel operations. The development included 369 hotel condominium units, 628 residential condominium units, retail shops, office spaces, a casino, and other amenities. Trump reportedly earned between $30 million and $55 million from the project.

In 2018, the Trump Organization was removed from managing the property, and the building was rebranded as the JW Marriott Panama. There were clear indications that Donald Trump and the Trump Organization were displeased with their removal from the Trump Ocean Club in Panama.

In early 2018, a protracted and contentious dispute unfolded between the Trump Organization and Orestes Fintiklis, the majority owner of the property. Fintiklis sought to terminate the Trump Organization's management contract, citing "declining revenues and alleged mismanagement".

The Trump Organization resisted these efforts, leading to legal battles in both U.S. and Panamanian courts. The situation escalated when Panamanian police escorted Trump Organization staff out of the building, and the Trump name was physically removed from the property.

The Trump Organization publicly condemned the actions taken by Fintiklis, accusing him of employing "mob-style tactics" and attempting a hostile takeover of the property. They also initiated legal proceedings to regain control of the hotel which were not successful.

Trump and Ukraine. If you want to know what Trump's real problem is with Zelensky of Ukraine, it is slightly because Trump said many times during his campaigning that he would end the war with Russia in the first 24 hours of his presidency, and he sees Zelensky as an impediment to that.

But more so look at the sole rights he wants for the vast precious minerals of Ukraine as his quid pro quo reward for ending the war. Trump is prepared to capitulate to Putin and sacrifice Ukraine's sovereignty in the deal by allowing Putin to keep all the lands he has illegally invaded, and Zelensky won't buy it.

Trump and Windmills. If you want to know why Trump is obsessed with windmills his description of "wind farms," and as such the Climate Movement, as seen in his campaign rhetoric, "they're killing the birds, they're killing the birds," look below the surface as to what Trump's real beef is.

Trump has frequently criticized climate change policy along with wind turbines, he calls them windmills, often referring to them as "ugly" or complaining that they kill birds. He has also argued that the push for renewable energy is misguided, stemming from what he considers the "mistaken belief" that carbon emissions cause global climate change.

Trump's real problem is that he sees wind turbines as detrimental to property values. Trump's aversion to wind turbines is a reaction to lost court case in an incident regarding his business ventures in Scotland. In 2006, he acquired a substantial portion of the Menie estate near Aberdeen to develop the Trump International Golf Links, Scotland.

When plans emerged for the European Offshore Wind Deployment Centre off the Aberdeenshire coast, Trump objected, claiming the turbines would mar the ocean view from his resort. He described the turbines as "ugly" and environmentally irresponsible, asserting that they would harm tourism and the natural beauty of the area.

Trump's legal challenges against the wind farm were unsuccessful. The Scottish government granted planning permission for the wind farm in March 2013, a decision Trump vehemently opposed, vowing to "spend whatever monies are necessary" to prevent its construction. However, his appeals were dismissed, and the wind farm proceeded as planned.

These incidents highlight the intersection of Trump's personal business interests with his broader policy positions, particularly his scepticism toward renewable energy and climate change initiatives.

In line with these views, Trump's administration has taken steps to curtail renewable energy initiatives. Notably, a recent directive halted offshore wind permits, critically impacting the U.S. offshore wind energy sector. This suspension affects over 90% of planned projects, totalling more than 60 gigawatts of potential capacity, thereby jeopardizing clean energy goals and grid reliability on the East Coast.

Trump and Gaza. If you say you want to understand Trump's fixation with Gaza don't look at the Palestinian and Israeli conflict and Trump's insistence that he wants to stop the war, look at the real estate value he now perceives that Gaza holds, that he would like to unlock in exchange for favourable treatment of Israel by the United States. Real estate that Israel as part of the agreement would freely give to the United States.

EMBRACE TRUTH, CHOOSE YOUR ELECTED OFFICIALS WISELY.

In societal and political discourse two great leaders in the concept of "truth without turmoil" were Mahatma Ghandhi and Dr. Martin Luther King Jnr. In the Indian continent's struggle against English Imperialism, Ghandhi embraced Satyagraha, a philosophy of nonviolent resistance, which aimed to "remove the sin from society," which may at times require "legitimately removing the sinner," who is habitually fuelling the sin. Similarly as did Dr. Martin Luther King Jnr. in the activities of the Civil Rights Movement of the 60's.

And many times this can only be achieved through elections, through governmental legislative means, or through new or enhanced laws, which is why every voter's vote matters. For example if you want to eliminate violence from your city you don't elect a mayor who has a history of violent behaviour. If you want to address racial inequality you don't elect a leader with fascist leaning tendencies.

If you want to address the prevalence of domestic violence or violence against women in general, you don't elect an accused wife abuser or a sexual predator to a position of power. If you want more equality for women, you don't elect an obvious misogynist to parliament.

If you want to make the tax system fairer to all you don't elect a billionaire with past dubious business dealings to government. If you want to improve your personal economic conditions, even something as simple as "lowering the cost of groceries," you don't elect a six times bankrupt person with an oligarchal assistant to lead your country.

If you want to see your cost of living improve you don't elect a leader who sits on a golden toilet in the morning, rides a golden escalator in the day, and sits under a crystal chandelier for their evening meal. One who seems to be obsessed with an insatiable need to surround himself with bright golden things. You elect a credible candidate as was seen with Abraham Lincoln, "honest Abe" as he was called,

There is often a moral duty for all of us to speak the truth, even when it is difficult or dangerous. And many of these historical figures that I have touched on have demonstrated this carriage. Socrates chose to die rather than bending his pursuit of truth. Mahatma Gandhi used truth as a weapon against colonial oppression. Martin Luther King Jnr. called for truth and justice in the face of racial inequality and gave his life for the Civil Rights cause.

Speaking truth to power requires integrity, wisdom, and resilience. It is not only an individual act but a social duty that upholds justice and promotes the common good. But if the voter doesn't do it through their vote, who will. Failure to do it opens the path to authoritarian rule, the eventual rise of a political dictator.

Truth is not only a philosophical or spiritual concern, but truth also carries deep social and ethical responsibilities. When individuals honour truth, they uphold integrity, and foster trust. When truth is disregarded, society risks falling into corruption, deception, and chaos. Honouring truth in one's personal life means practising honesty in thoughts, words, and actions.

This requires self-examination, the courage to admit mistakes, and the willingness to seek knowledge. Integrity is the act of living in accordance with truth, demonstrating consistency between what one believes, says, and does. This consistency builds credibility and respect, both in personal relationships in in societies at large, and builds cohesion.

You see societies function more cohesively and as a result more peacefully and effectively when truth is upheld in institutions such as law, politics, and education. When leaders and citizens commit to truth, political governance is just, laws are fair, and communities drive. However, when truth is manipulated for personal gain, societies suffer from misinformation, prejudice, injustice, and conflict.

History has shown that when truth is suppressed such as is seen in current political regimes in many nations, where citizens embrace authoritarian leaders, chaos, oppression and disorder will automatically follow. Conversely, movements based on truth such as civil rights struggles, have led even at times if slowly to justice and positive social change.

So truth is more than just a concept; it is a guiding principle that shapes individual character and social order. Philosophers and spiritual leaders have long emphasised its importance, offering different perspectives on what truth is and how it should be pursued. Primarily honouring truth requires a personal commitment to honesty, integrity, and moral responsibility by every citizen.

In a world where misinformation and deception increasingly threaten trust and justice, the duty of all citizens is to uphold truth. Truth remains as vital today as it ever was. By embracing truth in thought, word, and action, individuals as a whole can contribute to a more ethical, stable, and just society.

Truth is the foundation upon which the edifice of society stands; without it, the structure crumbles into chaos. A society that values truth above comfort is one that paves the way for genuine progress. It is the mirror in which society sees its true reflection, untainted by illusion. The strength of a society is measured by its commitment to uphold the truth, even when inconvenient. A society that fears truth is one that shackles itself to the chains of ignorance.

"A nation under the sway of a political cult must confront the uncomfortable truth that democracy demands vigilance, not complacency. When a political cult leader governs, democracy's greatest challenge is not the leader's power, but the people's unwillingness to reclaim their own. In a democracy, the power of the people is a sacred trust; under authoritarian rule, it becomes a mere tool for manipulation and control."

8

The Anatomy of Trumpism, a Political Cult.

The Myth, The Man, The Truth.

Chapter Contents.

"When a nation surrenders to the will of an authoritarian leader, it trades its moral compass for the illusion of certainty. When a political cult seizes control, the social fabric of a nation is stretched thin, as fear and division replace unity and dialogue. In the shadow of authoritarianism, the voice of the individual is thus often drowned out by the roar of the cult, leaving democracy gasping for breath."

THE ANATOMY OF TRUMPISM, A POLITICAL CULT.

Throughout history, religious and political movements have frequently intertwined, creating groups that can best be described as religious political cults. These organisations blend theological belief with political ambition, forming alliances that serve both religious, personal, and political ideological goals.

The key to their unity lies in a shared ideological framework often centred around their belief that their movement represents a divine mandate or a moral crusade against perceived enemies. The psychology of their supporters and the characteristics that elevate certain individuals involved in the group to leadership provide insight into how these groups function, manipulate the rhetoric, and maintain power.

At the heart of any religious political cult is a belief in a transcendent mission, one that positions the movement as an instrument of divine will or moral righteousness. This belief justifies the blending of religious doctrine with political or personal objectives.

In many cases, members see their cause as a battle between good and evil, not just a battle between opposing political parties, with their leaders acting as messianic figures or chosen representatives of a higher power. Trump has elevated this to a new level by regularly making statements such as, "I am the anointed one," and after the supposed assassination attempt, "God saved me for a reason."

This narrative strengthens the groups cohesion and moral conviction, making it difficult for outsiders to challenge or reason with them. The ideological foundation also fosters an "ends justify the means" mentality. Since the movement is seen as divinely sanctioned, any action taken to achieve its goals, whether through political manoeuvring, social coercion, or even violence, is rationalised as necessary and just.

This ideological unity enables the movement to attract both devout believers and individual opportunistic political actors and electoral candidates, who see the movement as a vehicle for personal and party influence and power.

Supporters of religious political cults often exhibit several defining psychological and behavioural traits. Members often placed blind faith in the movement's leadership, seeing them as infallible or divinely guided. Dissent is viewed as betrayal, and critical thinking is discouraged. They believe they are part of a righteous struggle, which then fosters an attitude of elitism, and fellow citizens outside the movement are often seen as misguided, corrupt, or even evil.

A strong "us versus them" mentality permeates these groups. They often perceive themselves as under siege from external sources, the enemy without, or even internal sources, those of their own political party, and label these people as the "enemy within." This will also include political adversaries, secularists, and those of competing religious or social factions.

Members subsume their personal identities under the larger movement, adopting group slogans, for example "Make America Great Again", as well as symbols and rituals that reinforce a group persona of unity. Many supporters crave strong leadership, preferring a top-down hierarchy where decisions are made by a central authority rather than through democratic or open discussion. These qualities create a highly motivated, disciplined, and emotionally invested base that is willing to sacrifice personal autonomy, and moral integrity, to ensure the success of the movement.

Within any religious political cult, a hierarchy inevitably forms, with certain individuals rising to positions of influence and control, "the first amongst equals," so to speak. The most successful leaders tend to exhibit a distinct set of traits that allow them to dominate the movement, including a type of "strongman persona."

A successful leader must have the ability to captivate and inspire followers, often through impassioned rhetoric, whether it makes sense or not, and a larger-than-life presence and persona that makes supporters feel protected and safe, as a shepherd does his sheep.

Ever mindful of the ambition of others in the group, the leader will continually portray themselves as the only one uniquely capable of guiding the movement to victory, then very quickly they will consolidate power by eliminating dissent and demanding obedience. The leader will create a culture of fear at times, ensuring that those within the movement do not challenge their authority.

Their ability to strategically use propaganda, religious doctrine and political alliances is also essential. These leaders craft narratives that reinforce their position while demonising opponents. While the rank and file may be driven by ideology, the leader often understands the necessity of political and emotional manoeuvring. They make calculated alliances, compromise when necessary, and adapt their messaging to maintain power.

Many leaders cultivate an image of personal sacrifice or martyrdom, portraying themselves as suffering for the cause, which they may describe as "political persecution." This creates emotional loyalty among followers who view any attack on the leader as an attack on the movement itself.

Donald Trump has become very adept at doing this, continually reminding his followers of the ongoing persecution of himself by legal authorities in the past and currently in the present, using terminology such as the "ongoing witch hunts against me", and publicly exploiting what is still regarded by some truth seekers as "a questionable assassination attempt," since the potential suspect in the incident was a registered member of the Republican party.

Ultimately, the leader who rises to dominance in a religious political cult is the one who can most effectively balance charisma with ruthless pragmatism. They manipulate the ideological fervour of their supporters, while maintaining strategic control over the group's direction, at times even adopting a group song as do sporting clubs, which is sung at events to create an emotional atmosphere of unity.

Civil Rights Movements of the past have adopted songs like "We Shall Overcome," Kamala Harris adopted the song, "Freedom," and Donald Trump exploited the song of the Village People, Y.M.C.A.

As mentioned before in a touch of irony considering the conservative political stance on the LGBTQ+ culture, whilst it was said that the song when written was inspired by the Young Men's Christian Association which, at the time, provided affordable housing, gym facilities and social programmes for young men, there has long been speculation about the song's subtext. On the surface, it celebrates the Y.M.C.A. as a place where young men can exercise, stay, and build friendships.

However, given the Village People's association with LGBTQ+ culture and its strong ties to the gay community, many interpret the song as a coded message about the Y.M.C.A.'s role as a meeting place for gay men. Whether intentionally or not Y.M.C.A. became an enduring anthem in the LGBTQ+ culture, and is often played at gay pride events, weddings and sporting events, and as witnessed now at Donald Trump's rallies and other celebratory events he holds, including his 2024 Christmas party at Mar-a Lago.

Religious political cults thrive on the fusion of faith and power, creating movements that are resistant to external criticism and highly motivated to achieve their goals. Their strength lies in their ability to instil a sense of divine purpose in their members while using fear, loyalty, and authoritarian structures to maintain control.

The rise of a dominant leader within such a movement is almost inevitable, as the psychological needs of the group and the intellectual shortcomings of many in the group, demand a figure who embodies their mission with absolute conviction.

Such movements can be highly disruptive, often rejecting democratic norms, suppressing dissent, and pursuing objectives that quite often lead to social conflict and social division. Understanding their ideological foundations, the psychology of their followers, and the "sometimes-mythological (made up) characteristics" of their leaders, is crucial in countering their influence and preserving pluralistic societies.

THE DIFFERENCE BETWEEN TRUMPISM AND MAGA-MANIA.

The terms Trumpism and Maga-Mania (my term for the MAGA Movement), refer to overlapping but distinct political and cultural phenomena. While both are rooted in the political movement surrounding Donald Trump, they differ in ideology, intensity, and the psychological and sociopolitical mechanisms that drive them. To break down these differences:

Trumpism is a political cult of personality. Trumpism refers to the ideological and policy-driven movement centred around Donald Trump's vision for America, which is basically, unbeknown to many, a carbon copy of the Project 2025 agenda. Trumpism represents a political cult of personality, where loyalty to Trump defines political identity and allegiance.

The cult itself could be described as one of authoritarian populism. Trumpism combines a strongman leadership style with a populist appeal. It emphasizes an "us vs. them" narrative, where Trump positions himself as the sole defender of the people against elites, immigrants, the Deep State, and globalists.

Trumpism thrives on cultural grievances. and intellectual ignorance. It attacks political correctness, LGBTQ+ rights, diversity efforts, and progressive movements, branding them as existential threats to "traditional America." It promotes an anti-establishment political view even whilst Trump's campaign coffers have been filled with elite finances. Trumpism markets itself as an insurgency against the Washington establishment, media, and bureaucracy, whilst accepting media promotions and millions of dollars of campaign donations from them.

Many adherents to Trumpism embrace conspiracy theories such as QAnon, election fraud narratives, and distrust of scientific institutions. They see Trump as a near-messianic figure, infallible in the eyes of his most devout supporters. His actions are justified regardless of legality or morality because his followers believe in their psychologically deceived state that he alone can "save America." Followers embrace Trump's disregard for democratic norms because they see him as a strongman fighting corrupt institutions.

Maga-Mania on the other hand is a mass psychological movement. Maga-Mania extends beyond Trumpism as an ideological movement and into the realm of mass hysteria, fervour, and emotional attachment. It operates more as a psychosocial phenomenon than a strictly political ideology.

Maga-Mania is less about policy and more about how Trump makes people feel. His rallies are akin to religious revivals, where emotional highs, anger, and euphoria drive collective behaviour. I discussed this in Chapter 5, Faith and Fervour, Manipulating the Masses. Maga- Mania functions like a social and cultural identity rather than a political stance. Wearing a MAGA hat, waving Trump flags, and engaging in performative patriotism (e.g., "Let's Go Brandon"), all these things signal belonging.

"Let's Go Brandon" is a euphemism for an expletive-laden anti-Joe Biden chant. It originated on October 2, 2021, during a NASCAR race at Talladega Superspeedway in Alabama. After driver Brandon Brown won the race, he was being interviewed by an NBC Sports reporter. In the background, the crowd was audibly chanting "F* Joe Biden.**"

The reporter, either misinterpreting or attempting to sanitize the chant, remarked, "You can hear the chants from the crowd: "Let's Go Brandon!" This quickly became an internet meme and a coded way for critics of President Biden to express discontent without using explicit language. The phrase spread rapidly across social media, political rallies, and merchandise, turning into a cultural and political slogan.

Trump supporters caught in Maga-Mania will reject any evidence contradicting their beliefs. No scandal, legal issue, or failure by Trump can shake their conviction. Any criticism of Trump is seen as an attack on MAGA itself. His indictments, impeachments, and electoral losses are reframed as proof that the Deep State is conspiring against him, fuelled also by Trump's continual use of the phrase, "it's a witch hunt."

Some adherents in an almost apocalyptic manner believe in a near-messianic future where Trump will "drain the swamp," defeat the Deep State, and restore America to greatness, even if it requires violence or civil unrest such as was seen with the January 6th. insurrection. Charismatic leaders like Trump manipulate emotions, demand loyalty, and isolate followers from conflicting information.

Maga-Mania has turned politics into a reality show where Trump is the hero, the Deep State is the villain, and followers are the righteous audience cheering for justice. While Trumpism is an ideological movement that seeks political power, Maga-Mania is a mass psychological phenomenon that transcends politics. Trumpism can survive beyond Trump if another leader carries its ideological torch, but Maga-Mania is uniquely tied to Trump's persona and performance.

DONALD TRUMP, THE MYTHIC MAN IN PERSON.

Political figures have long used myths to manipulate public perception and consolidate power. By crafting narratives that emphasize their strengths and downplay their weaknesses, they can create an image of infallibility and authority. Political dictators, in particular, have been known to use and promote myths to assert their credibility and justify their rule. Donald Trump is a prime example.

Donald J. Trump, the 45th President of the United States, and just recently confirmed 47th President, is arguably one of the most polarizing and influential figures in modern political American and perhaps even world history.

From his beginnings as a slumlord, a term used to describe a landlord who owns and manages rental properties that are in poor condition, often neglecting maintenance and repairs, whilst prioritizing profit over the well-being of their tenants, to his becoming an established real estate mogul and reality television star, to his unexpected rise to the presidency in 2016, and again in 2024, Trump has consistently defied conventional expectations.

To explore the key aspects of Donald Trump's life, career, and impact on American politics, is to discover the following. Donald John Trump was born on June 14, 1946, in Queens, New York, into a wealthy family. His father, Fred Trump, was a successful real estate developer, and Donald followed in his footsteps, joining the family business after graduating from the Wharton School of the University of Pennsylvania in 1968. Several of his teachers have when asked, described him as "an average student."

For many years Fred Trump in his real estate transactions held a reputation for having a good business acumen and reputable dealing with clients. However, a story has surfaced more recently regarding Fred Trump, with allegations of racial discrimination in housing projects. The story primarily stems from a legal case in the 1970's that saw the U.S. Department of Justice file a lawsuit against Fred Trump and his real estate company, Trump Management, accusing them of discriminating against potential tenants based on race.

The lawsuit alleged that the company had refused to rent apartments to black or Asian individuals and had misrepresented the availability of apartments to them. The case was based on evidence gathered by the New York City Human Rights Commission and the Urban League, which conducted tests to demonstrate discriminatory practices. Testers posing as potential tenants found that black applicants were often told that no apartments were available, while white applicants were offered leases.

Fred Trump and his company representatives and company lawyers led by Roy Cohn (remember that name), of course denied the allegations, and the case was settled in 1975 without an admission of guilt. As part of the settlement, Trump Management agreed to take steps to ensure compliance with the Fair Housing Act, including providing lists of vacancies to the Urban League and advertising vacancies in minority newspapers.

This case has been a point of discussion in the context of Donald Trump's later political career, as it highlights issues of racial discrimination in housing practices during that era.

Trump the son quickly made a name for himself in the New York real estate market, known for his ambitious projects and larger-than-life personality. He developed numerous high-profile properties, including Trump Tower in Manhattan, and expanded his brand into casinos, hotels, and golf courses all bolding bearing the name Trump. His brash style and self-promotion earned him widespread recognition, but also led to several bankruptcies and legal battles.

In the 1980's and 1990's, Trump's public persona grew through appearances in the media and his role as the host of the television reality show The Apprentice, which further solidified his self-framed myth of a successful and decisive businessman. This fame set the stage for his later entry into politics.

Trump's first foray into politics came in the late 1980's when he briefly considered running for president, but it wasn't until 2015 that he launched a serious campaign. His candidacy was initially dismissed by many as a publicity stunt, but Trump quickly gained traction with his unconventional style and populist rhetoric. His previous comments about Republican politicians being the dumbest group in Congress, were quickly denied when he was offered the opportunity from the Republican Party to run for president in 2016.

Running on a revived Reagan slogan, "Make America Great Again," Trump tapped into widespread discontent with the political establishment, promising to bring back jobs, secure the borders, and put "America First." His campaign was marked by controversial statements on immigration, trade, and foreign policy, which resonated with a significant segment of the non-college educated electorate, particularly white working-class voters who felt left behind by globalization and demographic changes.

In the Republican primaries, Trump defeated a crowded field of experienced politicians, defying expectations at every turn. In the general election, he faced off against Democratic nominee Hillary Clinton, a former First Lady, Senator, and Secretary of State, and despite losing the popular vote by nearly three million votes, Trump won the Electoral College vote, and as such was elected president.

Stories emerged at this time however some saying that it was not by chance that he won, but through assistance from the Russian government, and the saga of Russian interference in the 2016 United States presidential elections became a complex and multifaceted narrative that had significant implications for American politics and international relations at the time.

The episode involved the roles of key political figures, including Hillary Clinton and Donald Trump, and led to extensive investigations, notably by the F.B.I., which culminated in the controversial dismissal of its Director, James Comey, during Trump's first term in office.

The backdrop to this dramatic F.B.I. saga that resulted in James Comey's dismissal, began with the 2016 presidential election. During the campaign, U.S. intelligence agencies detected efforts by the Russian government to interfere in the electoral process. These efforts included hacking into the Democratic National Committee's (D.N.C.) emails and releasing them through platforms like WikiLeaks, as well as a sophisticated disinformation campaign aimed at influencing public opinion through social media.

Hillary Clinton's campaign was directly affected by these actions, as the leaked emails were used to sow discord and undermine her candidacy. The content of the emails, which included internal communications and strategy discussions, was used by opponents to fuel narratives of corruption and untrustworthiness. Clinton and her supporters argued that the Russian interference was a deliberate attempt to damage her campaign and aid Donald Trump, who was perceived to have a more favourable stance towards Russia.

Donald Trump, on the other hand, consistently downplayed the significance of Russian interference. During the campaign and after his election, Trump expressed scepticism about the intelligence community's findings, often referring to the investigations as a "witch hunt" and denying any collusion between his campaign office and Russian operatives. His stance created a political divide, with many of his supporters echoing his sentiments and dismissing the allegations as politically motivated attacks.

The F.B.I. under the leadership of Director James Comey, launched an investigation into the Russian interference, and its potential connections to the Trump campaign. This investigation was part of a broader effort to understand the extent of foreign influence in the election and to safeguard future electoral processes, however Trump took it all personally.

The investigation then became a focal point of controversy, particularly regarding Comey's handling of the inquiry into Hillary Clinton's use of a private email server during her tenure as Secretary of State. Comey's decision to publicly announce the reopening of the email investigation just days before the election, was criticized by many as having a detrimental impact on Clinton's campaign.

The situation escalated when President Trump dismissed James Comey in May 2017. The official reason given for Comey's dismissal was his handling of the

Clinton email investigation, however many speculated that it was related to the ongoing Russia investigation and Trump's desire to terminate it to avoid scrutiny of his own campaign office. Comey's firing led to the appointment of Special Counsel Robert Mueller to continue the investigation into Russian interference and any potential collusion with the Trump campaign.

Mueller's investigation, which lasted nearly two years, resulted in numerous indictments and convictions of individuals associated with the Trump campaign, though it did not establish a criminal conspiracy between the campaign and Russia. The investigation's findings were detailed in the Mueller Report, which outlined extensive Russian interference efforts and highlighted instances of potential obstruction of justice by President Trump.

As such the saga of Russian interference in the 2016 election remains a pivotal moment in American history, highlighting vulnerabilities in the electoral process and the challenges of addressing foreign influence in a digital age. It underscored the importance of cybersecurity, the impact of disinformation, and the need for transparency and accountability in political campaigns.

The roles of Hillary Clinton and Donald Trump in this narrative continue to be debated, as do the actions and decisions of James Comey and the broader intelligence community. The episode still serves as a reminder of the complexities of modern democracy and the ongoing struggle to protect its integrity. To gain some understanding of what a second Trump presidency might look like it is relevant to look at some of the on the ground operational details of his first presidency.

A Summary of Trump's First Presidency.

Trump's first presidency was characterized by a series of significant and often controversial actions. Trump implemented a major tax cut in 2017, which benefited corporations and the wealthy, and pursued deregulation across various industries. It was interesting then, to see in the 2024 campaign, Elon Musk, a strong vocal advocate for deregulation, aligning himself with Trump personally, politically, and financially, even to a point of taking up residence at Mar-a-Lago, Trump's Florida resort.

In his 2017 presidency, Trump took a hardline stance on immigration, making it a central issue of the presidency. His administration implemented a travel ban on several predominantly Muslim countries, increased border security, and attempted to build a wall along the U.S.-Mexico border. The administration's "zero tolerance" policy led to the separation of thousands of families at the border, sparking widespread criticism.

Immigration was a central theme of Trump's first campaign and presidency and continued in his 2024 campaign. His administration implemented strict immigration policies, including travel bans on certain countries, increased border security, and efforts to end the Deferred Action for Childhood Arrivals (DACA) program.

The construction of a border wall with Mexico was a symbolic and contentious issue throughout his term. Most of what he did however has had little impact on the border crossings and drug and people smuggling.

His foreign policy was characterized by an "America First" approach, emphasizing national sovereignty and reevaluating international alliances. His administration engaged in direct diplomacy with North Korea, such as his meetings with North Korean leader Kim Jong-un, though these efforts yielded few substantive results.

He withdrew from the Iran nuclear deal and moved the U.S. embassy in Israel to Jerusalem. Trump's "America First" foreign policy saw a withdrawal from several international agreements, including the Paris Climate Accord. and the Iran nuclear deal.

The final year of Trump's presidency was dominated by the COVID-19 pandemic, which led to widespread economic disruption and the deaths of over

400,000 Americans by the time he left office. Trump's handling of the crisis was heavily criticized, particularly his downplaying of the virus's severity, inconsistent messaging, and clashes with public health officials.

Perhaps realising the future of once again ascending to the political heights of a second presidency, and to ensure it worked out better for him the second time, as a type of political "get out of jail" card, Trump subsequently instigated the appointment of three Supreme Court justices Neil Gorsuch, Brett Kavanaugh, and Amy Coney Barrett, shifting the court to a solid conservative majority, who subsequently granted him presidential immunity for any offences carried out whilst in office.

This has further emboldened him in this his second term in office to test the limits of his presidential power. He also appointed numerous conservative judges to lower federal courts, leaving a lasting impact on the judiciary.

One of the most controversial things Trump did during his first term in office was to initiate the overturn of Roe v. Wade. Roe v. Wade was a landmark decision by the U.S. Supreme Court in 1973 that established a woman's legal right to have an abortion under the constitutional right to privacy.

However, on June 24, 2022, the Supreme Court overturned Roe v. Wade with its decision in the case of Dobbs v. Jackson Women's Health Organization. This decision effectively ended the federal constitutional protection of abortion rights and allowed individual states to regulate or ban abortion as they saw fit.

The groundwork for this decision was influenced by the appointment of those three conservative justices to the Supreme Court during Donald Trump's first presidency. Trump through his initiation of the over-turning, did not do it out of any kind of moral conviction, he did it merely to appease his Christian Nationalist and Evangelical supporters in reward for their vote at the election.

The Dobbs decision as it was called led to significant changes in abortion laws across the United States, with many states enacting strict bans, seeing doctors and medical staff liable for criminal prosecution not only for carrying out an abortion, but for assisting women who may have had a miscarriage and would die if not treated immediately. And women were not treated, and women died as a result.

Trump was impeached twice by the House of Representatives, first in 2019 over his dealings with Ukraine and again in 2021 for incitement of the insurrection following the January 6th Capitol riot. He was acquitted by the Senate both times. To be acquitted does not mean he was innocent of the charges.

After leaving office, Trump continued to wield significant influence within the Republican Party. He maintained a strong base of supporters and has been a key figure in shaping the party's direction, particularly through his endorsements in primary elections. Trump's false claims about the 2020 election being stolen have led to widespread efforts to challenge and undermine mid-term election results across the country, fuelling ongoing political polarization.

Despite facing numerous legal challenges, including investigations into his business practices and his role in the January 6th Capitol riot, Trump at the time hinted at a possible run for the presidency in 2024, which he eventually did, keeping his political future in the spotlight.

Donald Trump's impact on American politics is profound and far-reaching. He reshaped the Republican Party in his image, turning it into MAGA, a populist, nationalist movement. His presidency challenged norms and conventions, leading to a re-examination of the role of the media, the judiciary, and the rule of law in American democracy.

His presidency was marked by significant social and political polarization. His handling of issues such as racial tensions, healthcare, and climate change drew both support and criticism. The COVID-19 pandemic posed unprecedented challenges, with Trump's response becoming a focal point of debate.

Trump's tenure also deepened political polarization, with his supporters viewing him as a champion of the people against a corrupt establishment, while his critics see him as a threat to democratic institutions and norms. His legacy is likely to be debated for years to come, as scholars, politicians, and citizens grapple with the implications of his presidency for the future of American democracy.

Donald Trump remains a towering albeit controversial figure in American politics, embodying both the hopes and fears of a divided nation. His unconventional rise to power and turbulent presidency have left an indelible mark on the United States, reshaping the political landscape in ways that will be felt for generations.

Whether as a polarizing former president or a continually polarising now current second term president, Trump's influence on American politics is undeniable, ensuring that his legacy for good or bad will continue to be a central topic of discussion and debate for many years to come.

His influence on the United States democratic process has raised significant concerns among political analysts, scholars, and citizens alike. His presidency and subsequent actions have sparked debates about the integrity of democratic institutions, the rule of law and the norms that underpin American democracy, as well the dangers he poses to the democratic process, including the erosion of trust in electoral systems, and the potential for authoritarianism to gain a foothold in what was once regarded as the greatest democratic nation in the world.

Donald Trump's involvement in American politics has been transformative, reshaping the political landscape and challenging established norms. His first presidency left a lasting impact on domestic and international policies, and the potential legacy of his second term carries significant implications for the future of democracy not just in America, but in international politics as well.

Behind all the fanfare that has surrounded the myth of Donald Trump however, lies a long history of business failings, moral failings, political failures, and legal entanglements.

THE MYTH OF THE SUCCESSFUL BUSINESSMAN... TRUMP'S BUSINESS FAILINGS.

As most people well know, before entering politics, Donald Trump was primarily known as a real estate mogul and businessman, which helped reinforce in the public's eyes the myth that he was and is a successful self-made businessman, but the truth is far from this. Trump's business ventures have been the subject of various legal disputes over many years, and his companies have faced multiple lawsuits related to real estate transactions.

Throughout the 1980's and 1990's, Trump's business dealings were marked by a series of bankruptcies. His business career has included several high-profile bankruptcies, particularly in the casino industry. His casinos in Atlantic City, including the Trump Taj Mahal, filed for bankruptcy multiple times, leading to significant financial losses and legal disputes with creditors, raising questions about Trump's financial management and business acumen.

In numerous on the ground interviews with supporters during Donald Trump's campaign rallies we saw most believing that he was a successful businessman, and consequently believed he would be a good president. Most of Donald Trump's supporters had no idea of the number of his business failings, and no idea that Donald Trump or his businesses had declared bankruptcy six times. Those bankruptcies were all what are known as Chapter 11 bankruptcies, which allow a business to restructure its debts while continuing to operate.

The bankruptcies involved his casinos and hotels in Atlantic City and New York. Some key examples were The Trump Taj Mahal, The Trump Plaza Hotel, The Trump Castle, The Trump Plaza Casino, The Trump Hotels and Casino Resorts Company, and Trump Entertainment Resorts, its successor.

The Trump Taj Mahal casino in Atlantic City was financed with 675 million dollars in junk bonds at high interest rates. The casino struggled with debt and filed for Chapter 11 bankruptcy in 1991, less than a year after it opened. Trump had to sell assets and give up half his ownership to lenders.

The Trump Plaza Hotel in New York faced financial difficulties due to excessive debt. Trump filed for bankruptcy and gave up a 49% stake to the creditors in exchange for reducing his personal liability.

The Trump Castle was another Atlantic City casino. Trump Castle was unable to pay its debts, and the business was restructured under bankruptcy protection in 1992.

The Trump Plaza Casino in Atlantic City also faced financial trouble in 1992, and Trump's lawyers negotiated a restructuring deal similar to the one for his other properties.

The Trump Hotels and Casino Resorts company which owned multiple casinos as well as the Trump Marina and The Trump Plaza ended up with $1.8 billion in debt and filed for Chapter 11 bankruptcy. Trump gave up a significant portion of his company to creditors but remained chairman.

Trump Entertainment Resorts, the successor company to Trump Hotels & Casino Resorts struggled after the 2008 financial crisis. It filed for bankruptcy again in 2009 and as part of the arrangement with creditors Trump resigned as chairman and gave up much of his remaining stake.

Interestingly Trump never personally filed for bankruptcy, only his businesses did, for to do so would mean that he would ruin his personal credit rating. He used bankruptcy to get someone else to foot the bill for his poor business management so that he could still restructure his existing debts and move on. Unfortunately he left a trail of financial destruction and personal heartbreak for others in his wake, many times small business owners such as tradesmen and suppliers.

Donald Trump's six business bankruptcies have played a dual role in shaping both his business reputation and his political rise. While critics see them as evidence of serious business and financial mismanagement, Trump and his supporters in what could be described as a supreme act of cognitive dissonance, have framed them as examples of his capability for strategic deal-making.

Trump often defended his bankruptcies by saying they were standard business practice and that he used the legal system to his advantage, which in a sense later became a hallmark of his political career, using the legal system to stall his cases. However many financial experts saw his frequent bankruptcies as a sign of overleveraging and poor financial planning rather than the work of strategic genius he made them out to be.

After multiple bankruptcies, major Wall Street banks, such as Citibank and JPMorgan Chase, stopped lending to Trump. Instead, he had to turn to alternative financing sources, including high-risk junk bonds, foreign financing, including from Deutsche Bank, which remained one of the few major institutions willing to lend to him, and other institutions some say in Russia and Saudi Arabia.

Since Trump's repeated bankruptcies made it harder for him to secure finance for large real estate deals, he eventually pivoted toward licensing deals and branding, which is basically when a person allows a company to use their name to market a product and pay for the privilege.

This strategy allowed him to generate revenue with lower risk, as he could earn fees from licensing his brand to other businesses without the same level of financial commitment. And because he had falsely created this impression that he was the best businessman in America, businesses were ready to use his name to market their own products as the best, for example Trump buildings and Trump golf courses.

Some other notable products that have been associated with Trump, include a brand of vodka that was launched in the mid-2000's, a line of premium steaks that was marketed through various channels, Trump Ice, a bottled water brand, Trump Home, a line of home furnishings and decor, and Trump Magazine, a lifestyle magazine that featured luxury living and business advice. In addition to these we witnessed during his election campaigning Trump promoting a variety of products including gold sneakers, hats, badges, bibles, picture cards, and bitcoin.

Branding himself as a "comeback king" during his 2016 presidential campaign, Trump used his bankruptcies to frame himself as a fighter who always comes back stronger. His supporters saw him as a tough, battle-hardened businessman who could handle crises, whilst his critics argued that he was merely a con-man, a snake oil salesman, who had gained wealth while his investors, employees, and contractors suffered from his bankruptcies brought about by his business incompetence and lack of integrity.

The bankruptcies also influenced Trump's relationship with the media. He became adept at using media coverage to his advantage, turning negative press into opportunities for publicity. His appearances on reality television, particularly "The Apprentice," thus helped him rebuild his brand and reach a wider audience.

One of the most notable legal battles during Trump's business career was the lawsuit involving Trump University. Founded in 2005, Trump University was marketed as a real estate education program. However, it faced allegations of fraud, with former students claiming they were misled about the quality of education and the potential for financial success.

In 2016, Trump agreed to a $25 million settlement to resolve the lawsuits, which included claims from students and the New York Attorney General. This case not only tarnished his reputation but also raised questions about his commitment to ethical business practices.

He has been involved in multiple defamation lawsuits, both as a plaintiff and a defendant. Notably, he has sued media outlets and individuals for defamation, while also being sued by others who claim he made false and damaging statements about them.

Donald Trump's legal battles are a testament to the complexities of his career, blending business ventures with political ambitions. From allegations of fraud and discrimination in his business dealings to the legal challenges stemming from his presidency, Trump's life has been characterized by controversy and conflict.

As he navigates these legal issues, even if they are not dismissed, now that he has assumed his second presidency, their appearance in the first instance will likely still have lasting effects on his legacy and the political landscape of the United States. The interplay between his legal troubles and his public persona continues to shape the narrative surrounding one of the most polarizing figures in American history.

TRUMP'S POLITICAL / LEGAL ENTANGLEMENTS.

Trump's political career and actions during his first presidency have led to significant legal battles for himself personally, the extent of which is unsurpassed by any previous American president. His past and present legal battles are a complex and multifaceted aspect of his public life. They encompass a wide range of issues, from business practices and personal conduct to political actions and post-presidency controversies.

His past legal battles have not only shaped his public persona but have also had significant implications for his business empire and political aspirations. In exploring them a little further we see that his business practices have often drawn scrutiny.

In the 1970's, as I previously touched on, the Trump Organization faced allegations of racial discrimination in housing practices, leading to a lawsuit from the U.S. Department of Justice in 1973. The case was settled without admission of guilt, but it set a precedent for the legal challenges that would follow.

Trump's transition from businessman to politician brought a new wave of legal challenges. His campaign for the presidency in 2016 was marked by controversy, including investigations into his ties with Russia. The Mueller investigation, which examined Russian interference in the election and potential collusion with the Trump campaign, resulted in numerous indictments of Trump associates but did not establish that Trump himself conspired with Russia.

Further to all these things, in 2018 the New York Attorney General filed a lawsuit against the Trump Foundation, alleging it engaged in a pattern of illegal conduct. They lawsuit, filed on June 14, 2018, accused the foundation of engaging in illegal coordination with Donald Trump's 2016 presidential campaign, another violations of nonprofit laws. The case resulted in the foundation agreeing to dissolve, and in 2019, Trump was ordered to pay $2,000,000 in damages.

Following the 2020 presidential election, Trump faced investigations related to his efforts to challenge the election results. This included inquiries into his communications with state officials and the events leading up to the January 6th Capitol riot.

However, the legal scrutiny did not end with the conclusion of the Mueller investigation. Trump faced multiple lawsuits related to his actions while in office, including allegations of abuse of power and obstruction of justice. The impeachment proceedings against him in 2019 and 2021 were rooted in these legal controversies, with the first impeachment focusing on his dealings with Ukraine and the second on the January 6 Capitol riot.

Trump was impeached twice by the House of Representatives, first in 2019 over allegations of abuse of power and obstruction of Congress, and again in 2021 for incitement of insurrection following the Capitol riot. Although acquitted by the Senate both times, these proceedings were major legal and political events.

After leaving office, Trump had been under investigation for his handling of classified documents and potential obstruction of justice. These investigations then raised questions about presidential records and national security.

From 2023, Trump's legal challenges intensified. He has faced multiple criminal indictments, including charges related to business fraud, election interference, and mishandling of classified documents.

In 2024, former U.S. President Donald Trump was tried and convicted in New York on charges related to a $130,000 hush money payment to adult film actress Stormy Daniels during his 2016 presidential campaign. The payment was intended to silence Daniels about an alleged affair, aiming to prevent potential damage to his electoral prospects.

Trump faced 34 felony counts of falsifying business records. Prosecutors argued that these falsifications were made to conceal the true nature of the payments to Daniels, thereby influencing the 2016 election. On May 30, 2024, after a six-week trial, a 12-person jury unanimously found Trump guilty on all 34 counts. This marked the first time a former U.S. president was convicted of a felony.

On January 10, 2025, President-elect Trump was sentenced via video conference from his Mar-a-Lago residence. Judge Juan Merchan issued an unconditional discharge, meaning no imprisonment, fines, or probation were imposed. This decision considered the complexities of sentencing a president-elect and the potential implications for the nation. Despite the absence of immediate punitive measures, Trump remains a convicted felon and has indicated plans to appeal the verdict.

Whilst it was assumed that these cases would have significant implications for his political future, perhaps due to voter ignorance and aided by electoral indifference, they have had no significant impact, and as such Donald Trump was re-elected as President of the United States.

It appears that the legal battles, alongside Trump's continued rhetoric about witch hunts, has only galvanized his supporters, who, in their own ignorance of the facts, view the charges against him as all politically motivated.

DONALD TRUMP: A POLITICAL LEADER OR MERELY A FOOL MASQUERADING AS A PRESIDENT.

"Oh, and while the king was looking down, the jester stole his thorny crown."

I spoke in Chapter 1 of Don McLean's "American Pie," a reflective song on the decade of the sixties which he released in 1971. It was a type of nostalgic look back at the chaos, idealism and domestic tumult of the 1960's written as a type of musical metaphor of the day. A key line of the lyrics read, "oh, and while the king was looking down the jester stole his thorny crown."

This line could politically symbolize how over time media figures and entertainers have been entering politics and thus have begun shaping public opinion; primary high office examples being Arnold Schwarzenegger, a body-building champion, who was elected Governor of California in 2003. Schwarzenegger famously won the title of Mr. Olympia seven times, in 1970, 1971, 1972, 1973, 1974, 1975, and 1980. Before that, he also won titles like Mr. Universe (both amateur and professional versions) multiple times in the late 1960's.

We also saw Ronald Reagan, a former Hollywood actor, who rise to become the 40th. President ofThe United States, and Donald Trump, a real estate salesman, beauty pageant chairman, and former reality TV star, who became the 45th. President and now 47th. President of the United States. Both events exemplifying the fusion of entertainment and politics in modern governance.

This shift meant that politics was no longer just about intelligent governance, it was about spectacle, personality, and media dominance. As such the "jester" as in the term "court jester" who subtly stole the thorny crown in McLean's lyrics could be likened to a professional political clown, an elected fool, who took control of governance, totally changing the way in which the "court of congress" operated.

Throughout history, the figure of the fool has occupied a complex place in human society, in both leadership and subservience. Sometimes depicted as a court jester, other times as a naive wanderer, and often as an arrogant and destructive ruler, we find three things that are common at all times; the fool always embodies a lack of wisdom, the fool always demonstrates a profound lack of understanding, and the fool continually shows a lack of foresight.

In more recent times, certain world leaders primarily those of an autocratic nature, have made bizarre claims, rejected scientific evidence, or engaged in foolish reckless policies that defy rationality. The idea of the fool in politics is not merely theoretical, it is a real and dangerous phenomenon. A fool in theatre can be harmless, playing the role of an innocent or comic relief, but in the realm of governance and power, the consequences of a fool in control of decision making that affects a nation's populace, can be catastrophic.

The grouping of politicians that are classed as political dictators, in their essential nature fall into the category of fools. Some of the most infamous dictators in history have displayed these very traits, making decisions that seem almost absurd in hindsight. Their inability to see beyond their own egos and delusions of grandeur, often led to unnecessary wars, economic collapse, and the suffering of millions.

Many foolish dictators and political leaders have, in their arrogance and detachment from reality, made decisions that seem completely irrational, leading to ongoing suffering for a host of their people; and whilst this fool may be accepted as wise and selfless by some members of society, those with a lower intellectual level, the same fool will be laughed at by the informed and wise members of a community or nation, who see the fool for who he really is, basically a "halloween clown masquerading as a wise leader".

For example, Adolf Hitler's insistence on controlling military strategy despite lacking the expertise of his generals led to disastrous defeats. His foolish belief in his own infallibility blinded him to reality. Similarly, Joseph Stalin's paranoia led him to purge his own most capable advisors, leaving the Soviet Union vulnerable at crucial moments.

Idi Amin of Uganda, whose irrational and brutal rule was characterized by erratic decision-making, famously claimed he had won a "gold medal in diplomacy" from the Queen of England, something that never happened.

So, is foolishness a comedic art, or is it simply the manifestation of ignorance? It can be both. There is a distinction between "deliberate foolishness", as an art, such as that of a court jester or the likes of the silent movie hero Charlie Chaplin, who use humour to reveal truth, and the person who is "unconsciously foolish", lacking the appropriate measure of wisdom to recognize their own errors and stupidity.

Some political figures may engage in performative foolishness, acting absurd or unpredictable to manipulate public perception, distract from deeper issues, or consolidate power through populist rhetoric. However, genuine foolishness, stemming from arrogance and ignorance, is far more dangerous.

We also see occurring at times a confluence between unconscious foolishness and deliberate foolishness, not initiated by the fool themselves, but by people in a state of indecision as to whether something someone has said is merely just that person "playing the fool," or whether the person who made the statement actually believes what they themselves have said.

For instance during his election campaigns, Donald Trump has made numerous statements that have been widely criticized for their inaccuracy and absurdity. It's important to distinguish between statements that are outright falsehoods, claims that contradict verifiable facts, and those that are foolish or absurd, illogical, and nonsensical.

The key distinction between these categories lies in their nature: falsehoods are factually incorrect statements that can be disproven with evidence, while foolish or absurd statements may not be factually wrong but are illogical, inappropriate, or demonstrate a lack of understanding. Both types of statements have been prominent in Trump's public discourse, contributing to ongoing debates about his credibility and judgment.

Here are some notable examples of his absurd and foolish statements. Read these whilst remaining aware that this man is now the President of the United States.

At a November 1 rally in Milwaukee, Wisconsin, during his 2024 campaigning, Trump fumed for several minutes about some issue with his microphone. Initially this rant didn't seem that bad. Trump was angrier and cursed more than usual, but his point was clear. "I get so angry," he said. "I'm up here seething. I'm seething! I'm working my ass off with this stupid mic." Then around three minutes in, Trump bent over and pretended to fellate his microphone stand. He simulated having oral sex with the microphone.

In the same rally, he made an inexplicable remark about the size of the late golfer Arnold Palmer's genitalia, leaving many attendees baffled. The comment just came out of nowhere during his speech.

His foolish rhetoric surfaced again when in a misunderstanding of basic physics he claimed that "magnets don't work underwater," a statement that contradicts basic scientific principles, as magnets do function underwater. He also expressed pride in his ability to put on his pants, a comment that seemed out of place and raised questions about his focus on substantive policy issues.

Trump many times during his campaign rallies shared an odd preference for being electrocuted rather than eaten by a shark, a statement that seemed irrelevant and bewildering in the context of his speech. He continually praised the fictional serial killer Hannibal Lecter, often confusing the character with the actors who portrayed him, which raised concerns about his grasp on reality.

He openly praised America's most notorious gangster, Al Capone at least four different times in the rallies I watched saying, "Al Capone, the greatest of all gangsters, he was indicted once. I've been indicted four times!" Trump also falsely accused Haitian immigrants in Springfield, Ohio, of eating people's pets, a claim that was quickly debunked and highlighted his tendency to spread baseless rumours.

Donald Trump's rally speeches have always been a dizzying mix of foolish statements, fearmongering, conspiracy theories, threats against his enemies, and laments about how America is a "nation in decline," yet Trump's rallies nowadays are weirder than ever as the list of his foolish and rambling statements above demonstrate.

In reply to comments from journalists about this incoherent and sometimes foolish rambling, whilst first stressing his high level of intelligence, Trump insisted that he isn't incoherent; he's just misunderstood, and that he's not rambling, he's simply using a "genius" rhetorical device he invented which he calls "the weave."

Trump also criticized President Abraham Lincoln for not negotiating to avoid the Civil War, displaying a lack of understanding of the historical complexities leading to the conflict, and during a speech about Gettysburg, he performed a pirate impression of Confederate General Robert E. Lee, an act that was widely viewed as disrespectful and perplexing.

You see the fool is not merely a figure of amusement but a deeply problematic force in society, especially when they ascend to power. Whether out of arrogance, ignorance, or sheer recklessness, the fool ignores wisdom, acts impulsively, and often leads themselves and others to ruin.

The lessons of history and philosophy remind us that true wisdom comes not from assuming one's own superiority but from recognizing one's limitations. A fool is dangerous not because they lack intelligence, but because they lack the humility to understand their own ignorance.

TRUMP'S SECOND TERM: THE ROAD AHEAD FOR AMERICAN POLITICAL GOVERNANCE.

As Trump commences his second term in office and as such continues to be a prominent figure in American politics, understanding his influence and the potential consequences of his past leadership remains crucial for comprehending the evolving political climate in the coming years, his future leadership of America.

Trump's leadership style and rhetoric have contributed to deep political divisions. His second term may well exacerbate these divisions, impacting social cohesion and political discourse. Trump's approach to governance has challenged traditional norms and institutions. His second presidency could further reshape the executive branch's role, the relationship with the media, and the balance of power among government branches.

One of the most pressing dangers Trump poses is the erosion of trust in the electoral process. Following the 2020 presidential election, Trump repeatedly claimed, without evidence, that the election was stolen from him. These unfounded allegations have led to a significant portion of his supporters questioning the legitimacy of elections, which undermines public confidence in democratic institutions.

This scepticism can have long-lasting effects, as it may discourage voter participation and foster a culture of cynicism regarding electoral outcomes. Additionally, Trump's actions have raised alarms about the undermining of institutional checks and balances. His first administration often displayed a disregard for the norms and practices that ensure accountability and transparency in government.

For instance, Trump's attempts to influence the Department of Justice and his dismissal of officials who opposed his directives signal a troubling trend toward consolidating power and diminishing the role of independent institutions. This behaviour poses a risk to the foundational principle of separation of powers, which is essential for a functioning democracy.

Moreover, Trump's use of divisive rhetoric has exacerbated political polarization in the United States. His tendency to label opponents as enemies and to promote a narrative of "us versus them" has deepened societal divides. This polarization not only hampers constructive political discourse, but also fosters an environment where violence and extremism can thrive.

The January 6th Capitol riot exemplified the potential consequences of such rhetoric, as it demonstrated how inflammatory language can incite individuals to take drastic actions against democratic institutions.

The potential for authoritarianism is another critical concern associated with Trump's influence. His admiration for autocratic leaders and his willingness to flout democratic norms raise questions about his commitment to the principles of democracy.

The normalization of authoritarian tactics, such as attacking the press, undermining judicial independence, and promoting loyalty over competence, poses a significant threat to the democratic fabric of the nation. If such behaviours are left unchecked, they could pave the way for a more authoritarian governance style, fundamentally altering the nature of American democracy.

Donald Trump has made various statements throughout his political career that have raised concerns about his views on presidential power and authority. Notable he has explicitly stated at every opportunity at his rallies that he would be a dictator on day one of his presidency.

His rhetoric often emphasized a strong executive role and a willingness to bypass traditional political norms, and at this the beginning of his second term in office, by introducing in the first few weeks a flurry of Executive Orders he has demonstrated his intent to test the waters of this.

During his campaign rallies, Trump often spoke about his desire to take decisive action and criticized the political establishment, suggesting that he would act unilaterally if necessary. Trump frequently mentioned his intention to use executive orders to implement his policies quickly, which some interpreted as a willingness to exert strong executive power. He has expressed admiration for authoritarian dictators like Vladimir Putin and Kim Jong-un, which has led to speculation about his views on governance and authority.

After the 2020 election, Trump made various claims about election fraud and suggested that he could take extraordinary measures to contest the results, which some viewed as an attempt to undermine democratic processes. While these instances reflect a tendency towards strong executive action, they do not constitute a direct declaration of intent to be a dictator, so it remains to be seen whether he would cross that line. It's important to analyse his statements in context and consider the broader implications of his approach to governance.

In his first term we saw Trump slowly dip his toes in the water of the Project 2025 agenda. The second term, under the guidance of the Heritage Foundation and the architects of Project 2025, it is likely he will put his goggles and flippers on and completely immerse himself.

Some of his early decisions in selecting a cabinet to government have been controversial to say the least which does not bode well for a smooth period of capable governance ahead. President Donald Trump's 2025 cabinet nominations have sparked significant controversy, with several appointees drawing criticism over their qualifications, past actions, and ideological positions. The most contentious picks were:

Matt Gaetz for Attorney General (Withdrawn). Gaetz, a former Florida congressman, faced intense scrutiny due to a past federal investigation into alleged sex trafficking, which concluded without charges. His limited legal experience further fuelled concerns about his suitability for the role. Amid mounting criticism, Gaetz withdrew his nomination, stating that his confirmation process had become a distraction.

Robert F. Kennedy Jr. for Secretary of Health and Human Services. Kennedy's history of vaccine scepticism and promotion of medical misinformation raised alarms among public health experts. His stance on COVID-19 vaccines and opposition to processed foods were particularly contentious. Kennedy underwent multiple Senate hearings, facing tough questions about his views on public health and science.

Tulsi Gabbard for Director of National Intelligence. Gabbard's past meeting with the dictatorial Syrian President Bashar al-Assad and her comments perceived as sympathetic to Russia led to bipartisan concerns about her suitability to lead the intelligence community. Despite the controversies, Gabbard was confirmed by the Senate on February 12, 2025.

Kash Patel for Director of the FBI. Patel's close ties to Trump and his previous efforts to undermine the FBI's independence raised questions about his ability to lead the bureau impartially. Patel faced rigorous questioning during his confirmation hearings, with concerns centred on his loyalty to Trump and potential politicization of the FBI.

Pete Hegseth for Secretary of Defence. Hegseth, a former Fox News contributor, faced allegations of sexual misconduct and was criticized for his lack of military leadership experience. His nomination was seen as part of Trump's pattern of appointing media personalities to key roles.

Elise Stefanik for Ambassador to the United Nations (Withdrawn). Stefanik's nomination faced opposition due to her perceived lack of foreign policy experience and partisan approach to diplomacy. Stefanik withdrew her nomination on March 27, 2025, after facing significant resistance during the confirmation process.

Dr. Mehmet Oz for Administrator of Centres for Medicare and Medicaid Services

Dr. Oz's promotion of unproven medical treatments and his support for Medicare privatization raised concerns about his commitment to evidence-based healthcare policies.

Elon Musk for Administrator of the Department of Government Efficiency. Musk's appointment to lead a new agency aimed at reducing government waste was criticized due to potential conflicts of interest, given his business ventures that rely on government contracts

These nominations reflect Trump's preference for loyalists and unconventional choices, often prioritizing personal allegiance and media presence over traditional qualifications. The controversies surrounding these appointments have led to intense debates about the direction and integrity of the administration in his second period of governance.

A second term will also likely solidify shifts in international alliances and trade relationships, influencing global dynamics for future generations. A second term will most likely so damage the flailing remnants of the democratic process in America that the entrails of its carcass will be dragged along impacting on American democracy for centuries to come.

"When religious nationalism weds the cold calculations of think tanks, governance ceases to be a balance of reason and faith, it becomes a crusade wrapped in policy papers. A nation where ideology dictates policy and faith determines law will not progress, it will march backward, convinced it is fulfilling a sacred duty. When faith is drafted into policy by intellectual mercenaries, theocracy no longer needs priests; it wears the mask of democracy and calls itself reform."

9

Project 2025: The Master Plan for Permanent Power.

Manufactured Amnesia....How Trump's Campaign Denied Project 2025 Existed Until it Mattered.

Chapter Contents.

The Primary Architects of The Heritage Foundation: The Direct Link Between Christian Nationalism and The Heritage Foundation: The Trump Administration's Project 2025 Team, Russell Voight, Stephen Miller, Karoline Leavitt, Tom Homan, and Brendon Carr: The Project 2025 Trump-Vance Pre-Election Cover Up, The True Facts on The Ground.

"A state built on the synthesis of religious nationalism and policy wonkery will legislate morality, criminalize difference, and call it governance in the name of the greater good. The fusion of religious nationalism and policy elites creates a machine that claims divine right while wielding academic rigor, a dictatorship disguised as destiny. The more policy is shaped by religious nationalism, the less room there is for cultural diversity, intellectual freedom, and the unpredictable brilliance of human progress."

THE PRIMARY ARCHITECTS OF THE HERITAGE FOUNDATION.

The Heritage Foundation is a prominent American conservative think tank based in Washington, D.C, founded in 1973 by Paul Weyrich, Edwin Feulner, and Joseph Coors. With a mission to promote conservative principles such as limited government, individual freedom, free markets, and a strong national defence, the Heritage Foundation has become a key player in the political landscape, influencing both public opinion and policymaking.

The foundation is led by a team of scholars, policy experts, and political strategists who contribute to its research and advocacy efforts. As of 2025, the president of the Heritage Foundation is Kevin Roberts, who took on the role in 2021. Under his leadership, the organization has continued to focus on its core mission while adapting to the evolving political environment.

The original founders of The Heritage Foundation, Weyrich, Feulner, and Coors, were key figures in the rise of the modern conservative movement in the United States, particularly in shaping the institutional infrastructure that has helped drive right-wing policy agendas. Their influence is deeply connected to Project 2025, a far-right policy initiative aimed at reshaping the federal government under a Republican administration.

The primary connection between Weyrich, Feulner, and Coors lies in their joint creation of the Heritage Foundation and the broader conservative policy network that underpins Project 2025. Weyrich had the vision, Feuler had the influence, and Coors had the finance. Their background details are as follows:

Paul Weyrich (1942–2008), was a conservative activist and strategist. Weyrich co-founded the Heritage Foundation, the American Legislative Exchange Council (ALEC), and the Moral Majority, the primary arm of the Religious Far Right that I spoke of in Chapter 2.

Weyrich as co-founder of the Moral majority alongside Jerry Falwell, played a major role in integrating religious conservatives into the Republican Party and was instrumental in creating the New Right.

Edwin Feulner is a policy expert and co-founder of the Heritage Foundation. Feulner helped shape conservative think tanks into influential policy-making institutions. Under his leadership, Heritage became a dominant force in Republican policymaking.

Joseph Coors (1917–2003) was an heir to the Coors beer fortune, an oligarch, and a major financial backer of right-wing causes, funding the Heritage Foundation and other conservative organizations. His wealth helped create the infrastructure needed to drive conservative policy agendas.

Weyrich's vision was "to infiltrate government with ideological loyalists". It stemmed from an almost obsessive belief that conservatives needed to control institutions to wield power effectively.

Feulner's influence was seen as essential by Weyrich to get the vision moving. As a political policy architect, Feulner had built Heritage into a policy powerhouse. But oligarchal money was needed to finance the vision and so entered Joseph Coors. Without Coors' financial support, the Heritage Foundation (and later Project 2025) wouldn't have been possible.

The Heritage Foundation as such, founded in 1973 with Coors' funding and Feulner and Weyrich's strategic direction, was designed to institutionalize conservative policy-making, a mission that continues through Project 2025. In short, Project 2025 is a modern extension of their original vision, seizing control of government to implement a long-term conservative agenda.

Project 2025, spearheaded by the Heritage Foundation, is a plan to reshape the federal government by staffing it with loyalists, dismantling regulatory agencies, and implementing sweeping conservative policies. It is essentially a blueprint for future ongoing Republican administrations, aiming to ensure that government institutions align with right-wing priorities. Donald Trump's personal goal however, takes it a bit further. He sees it as a tool to establish himself permanently as "a president for life."

THE DIRECT LINK DIRECT BETWEEN CHRISTIAN NATIONALISM AND THE HERITAGE FOUNDATION.

I spoke in Chapter 4 of the rise of the Religious Far Right, in the 70's and 80's, a political movement that sought to mobilize evangelical Christians in support of conservative policies. It was a religious political movement that laid the groundwork for the current wave of Christian Nationalism, and it established a framework for political engagement primarily based on religious beliefs. That rise of the Religious Far Right marked a significant shift in the political landscape, as religious conservatives became a powerful force in American politics.

I also mentioned that one of the most prominent figures in the rise of the Religious Far Right was Jerry Falwell, a Baptist minister who founded the Moral Majority in 1979. The Moral Majority aimed to mobilize conservative Christians as a political force, advocating for issues such as opposition to abortion, the promotion of school prayer, and the defence of what they described as "traditional family values". Here's the link:

Paul Weyrich the co-founder of the Heritage Foundation, the think-tank architects of Project 2025, was closely associated with Jerry Falwell, and their connection was pivotal in the rise of the Religious Right as a powerful political force in the United States. While Jerry Falwell officially founded the Moral Majority in 1979, a religious far-right group, Weyrich was one of the key strategists who convinced Falwell to enter the political arena in the first place.

You see Weyrich, had long sought to unite conservative evangelicals into a voting bloc, and so he recruited Falwell and other Christian leaders, such as Pat

Robertson, urging them to mobilize their congregations around conservative politics.

Before the late 1970's, many evangelicals were politically disengaged. Weyrich, seeing an opportunity, identified issues like abortion, school prayer, and opposition to LGBTQ+ rights as rallying points to bring evangelicals into the Republican Party. Falwell, with his national religious influence, became the perfect figurehead for this movement. What you could describe as "a type of religious version of Donald Trump."

Weyrich helped connect Falwell to major conservative donors and think tanks, ensuring that the Moral Majority had the resources to launch voter registration drives, media campaigns, and political lobbying efforts. Their collaboration helped elect Ronald Reagan in 1980, marking a major shift in American politics by aligning the Republican Party with religious conservatism.

The Moral Majority became a dominant force throughout the 1980's, pushing policies that reflected both Weyrich's ideological vision and Falwell's religious institutional values, which were not necessarily Christlike. In short, "Weyrich was the mastermind, and Falwell was the messenger", and together they helped forge the modern Religious Right. In today's political arena, Project 2025 is the policy, and Donald Trump is the messenger, not the architect.

However the assistant architects of Project 2025, the Heritage Foundation's blueprint for a Republican government include a coalition of former Trump administration officials, policy experts, and other Republican conservative think tanks. Notable figures involved in the project include Stephen Miller, former Senior Advisor to Trump, known for his influence on immigration policy, and Russell Vought currently the 2025 Director of the Office of Management and Budget.

Other key Project 2025 assistant architects who have taken up positions in Trump's 2025 administration include Karoline Leavitt, the White House Press

Secretary, Tom Homan, who is now "the border czar", and Brendan Carr who is currently the Chairman of the Federal Communications Commission (FCC).

THE CURRENT TRUMP ADMINISTRATION'S PROJECT 2025 TEAM.

> "In every empire, the real rulers are not those in palaces or parliaments, but those who write the rules behind closed doors. The bureaucrat who outlasts a dozen presidents has more power than any elected official, for his influence is neither debated nor questioned. When secret power governs, the law bends to serve it, and morality becomes an obstacle rather than a guide."

Russell Vought. Russell Vought is an American political analyst, who served as the Director of the Office of Management and Budget (OMB) under Donald Trump from July 2020 to January 2021. He was prior to this role Vice-president of Heritage Action for America, the lobbying arm of the Heritage Foundation, and served as the executive director of the Republican Study Committee in 2021.

Vought founded the Centre for Renewing America, an organisation focused on promoting conservative policies and opposing critical race theory. He also played a significant role in the construction of Project 2025, aimed at advancing conservative policies and reshaping the federal government. In November 2024, Donald Trump announced his intention to renominate Vought as Director of the OMB for his second term, whilst all the while claiming that he knew nothing about Project 2025.

Russell Vought is now responsible for developing the president's proposed budget and executing the administration's agenda. That agenda includes expanding presidential authority to a more autocratic (dictatorial) type of government and to implement its policy goals. When he previously served as OMB director during

Trump's first term, he played a significant role in drafting Project 2025's strategies for the initial 180 days of a new administration should Trump win the 2024 election, and he received Trump's tick of approval for it.

You see in truth the American people did not voluntarily elect Donald Trump in the 2024 presidential election, for, long before election day, over a period of some years, they were being digitally manipulated to do so. Trump, who throughout his campaigning continually publicly denied having any knowledge of Project 2025, is now merely the presidential puppet whose strings the architects of Project 2025, a religious ideologically driven group are pulling.

Behind the scenes Russell Vought is now making most of the decisions in the running of the United States. He is the de-facto President, alongside the richest man in the world, billionaire Elon Musk, who has become Vought's enforcer. It's a type of White House Al Capone/ Frank Nitti relationship.

Donald Trump publicly signs executive orders that Vought has drafted, and does this at media events, as a means of throwing breadcrumbs to his supporters and fuelling the fears of his detractors, while appeasing his own egoic madness, in an insane narcissistic way convincing himself as seen with his rhetoric, that he actually constructed the policy.

If you look closely at some of the videos of him signing his executive orders you can see that he is reading most of them for the first time, he looks surprised, with comments such as, "oh, this looks like a good one, " as if he looking at a replay of an episode of The Apprentice. After the public media signing, he then quietly returns to his safe place, his Mar-a-Lago golf course.

Stephen Miller. Stephen Miller is a prominent American political advisor known for his conservative views and significant influence on U.S. immigration policies. Miller himself appeared in a promotional video for Project 2025. Early in his career, Miller served as press secretary for Congresswoman Michele Bachmann and later as communications director for Senator Jeff Sessions. In these roles, he established a reputation for his hardline stance on immigration and national security.

In 2016, Miller joined Donald Trump's presidential campaign as a senior policy advisor and speechwriter, playing a pivotal role in shaping the campaign's messaging. Following Trump's election, Miller became a senior advisor to the president, where he was instrumental in crafting key policies, including the travel ban affecting several predominantly Muslim countries and the reduction of refugee admissions. He also advocated for the policy of separating migrant children from their parents at the U.S.-Mexico border.

Regarding his involvement with the Heritage Foundation and Project 2025. Millers' organization, America First Legal Foundation, was previously listed as a supporter of Project 2025 and appeared on its advisory board. However, after adverse public scrutiny of Project 2025 surfaced during the 2024 presidential campaign, the group later requested its name be removed from the advisory board.

Karoline Leavitt. Karoline Leavitt is an American political aide and government official currently serving as the White House Press Secretary in President Donald Trump's administration since January 20, 2025. During college, Leavitt interned at Fox News, Rupert Murdoch's far-right news propaganda network, and at the White House Office of Presidential Correspondence.

Post-graduation, she joined the White House Press Office as an assistant press secretary under Kayleigh McEnany. After the conclusion of President Trump's first term, she served as communications director for Representative Elise Stefanik of New York.

In 2022, Leavitt ran for the U.S. House of Representatives in New Hampshire's 1st Congressional District. She secured the Republican nomination but lost in the general election to incumbent Democrat Chris Pappas. Following this, she became a spokesperson for MAGA Inc., a pro-Trump Super PAC, and later served as the national press secretary for Donald Trump's 2024 presidential campaign.

Leavitt was an instructor for Project 2025's "Conservative Governance 101" training program, an initiative by the Heritage Foundation aimed at preparing individuals for roles in conservative governance. This program educates aspiring political appointees on the fundamentals of conservative governance, including staffing, budgeting, and media manipulations and relations.

As White House Press Secretary, Leavitt serves as the primary spokesperson for President Trump and the administration. Her role involves conducting daily press briefings, at which she fends off legitimate media questions, defends Trump's policy implementation, in a very controlled but arrogant manner, communicating the administration's policies and positions, and managing interactions with the media.

Leavitt's tenure has included both notable initiatives and controversies. For instance, she announced changes to the James S. Brady Briefing Room to better accommodate new media dynamics. Which basically meant that if you as a journalist asked too many difficult questions your press pass was revoked. She also faced criticism for disseminating inaccurate information regarding U.S. aid to Gaza, which was subsequently corrected by fact-checking organizations.

Tom Homan. Thomas Douglas Homan is an American law enforcement officer with a distinguished career in immigration enforcement. He began his law enforcement journey as a police officer in New York before joining the U.S. Border Patrol in 1984.

Homan has been associated with Project 2025, the comprehensive plan developed by conservative groups to prepare policy recommendations for a future conservative administration. His involvement included contributing to the project's initiatives and advocating for policies aligned with its objectives.

Over the years, Homan held various positions within the Immigration and Naturalization Service (INS) and later U.S. Immigration and Customs Enforcement (ICE), including roles as an investigator, supervisory special agent, assistant district director for investigations, and assistant agent in charge.

In 2013, he was appointed as the executive associate director for Enforcement and Removal Operations (ERO) at ICE. In January 2017, President Donald Trump appointed Homan as the acting director of ICE, a position he held until his retirement in June 2018. During his tenure, Homan was known for advocating stringent immigration enforcement policies.

In November 2024, President-elect Donald Trump designated Homan as the "border czar" for his second administration. This role, situated within the White House rather than a specific agency, underscores the administration's emphasis on immigration and border policy. As border czar, Homan is responsible for coordinating efforts across various agencies to implement the administration's immigration policies, focusing on enhancing border security and enforcing immigration laws.

In his current role as border czar, Homan's responsibilities involve overseeing and coordinating the administration's border security and immigration enforcement strategies. This includes addressing issues related to illegal immigration, enhancing border infrastructure, and collaborating with federal and state agencies to implement policies aimed at securing the nation's borders.

Brendan Carr. Brendan Carr is an American lawyer and government official currently serving as the Chairman of the Federal Communications Commission (FCC) under President Donald Trump's administration since January 20, 2025.He is recognized for his conservative stance on telecommunications policy and his advocacy for deregulation within the industry.

Carr contributed to the Heritage Foundation's Project 2025 by authoring a chapter outlining his vision for the FCC. In this chapter, he emphasized the need for the FCC to reinterpret Section 230 of the Communications Decency Act, aiming to reduce the immunity granted to online platforms and address concerns about content moderation practices.

As FCC Chairman, Carr oversees the regulation of broadcasting, telecommunications, and broadband industries. His tenure has been marked by initiatives to investigate diversity, equity, and inclusion (DEI) practices within media companies. Notably, he announced investigations into Disney's DEI policies to ensure compliance with FCC equal employment opportunity regulations.

Carr has also stated that companies seeking regulatory approval for mergers and acquisitions must eliminate DEI practices, asserting that such initiatives may not serve the public interest.

THE PROJECT 2025 TRUMP-VANCE PRE-ELECTION COVER UP.

Despite Donald Trump's frequent public distancing of himself from Project 2025, due to fears it might damage his electoral chances, reports indicate that Kevin Roberts, the president of the Heritage Foundation and Trump have interacted many times, including on a private flight in April 2022 on Trump's jet, where Roberts discussed the project with Trump.

This suggests a cover up of a strong but cleverly concealed level of engagement between the two regarding the project's objectives, that was in play during all of Trump's campaigning denials.

From the moment the Project came to public attention Donald Trump had been careful to distance himself from Project 2025, the Heritage Foundation's radical plan to remake the federal government under his presidency. "I have no idea who is behind it," he stated when questioned about his knowledge of the plan, by a journalist, a plan which would include the replacement of thousands of federal workers with partisan loyalists, ban abortion, and disband the Department of Education.

A couple of weeks later, he said of the people behind Project 2025, "They are extreme, they're seriously extreme, but I don't know anything about it."

However between those two denials, on July 15th. 2024, Trump made a decision that would evidence his deliberate attempt to cover up from the American public his involvement with the architects of Project 2025, and his plans to implement their policies should he be re-elected. But very few of the media picked up on it nor pursued it. The decision…he picked Senator J.D. Vance as his running mate.

Vance has deep ties to the Heritage Foundation, particularly to Kevin Roberts, who has been president of the right-wing think tank since 2021 and is the chief architect of Project 2025. Vance has praised Roberts privately and publicly for helping to turn the organization "into the de facto institutional home of Trumpism," and has often endorsed many elements of Project 2025.

As such after his selection as Donald Trump's running mate, the same Donald Trump who had consistently denied having any knowledge of Project 2025 or its architects, things started to, under journalistic scrutiny, get a little messy for both Vance and Trump, which necessitated the activation of a cover up to avoid their lies being revealed to the American voting public.

You see Vance, before his selection by Trump, had not only aligned himself with the policies of Project 2025, but he had also actually written a Forward to the soon to be published book written by Kevin Roberts titled, "Dawn's Early Light: Burning Down Washington to Save America," featuring a "lit match" on the cover. Kevin Roberts, president of hard-right Heritage Foundation, said, it's "time to put down the books and go fight like hell".

Something had to be done therefore before the American public got wind of Trump and Vance's deception, and Vance's deep ties to Roberts, otherwise it would influence the voting choices of those who put democracy ahead of personal ideological needs. What do we need to do they thought? I know, we need to soften the title of the book and delay its publication.

And as such the book originally titled, "Dawn's Early Light: Burning Down Washington to Save America", was re-titled, "Dawn's Early Light: Taking Down

Washington to Save America, and the "lit match" which was imaged on the front cover was removed, and its publication date set back. As well as this emotional promotional language invoking conservatives on the "warpath" to "burn down institutions" like the FBI, the Department of Justice, and certain universities was removed or toned down.

In his foreword in Robert's book, Vance makes it clear that he is extremely close with Roberts and that he sees him as a strong ally in a shared political project. The foreword opens with the parallels in their biographies: Over the three-page foreword, Vance singles out Roberts in the areas where the two most strongly align politically.

First, he praises Roberts for his willingness to criticize corporations and break with the GOP's free-market orthodoxy; he then praises Roberts for his strong emphasis on the family. Vance writes, "Roberts is articulating a fundamentally Christian view of culture and economics, by recognizing that virtue and material progress go hand in hand."

Vance's foreword is also, notably, a call for revolution. He writes, "The old conservative movement argued if you just got government out of the way, natural forces would resolve problems, he continues, "we are no longer in this situation and must take a different approach, and that is where the muskets come in". For those who are not old enough to remember, a musket is a long-barrelled firearm, widely used from the 16th. to the 19th. century.

In speaking of Robert's book Vance wrote, "as Kevin Roberts writes, it's fine to take a laissez-faire approach when you are in the safety of the sunshine. But when the twilight descends and you hear the wolves, you've got to circle the wagons and load the muskets. We are now all realizing that it's time to circle the wagons and load the muskets. In the fights that lay ahead, these ideas, (meaning the ideas in Robert's book), are an essential weapon".

The Trump Media people also went into extreme cover-up mode instituting public attacks on Project 2025 in a hasty but deliberately deceptive way, to distance themselves from Project 2025 in the public's eyes. They subsequently issued the following statement:

"The project is shutting its policy operations, and its director, Paul Dans, is resigning, reports of Project 2025's demise would be greatly welcomed. This should serve as notice to anyone or any group trying to misrepresent their influence with President Trump and his campaign, it will not end well for you." And the public bought it. We now know that this statement given to the press by the Trump Campaign organization, was also just a part of the big Trump-Vance cover up, a deliberate ongoing litany of lies.

THE TRUE FACTS ON THE GROUND.

In July 2024, Donald Trump issued a statement on his Truth Social platform, distancing himself from Project 2025 and labelling its authors as part of the "far-right establishment." In August 2024, during a Republican presidential debate with Kamala Harris, Trump reiterated his lack of involvement with Project 2025, stating he had not read the playbook crafted by the Heritage Foundation. These denials contrast with reports suggesting that Trump has privately expressed support for the project's objectives.

The facts of the matter are unambiguous. "Trump consistently wilfully lied to the American people" about his knowledge of the Heritage Foundation's Project 2025. President Trump has in fact participated in many events hosted by the Heritage Foundation, reflecting his long engagement with conservative policy circles and these the architects of Project 2025.

In October 2017 Trump delivered remarks at the Heritage Foundation's President's Club Meeting, where he praised the organization's contributions to conservative policy development. In April 2022 in a speech at a Heritage Foundation event, Trump commended the group for laying the groundwork for future conservative initiatives, stating, "This is a great group and they're going to lay the groundwork and detail plans for exactly what "our movement' will do." Note he termed it "our movement."

The Heritage Foundation, this prominent conservative think tank, has in fact played a significant role in shaping policy agendas, in Trump's two presidencies, particularly through its "Mandate for Leadership" series and the more recent "Project 2025" initiative. These efforts have influenced both Donald Trump's first presidency (2017–2021) and his current administration.

During his first term, President Trump incorporated numerous policy recommendations from the Heritage Foundation's "Mandate for Leadership," and notably, approximately 70 former Heritage employees joined the Trump transition team or served within the administration. This collaboration led to the adoption of nearly two-thirds of Heritage's policy prescriptions, including:

The Withdrawal from the Paris Climate Accord: In August 2017, Trump announced the U.S. exit from the agreement, aligning with Heritage's stance on climate policy.

The Repeal of Net Neutrality: The Federal Communications Commission, under Trump's appointees, moved to end the 2015 net neutrality rules in December 2017, reflecting Heritage's recommendations on telecommunications policy.

The Reshaping of National Monuments: Trump issued executive orders to reduce the size of national monuments in Utah, consistent with Heritage's advocacy for limiting federal land ownership.

And despite President Trump's public disavowal of direct involvement with Project 2025, as mentioned many individuals associated with the project have been appointed to key positions in his current administration. These appointments illustrate the integration of Project 2025's architects into influential roles within the current administration, suggesting a continuing alignment with the project's conservative policy objectives.

While Trump has publicly denied, and lied, about having a direct involvement with Project 2025, when he thought it might hurt his electoral campaign, the appointment of several of its contributors to key positions proves his strong alignment with the project's conservative policy goals. Additionally, Trump's ongoing participation in Heritage Foundation events underscores his deep commitment to and connection with the organization's policy agenda.

The truth is that Donald Trump and J.D. Vance have together in their Project 2025 cover up taken the deliberate act of lying to the public out of self-interest to a whole new level. Lying in politics erodes public trust, polarises the electorate, and damages democratic institutions.

When politicians repeatedly mislead voters, cynicism increases, and people become less likely to engage in the political process. The spread of misinformation also makes it harder for voters to make informed decisions, leading to elections based on emotion rather than fact, as was witnessed in the re-election of Donald Trump in the 2024 presidential election.

On the campaign trail last summer, Trump disavowed Project 2025, saying he knew nothing about it. But many of the conservative blueprint's ideas have made their way into the first two weeks of his executive orders, signalling the sweeping impact the Heritage Foundation document has already had on the Trump administration's 2025 policy making agenda.

In a recent side by side review by a news organisation, the review revealed dozens of cases where the president's early executive actions have aligned with portions of the 922-page policy statement of Project 2025, including some instances with nearly verbatim language lifted from the report and transcribed directly on to the executive orders issued from Trump.

Some of the more unconventional strategies outlined in the document, such as reclassifying federal employees to make them easier to fire and installing loyalists in senior government positions, have also shown up in Trump's initial executive orders. There have also been other administration moves outside of his executive orders, that appear to come directly from Project 2025, such as directing the Federal Communications Commission to investigate NPR and PBS for alleged violation of sponsorship advertising rules.

"The hallmark of a political dictator is a distorted self-image, akin to malignant narcissism, where the leader believes they are infallible and above reproach. A dictator's supposed charm can mask their malignant narcissism, drawing followers into a web of loyalty that ultimately serves the leader's insatiable need for validation. When malignant narcissism takes the helm of a nation politically, the result is a dictatorship characterized by paranoia, aggression, and a profound disconnect from the reality of the people's struggles, even what may seem to some simple struggles, such as the affordability of eggs."

10

The Mirror of Tyranny, Echoes of the Past in the Present.

A Psychological and Political Inquiry into the Authoritarian Narcissism of Hitler and Trump.

Chapter Contents.

The Dictator and The Ego: The Egoic Traits of A Political Dictator: The Malignant Narcissist; Adolf Hitler...A Political Dictator in Play: Hitler's Nazi Regime, A Pathological Need for Dictatorial Dominance and Control, Trump's MAGA Regime: The Signs are Already Appearing.: Gleichschaltung...Hitler the Dictator's Governance Manifesto, Mirrored in the Project 2025 Agenda: The Hitlergruß, Hitler the Dictator's Infamous Nazi Salute: Schutzstaffel...The SS: Hitler the Dictator's Feared Mobile Killing Squads.

§

"A malignant narcissist thrives on power and control, often mirroring the traits of a dictator who sees the state as an extension of their own ego. In the realm of politics, malignant narcissism manifests as a relentless pursuit of admiration, where the dictator demands loyalty not from love, but from fear. Malignant narcissism fuels the dictator's delusion of grandeur."

THE DICTATOR AND THE EGO.

Political dictators have been a recurring phenomenon throughout history, often leaving indelible marks on their nations and the world. While each dictator is unique, many share common personality traits that influence their governance style, policy implementation, rule of law, freedom of expression, and foreign relations. Understanding these traits provides insight into the mechanisms of authoritarian rule and its impact on societies.

Dictators typically exhibit a strong desire for control and power. This authoritarian nature manifests in their governance through centralized decision-making and the suppression of dissent. They often view themselves as the ultimate authority, with little tolerance for opposition or alternative viewpoints.

The annals of history are replete with figures who have risen to power through sheer force of will, charisma, deception, and often, a ruthless disregard for the welfare of others. One of the most well-known being Adolf Hitler. Political dictators, in particular, have been subjects of intense scrutiny, with scholars and psychologists alike attempting to unravel the complex web of personality traits that define their leadership. Central to this discourse is "the role of the ego", and particularly in how an overinflated ego can lead to narcissistic behaviours and bolster authoritarian tendencies.

The term "ego" has a rich and multifaceted history, originating from the Latin word for "I." In contemporary discourse, it is often associated with the self, identity, and the conscious mind, all active participants in this our ephemeral reality, our ever-evolving transitory journey through life. However, its implications stretch far beyond mere self-reference, encompassing philosophical, psychological, and sociological dimensions.

In ancient philosophy, the concept of the ego was not explicitly defined as it is today, but it was implicitly present in discussions about the self and consciousness. Philosophers like Socrates and Plato explored the nature of the self, emphasizing the importance of self-knowledge and introspection. Socrates famously stated, "The unexamined life is not worth living," highlighting the significance of understanding one's own identity and motivations.

In Eastern philosophies, such as Buddhism, the ego is often viewed as an illusion or a source of suffering. The Buddhist concept of "anatta," or non-self, that clinging to a fixed identity leads to attachment and dissatisfaction. Spiritual leaders like the Buddha taught that transcending the ego is essential for achieving enlightenment and inner peace.

The modern understanding of the ego was significantly shaped by the work of Sigmund Freud, who introduced a structural model of the psyche comprising the id, ego, and superego. In Freud's framework, the ego serves as "the mediator between the primal desires of the id, and the moral constraints of the superego".

It is responsible for rational thought, decision-making, and navigating the complexities of the ephemeral reality. Freud's perspective emphasized the ego's role in maintaining psychological balance and as such functioning effectively in society.

Contemporary psychologists have expanded upon Freud's ideas, exploring the ego's relationship with personality traits and behaviours. The ego is often seen as a crucial component of self-esteem and self-concept. A well-developed ego can lead to healthy self-assertion and confidence, while an underdeveloped or overinflated ego can result in various psychological issues.

The notion of a "small ego" typically refers to individuals who may lack confidence or self-worth, often leading to submissive behaviours or an inability to assert themselves. This can manifest in social anxiety, low self-esteem, and a tendency to seek validation from others.

Conversely, an "out-of-control ego" describes individuals with an inflated sense of self-importance, often characterized by arrogance, entitlement, and a lack of empathy. Such individuals may struggle with interpersonal relationships and exhibit narcissistic tendencies.

Both extremes can hinder personal growth and social interactions. A balanced ego, which allows for self-awareness and humility, is essential for healthy relationships and personal development. The goal is not to eliminate the ego but to cultivate a healthy sense of self that acknowledges both strengths and weaknesses.

The relationship between the ego and personality traits is complex. The ego influences how individuals perceive themselves and as such interact with the world, shaping traits such as assertiveness, openness, and resilience. For instance, individuals with a strong, balanced ego may exhibit higher levels of self-confidence and emotional stability, while those with a fragile ego may display traits associated with insecurity and defensiveness.

Moreover, the ego can impact behaviour in various contexts. In professional business settings, and in politics, a well-regulated ego can foster collaboration and leadership, while an unchecked ego may lead to conflict and competition. In personal relationships, a healthy ego allows for vulnerability and intimacy, whereas an inflated ego can create barriers to connection and understanding.

The ego is a multifaceted construct that has evolved through philosophical, spiritual, and psychological lenses. Understanding its origins and implications can provide valuable insights into human behaviour and personality. Striking a balance in our ego, meaning neither too small nor out of control, can lead to healthier relationships, greater self-awareness, and a more fulfilling life. As we navigate the complexities of our identities, recognizing the role of the ego can empower us to cultivate a more authentic and harmonious existence.

THE EGOIC TRAITS OF A POLITICAL DICTATOR.

The ego, in psychological terms, is the part of the human psyche that mediates between the conscious and unconscious mind, balancing the demands of reality with instinctual desires. In the context of a political dictator, the ego often becomes overinflated, leading to a distorted self-image characterized by grandiosity, entitlement, and a lack of empathy. This can further be exacerbated, when the political dictator is given absolute immunity from prosecution for crimes committed whilst in office, by the highest court in the nation, as has been witnessed in the United States with Donald Trump, and the Supreme Court's 2024 decision.

The over- inflated ego is not merely a personal trait, but a driving mind-altering force that shapes a politician's political ideology and governance style, and for the dictator a "legal free pass" further entrenches in their behaviour an authoritarian style of leadership, an "I can do anything and get away with anything" type of attitude.

Now narcissism, a personality trait marked by an excessive need for admiration and a lack of empathy, is often found working in conjunction with an overinflated ego. For dictators, narcissism manifests in a belief that they are uniquely qualified to lead, more so than anyone else, often viewing themselves as saviours of their nation. Donald Trump has frequently expressed publicly that he is "the anointed one, sent by God to fix all of America's problems and make America great again."

This self-perception justifies their authoritarian behaviours, as they see dissent as not just a challenge to their authority but a personal affront. Consequently they may resort to extreme measures to maintain control, including censorship, propaganda, and the suppression of political opposition, and if necessary, use the law to their advantage by taking legal action against those who would oppose them, particularly if the courts have demonstrated they are sympathetic towards them.

Paradoxically, beneath the veneer of confidence and superiority, many dictators harbor deep-seated insecurities. These insecurities fuel their need for control and validation, driving them to seek constant reinforcement of their power and status. This can lead to a cycle of increasingly authoritarian behaviour, as the dictator becomes more isolated and paranoid, perceiving threats where none actually exist. The need to protect their fragile ego often results in a governance style that is rigid, oppressive, and intolerant of dissent.

The egoic traits of a dictator have profound implications for governance. An overinflated ego can lead to decision-making that is impulsive and self-serving, prioritizing personal legacy over the welfare of the populace. Policies may be enacted not for their efficacy, but for their potential to enhance the dictator's image. Furthermore, the centralization of power in the hands of a single individual stifles innovation and dissent, leading to a stagnation of political and social progress.

The egoic traits of political dictators are also a critical factor in understanding their rise to power and the nature of their rule. An overinflated ego, coupled with narcissistic tendencies, not only shapes their personal identity, but also influences their approach to governance. This often results in authoritarian behaviours that prioritize personal power over the collective good, over time resulting in devastating consequences for the societies they govern.

Understanding these traits is essential for recognizing the warning signs of emerging dictatorships thus preventing the erosion of democratic institutions. As history has shown, unchecked ego and power can lead to tyranny, making it imperative to remain vigilant against the allure of authoritarianism.

The common personality traits of political dictators are authoritarianism, paranoia, and lack of empathy, traits which eventually manifest in centralized and repressive policies, the erosion of the rule of law, suppression of freedom of expression, and self-serving foreign relations.

However perhaps even far more impactful on their governance style is the dictator who possesses extreme "narcissistic tendencies", the dictator who fits into the criteria of a "malignant narcissist". Many psychologists have expressed their firm belief that Donald Trump's behaviours demonstrate that he is in actual fact what is termed in psychological circles as "a malignant narcissist".

THE MALIGNANT NARCISSIST.

The word "malignant" in the term refers to a behavioral quality which is passionately malevolent, and aggressively malicious. Understanding malignant narcissism is crucial for recognizing its impact on relationships, workplaces, governance, and society at large.

The term malignant narcissism itself describes a particularly severe form of narcissistic personality disorder (NPD) characterized by a combination of narcissistic traits, antisocial behaviour, and a lack of empathy. This complex personality disorder poses significant challenges not only for those who exhibit these traits but also for the individuals and communities around them.

Understanding the dynamics of a malignant narcissist is crucial for recognizing the signs of emerging authoritarianism, and the best time to determine this is when the political candidate is under the spotlight, in full view physically and vocally in full pre-election campaigning mode.

Most dictators possessing malignant narcissistic traits, are characterized by an inflated sense of self-importance and a need for admiration. This can lead to the creation of a cult of personality, where the dictator is portrayed as a heroic and indispensable leader, a "strongman for the nation." Such narcissism often results in policies that prioritize the leader's image over the welfare of the populace.

Malignant narcissism encompasses several key traits that distinguish it from other forms of narcissism: Individuals with malignant narcissism often exhibit an inflated sense of self-importance and entitlement. They believe they are superior to others and expect special treatment, not just from normal citizens but from judicial systems as well, often disregarding the feelings and needs of those around them, and the rule of law.

A hallmark of malignant narcissism is a profound inability to empathize with others. This lack of empathy allows individuals to manipulate and exploit others without remorse, often leading to harmful behaviours. Malignant narcissists may engage in deceitful, manipulative, or aggressive behaviours, and they may violate the rights of others and show little regard for societal norms or laws, often displaying traits associated with antisocial personality disorder.

Individuals with malignant narcissism may exhibit paranoid tendencies, believing that others are out to undermine or harm them, quite often expressed with the words, "it's a witch hunt." This paranoia can lead to aggressive reactions, including verbal or physical confrontations, and on occasions a revenge filled counterattack. Malignant narcissists also often use others as tools to achieve their own goals. They may charm and manipulate individuals to gain power, control, or resources, discarding them once they are no longer useful.

The presence of malignant narcissists can have profound effects on individuals and communities: Malignant narcissists often create toxic environments in personal and professional relationships. Their manipulative and exploitative behaviours can lead to emotional abuse, conflict, and a breakdown of trust.

In professional settings, malignant narcissists can undermine team cohesion and morale. Their need for control and recognition can stifle collaboration and innovation, leading to a toxic workplace culture.

On a larger scale, malignant narcissism can influence societal structures and norms. Leaders with these traits may prioritize their interests over the common good, leading to policies and practices that harm communities and perpetuate inequality.

The progressive development of malignant narcissism is believed to be influenced by a combination of genetic, environmental, and psychological factors. Some research suggests that certain personality traits, including malignant narcissism, may have a genetic component. Individuals with a family history of personality disorders may be more susceptible to developing malignant narcissism, as the genetically transmitted psychological illness is passed down from one generation to the next, as in father to son.

Early childhood experiences, environmental factors, such as childhood trauma, neglect, or excessive pampering, can also contribute to the development of narcissistic traits. Children who are either overly criticized or excessively praised may struggle to form a healthy self-image, leading to maladaptive coping mechanisms.

Cultural influences can also play a part. Societal values that emphasize individualism, competition, and success can foster narcissistic traits. In cultures that prioritize personal achievement over community well-being, individuals may develop a sense of entitlement and superiority.

The election of a politician with a malignant narcissistic personality disorder to a leadership position in a democratic nation can have profound and detrimental effects on social justice, equality, and civil rights, not just domestically but internationally as well. Malignant narcissistic leaders will prioritize their own interests and self-image over the collective needs of the populace, leading to policies and behaviours that undermine the very foundations of a just and equitable society.

Social justice is predicated on the principles of fairness, equity, and the protection of marginalized groups. Narcissistic leaders tend to exhibit a lack of empathy and an inflated sense of entitlement, which can result in policies and subsequent legislation that favours the privileged while neglecting the needs of the disadvantaged.

For instance, a malignant narcissistic leader may prioritize tax cuts for the wealthy or deregulation that benefits large corporations, such as those being proposed by Elon Musk and other tech giants in the United States, thereby exacerbating economic inequality. This disregard for the welfare of marginalized communities can lead to systemic injustices, where the voices of the oppressed are silenced and their struggles are ignored.

Moreover, malignant narcissistic leaders often engage in divisive rhetoric that polarizes society. By framing social issues in a manner that pits groups against one another, they can distract from the underlying injustices that need to be addressed. This manipulation of public discourse can hinder social movements aimed at achieving justice, as the focus shifts from collective action to individualistic narratives that serve the leader's agenda.

You see equality is a cornerstone of democratic societies, ensuring that all individuals have equal rights and opportunities. However, the leadership of a malignant narcissistic politician can lead to the erosion of these principles. Such leaders may implement policies that disproportionately benefit certain demographics while marginalizing others, often based on race, gender, or socioeconomic status.

Additionally, malignant narcissistic leaders often surround themselves with loyalists or organizational advisors who reinforce their worldview, leading to a lack of diverse perspectives in decision-making processes. This is being witnessed currently in the United States with the appointment of key players in the Heritage Foundation's Project 2025, into the new Trump White House administration. This homogeneity can result in policies that fail to consider the needs of all citizens, further entrenching systemic inequalities.

Furthermore narcissistic leaders may seek to consolidate power by undermining the judiciary, attacking the press, or delegitimizing dissenting voices.

Such actions can create a climate of fear and repression, where individuals are discouraged from exercising their rights or advocating for social change.

They often engage in scapegoating, targeting specific groups as a means of deflecting criticism or rallying support. I spoke of this in a previous chapter as "the deliberate act of distraction" in political rhetoric. This can lead to increased discrimination and violence against marginalized communities, as the leader's rhetoric legitimizes harmful stereotypes and fosters a culture of intolerance.

All this being true, then this complex personality disorder called "malignant narcissism" with regards to Donald Trump poses significant challenges not only for himself but also for all citizens of the United States, the individuals and communities around him, as they do similarly with the personalities of other authoritarian dictators around the world, such as those in Russia and Hungary.

ADOLF HITLER...A POLITICAL DICTATOR IN PLAY.

A dictators' authoritarian nature leads to policies that centralize power and limit checks and balances. The dictator often bypasses democratic institutions, ruling by decree (executive orders), and manipulating legal frameworks (appointment of specific judges), to legitimize their actions. As well as this, economic policies may focus on short-term gains that bolster the regime's stability, often at the expense of long-term development and public welfare.

Under dictatorial regimes, the rule of law is frequently undermined. Legal systems are manipulated to serve the interests of the dictator, with laws applied selectively to suppress opposition. Judicial independence is compromised, and legal processes are used as tools of repression rather than justice. This erosion of the rule of law creates an environment where arbitrary arrests, detentions, and extrajudicial actions become commonplace.

Freedom of expression is also severely curtailed in dictatorial regimes. The media is often controlled or censored, with propaganda used to shape public perception and maintain the dictator's image. Independent journalism is stifled, and dissenting voices are silenced through intimidation, imprisonment, or worse. This suppression of free expression stifles public discourse and prevents the emergence of alternative political ideas.

In early 2025, White House Press Secretary Karoline Leavitt implemented significant changes to press access protocols, leading to the exclusion of certain journalists and media organizations from presidential events.

Leavitt announced that the White House would assume control over the selection of reporters granted access to high-profile events, such as those in the Oval Office and aboard Air Force One. This move ended the longstanding practice where the White House Correspondents' Association (WHCA) managed press pool rotations.

In addition, a dictators' foreign relations are often characterized by a focus on regime survival and self-interest. They may seek alliances with other authoritarian regimes, (Trump's pro Putin approach), engage in aggressive posturing, such as is being currently seen with Donald Trump's trade tariff agenda and verbal attacks on Canada and Mexico, or use foreign policy as a tool to distract from domestic issues (the war in Ukraine).

A dictator's paranoia can lead to isolationist tendencies, as seen in Trump's move to leave the Climate Accord, the World Health Organization, and NATO, whilst at the same time in a type of psychologically insecure way the dictator may strive for international recognition and legitimacy. Diplomatic relations nevertheless are always transactional, with little regard for international norms or cooperation.

And probably as history has witnessed time and time again the trait most damaging to social cohesion and international relations is the pathological need for all dictators to have complete dominance and control at all times in all situations.

Hitler's Nazi Regime: A Pathological Need for Dictatorial Dominance and Control.

Trump's MAGA Regime: The Signs are Already Appearing.

The phenomenon of a political dictator's insatiable need for dominance and control is a complex interplay of power, insecurity, and the desire for absolute authority, and in terms of a primary example of a political dictator in persona and action, one needs to look no further than the political life and times of Adolf Hitler of Nazi Germany notoriety.

Adolf Hitler, one of history's most infamous dictators, exemplifies this need for dominance and control in a manner that is both comprehensive and chilling. His regime sought to dominate every aspect of German life, from politics and education to culture and religion, despite his own limitations in intellectual capacity and little to no expertise in these areas.

Hitler's rise to power was marked by his ability to manipulate the political narrative to his advantage. He was not the architect of every policy or the mastermind behind every strategy; rather, he was a master of propaganda and a charismatic orator who could sway public opinion and rally support. His control over the political agenda was achieved through a combination of fear, coercion, deception, and the strategic use of scapegoats, most notably the Jewish population, whom he blamed for Germany's woes.

In education, Hitler's regime sought to indoctrinate the youth with Nazi ideology. The curriculum was altered to emphasize racial purity, Aryan superiority, and loyalty to the Führer. Teachers were required to join the National Socialist Teachers League, ensuring that they adhered to the party line.

This control over education was not born out of a deep understanding of pedagogy or intellectual discourse, but rather from a desire to mould future generations into obedient followers of the Nazi regime. Social and cultural practices were similarly commandeered to serve the Nazi agenda.

In the 19th and 20th centuries, European racial theorists misappropriated the term Aryan to promote a false idea of racial superiority. The Nazis and other White Supremacists wrongly used Aryan to describe a so-called "pure white, Nordic race", which had no historical or scientific basis.

The Nazi regime under Hitler promoted this homogeneous Aryan culture, a culture where people share the same colour, the same language, ethnicity, values, traditions, and customs. There is little if any cultural diversity, and as such laws are enforced suppressing any form of expression that deviated from its ideals.

Hitler's reign was characterised by what you could describe as a paranoid need for control of and dominance over everything, not just people and laws, but their cultural pursuits, their education, their religion, and their health outcomes.

"Have any of the American public or news media thought carefully about the sudden Trump takeover of the John F. Kennedy Centre of Performing Arts, appointing himself as the board chairman, "so early in his second presidency", and his termination of all board members, replacing them with Trump loyalists?"

In Hitler's regime art, music, and literature were censored, with only those works that glorified the regime or conformed to its racial ideology being permitted. The infamous book burnings of 1933 symbolized this cultural control, as works by Jewish authors and other "undesirables" were destroyed. The book burnings of 1933 were a series of events organised by the Nazi party, aimed at purging the country of what was termed un- German literature.

The most infamous burning took place on May 10th, 1933, when Nazi student groups, supported by party officials and the German Student Association

(DSTA) and led by Joseph Goebbels, the Nazi Minister for Propaganda, burned thousands of books in Berlin's Opernplatz. Similar burnings occurred in 34 university towns across Germany. Books by Jewish, communist, socialist, pacifists, and liberal authors, were targeted.

The book burnings symbolised the Nazi regime's broader efforts to censor dissent, control thought, and suppress intellectual freedom. The Nazi Minister of Propaganda Goebbels stated that the purpose of the book burning was to eliminate what they termed "degenerate ideas," and establish Nazi ideological control over German culture and education. It foreshadowed the persecution of Jews, intellectuals, and political opponents, eventually leading to the Holocaust itself.

Notable authors who were banned were Albert Einstein, because of his scientific writings, Sigmund Freud because of his psychology theories, Karl Marx because of his writings about socialism, Erich Maria Remarque for her writing of All Quiet on the Western Front, a story which was critical of war, Heinrich Heine who famously wrote "where they burn books, they will also burn people," and H.G. Wells who wrote The War of The Worlds, whose Classic Comic edition I read as a young child.

The creative arts were also tightly controlled, with the Reich Chamber of Culture overseeing all artistic endeavours. Artists were required to be members of this organization, and their work had to align with Nazi ideals. This stifling of creativity was not due to Hitler's own artistic vision he didn't have one, and his failed career as an artist is well-documented, but rather his desire to use art as a tool for propaganda.

"Have any of the American public or news media thought carefully about the early establishment of the White House Faith Office, a type of "state sanctioned religious priority" and the installation of a Trump loyalist of the Evangelical kind to head it up?"

Religious practices also were not immune to Hitler's pathological need for control. The regime sought to align Christianity with Nazi ideology, creating a distorted version of the faith that supported its racial policies.

The German Christian movement attempted to reconcile Nazi beliefs with Protestantism, while the Confessing Church resisted such efforts, leading to a tense relationship between the state and religious institutions. To deal with this Hitler created a state sanctioned religious institution which he called the "Reich Church."

In February 2025, President Donald Trump established the White House Faith Office, appointing Pastor Paula White-Cain as its Senior Advisor. This office is supposedly designed to empower faith-based entities, community organizations, and houses of worship to serve families and communities.

Paula White-Cain, 58, is a pastor and televangelist from Tupelo, Mississippi and a Trump loyalist. She is the founder and president of Paula White Ministries and the National Faith Advisory Board.

White-Cain's religious background is rooted in evangelical Christianity. She is known for her association with the "prosperity gospel", a false belief that financial success is a sign of God's favour. Critics have accused her of promoting this theology, which she denies. President Trump's decision to appoint White-Cain to lead the Faith Office reflects their longstanding relationship and her influence within evangelical circles.

"Have any of the American public or news media thought carefully about the reason for the appointment of Robert F. Kennedy Jr. a converted Trump loyalist, with no medical or scientific experience, as the U.S. Secretary of Health and Human Services?"

In Nazi Germany, in the realm of health, the Nazi regime implemented policies that reflected its obsession with racial purity not good health outcomes for the German people. The eugenics program, which included forced sterilizations and the euthanasia of those deemed "unfit," which I spoke of previously, was a horrific manifestation of this control. These policies were "not based on scientific rigor" but rather on a perverse interpretation of genetics and social Darwinism.

Robert F. Kennedy Jr. was appointed as the United States Secretary of Health and Human Services (HHS) under President Donald Trump, with his confirmation by the Senate occurring on February 13, 2025.

Kennedy has a longstanding history of scepticism toward vaccines and certain aspects of scientific medical research. During his Senate confirmation hearings, he called for a return to "gold standard science" and expressed doubts about existing vaccine safety data, even when presented with compelling research.

His tenure at HHS has been marked by actions reflecting his critical stance on vaccines. For instance, during a measles outbreak in the southwestern U.S., Kennedy downplayed the severity of the situation and promoted alternative treatments such as vitamin A supplementation, despite a lack of robust scientific evidence supporting their efficacy in this context.

He also overstated potential harms of the measles vaccine and suggested that natural immunity from contracting the disease might be preferable, contradicting established public health guidance. Furthermore, Kennedy's leadership has led to significant resignations within health agencies. Dr. Peter Marks, the head of the FDA's vaccine program, resigned citing Kennedy's spread of "misinformation and lies" about vaccines.

These developments have raised concerns among public health officials and scientists about the potential erosion of scientific standards and the undermining of public confidence in vaccines and other medical interventions.

To implement his overall agenda, Hitler the fascist dictator relied on a cadre of loyal followers some more capable than himself in their respective fields. Figures like Joseph Goebbels, Heinrich Himmler, and Hermann Göring were instrumental in executing the policies that Hitler envisioned. These individuals, while often sharing Hitler's ideological fervour, were the true architects and implementers of the regime's agenda.

Not dissimilar in strategy from what we are witnessing with the current White House administration, with Trump due to his inability to create and define a political agenda enlisting the help of Project 2025 architects and devotees in his administration team to not only create his agenda but implement it into his governance mixed in with some of his own ego driven ideas.

Adolf Hitler's insatiable need for control and dominance was driven by a combination of personal ambition, ideological fanaticism, and a desire for absolute power. His regime's reach into every facet of German life was not a testament to his own intellectual prowess, but rather his ability to manipulate, coerce, and delegate. The legacy of his dictatorship serves as a stark reminder for every democratic nation of the dangers of unchecked power and the human cost of a leader's unrelenting quest for control.

Gleichschaltung...Hitler the Dictator's Governance Manifesto. Mirrored in The Project 2025 Agenda.

Gleichschaltung, was the title given to Hitler's political agenda for seizing control over intellectual property, education policy, health policy, the arts, and religious rights. Gleichschaltung means "coordination or synchronization." Gleichschaltung was the process by which the Nazi regime systematically took control of all aspects of society, aligning institutions, organisations, and cultural life with Nazi ideology.

It included seizing control of the country's "Health Policy" and instigating a programme of promoting eugenics and racial hygiene, leading to forced sterilisations and euthanasia programmes. It included seizing control of the countries "Education Policy", and subsequently indoctrinating youth through the education system and organisations like the Hitler Youth Movement.

It included seizing control of all "Arts and Culture Programmes", enforcing strict censorship and promoting propaganda through the Reich Chamber of Culture. It included an attack on "religious rights", attempting to subordinate churches under state control through efforts like the "Reich Church", whilst at the same time suppressing religious opposition.

Gleichschaltung effectively eliminated independent institutions and ensured that all aspects of German life served Nazi objectives, specifically education policy, health policy, the arts policy, and religious policy.

In what only could be described as a "remarkable coincidence", as of February 13, 2025, the current White House administration has enacted several similar executive orders and policies affecting health, education, arts and culture, and religious education.

President Trump has issued executive orders that have mandated the removal of reference to race, gender, sexual orientation, disabilities, and other terms from U.S. Health Agency websites. Experts warned that this move would undermine scientific research and the health of various communities, including trans and intersex people, people of colour, LGBTQ+ individuals, women, and disabled individuals including disabled veterans.

President Trump has expressed a desire to close the Department of Education, describing it as "a big con job". He advocates for returning control of education to the states and has flagged that he is considering issuing an executive order to transfer many of the department's functions to other agencies. The catch?

The states then in order to qualify for federal funding will have to implement the Trump administration's curriculum changes.

He has signed in his first two weeks in office, an executive order aiming to promote "patriotic education in schools," and advised the establishment of the 1776 Commission within the Department of Education to advance this initiative. Something to watch for the future once this is enacted will be if the states are threatened with reduced funding if they don't adhere to federal education suggestions.

President Trump's creation of the White House Faith Office supposedly to "assist" faith-based entities, community organisations, and houses of worship in strengthening American families, promoting work, and self-sufficiency, and supposedly protecting religious liberty, has given his administration some measure of influence and thus control. Remember Hitler established the Reich Church.

In terms of Arts and Culture, Trump's National Endowment for the Arts (NEA) as of 2025 have been given funding restrictions. The NEA has announced that all 2026 projects must ensure compliance with legal, regulatory, and policy requirements, including not promoting gender ideology. This move aligns with recent executive orders and may limit funding for programmes that promote diversity and gender education.

On January 20, 2025, during a celebration at Capital One Arena in Washington, D.C., following President Donald Trump's second inauguration, Elon Musk, the person Trump tasked with putting a blowtorch to programs and people in the areas of arts and culture, education, justice, religion, and health, supposedly to reduce costs, delivered a speech that sparked controversy due to a gesture he made, which some interpreted as resembling a Nazi salute.

While addressing the crowd, Musk slapped his chest with his right hand and then extended his arm outward with his palm facing downward. He repeated this gesture toward the audience seated behind him, stating, "My heart goes out to you".

This action drew immediate comparisons to the Nazi salute, leading to widespread criticism on social media and in the press.

In response to the allegations, Musk dismissed the criticism as a "dirty trick" by his political opponents and clarified that the gesture was meant to symbolize giving his heart to the crowd, not a Nazi salute. The gesture elicited mixed reactions.

Some commentators and organizations, such as the Anti-Defamation League, suggested it was a moment of enthusiasm rather than an intentional Nazi salute. Conversely, various media outlets and public figures criticized the gesture, with some noting that far-right and neo-Nazi groups embraced it as a sign of support.

Politicians such as Yolanda Diaz, Alexandria Ocasio-Cortez, and Jerry Nadler, along with historian Ruth Ben-Ghiat, condemned the gesture. Political parties in Austria and Germany called for Musk to be banned from entering their countries, citing his support for right- wing extremism and interference in European politics. In contrast Israeli Prime Minister Benjamin Netanyahu defended Musk, stating he was falsely smeared.

Musk responded to the allegations naturally by dismissing them as politicised attacks, or as Donald Trump might put it, "a witch hunt," stating the words "the everyone is Hitler attack is so tired", but he did not explicitly deny the claims. He also posted a series of puns about Nazis on social media, which the Anti-Defamation League (ADL) condemned as inappropriate and highly offensive.

Regardless of intent, the gesture was widely embraced by right wing extremists and neo- Nazis. The incident has intensified debates about political affiliations and the influence of high-profile figures with perhaps a hidden ideological agenda in shaping political and public discourse. The American people have a responsibility to their founding fathers to wake up and smell the rot. Their country is subtly transitioning from a democratic republic to an autocracy through the ideological agenda of both Musk and Trump.

THE HITLERGRUß.
HITLER THE DICTATOR'S INFAMOUS NAZI SALUTE.

The Hitlergruß, the infamous Nazi salute, served multiple ideological and psychological functions. It was a symbol of swearing loyalty to Adolf Hitler, personally, not just the state or the military, it demonstrated unity and submission to the Nazi regime and its worldview, it was a symbol of public identification, and as such not saluting could mark someone as politically unreliable, subversive, or even treasonous.

The infamous Nazi salute, commonly recognized as the outstretched right arm raised upward with a straightened hand, was a powerful symbol of allegiance and submission within Nazi Germany. It achieved its aim creating a culture of fear and conformity, as failing to perform the salute could lead to ostracism, job loss, arrest, or worse. And it functioned less like a traditional patriotic salute and more like a ritual of obedience and ideological purity, a public performance of allegiance to fascist rule.

The Nazi salute drew inspiration from the ancient Roman salute, though this connection is largely mythologized. Fascist movements in Italy and Germany appropriated the concept of an arm-raising gesture to symbolize imperial grandeur and martial discipline. In Italy, Mussolini's Fascists were already using a similar gesture by the early 1920's. In Germany, the Nazi Party adopted the salute in the 1920's as part of its political theatre, creating a sense of militarized unity among followers.

After Hitler's appointment as Chancellor in 1933, the salute began transitioning from party ritual to national requirement. Once the Nazis consolidated power, the salute was mandatory in many public and private contexts. Civil servants, teachers, police officers, and soldiers were required to use it. Schoolchildren were taught to say "Heil Hitler" as a morning greeting.

Ordinary citizens were expected to salute in public ceremonies, to police or military officers, and especially during any mention of Hitler. Refusing to give the salute could result in denunciation by neighbours or coworkers. It could lead to interrogation, job loss, arrest, or worse (particularly after 1934, when the Gestapo became more active). Some religious groups, notably the Jehovah's Witnesses, refused to give the salute and were sent to concentration camps.

There were however acts of defiance. Some Germans quietly resisted by using traditional greetings or simply avoiding eye contact. The famous image of August Landmesser, who refused to raise his arm during a rally in 1936, became an enduring symbol of silent defiance. Similar Sophie Scholl, and the White Rose resistance movement, which I speak of further in Chapter 12, resisted not only with words but by rejecting all the formative rituals of loyalty expected of young Germans.

The dangers of electing leaders with malignant narcissistic tendencies are not confined to history; they remain an ever-present threat to democratic nations. As witnessed in Hitler's rise to power, such individuals seek not just political control but dominance over every facet of society, arts and culture, education, justice, religion, and health, ensuring that no institution remains independent of their will.

Their unchecked egos demand absolute authority, and their insatiable need for validation leads them to dismantle democratic safeguards, replacing them with mechanisms of personal power and ideological conformity.

The lesson from history is clear: democracies are not immune to authoritarian drift, especially when a nation, disillusioned or desperate, embraces a leader who promises strength but delivers subjugation. A narcissistic demagogue does not simply govern; he reshapes society in his own image, silencing opposition, distorting truth, and cultivating a culture of fear and loyalty. In doing so, he corrodes the very institutions meant to serve the people, transforming them into instruments of control.

The erosion of democracy does not happen overnight; it is a slow, insidious process, enabled by complacency, apathy, and the misguided belief that "it could never happen here." But history has shown otherwise. The question is not whether such leaders will emerge again, but whether democratic societies will recognize the warning signs in time, and whether they will have the will to resist before it is too late.

SCHUTZSTAFFEL...THE SS.
HITLER THE DICTATOR'S FEARED MOBILE KILLING SQUADS.

The SS (Schutzstaffel) was one of the most powerful and feared organizations in Nazi Germany, serving as Adolf Hitler's elite paramilitary force. Initially created as a "personal bodyguard unit for Hitler" in the 1920's, similarly you could say as is the Secret Service (SS) in the United States.

Initially, the SS was a small, elite guard unit to protect Hitler and top Nazi officials. It eventually expanded under Heinrich Himmler into a vast organization that played a central role in both Nazi terror and the administration of the Holocaust. One could similarly see, if not contained, Donald Trump expanding the involvement of his own SS, the Secret Service in a similar way.

The SS was portrayed as an elite, almost mystical order, which added to their aura of invincibility. It was not just a military force however, but also a tool for enforcing Hitler's totalitarian control, racial ideology, and climate of fear throughout Nazi Germany. It later evolved into the Waffen-SS, a military branch that fought alongside the regular German army (Wehrmacht).

The Gestapo (secret police) worked closely with the SS to crush political opposition and eliminate threats to the Nazi regime. Combined with this the SD (Sicherheitsdienst), the SS's intelligence agency, a type of Nazi CIA, monitored civilians and carried out covert operations.

Hitler used the SS as a tool of fear and psychological warfare. The black uniforms, skull insignia, and rigid discipline made the SS a symbol of absolute authority and terror. Massive SS parades, executions, and public punishments created fear and obedience. The SS (often via the Gestapo) made thousands "disappear," reinforcing the idea that opposition to Hitler's authoritarian rule would result in a death sentence.

Eventually the SS grew rapidly seeing it put in charge of the concentration camps and extermination camps such as Auschwitz. The Einsatzgruppen, the SS mobile killing squads, were responsible for mass shootings of Jews, political dissidents, and other groups in Eastern Europe. They were heavily involved in eugenics programs, including forced sterilizations and racial experiments. The SS controlled businesses and industries using slave labour from concentration camps.

"When wealth becomes the voice of power, democracy fades into a whisper, drowned out by the clamour of the few; thus in a nation where money speaks louder than the vote, the true essence of democracy is sacrificed at the altar of greed. The greatest threat to liberty is not the tyranny of the majority, but the silence of the many under the weight of oligarchic influence. A government of the people, by the people, and for the people then slowly fades into a mere façade of its former self."

11

Drinking the Nectar of The Golden Chalice.

The Unholy Alliance of Oligarchs and Governance.

Chapter Contents.

The Golden Chalice: The Poisoned Chalice: The Historical Rise of the Oligarchy: Present Day Oligarchal Influence, The Russian Oligarchy, The American Oligarchy: The Technogarchy: The Quid Pro Quo Oligarchal Arrangement: The Silicon Valley Oligarchy. Musk, Thiel, and Others, The PayPal Mafia Connection: The Musk Trump Oligarchal Connection: The Musk, Thiel, Vance Connection, an Alliance of Governance, Greed, Ideology, and Political Ambition, with a Goal for a Trump/Vance Project 2025 Style Permanent Presidency.

"The true danger of an oligarchy lies not just in its power, but in its ability to reshape the narrative, turning citizens into mere spectators of their own governance. Money in politics is like poison in a well; it contaminates the very source of democracy, leaving the populace thirsty for the pure waters of honest representation."

THE GOLDEN CHALICE.

I have coined a phrase "Drinking the Nectar ofThe Golden Chalice" for the title of this chapter. "Drinking the Nectar ofThe Golden Chalice" can be interpreted as a celebratory metaphor for "a joint toasting to the oligarch's financial and political benefits and rewards that come their way from the accomplishment of morally questionable or totally corrupt political and business arrangements".

To me this phrase carries a rich and evocative imagery. Chalices are often associated with ceremonial or religious significance, and a golden chalice would suggest something of great value or importance has been achieved, so let all political leaders, corporate leaders, and church leaders stand up and toast to that success.

With this phrase I am suggesting that certain wealthy individuals, large business corporations, and religious institutions, are deliberately and with intent partaking in "quid pro quo arrangements," the "something for something" type of deal, with a sense of greed and self-indulgence, secretly passing the golden goblet, sharing the wine of success, achieved at the expense of a large proportion of a nation's populace.

These arrangements see oligarchal individuals, corporations, or organisations prioritizing their own corporate, financial, religious, political, or ideological needs, by offering some sort of reward to a government or an individual in the government, to shift their stance on things that affect them, even if it sees the official sacrificing ethical and moral considerations to do so. And in the pursuit of power, many individuals or governments will bend the ethical and moral knee, if individuals or corporations are prepared to pay the price for it.

The "Golden Chalice" symbolizes the allure and temptation of power, wealth, and influence that these entities, whether financial, religious, corporate or political, are willing to pursue, even at the cost of integrity and justice, to reap the desired results. This imagery highlights the opulence and desirability of the rewards, while also implying a sense of complicity and shared guilt among those who partake in the toasting.

However all that glitters is not gold, and history continues to reveal how quickly the supposed golden chalice slowly morphs into a poisoned one.

THE POISONED CHALICE.

The term "a poisoned chalice" refers to something that appears desirable or beneficial but is, in reality, harmful or damaging to the recipient. It is often used in political and professional contexts to describe a position, honour, or responsibility that comes with hidden dangers or inevitable failure.

The phrase has its roots in Shakespeare's Macbeth. In Act 1, Scene 7, Macbeth wrestles with his conscience about murdering King Duncan and reflects on the consequences. Here, Macbeth acknowledges that by committing murder to gain the throne, he may ultimately face the same fate. The metaphor of a poisoned chalice suggests that an apparent reward, the throne, carries a fatal cost, sometimes psychological, sometimes physical, in retribution or guilt.

Over time, "a poisoned chalice" has evolved into a common phrase to describe burdensome responsibilities disguised as opportunities. For example we see in politics a high-profile political position, such as becoming Prime Minister or President in a time of crisis, can be a poisoned chalice if it leads to inevitable failure or backlash. For example, Theresa May's leadership after Brexit in Britain was widely considered a poisoned chalice.

In business leadership CEO's or executives who take over failing companies may be seen as inheriting a poisoned chalice, as their chances of success are slim despite the prestige of the role. In sports, a coach or manager inheriting a failing team, or unrealistic expectations, may find their position to be a poisoned chalice.

In the world of politics more than anywhere else, the concept of a poisoned chalice, where individuals punching above their own intellectual weight and subsequent intelligence levels, have accepted positions or responsibilities that seemed prestigious at first, but ultimately led to their downfall, and the downfall of those who poured the wine into the chalice. History has borne witness to the following:

Julius Caesar, the Roman Dictator (49–44 BCE). Caesar's rise to power made him Rome's most powerful figure, granting him control over the republic and the opportunity to enact major reforms. His consolidation of power angered the Roman Senate, leading to his assassination in 44 BCE. Despite his military and political genius, his ambition ultimately made him a target, proving that absolute power often comes with fatal consequences.

Neville Chamberlain, the British Prime Minister (1937–1940). Chamberlain became Prime Minister at a time when Britain was still a major world power. His goal of securing peace in Europe made him initially popular. His policy of appeasement towards Hitler, best symbolized by the 1938 Munich Agreement, where he claimed to have secured "peace for our time", proved disastrous when Nazi Germany invaded Poland in 1939, triggering World War 2. Chamberlain was forced to resign in 1940, his legacy forever tarnished. Donald Trump is following a similar pattern as Chamberlain's in his attempts to appease Putin; time will tell.

Lyndon B. Johnson, the U.S. President (1963–1969). Johnson assumed the presidency after John F. Kennedy's assassination, a role that offered immense power and the opportunity to shape America's future. His Great Society programs aimed to eliminate poverty and racial injustice. Despite his domestic achievements, his presidency was overshadowed by the Vietnam War. As the war escalated, public opinion turned against him, leading to protests, political turmoil, and his decision not to seek re-election in 1968. His legacy remains deeply controversial.

Richard Nixon, the U.S. President (1969–1974). Nixon won the presidency during a period of social unrest but managed to secure major foreign policy achievements, including opening relations with China and negotiating arms control with the Soviet Union. The Watergate scandal led to his resignation in 1974, making him the first U.S. president to leave office in disgrace, but perhaps not the last. What began as a successful presidency ended in political ruin, forever associating his name with corruption and scandal.

Mikhail Gorbachev, the last leader of the Soviet Union (1985–1991). When Gorbachev became General Secretary of the Communist Party in 1985, he inherited one of the two global superpowers, the Soviet Union. His leadership position offered the opportunity to modernize the USSR and shape global politics.

His attempts at reform glasnost and perestroika backfired, leading to political instability, economic collapse, and ultimately the dissolution of the Soviet Union in 1991. Instead of being remembered as a reformer who revitalized the USSR, he was seen by many as the leader who presided over its collapse.

Boris Yeltsin, the First President of Post-Soviet Russia (1991–1999). Yeltsin became Russia's first democratically elected president after the collapse of the USSR, offering him a chance to reshape the country's future. He inherited a crumbling economy, political instability, and oligarchic corruption. His presidency saw the rise of Russian oligarchs, economic chaos, and the eventual transfer of power to Vladimir Putin in 1999. Many Russians viewed his tenure as disastrous, leading to his deep unpopularity.

Theresa May, the British Prime Minister (2016–2019). After the Brexit referendum in 2016, May became Prime Minister, inheriting the historic task of leading Britain through its departure from the European Union. She was unable to unite her party or secure a Brexit deal that satisfied both the EU and the British Parliament. Her repeated failures to pass a withdrawal agreement forced her to resign in 2019, leaving her tenure defined by political paralysis and public frustration.

Positions of power, prestige, or influence whether they be of the political or oligarchal kind, can be poisoned chalices, offering glory at first, but ultimately leading to downfall, disgrace, or failure. This concept is especially relevant in politics, where the burden of responsibility can make a euphoric victory feel like a dysphoric curse.

THE HISTORICAL RISE OF THE OLIGARCHY.

The term "oligarchy" refers to a small group of people having control of a country or organization. In the context of American politics, this often includes billionaires, corporate executives, media executives, and influential lobbyists who wield significant power over political processes through financial contributions, strategic alliances, and what are known as "quid pro quo" arrangements.

The word "oligarchy" derives from the Greek words "oligos" (few) and "arkhein" (to rule), meaning "rule by a few." Unlike democracy, where power is theoretically distributed among the populace, oligarchy concentrates power in the hands of a privileged minority. This minority often consists of wealthy individuals, business or media magnates, political elites, or military leaders who exercise control over government institutions, the economy, and society at large.

The concept of oligarchy dates back to ancient Greece, particularly in the writings of philosophers such as Aristotle and Plato. Aristotle categorized government structures into monarchies, aristocracies, and oligarchies, with the latter representing rule by the wealthy elite.

In terms of the historical rise of the oligarchy we can see their influence in various contexts over a long period of time. We see them functioning in Ancient Sparta and Athens, in Medieval Feudalism, during the Industrial Revolution, and now in Modern Corporations, where single wealthy individuals, multinational corporations, financial institutions, political powerbrokers, and religious leaders exert significant control over political parties, government policies, global trade, and regulatory frameworks.

Ancient Sparta and Athens were two of the most powerful city-states in ancient Greece, but they were fundamentally different in their political structures, societal values, and military focus. Sparta was oligarchic and militaristic. It was ruled by two hereditary kings and a council of elders with significant power held by the Ephors (overseers). Democracy had little role in governance.

Athens on the other hand was a democracy, well at least for male citizens. Athens developed one of the earliest forms of direct democracy, with a popular assembly and a system of random selection for many public offices.

In terms of societal norms and culture, Sparta focused on military discipline and obedience. Boys were taken at age seven to be trained in the agoge system, emphasizing endurance, combat skills, and loyalty to the state. Individualism and intellectual pursuits were discouraged. Women in Sparta had more freedom and physical training than in Athens.

Athens on the other hand valued philosophy, arts, and education. Thinkers like Socrates, Plato, and Aristotle thrived there. The city was a hub for literature, drama, and architecture. Women, however, had far fewer rights compared to Spartan women.

With regards to military strength Sparta was a land-based military powerhouse, renowned for its disciplined and highly trained hoplite warriors. The Spartan army was feared throughout Greece. Whilst Athens excelled in naval power, boasting the strongest fleet in Greece. The Athenian navy was crucial in victories like the Battle of Salamis against the Persians.

In terms of the economy Sparta relied on a rigid system of agriculture, with a subjugated class forced to farm and support the warrior elite. Trade and luxury were discouraged, whereas Athens had a thriving economy based on trade, craftsmanship, and a strong maritime presence. Athens was known for its wealth and its bustling marketplaces.

In an almost ancient metaphoric picture of the current Republican (Conservative) versus Democrat political and social environment, Sparta was a war-driven society focused on obedience and strength, whereas Athens championed democracy, culture, and intellectual achievement.

Their opposing values and ambitions made them natural rivals, shaping much of ancient Greek history. Sparta (conservatism) maintained a rigid oligarchic structure dominated by a small warrior elite, and even though Athens prided itself on its status as a democracy, with a type of arrogant self-serving attitude, oligarchic factions still frequently disrupted its governance trying to infiltrate.

In the Medieval Feudal system in Europe there was an inherently oligarchical influence as a landed aristocracy controlled vast economic and military resources, and during the Industrial Revolution, the rise of industrial capitalism in the 19th and 20th centuries saw the emergence of powerful business moguls who influenced policy and economic direction.

These factors were masterfully illustrated in Leo Tolstoy's magnificent work "War and Peace", and Charles Dicken's classic novel "A Tale of Two Cities" which I read and reread at a very young age. Both War and Peace by Tolstoy, and A Tale of Two Cities by Dickens, explore themes of oligarchic power and the struggles of the common people, but they do so in different ways and with distinct philosophical and political nuances.

War and Peace is set during the Napoleonic Wars and primarily follows the Russian aristocracy. The novel does not depict a direct battle between a far-right oligarchy and a democratic left in modern terms, but it does highlight the corruption and self-interest of the Russian aristocracy, a nobility that is largely detached from the needs of the common people and prioritizes its own survival over national well-being. The Russian court and military leadership are often ineffective, detached from reality, or self-serving.

Tolstoy portrays a shift away from oligarchic dominance toward a more collective, patriotic resistance (exemplified in the character of General Kutuzov and the peasant-driven war effort), similar to what we saw with the anti-Vietnam war protests of the 60's with the hippies and beat generation alongside the public leading the charge. Tolstoy argues that individuals (whether rulers or revolutionaries) have limited control over historical movements, subtly undermining the idea of strong oligarchic rule.

A Tale of Two Cities, set during the French Revolution, presents a clearer battle between oligarchic oppression and revolutionary forces, focusing on the cruelty of the aristocracy (oligarchy), the vengeance of the revolutionaries (freedom fighters), and the necessary sacrifice by many for the greater good.

The opening chapters show how the French nobility exploits and dehumanizes the common people (e.g., the Marquis' carriage running over a child without consequence). The book sympathizes with the plight of the poor, but also warns against the excesses of revolutionary violence (e.g., Madame Defarge and the Reign of Terror).

Perhaps most importantly Dickens emphasises the principle of sacrifice for a greater good. Sydney Carton's sacrifice reflects Dickens' belief that "redemption and personal morality matter more than blind ideology". Whilst Dickens does not fully endorse the revolution, he emphatically critiques the conditions that made it inevitable. His novel can be seen as a warning about how "unchecked oligarchic rule eventually leads to violent backlash".

We are seeing pockets of this happening in America in this current day with the burning of Tesla cars and dealerships in response to Elon Musk's involvement and influence in the Trump administration.

If we map these themes onto a modern left-right framework: The aristocracy in both novels represents far-right oligarchic rule, prioritizing power, privilege, and hierarchy. The common people represent leftist revolutionary forces, whether in the form of Russian patriotism (War and Peace) or French revolutionaries (A Tale of Two Cities).

Both novels warn against extremes, whether the arrogance of the aristocracy or the violence of revolutionary movements. So yes, protest and resist but do so in a highly visible but non-violent way as was exemplified in the protest movements led by political and social "activist revolutionaries" such as Dr. Martin Luther King Jnr. and Mahatma Ghandi.

PRESENT DAY OLIGARCHAL INFLUENCE.

Today, in modern corporatism, multinational corporations and financial institutions exert significant control over government policies, global trade, and regulatory frameworks. There are different types of oligarchs which could probably be divided down into five basic oligarchy types, based on their source of power and sphere of influence, the fifth one being relatively new, but fast becoming an emerging contender for top position.

The five are: Industrial Oligarchs, Financial Oligarchs, Political Oligarchs, Military Oligarchs, and perhaps what one could describe as the newest member of the "oligarchy club", the Technological Oligarchy. And also, whilst not strictly an oligarchy in the classic sense, in certain circumstances through its increasing involvement in lobbying political powers, Christian Nationalism as a religious oligarchy could be added to the pack.

Industrial Oligarchs are individuals or groups who control major industries, such as oil, steel, or manufacturing. Historical examples in the United States include Andrew Carnegie and John D. Rockefeller. Financial Oligarchs are bankers and investors who control vast sums of wealth and influence monetary policies. For example, institutions such as JPMorgan Chase and Goldman Sachs wield enormous global influence.

There are also Political Oligarchs who manipulate governance structures to maintain control, often merging business and political interests. A political dictator could be considered an oligarch if they amass wealth and power alongside a select group of elites who reinforce their rule. e.g. the Trump-Musk-Murdoch oligarchy.

There are Military Oligarchs, where in some regimes, military elites maintain disproportionate control over state affairs, as seen in juntas and military-led governments. And lastly more recently emerging are Technological Oligarchs, tech moguls who dominate digital infrastructure, social media, and artificial intelligence. Figures like Elon Musk, Mark Zuckerberg, and Jeff Bezos exemplify this class of oligarchs whilst Musk could technically even be described as an Industrial/ Technological oligarch.

Whilst Oligarchies exist in various forms worldwide, quite often certain ones are intertwined with state/national governance. For example with Elon Musk's entrenchment in the White House administration, he has become increasingly involved in decisions relating to America's military, economic, and social landscape.

Some notable examples of oligarchal led countries would include Russia, a prime example of a modern oligarchy, where business tycoons with ties to the Kremlin exert significant influence over politics and the economy, the United States, which while officially a democracy, exhibits increasingly and growing oligarchic tendencies through lobbying, campaign financing, and corporate influence in policymaking.

China, where we see the Chinese Communist Party, while nominally communist, functioning as an oligarchy, with elite families and business magnates shaping economic and political policies. India, where business dynasties and political elites maintain significant control over key industries and governance structures, and Saudi Arabia, where a hereditary monarchy with an oligarchic elite control oil wealth, and state decision-making.

THE RUSSIAN OLIGARCHY.

The rise of Vladimir Putin to the presidency of Russia in 2000 marked a significant turning point in the country's post-Soviet history, and as such it is, in the pursuit of understanding the current moral and political crisis occurring around the world, worth exploring a little more closely. Central to Putin's ascent to dictatorship was the role of the "Russian oligarchy", a group of powerful businessmen who had amassed significant wealth and influence during the chaotic privatization processes of the 1990's.

The oligarchs' role in Putin's initial election and their subsequent influence on his policy agenda when explored reveal this. In the aftermath of the Soviet Union's collapse, Russia underwent a rapid and often tumultuous transition from a centrally planned economy to a market-oriented one. This period was characterized by the privatization of state assets, which, due to a lack of regulatory frameworks and oversight, led to the concentration of wealth in the hands of a few individuals.

These newly minted oligarchs wielded significant economic power and, by extension, political influence. By the late 1990's, they had become key players in Russian politics, often using their resources to support candidates and policies that aligned with their interests. The Russian 1996 presidential election was a pivotal moment that underscored the oligarchs' influence.

Faced with the possibility of a Communist resurgence, the oligarchs rallied behind Boris Yeltsin, providing financial support and media backing to ensure his re-election. This alliance between Yeltsin and the oligarchs set a precedent for the role of money and media in Russian politics, a dynamic that would later benefit Vladimir Putin. When Yeltsin's presidency was nearing its end, the oligarchs were instrumental in facilitating Putin's rise to power.

Initially Putin was seen as a compromise candidate who could maintain stability and protect the oligarchs' interests. His background in the KGB and his reputation for decisiveness appealed to those seeking a strong leader who could restore order and continue economic reforms.

The oligarchs, leveraging their control over major media outlets, played a crucial role in shaping public perception and garnering support for Putin's candidacy. Once in office, Putin's relationship with the oligarchs evolved. While initially reliant on their support, he quickly moved to consolidate power and reduce their influence over the state, furthering his dictatorial tzarist ambitions. Does this look familiar?

This shift was exemplified by the high-profile arrest of Mikhail Khodorkovsky, one of Russia's wealthiest oligarchs, in 2003. Khodorkovsky's arrest sent a clear message that the era of oligarchic dominance was over, and that political power would be centralized under one man, this dictator, Vladimir Putin. One would be inclined to watch if once Donald Trump consolidates his presidency how the Musk/Trump relationship plays out; will the old adage "honour amongst thieves" prevail or not.

Despite this crackdown, the oligarchs continued to play a significant role in shaping Putin's policy agenda, albeit in a more subdued and co-operative manner. Many oligarchs aligned themselves with Putin's vision of a strong, centralized state and supported his efforts to reassert Russia's influence on the global stage. In return, they were "allowed to maintain their business empires", provided they did not challenge the Kremlin's authority, witnessing "the power of the quid pro effect" being cemented in.

Under Putin, the relationship between the state and the oligarchs became symbiotic. The government relied on the oligarchs for economic growth and development, while the oligarchs depended on the state for protection and favourable business conditions, such as increasing deregulation and bigger tax cuts. This mutual dependency facilitated the implementation of key policies, such as the consolidation of strategic industries under state control and the expansion of Russian influence through state-backed enterprises.

The Russian oligarchy played a crucial role in Vladimir Putin's rise to power and has continued to influence his policy agenda since. While Putin has curtailed their political power, the oligarchs remain integral to the functioning of the Russian economy and, by extension, the state's geopolitical ambitions.

This complex interplay between wealth and power highlights the enduring legacy of the oligarchs in shaping modern Russia and underscores the challenges of balancing economic interests with political authority in a rapidly changing world.

THE AMERICAN OLIGARCHY.

With regards to America and the growing presence of an oligarchy in play. The election of Donald Trump as the 45th president and now 47th President of the United States both times has marked a significant turning point in American politics.

While many factors contributed to his victory, the influence of the American oligarchy, wealthy individuals, powerful corporations, and influential institutions, including those of the religious far right, has played a crucial role in shaping the political landscape that facilitated his rise.

My metaphor of "drinking from the golden chalice" aptly captures the allure of unfettered wealth, unbridled power, and the seductive promises of economic freedom that drive the oligarchic elite in America. This gilded vessel symbolises the short-term gains of deregulation, a seductive promise that blinds its holders to the long-term consequences of the impacts on inequality, environmental degradation, and the erosion of democracy.

For America's oligarchs, the presidency of Donald Trump represented a golden moment to participate in the quid pro quo effect, to tip the golden chalice to their lips and drink deeply, ensuring their fortunes grew and their influence remained unchallenged.

Deregulation has long been a siren call for America's wealthiest, promising to strip away governmental barriers that limit corporate profit. For billionaires and corporations, the government, particularly democratic government, is often seen as an impediment to their aspirations, a meddlesome force imposing environmental protections, labour rights, and financial oversight. This is similarly witnessed in Australian politics.

When Donald Trump stormed into the Oval Office in 2017 with a promise to drain the swamp, what he really offered was a swamp of a different kind, one where industry leaders and financiers including the technogarchy, could shape policy to suit their desires.

Trump's White House administration, stocked with corporate insiders and lobbyists, became a playground for the oligarchs. The golden chalice of deregulation was held high as environmental protections were dismantled, labour rights were curtailed, and financial oversight was relaxed.

The wealthy elite, secure in the power of their own financial influence capability, and Trump's insatiable need for campaign financing, saw in Trump and opportunity to cement their dominance. In return, Trump found in them a reliable financial base of support, not necessarily for his personal charisma, but for the policy's he delivered.

You see Trump's meteoric rise to conservative party dominance, was not a solo endeavour. It was fuelled by an oligarchic class that recognised his appeal as a populist figurehead who could without conscience deceptively mask their intentions behind the rhetoric of nationalism and economic revival.

While Trump deceptively rallied the working class with promises to bring jobs back, reduce the price of groceries, "make eggs cheaper," and restore American greatness, the oligarchs worked quietly behind the scenes, hidden from media and public scrutiny, ensuring the tax cuts and regulatory rollbacks would benefit their interests.

In pursuing his personal interests one oligarch in particular, Elon Musk, ensured for a mere donation of 277 million dollars to Trump's campaign coffers, that he had as part of his quid pro quo arrangement with Trump, a front row seat in the White House, an "advisory position in Trump's new administration that had no legal consequences to himself," to not only pursue his personal corporate agenda, but also as a means of watching up close that his personal agenda was being carried out as per his quid pro quo arrangement.

The Oligarchy, in its various manifestations, remains a persistent and influential force in both American and global governance. The interplay of quid pro quo arrangements ensures that power remains concentrated, challenging democratic ideals and economic fairness. Understanding and addressing oligarchic influence is crucial for those who seek more equitable and transparent governance structures in the modern world.

Oligarchs fund political campaigns, ensuring favourable policies and regulatory advantages. Business elites gain control over state assets through privatization deals that serve their interests. Wealthy individuals use their resources to sway judicial outcomes and maintain legal immunity, and ownership of news outlets and social media platforms allows oligarchs to shape public perception and control narratives.

This has been perfectly witnessed in recent American politics with the oligarchal influence held by Rupert Murdoch, the Australian born billionaire owner of the Fox News Corporation, and Mark Zuckerberg the billionaire owner of Meta (Facebook), and Elon Musk the South African billionaire owner of X (Twitter), in shaping political and public discourse, public perception of candidates, and subsequent political election outcomes.

The Technogarchy, The New Wave of Oligarchal Influence: The Key Players.

In recent years, the United States has witnessed the ascent of tech entrepreneurs who have evolved into influential figures, often termed "technological oligarchs." These individuals not only helm some of the most powerful technology companies in the world, but also wield significant economic and political influence, which is not necessarily dangerous in itself if the company has a firm moral footing to begin with.

The true danger of a technological oligarch lies not just in their influential geographical reach, but in their ability to redirect without hesitation and consequence, the collective digital narrative of societies and nations, turning brother against sister, husband against wife, neighbour against neighbour and nation against nation: progressively turning all citizens into mere spectators of their own ephemeral reality, poisoning the soil of democracy.

According to the New York Post the five key figures and their enterprises who have become the new billionaire breed of technological oligarchs, what I have termed as techno-garchs, in descending order of their personal financial status are: Elon Musk, Jeff Bezos, Mark Zuckerberg, Larry Ellison, and Alex Karp.

The richest is Elon Musk the owner of X (formerly Twitter), and the CEO of Tesla and SpaceX; Musk's ventures span social media, electric vehicles and aerospace technology. His net worth is estimated at $433 billion, according to the New York Post.

The second richest technogarch is Jeff Bezos the founder of Amazon. Bezos has expanded the company from an online bookstore to a global e-commerce and cloud computing giant. His net worth stands at $239 billion according to the New York Post.

The third richest is Mark Zuckerberg, the founder of Meta Platforms, formerly Facebook. Zuckerberg oversees a vast social media empire. His net worth is approximately $211 billion, according to the New York Post.

The fourth richest is Larry Ellison, the co-founder and Executive Chairman of Oracle Corporation. Ellison has been instrumental in shaping the enterprise software industry. His net worth is $185 billion, according to The Tech Society.

And the fifth richest is Alex Karp the CEO of Palantir Technologies. Karp leads a firm specializing in data analytics with strong ties to U.S. Defence and Intelligence sectors. Palantir is valued at over $260 billion according to The Wall Street Journal.

These tech magnates have increasingly engaged in the political arena, often aligning with policies that favour technological advancement and deregulation.

Elon Musk, for instance, has assumed a governmental role as the head of the Department of Government Efficiency (DOGE), in Trump's second presidency, granting him substantial influence over federal agencies that intersect with his business interests. Mark Zuckerberg and Jeff Bezos have also shown a willingness to engage with political leadership, a readiness to collaborate with the administration, and Alex Karp, has been vocal about his support.

All four of the five were present at President Donald Trump's second inauguration, signalling for American interests and Western values, urging the tech industry to align more closely with national security objectives. Whilst Larry Ellison was not present, the following day Ellison appeared at the White House alongside President Trump to announce the Stargate Project, a partnership between Open AI, Oracle, and SoftBank, aiming to invest up to $500 billion in artificial intelligence infrastructure.

THE QUID PRO QUO OLIGARCHAL ARRANGEMENT.

The quid pro quo effect is a term commonly used in political and business circles which relates to this imagery of a shared sipping of the contents of the golden chalice. It refers to a mutual exchange where one party provides goods, a service, or a favour in return for something seen as of equivalent value from another party.

The concept is deeply embedded in human interactions and has evolved over centuries, influencing various sectors such as commerce, politics, and international relations. Oligarchs secure and maintain their influence by offering financial support, political endorsements, or economic concessions in exchange for preferential treatment. The origin of the term dates back to the medieval period, where it was initially used in the context of medicine.

Apothecaries (chemists/pharmacists) would substitute one medicine for another, and the term was used to describe this exchange. Over time, the phrase perhaps to project some veneer of respectability in deals that may appear to be verging on corrupt conduct, has expanded beyond the medical field to encompass any reciprocal exchange, including "cash for comment in media circles, and cash for concessions" in business/political circles.

Throughout history, the quid pro quo effect between governments and corporate and religious institutions has manifested in various forms, from political alliances to financial transactions. These relationships have been driven by mutual interests, with governments seeking legitimacy and support, while corporations and religious institutions aim to maintain influence and secure resources and increase wealth.

The relationship between the British monarchy and the Church of England is a prime example of a historical quid pro quo arrangement. Established in the 16th century during the reign of Henry VIII, the Church of England was born out of a political necessity rather than purely theological differences with the Catholic Church as many people believe.

The Act of Supremacy in 1534 declared the monarch as the Supreme Head of the Church of England, effectively intertwining the church with the state. In return for its loyalty and support, the church received protection and endorsement from the monarchy.

This relationship ensured that the church maintained significant influence over English society and politics, while the monarchy secured religious legitimacy and control over ecclesiastical appointments. The exchange was not merely about electoral support, as the monarchy was not elected, but rather about mutual reinforcement of power and authority.

The relationship between the church and military or political powers has also seen instances of quid pro quo. During World War II, there were controversial discussions about the Vatican's role and its interactions with Nazi Germany. While there is no definitive evidence of a formal alliance or exchange of treasures for silence, the Vatican's diplomatic stance during the war has been a subject of much historical debate.

While in Russia, the relationship between the government and the Russian Orthodox Church has been marked by periods of cooperation and conflict. During the Tsarist era, the church was a pillar of the autocratic regime, providing spiritual justification for the Tsar's divine right to rule, regardless of how oppressive that rule was. In return, the church enjoyed state patronage and influence over the moral and social fabric of the nation.

However, this relationship was disrupted during the Soviet era, when the state sought to suppress religious influence. In recent years, under Vladimir Putin's leadership, there has been a resurgence of the church's influence in Russian politics.

The government has leveraged the church's authority to promote nationalism and social conservatism, while the church has gained increased visibility and support from the state. This modern quid pro quo involves both political and financial exchanges, as the church receives state funding and advocates for Putin's ongoing re-election.

In the United States, the relationship between the government and the Christian Nationalist and Evangelical movement has become increasingly prominent in recent decades. This alliance has been particularly evident in the political landscape, where evangelical leaders and organizations have mobilized significant electoral support for candidates who align with their values, as previously discussed.

In return, these political figures often advocate for policies that reflect evangelical priorities, such as opposition to abortion and same-sex marriage, and the promotion of religious freedom. While the exchange is primarily centred around electoral support, financial transactions also play a role, as religious organizations contribute to political campaigns and, in some cases, receive government funding for faith-based initiatives and tax breaks.

Historically, the quid pro quo effect has been evident also in specific military alliances, and in religious / political alliances. In terms of military alliances, throughout history nations have often formed alliances with the understanding that mutual support would be provided in times of conflict, and in specific alliances that the division of the spoils of war would be part of the arrangement, where victorious allies would carve up territories or resources as part of their agreement, and the death of the soldiers seen as merely collateral damage.

Some of the major ones historically were: The Peloponnesian War (431–404 BC), between Athens and Sparta, where tens of thousands of soldiers and citizens died, saw various city-states align with either side, often with the expectation of territorial gains or increased influence in the Greek world. Sparta, for instance, promised Persians support in exchange for ceding control of Ionia.

The Crusades (1096–1291), where nearly 200 years of conflict saw up to 9 million people killed. In the Crusades European knights and nobles were motivated not only by religious fervour as has been historically reported, but also by the promise of land, wealth, and titles in the Holy Land. The leaders of the Crusades often negotiated with local powers, promising protection or shared control in return for support.

In the Italian Wars (1494–1559), where historians estimate hundreds of thousands of soldiers and civilians died, we saw shifting alliances among France, Spain, the Holy Roman Empire, and various Italian states. These alliances were frequently formed with the promise of territorial expansion or control over key cities and regions in Italy.

The Napoleonic Wars (1803–1815), estimated to have caused the death of between 3.5 and 6 million people, saw Napoleon Bonaparte form alliances with various European states, promising them territorial gains or political influence in return for military support. The Confederation of the Rhine is an example, where German states allied with France in exchange for autonomy and expansion.

In World War I (1914–1918) where estimates are given that between 15 and 22 million people died, we witnessed the complex web of alliances being partly driven by promises of territorial gains. For instance, Italy joined the Allies after being promised territories in the Treaty of London (1915).

And in World War II (1939–1945), with a death toll of between 70 to 85 million, we saw the Axis powers, particularly Germany and Japan, form alliances with countries like Italy and Hungary, promising them territorial expansion and resources from conquered lands. Similarly, the Allies promised post-war reconstruction and territorial integrity to nations like Poland and Czechoslovakia.

Not forgetting that in this modern day with regards to the Israel Palestine conflict and a peace plan we have Trump's quid pro quo arrangement with Israel's Benjamin Netanyahu, which sees the United States supporting Israel's military objectives, and in return Netanyahu supporting Trump's "grand plan" to remove the remaining residents of Gaza to another country, and to turn a destroyed Gaza into a Trump Gaza Plaza, a new Riviera of the East, which would include Trump Beaches, Trump Casinos, Trump Marketplaces, and Trump Hotels, such is the megalomaniacal madness of the man.

In commerce and industry, the quid pro quo effect is prevalent. It is the foundation of contractual agreements where businesses exchange goods and services for payment. In the corporate world, it can manifest in partnerships, mergers, and acquisitions, where companies trade resources, technology, or market access. The tech industry, in particular, has seen a rapid growth of quid pro quo arrangements, especially in data sharing and collaborative innovation.

The tech industry is a notable area where the quid pro quo effect is growing. Companies often engage in data exchanges, where user information is traded for access to services or technological advancements. Companies donate vast amounts of money to various political organizations in return for regulatory support for their organization or industry. This raises questions about privacy and the ethical implications of such exchanges.

Critics argue that the quid pro quo effect can sometimes resemble bribery, where the exchange is not transparent or equitable, leading to a moral decline in institutions. When used to mask unethical practices, it undermines trust and integrity in both religious and political spheres.

Whilst the quid pro quo effect is a fundamental aspect of human interaction, with both positive and negative implications, and as such it facilitates cooperation and mutual benefit, it also poses ethical challenges, particularly when it blurs the line between legitimate exchange and corruption. As society evolves, it is crucial to maintain transparency and ethical standards to ensure that quid pro quo arrangements serve the greater good rather than individual interests.

Trump's 2017 Tax Cuts and Jobs Act is a prime example of this relationship in action. Framed as a boon for the middle class, the bill overwhelmingly benefited the wealthiest American corporations and their owners. Trump's rhetoric emphasized job creation and economic growth, but in reality, it allowed the oligarchy to hoard wealth at unprecedented levels.

By drinking from the chalice of tax cuts and deregulation, they ensured a windfall of capital, while workers saw stagnant wages and rising economic precarity. For as enticing as the "golden chalice of deregulation and tax cuts" may be for the rich, its delivery is not without its dangers. The short-term gains for the oligarchy can come at the expense of long-term economic, environmental, and societal stability.

Deregulation legislated in his first presidency allowed corporate monopolies to grow unchecked, stifling innovation and creating systemic vulnerabilities. Moreover, the oligarchs uncritical support of Trump, aligned them with his divisive and anti-democratic tendencies. By prioritising profit over principle, they tacitly endorsed his attacks on institutions, the rule of law, and the democratic process. While their business and as such personal fortunes soared, the foundations of the nation cracked under the weight of political polarisation and social unrest.

Drinking from the golden chalice of deregulation may offer Americans oligarchs a fleeting sense of invincibility, but it comes with a bitter after taste. Donald Trump's presidency was a moment of triumph for the wealthy elite, a chance to shape the country in their image.

Yet, in their underlying pursuit of profits, they fail to recognise the brutal consequences of their actions. The metaphor of the golden chalice is to remind us that the lure of gold blinds those who hold it to the moral responsibility each and every oligarch owes to society.

THE SILICON VALLEY OLIGARCHY.

MUSK, THIEL, AND OTHERS: THE PAYPAL MAFIA CONNECTION. AN OLIGARCHAL QUID PRO QUO ALLIANCE OF GREED AND IDEOLOGY.

The PayPal Mafia refers to a group of former PayPal employees and founders who went on to become highly influential figures in the tech industry after eBay acquired PayPal in 2002. Many of them became successful entrepreneurs, venture capitalists, and industry leaders, shaping Silicon Valley's landscape over the following decades.

The group was dubbed the "PayPal Mafia" because of their tight-knit network, ability to support each other in business, and their dominant role in tech startups, plus, a Fortune magazine photo shoot once depicted them dressed as mobsters, further cementing the nickname.

Two of the key members of the PayPal Mafia were Elon Musk and Peter Thiel. Musk was the co-founder of X.com (not Twitter X), which later became PayPal. He then went on to found Tesla, SpaceX, Neuralink, and The Boring Company. Peter Thiel, also a co-founder of PayPal, co-founded Palantir and became an early investor in Facebook. Thiel funded Vance's political entry and also Vance's first business venture.

Others included Reid Hoffman, an early PayPal executive who co-founded LinkedIn, Max Levchin, a co-founder of PayPal, who went on to found Affirm and was involved with Slide and Yelp, David Sacks, the former COO of PayPal who co-founded Yammer, which was sold to Microsoft, and Roelof Botha, the former CFO of PayPal; who became a prominent partner at Sequoia Capital

As well as Keith Rabois, an early PayPal executive who became a venture capitalist and was involved with Square, OpenDoor, and Founders Fund, Luke Nosek a co-founder of PayPal who became a partner at Founders Fund, Russel Simmons who co-founded Yelp, and notably Chad Hurley, Steve Chen, and Jawed Karim, who left PayPal to co-found YouTube.

The PayPal Mafia is notable for its deep connections in Silicon Valley and its influence on the modern tech world. Many of these figures have funded or built some of the most important companies in the past two decades, from social media (Facebook, LinkedIn, YouTube) to AI and fintech (OpenAI, Affirm, Palantir), and the PayPal Mafia is a perfect example of oligarchy and political influence.

While they began as a group of tech entrepreneurs revolutionizing online payments, many of them went on to wield enormous economic and political power, shaping Silicon Valley, venture capital, and even national governance. Their rise embodies the transformation of tech billionaires into oligarchs, blending financial power (gold) with governmental influence (governance).

Unlike traditional oligarchs who emerged from industry (Rockefellers, Carnegies) or finance (Rothschilds, Kochs), the PayPal Mafia came from technology, positioning themselves as "disruptors." However, their disruption ultimately centralized power into a new elite class rather than democratizing it. Their companies Facebook, LinkedIn, YouTube, Palantir, Tesla, and SpaceX control vast swaths of the internet, surveillance, and even defence contracts.

Peter Thiel, perhaps the most openly political of the group, has been a major funding force behind right-wing populism and techno-authoritarianism. He backed Trump in 2016 and has financially supported candidates pushing for "national conservatism." His company Palantir has deep ties to government surveillance, providing data analysis for various intelligence agencies. (CIA, NSA, ICE).

Thiel has openly questioned democracy, once saying, "I no longer believe that freedom and democracy are compatible." He also funds secessionist and radical futurist movements, including transhumanist initiatives and breakaway tech enclaves like Seasteading. Thiel's vision represents a fusion of billionaire libertarianism and authoritarianism, rule by an elite technocratic class that controls both economic and state power.

Musk on the other hand is often portrayed as a tech genius disrupting industries, he has also become one of the most politically influential oligarchs. Musk's intentional purchase of Twitter allowed him to control a key platform of discourse, reshaping narratives on free speech, media bias, and political influence. His dominance in aerospace (SpaceX) and AI (xAI) gives him leverage over national security, space militarization, and AI governance.

Like Thiel, Musk has amplified conservative and anti-establishment messaging, aligning himself with the populist right. His transformation from entrepreneur to political kingmaker, has seen him inserting himself into governance structures, not as an elected leader, but as an oligarchical overlord shaping the political policy landscape of a second Trump presidency.

Companies like PayPal and Affirm pioneered online financial transactions, but they've also wielded censorship power, e.g., freezing accounts for political reasons. This foreshadows how private companies, not governments, increasingly dictate financial access.

Thiel (Facebook), Rabois (LinkedIn), and Hurley/Karim/Chen (YouTube) helped build the platforms that control public discourse. Their early investments in AI and surveillance tools show how tech oligarchs are centralizing control over thought and finance. The PayPal Mafia essentially privatized critical public functions, banking, surveillance, media, and political discourse.

In many ways, the PayPal Mafia represents a new form of feudalism. Instead of kings and barons, we have tech oligarchs who control the economy, information, and political discourse. Their alliances with governments (Palantir-NSA, SpaceX-

Pentagon, Twitter-politics) blur the line between private enterprise and state power, forming a new aristocracy.

The Musk Trump Oligarchal Connection, An Alliance of Governance and Greed.

The most dominant oligarchal figure to help get Donald Trump elected at the 2024 election and the one who gave the greatest financial and social media help to the Trump election campaign when Trump's finances were falling due to his massive legal bills was Elon Musk.

One could reasonably suggest that Elon Musk's acquisition of Twitter in October 2022, a purchase which sparked widespread debate about the moral and political implications of such concentrated control over a major social media platform, was more of a strategic move than a financial move. Twitter (X) was a digital media force in social dialogue, that could be used advantageously in political campaigning.

As a powerful figure with significant influence, Musk's ownership raises questions about the balance between free speech and censorship, the promotion of personal policy agendas, and the broader impact on individuals and society.

Elon Musk is known for his ambitious vision and policy agendas, particularly in areas such as renewable energy, space exploration, and artificial intelligence. His ownership of Twitter provides a powerful platform to promote these agendas, potentially influencing public opinion and policy decisions. While this can be seen as an opportunity to advance important causes, it also raises ethical concerns about the concentration of influence.

The ability to shape narratives and sway public discourse through a platform as influential as Twitter (X) can lead to an imbalance in the marketplace of ideas. Musk's personal interests may overshadow other important issues, skewing public attention and resources. This concentration of power in the hands of a single individual challenges democratic principles, where diverse voices and perspectives should ideally contribute to policy development and societal progress.

The implications of Musk's ownership extend beyond political and ethical considerations to affect individuals and society at large. For users, changes in Twitter's policies and algorithms can alter their online experience, affecting how they access information and interact with others. This can have broader societal impacts, influencing public opinion, electoral outcomes, and even social movements.

Moreover, the role of super PACs (Political Action Committees) which Elon Musk oversees, cannot be overlooked. These organizations, which can raise unlimited sums of money from individuals, corporations, and unions, played a pivotal role in amplifying Trump's message.

In his first bid for the presidency, the support from these entities allowed Trump to compete effectively against the well-funded campaign of Hillary Clinton, the Democratic nominee. The oligarchs' financial contributions helped to create a robust media presence and grassroots mobilization that were essential to Trump's electoral success. And of course in his second campaign it was all about Musk's $277 million donation to Trump.

Both times the support of the American oligarchy for Trump was not merely an act of political patronage; it was a strategic investment that yielded significant returns. In 2016 once in office, Trump implemented a series of policies that aligned closely with the interests of his wealthy backers. It is speculated that this is Musk's primary purpose in supporting Trump, to get greater deregulation that suits his business interests and even greater exposure to lucrative government defence contracts.

One of the most notorious but nevertheless notable achievements of the Trump administration was the passage of the Tax Cuts and Jobs Act in 2017. This legislation significantly reduced the corporate tax rate from 35% to 21%, benefiting large corporations and wealthy individuals. Many oligarchs and business leaders saw their tax burdens decrease substantially, leading to increased profits and wealth accumulation.

The tax cuts were framed as a means to stimulate economic growth, but the primary beneficiaries were often those at the top of the economic ladder. Additionally, Trump's deregulatory agenda appealed to many oligarchs who sought to minimize government oversight and intervention in their businesses.

The administration rolled back numerous regulations across various sectors, including environmental protections and financial regulations. This deregulation not only facilitated greater profit margins for corporations, but also aligned with the interests of oligarchs who preferred a less restrictive business environment. This same agenda is now re-surfacing in his 2025 governance.

Furthermore, Trump's foreign policy decisions, such as withdrawing from the Paris Agreement and renegotiating trade deals, were often viewed favourably by business leaders who prioritized short-term economic gains over long-term global cooperation. The emphasis on "America First" resonated with many oligarchs who sought to protect their domestic interests, even at the expense of international alliances.

The election of Donald Trump in 2016 was significantly influenced by the support of the American oligarchy, which recognized an opportunity to advance its interests through his candidacy. The financial backing and strategic alliances formed during the campaign laid the groundwork for a presidency that ultimately benefited these powerful individuals and corporations.

Through tax cuts, deregulation, and a foreign policy focused on national interests, the oligarchs reaped substantial rewards from their investment in Trump's political ascent. This dynamic underscores the intricate relationship between wealth, power, and politics in the United States, raising important questions about the future of democracy and the influence of money in shaping political outcomes.

The oligarchal support of Trump during his two presidential campaigns, revealed a willingness of an elite few to sacrifice democratic principles and social cohesion for the nation, simply for their own economic gain. But as history shows, no chalice, no matter how gilded, can remain unbroken forever. The question is not whether the chalice will shatter, but when it does who will bear the cost of the spill.

One of the most notable aspects of Trump's campaign was his appeal to populist sentiments, which resonated with a significant portion of the electorate disillusioned with traditional political elites. However, this populist rhetoric was often underpinned by substantial financial backing from specific wealthy donors. Figures such as Robert Mercer, a hedge fund magnate, and his daughter Rebekah Mercer were instrumental in providing financial support to Trump's campaign coffers.

The Mercers, along with other fellow oligarchs, saw in Trump a candidate who could disrupt the status quo and advance policies that aligned with their interests, in return for their financial support of his campaign. In other words, they saw that with regards to his previous business dealings, and his obvious insatiable quest for power, he was potentially corruptible.

The Musk, Thiel, Vance Connection, an Alliance of Governance, Greed, Ideology, and Political Ambition, with a Goal for a Project 2025 Trump/Vance Permanent Presidency.

Elon Musk, Peter Thiel, and J.D. Vance are connected through their shared involvement in technology, venture capitalism, and right-leaning political circles. Here's how they are linked:

As mentioned Thiel and Musk were co-founders of PayPal. Musk originally founded X.com, which later merged with Confinity, which was Thiel's company, to form PayPal. J.D. Vance in his career as a venture capitalist, joined Peter Thiel the co-founder of Palantir in his sales venture capital firm, Mithril Capital, as a principle.

Later with backing from Thiel and other investors, in 2021 Vance launched his own venture capital firm Narya Capital, based in Cincinnati Ohio. Vance also received significant financial backing from Thiel to at least $15 million supporting Vance's political ambitions, helping him win a competitive Republican primary in Ohio.

It is interesting to note that it appears both Thiel and Vance share a love of Lord of The Rings. The name of Thiel's' company Palintir comes from Tolkein's Lord of The Rings, it means "far-seeing", and Vance's company name Narya is also from Lord of the Rings, it refers to one of the Three Elven Rings of Power, specifically known as the Ring of Fire.

After PayPal's acquisition by eBay in 2002, both men Musk and Thiel, became wealthy and influential investors. While their business paths have diverged, they both hold libertarian and contrarian views on technology, free speech, and government regulations.

For a period of time Thiel has funded hard-right candidates in the conservative movement. In 2022, he funded Blake Masters, an Arizona Senate candidate. Masters, a former Thiel Capital executive, ran as a far-right candidate emphasising immigration restrictions and economic nationalism. Thiel poured at least $15 million into his campaign, however Masters lost to Democrat Mark Kelly.

He has also funded Josh Hawley for the Missouri Senate. Whilst not directly funded by Thiel at the same level he funded Vance or Masters, all these men share similar ideological views, particularly on big tech regulation and economic nationalism. Thiel's willingness to spend tens of millions of dollars on these races suggest a long-term strategy to reshape the Republican Party into a more nationalist, anti-globalist movement, that is sceptical of traditional corporate power, and interventionist foreign policy.

Peter Thiel was a vocal supporter of Trump in 2016. He donated $1.25 million to pro-Trump efforts, including a contribution to the Trump campaign and a pro-Trump super PAC. He also spoke at the Republican National Convention, endorsing Trump. Elon Musk, on the other hand, did not financially support Trump's first campaign, but did become his largest donor during Trump's second campaign.

While he later served on Trump's advisory councils during Trump's first administration, keeping well below the radar, Musk was at that time initially critical of Trump and opposed some of his policies, especially on climate change, perhaps because it interfered with his electric car venture. He ultimately resigned from Trump's advisory councils in 2017 after the U.S. withdrew from the Paris Climate Agreement.

Thiel too had some issues with Trump, and whilst he didn't change his opinion of Trump, he shifted his allegiance from Trump to Vance, perhaps one could suggest, to insulate his personal oligarchal future, eyeing Vance as a future President of the United States.

Musk also endorsed Vance for the Senate, calling him the "most sane candidate". They both oppose woke culture and government overreach, frequently criticizing elites despite being elites themselves. Vance praised Musk's Twitter takeover as a win for free speech. It was in fact not a win but a loss for free speech, giving Musk grand censorship of a great proportion of public viewpoints.

Both advocate for less government interference in innovation and economic growth. Vance, like Musk, is wary of China's influence on American manufacturing and technology. While Musk benefits from government subsidies (SpaceX, Tesla), he criticizes bureaucratic inefficiencies, similar to Thiel's anti-regulation stance.

By 2023, reports suggested that Thiel had distanced himself from Trump, presumably having watched Trump's performance in his first presidency, sighting disillusionment with the GOP's focus on cultural issues over technological and economic progress, which saw Thiel shifting his support totally to J.D. Vance.

All three Musk, Thiel, and Vance are sceptical of government intervention, particularly in business and technology. They champion populist, anti-elite rhetoric, despite being elite figures themselves. They are involved in conservative-aligned politics, with Thiel and Vance explicitly supporting Trump and Musk engaging in political discourse favouring right-leaning policies.

Vance, who was initially harshly critical of Trump, having once likened Trump to Adolf Hitler, subsequently did a complete about face and aligned himself with Trump's populist movement, securing Trump's endorsement for Vance's entry and support in the race for Vice-President, which he received, after Theil had a little whisper in Trump's ear. And as such we saw J.D. Vance, having limited political experience, but deep personal and business ties to Peter Thiel and Elon Musk, become Vice-President of the United States.

His initial criticisms of Trump highlighted genuine concerns about Trump's character and policy proposals and were not limited to personal attacks alone. He also challenged Trump's policy positions and argued that Trump's proposals ranged from immoral to absurd and deemed him unfit for the nation's highest office.

Vance likened Trump's appeal to voters to "cultural heroin" 'suggesting that Trump's rhetoric provided a temporary escape without addressing underlying societal issues. By 2021, as he prepared to enter the political arena himself, Vance had a Judas Iscariot moment, and publicly apologised for his past remarks about Trump, saying, "I got it wrong."

He acknowledged his earlier remarks as misjudgements and emphasised his newfound appreciation for Trump's leadership and the movement he inspired. As the newly minted Vice-President of the United States Vance now has an open pathway to a presidency himself, much to the delight of Peter Thiel and Elon Musk. Vance is the guy they want in the Oval Office once Trump has worn out his welcome.

Vance's hypercritical backflip from a staunch critic to a key ally of Trumps reflects a broader trend in American politics, where personal, moral convictions and even religious beliefs often yield to political expediency and self-promotion.

His initial criticisms highlighted genuine concerns about Trump's character and policy proposals, however, as Vance's political ambitions grew, and perhaps with encouragement from Thiel, he re-calibrated his stance, aligning himself with Trump securing for the moment anyway his political future, but time will tell.

One could reasonably suggest that Vance was a mere back door entrance for Thiel into a present White House administration's agenda, but more importantly in a post-Trump era, a future one, perhaps even holding a similar position to the one Musk holds now with his DOGE appointment, a position of all authority but no legal responsibility.

However the Silicon Valley oligarchal influence, the techno-oligarchy of the Theil, Musk, Vance alliance was not yet complete, there was one more step to go. You see the domination of political institutions was only the beginning. True power does not merely reside in law or legislation, it thrives in narrative, in the shaping of what people believe is real, what they fear, and whom they trust. And as such who they vote for. The end goal was to get Trump and Vance into office.

The oligarchs, ever shrewd in their pursuit of total influence, turned their gaze to the Fourth Estate. Once the watchdog of democracy, the press had long been revered as the pillar that stood between power and the people. But in an age of spectacle, outrage, and algorithm, this pillar proved vulnerable, crumbling under the weight of profit motives, corporate consolidation, and the seductive pull of access journalism.

With chilling precision, the alliance moved to colonize the very mechanisms of public perception, to create a new "red pill reality." I spoke to this in Chapter 3 The Unholy Algorithms of Our New Moral Reality. Rupert Murdoch's Fox News became a prototype: not a news network, but a theatre of grievance, wrapping propaganda in the veneer of patriotism and turning truth into a casualty of the culture war.

And Mark Zuckerberg and Elon Musk seized control of the algorithmic nervous system of modern society, transforming platforms that once promised connection into echo chambers of disinformation and division.

By tweaking a line of code or elevating a certain voice, they could amplify paranoia, erase context, or rewrite reality itself. The result was a media landscape where spectacle replaced substance, where rage became currency, and where those with the most power could shape not only the story, but the storyteller.

Now we turn our focus to this silent conquest: how the institutions designed to speak truth to power were slowly rewired to whisper only its praises, and what happens to a democracy when its mirrors no longer reflect reality, but only the curated illusions of those oligarchs who bought the frame.

"When media ceases to report and begins to convert, truth becomes a casualty, and the nation loses its way. A press that serves an ideology rather than the truth is not a watchdog but a shepherd leading the public astray. Propaganda does not always come with a dictator's decree; sometimes it arrives in the guise of a trusted newsroom. A nation fed only curated truths will eventually become blind to lies".

12

The Echo Chamber of an Empire: How Oligarchs Captured the Fourth Estate and Turned It Into a Mirror.

Chapter Contents.

"In the cacophony of voices, the media must be the clarion call of truth, resonating with integrity and purpose. A responsible media is the cornerstone of a just society, where the light of truth dispels the darkness of misinformation and cluelessness. In the digital age, the media's moral responsibility is not just to inform, but to enlighten, fostering a world where knowledge and understanding triumphs over ignorance and governmental abuse".

The Term Estate.

Before the modern world fractured into networks, algorithms, and soundbites, society was shaped by a more visible architecture of power known as "estates." The term "estate" in the context of the Five Estates (or more traditionally, the Three Estates) originates from the Latin word "status", which means "condition" or "state" as in a person's legal or social standing. In medieval French, it became '*estat*', and then "*estate*" in English, carrying the meaning of a distinct class or order in society.

An estate is a broad social category or division of people based on their role in society, function, or legal privileges and obligations. These were not merely economic classes, but were tied to ideological, legal, and even theological frameworks that justified the social order.

In essence, an estate is a structural pillar of society, grounded in a specific function, authority, and influence. The evolution from three to five estates reflects the shift from a feudal, religious order to a modern, media-driven, and information-based society.

The Estates of Power and the Collapse of the Mirror.

Once upon a time, the world was neatly divided. There were those who prayed, those who fought, and those who toiled, those three groups being subsequently named the First Estate, the Second Estate, and the Third Estate. The First Estate held the soul of the world; the Second wielded the sword; and the Third bore the weight of them both. For centuries, this triptych of power, these three distinct sections governed the "moral, martial, and material realities of humankind".

But time, like empire, does not stand still. The printing press cracked the priest's monopoly on truth. Revolution unseated the nobility. The labouring masses rose, only to be consumed by machines and markets. And as new forms of power emerged, so too did new "Estates", new pillars holding up the façade of freedom, namely the Fourth and Fifth Estates.

The Fourth Estate, the Press, was once imagined as the people's last defence. It was not meant to rule, but to reveal. It stood apart, a mirror held up to power, meant to reflect the truth, unflinching, unowned, unsilenced. But the mirror has cracked. In our time, the Fourth Estate has become less a reflection than a refraction, a warped funhouse of headlines and hidden hands.

The press, once the guardian of public truth, now too often serves private empires. In boardrooms, not newsrooms, the stories are shaped. Billionaires, such as the likes of Rupert Murdoch, do not need to storm the gates when they can simply buy the castle. Today's oligarch does not need to censor the press, only to fund it. A captured media does not silence dissent; it floods it, fragments it, buries it beneath opinion, outrage, and endless scroll.

The Fifth Estate, born from the code and chaos of the digital age, tried to break the mirror, to scatter truth across a thousand screens. But with no guardrails and no gatekeepers came no guarantees. The democratization of speech unleashed a cacophony, where everyone speaks, and no one hears. In the static, the oligarch smiles. And so we enter the "Echo Chamber of an Empire", where the Fourth Estate no longer watches power, but wears its face.

Where journalism has been transformed from the watchdog of democracy into a hall of mirrors curated by those it was meant to expose. And where the truth, like power itself, has been privatized.

THE FIVE ESTATES EXPLAINED.

It began with three. In the medieval order, power was divided among Three Estates: The **First Estate, the Clergy**, held sway over the soul, the invisible kingdom of heaven. The **Second Estate, the Nobility**, wielded the sword and crown, protectors, rulers, enforcers of law and privilege. The **Third Estate, the Commoners** as they were known, toiled under the weight of both; these were the labouring mass upon which the first two stood. They had little voice, but they bore the body of the realm.

This hierarchy collapsed, or rather, exploded with the French Revolution, as the Third Estate rose, and the idea of "popular sovereignty" was born. Yet the architecture of power did not disappear. It evolved. As democracy spread and literacy became widespread, a new power emerged, **"the Press"**.

The voice of the people found amplification not in pulpits or thrones, but in printing presses and editorial rooms. This became known as the **Fourth Estate**, a term coined in the 18th century to describe journalism's role as watchdog, counterbalance, and chronicler of power. But power structures don't stop evolving.

In the digital age, a **Fifth Estate** has emerged, less centralized, more chaotic. It is the domain of hackers, bloggers, influencers, and whistleblowers. It operates outside traditional institutions, often in opposition to them. It spreads truth and lies at speeds unimaginable to the past scribes of the Fourth Estate.

To understand the current unravelling of trust, governance, and truth itself, witnessed in the chaotic events that have materialised since Donald Trump ascended the throne in the Oval Office for the second time, we must begin with the rise, and the **"hollowing of the Fourth Estate".** For when journalism falters, democracy staggers. And when it is captured, the people are left with shadows on the wall and no candle to hold.

THE FOURTH ESTATE.

PRACTICES, MODELS, AND TECHNOLOGIES AS GUARDIANS OF DEMOCRACY.

In democratic societies, the architecture of governance is traditionally composed of three primary branches: the executive, the legislative, and the judiciary. Yet, history has taught us that these institutional powers, while designed to provide checks and balances upon one another, are not immune to corruption, capture, or collusion.

Into this dynamic steps the Fourth Estate, a term historically used to describe the free press, but whose modern meaning encompasses a broader set of practices, organizing models, and technologies dedicated to holding power to account. The Fourth Estate is not merely a profession or an industry, it is an evolving institutional force with a democratic mandate rooted in transparency, accountability, and the public interest.

THE PRACTICE OF JOURNALISM AS DEMOCRATIC INFRASTRUCTURE.

At its core, the Fourth Estate is defined by journalistic practices that prioritize investigation, verification, storytelling, and the amplification of voices otherwise excluded from official channels of power. Investigative reporting, in particular, serves as a watchdog over public and private institutions. From exposing political scandals like Watergate, to unearthing global networks of corruption in the Panama and Pandora Papers, investigative journalism has functioned as a de facto check on abuses of power.

The ethical principles underlying these practices, accuracy, fairness, and independence, create a civic scaffolding through which citizens are informed about the conduct of their government. Journalism also plays a pivotal role in constructing public memory: the practice of chronicling events shapes how societies remember their past and orient toward their future. When these practices are allowed to flourish, the Fourth Estate becomes a bulwark against authoritarian drift.

Historically, the Fourth Estate operated through centralized institutions: the newspaper, the radio station, the broadcast network. These models carried a degree of stability and institutional authority, but also left journalism vulnerable to monopolization and corporate influence. In the 21st century, the digital revolution has decentralized the organizing model of the press, allowing for new modes of journalism to emerge.

Today's Fourth Estate includes legacy institutions like The New York Times and the BBC, but also digital-first outlets like ProPublica, The Intercept, and Bellingcat, as well as grassroots platforms and independent media collectives. These models reflect an increasingly networked ecology of journalism, where collaborative reporting across borders and platforms is both necessary and common.

Nonprofit models have also gained traction, removing the profit motive from investigative journalism and restoring the mission of serving the public good. Crowd funded journalism, foundation-supported reporting, and reader-sustained platforms demonstrate a growing recognition that journalism must be structurally independent from both state control and market imperatives if it is to serve its democratic function.

Technologies of the Fourth Estate: Surveillance and Counter-Surveillance.

Just as state and corporate actors have adopted increasingly sophisticated surveillance tools, the technologies of the Fourth Estate have evolved in response.

Journalists now use encryption software, anonymized digital drop boxes, and blockchain authentication to protect sources and verify materials. Secure communication technologies like Signal and Tor are not only tools of the trade, but they are also lifelines in environments where press freedom is under siege.

Moreover, data journalism and open-source intelligence (OSINT) have expanded the investigative capacities of journalists. Organizations like Bellingcat have demonstrated that publicly available data, satellite imagery, metadata, and social media posts can be used to hold military powers, authoritarian regimes, and corporations accountable. These technological advancements reinforce the Fourth Estate's ability to conduct independent verification and resist information warfare.

The press is also now engaged in an epistemological struggle: combating disinformation, deepfakes, and algorithmic bias requires the development of new tools for digital forensics and fact-checking. In this new media terrain, technologies are not neutral, they are battlegrounds in the contest between democratic accountability and autocratic control.

To function as a genuine check on power, the Fourth Estate must be seen not merely as a commercial entity or professional guild, but as a civic institution, one that serves the public rather than panders to consumer demographics or partisan audiences. This requires public investment in press freedom and media literacy, as well as the legal protections necessary to shield journalists from repression and retribution.

Whistleblower protections, shield laws, and access to public records are all necessary conditions for the press to perform its role. But equally important is the cultural infrastructure that values truth-seeking, investigative rigor, and journalistic courage. In societies where the Fourth Estate is strong, journalism is not an enemy of the people but a conduit through which the people hold the powerful to account.

In an age of disinformation, autocratic resurgence, and deepening political polarization, the role of the Fourth Estate is more vital than ever. It is a living institution composed not just of newsrooms and reporters, but of practices rooted in ethics, organizing models designed for resilience, and technologies forged in the crucible of modern surveillance and digital warfare. At its best, the Fourth Estate is not a passive observer of power, but a form of power itself, public power, held in trust for the people.

To protect and strengthen the Fourth Estate is not merely to defend journalists, it is to defend democracy itself. In theory, the Fourth Estate functions as a critical watchdog over the other three branches of government, serving as a conduit for truth, a defender of transparency, and an institutional force that keeps democratic governance accountable to the public. In practice, however, the terrain of information has become a battlefield, where truth is contested, trust is eroded, and propaganda is packaged in the aesthetic of journalism.

As traditional models of the Fourth Estate struggle to sustain themselves in an era of algorithmic media, they face a growing onslaught from entities that mimic the language and form of journalism while abandoning its core democratic purpose. Fox News, hyper-partisan digital outlets, and influential podcast personalities are among the most powerful of these forces.

At its best, the Fourth Estate is not just about disseminating news, it is a civic institution. Its legitimacy comes from the rigor of its methods (fact-checking, source verification, editorial oversight) and its commitment to the public interest. Traditional newsrooms follow ethical guidelines: separating editorial content from opinion, issuing corrections when errors occur, and resisting overt alignment with political or corporate agendas.

Public interest journalism functions as a kind of democratic immune system. Investigative reports uncover abuses of power, expose corruption, and elevate suppressed voices. Its purpose is not to comfort its audience but to challenge it, to inform citizens in ways that enable thoughtful civic participation. Its organizing models, whether corporate or nonprofit, are (ideally) structured around values of independence and accountability.

By contrast, propaganda-based media, whether in the form of cable news echo chambers or viral podcast empires, operate on a fundamentally different logic. Their primary loyalty is not to truth, but to narrative. These outlets often frame reality not through verification but through ideological storytelling, prepackaged for outrage and emotional reward.

Fox News offers a prime example. While it presents itself as a journalistic outlet, its internal memos, editorial choices, and host commentaries reveal an allegiance not to the Fourth Estate tradition but to partisan power. From its role in amplifying false claims about election fraud to its function as an informal PR arm of political figures, such as Donald Trump, Fox News has operated as a propaganda machine cloaked in the aesthetics of journalism.

Its power lies not in uncovering the truth but in constructing a "red pill Matrix type reality" that keeps its audience loyal, enraged, and politically mobilized. Similarly, a new wave of digital commentators, often described as "alternative media", has emerged on platforms like YouTube, Rumble, and Spotify.

Many of these figures reject mainstream journalism as "elitist" or "corporate," but what they offer in its place is not evidence-based reporting; it is performance, grievance, and ideology. They blend conspiracy theories with kernels of truth, cater to algorithmic incentives, and build monetized brands on distrust. The message is less "here is what is happening" and more "they are lying to you, and we are the only ones who will tell you the truth."

The Fourth Estate is a system of checks and balances; its credibility comes from transparency, methodology, and editorial discipline. It is not built on personal loyalty, but on institutional trust. A newspaper or broadcaster might survive even if a particular journalist fails or a scandal erupts, because the institution, ideally, holds itself to standards beyond any single figure.

In contrast, propaganda media is often personality-driven. Loyalty is not to the truth, or to institutional norms, but to the figurehead, whether it's a prime-time Fox News host such as Sean Hannity or Tucker Carlson, or a podcast influencer. These media ecosystems resemble cults of personality more than democratic institutions.

And because they often reject editorial oversight, fact-checking, or professional ethics, they are able to move faster, take more risks, and adapt more fluidly to audience demands. What they trade for speed and loyalty, however, is epistemological integrity.

Fox News and the Machinery of the Big Lie.

If the Fourth Estate is meant to be a pillar of democracy, then its collapse can be measured in the tremors of complicity. Few institutions better exemplify this fall than Fox News, whose transformation from a news outlet into a propaganda engine reveals the dangerous convergence of power, profit, and political deception.

At the centre of it all stands Rupert Murdoch, the media mogul whose empire spans continents and whose influence warps the boundaries between journalism and ideological warfare.

Murdoch did not merely report the news, he reshaped it, moulding narratives to serve his interests and those of the political movements he cultivated. His media holdings became echo chambers, rallying cries, and shields for the powerful. Nowhere was this clearer than in the months following the 2020 U.S. presidential election.

As Donald Trump lost the popular and electoral vote, a lie was born. The Big Lie, the baseless claim that the election was stolen, was not the spontaneous cry of a delusional leader. It was a calculated fabrication, sustained and legitimized by a media ecosystem that knew better.

Fox News executives and anchors, as internal messages would later reveal, knew Trump's claims were false. They admitted as much in private. And yet, they gave airtime to conspiracy theorists, aired baseless accusations, and fanned the flames of doubt. Why? To preserve their ratings. To keep their audience. To protect the brand. This wasn't journalism, it was cowardice in pursuit of capital.

The consequences were historic. The Big Lie metastasized into violence. It laid the groundwork for the January 6th insurrection. It undermined faith in democratic institutions and gave rise to a permanent, radicalized segment of the electorate who live in an alternate reality, one built not by ideology alone, but by media malpractice.

Fox News would later settle a defamation lawsuit for nearly $800 million with Dominion Voting Systems. A staggering sum, yet still less than the cost of truth. For once the public trust is broken, no payout can restore it. Murdoch, like so many oligarchs cloaked in media power, escaped relatively unscathed. He offered no genuine contrition. His legacy remains intact among those who see the world not as it is, but as it is narrated to them, hour by hour, screen by screen, rage by rage.

This is not just a story about Fox News. It is about the weaponization of the Fourth Estate. It is about the commodification of outrage, the monetization of lies, and the quiet death of accountability. When a press empire chooses profit over principle, the people are not informed. They are conditioned.

The Murdoch model proved something devastating: that truth is no longer a prerequisite for media power. It simply needs to be profitable, polarizing, and persistent. Others have picked up the blueprint, and in the digital age, they've made it faster, bolder, and more dangerous. At the centre of this next phase stands Tucker Carlson, Murdoch's most successful weapon until he became too volatile even for Fox News.

Carlson mastered the dark art of rhetorical laundering: taking white nationalist talking points, conspiracy theories, and anti-democratic propaganda and repackaging them in primetime with a polished smirk and a patriotic frame. He didn't just report. He performed grievance, nightly monologues designed not to inform but to enrage, to isolate, and to create an alternate moral universe in which the enemy was always the other: the immigrant, the progressive, the globalist, the truth-teller.

When he was finally ousted from Fox News, it was not because he lied, it was because he became a liability. And like all ideologues unbound by institutional limits, Carlson found his next stage, Twitter, soon to be renamed X, under the ownership of Elon Musk. Under Musk, Twitter didn't just become a platform for "free speech,": it became a tool of strategic narrative warfare.

When Musk released the so-called Twitter Files, a series of cherry-picked internal emails intended to expose "deep state censorship," he did so not in the interest of journalistic transparency, but to weaponize suspicion and delegitimize prior leadership.

The Twitter Files refer to a series of internal documents and communications from Twitter that were released to the public starting in December 2022. These files were shared with a few selected journalists, most notably Matt Taibbi and Bari Weiss, who published their findings on social media.

The files suggested that pre-Musk Twitter had engaged in censorship practices, particularly around political events such as the 2020 U.S. presidential election and the Hunter Biden laptop story. It highlighted discussions about blocking certain narratives or suppressing content that was deemed problematic or controversial, often based on pressure from political figures or government agencies.

There were also reports suggesting that Twitter had been working with various government entities, including the FBI and DHS, to monitor and sometimes suppress certain content. Critics of the Twitter Files have argued that this could have violated principles of free speech and raised questions about the power of tech companies to influence public discourse.

The release also emphasized claims of bias in Twitter's content moderation policies, particularly allegations that conservative voices and perspectives were disproportionately targeted for suspension or shadow banning, with some suggesting a left-leaning bias in the platform's decision-making process.

Musk's acquisition of Twitter marked something profound: the merger of platform and propaganda, a new fusion of tech oligarchy and information control. Like Murdoch before him, Musk presents himself as a populist outsider even as he consolidates unprecedented power over public discourse.

But unlike Murdoch, Musk is not merely a media baron, he is also a defence contractor, a transportation czar, and a spacefaring monopolist. He does not just shape opinion; he builds the infrastructure of the future and positions himself as its gatekeeper. In his hands, media becomes not just a fourth estate, but a "tool of techno-authoritarianism".

By controlling the flow of information, Musk does not need to silence everyone. He simply tilts the algorithmic terrain, amplifying voices that serve his worldview, shadow-banning those that challenge it, and framing himself as the ultimate arbiter of truth.

Where Murdoch corrupted the Fourth Estate, Musk now threatens to absorb the Fifth, the last realm of decentralized speech into his empire. The result is a media environment where dissent is either co-opted or buried, and where truth must now shout to be heard over the thunder of wealth and machines.

Global Narratives, Algorithmically Tilted.

When Elon Musk took control of Twitter, renamed it X, rebranded "trust and safety" as "censorship," and gutted moderation teams worldwide, he didn't just change a company. He changed the vector of global narrative control. What was once a decentralized public square became an engine of algorithmic distortion. Across the globe, authoritarian regimes watched and learned: misinformation now had the blessing of chaos, and chaos had a new benefactor.

In the case of Ukraine, Russian propaganda suddenly found more traction. Verified Ukrainian officials were stripped of blue checks while Kremlin mouthpieces regained them. Disinformation about war crimes, refugee crises, and Western involvement surged, often unchallenged, often amplified. Musk's own tweets undermined the Ukrainian cause, suggesting "peace deals" eerily aligned with Putin's strategic goals.

In Gaza, the chaos deepened. On-the-ground journalists were drowned out by viral lies, deepfakes, and outrage loops. The human toll of war became a backdrop for digital clout-chasing, as Musk's changes to the platform rewarded engagement over accuracy, virality over verification.

X became a new kind of battlefield: one where information, identity, and empathy were weaponized. Musk had not created this dynamic, but he accelerated it, enabled it, and removed the last institutional guardrails against it. This is what happens when one man with opaque motives and unaccountable power becomes the de facto editor-in-chief of global discourse?

You see democracy requires more than votes. It requires a shared space where people can see the same world, even if they disagree on what to do about it. This was once the dream of the Fourth Estate, to act as a public square, a town hall, a mirror to the moment. Even flawed, it was something. You could open a newspaper and know your neighbour was reading the same headlines. You could watch a debate and know the facts, at least, were common ground.

But in our current era, that commonality has been shattered. Fragmented by algorithmic feeds, polluted by monetized rage, and colonized by corporate interests, our media ecosystem no longer informs, it isolates. We are not debating different ideas, we are living in different realities.

This is not just a crisis of information. It is a crisis of democratic coherence. Without a shared foundation of truth, there can be no meaningful debate, no compromise, no accountability. Only friction. Only spectacle. Only collapse. Musk's control of X is not the cause of this collapse, but it is the symbol of its final stage: when the public square becomes a personal brand, when the town crier is also the king, and when truth is whatever the algorithm rewards.

The Dangerous Convergence: News as Entertainment, Politics as Identity.

One of the most insidious dynamics at play is the merging of news and entertainment. The Fourth Estate historically drew a line between the two, informing was not the same as amusing. But the propaganda model collapses that distinction. When news becomes identity-driven entertainment, the goal is not to engage citizens but to inflame consumers. Viewers become fans. Stories become weapons. The very idea of shared truth erodes.

As this model spreads, the Fourth Estate is not just under political pressure, it is under existential threat. When large portions of the population believe that every media outlet is "biased" or "fake," then no institution can serve as a neutral reference point for democratic debate. The erosion of media trust is not just a crisis for journalism, it is a crisis for democracy itself.

To resist this descent into post-truth media warfare, we must reinvest in the principles and practices of the Fourth Estate. This means supporting nonprofit journalism, demanding platform accountability, funding local newsrooms, and cultivating media literacy across all age groups. It also means confronting the incentives, both economic and psychological, that fuel propaganda media.

Most importantly, we must reaffirm that journalism is not just a profession. It is a public good. And like clean water or free elections, it must be protected from those who would pollute or exploit it.

The Fourth Estate and propaganda media are not simply competing narratives, they are competing visions of what truth is, who can be trusted, and how democracy functions. One is rooted in public accountability, the other in private manipulation. One seeks to inform; the other seeks to inflame. As we stand on the precipice of deepening political polarization and technological manipulation, the future of the Fourth Estate may well determine the future of democracy itself.

THE HOLLOWING OUT OF THE FOURTH ESTATE, TRUTH ON TRIAL.

There is a quiet kind of surrender that destroys nations: not the gunshot or the coup, but the shrug. The refusal to ask questions. The wilful silence in the face of creeping lies. The soft erosion of vigilance dressed up as civility. This is where power slips through the cracks, not with thunder, but with apathy.

The Fourth Estate was never meant to be neutral. It was meant to be watchful. A check on power. A witness to abuse. A mirror to society's contradictions and a voice for those written out of the official story. At its best, journalism is a light in the cave, a flickering but defiant resistance to the shadows cast by the powerful. But what happens when that light is dimmed? Or worse still, bought?

As media conglomerates consolidated and advertising dollars flowed to algorithms, the soul of the Fourth Estate began to hollow. Truth gave way to ratings. Investigation yielded to access. Newsrooms shrank. Sensationalism rose. And slowly, the press, the great mediator between power and the people, began to serve the former while placating the latter.

We find ourselves now in an age of fractured realities. Cable news peddles outrage. Social media floods the zone with noise. Billionaire oligarchs buy platforms and newspapers like chess pieces. What was once the estate that informed democracy now teeters on becoming an instrument of oligarchy.

The philosopher's question becomes urgent again: What is truth? In a world of curated narratives and weaponized doubt, truth is no longer a given, it must be fought for. Silence is never neutral. To stand aside while truth is bent, erased, or sold is to become complicit in the machinery that devours it.

So we begin here, not with nostalgia for the golden age of journalism, but with an unflinching look at its capture, its failures, and its flickering hope. For if there is to be a resistance, it must begin with the reclamation of truth. Not just as fact, but as moral courage.

THE SILENT GUILLOTINE: HOW HITLER AND PUTIN DISMANTLED THE FOURTH ESTATE.

In any functioning democracy, the Fourth Estate, journalism, acts as a counterbalance to power. It is the watchdog, the mirror, the voice of dissent, and the chronicler of truth. But for autocrats and aspiring dictators, a free press is an existential threat.

History bears witness to how two of the most consequential authoritarian figures of the 20th and 21st centuries, Adolf Hitler and Vladimir Putin, methodically dismantled the Fourth Estate to centralize control and shield their regimes from scrutiny. Though separated by time, geography, and ideology, the strategies employed by both men reveal a chilling continuity in the anatomy of authoritarianism.

THE NAZI BLUEPRINT: HITLER'S ASSAULT ON TRUTH.

When Adolf Hitler rose to power in 1933, Germany still retained a vestige of press freedom inherited from the Weimar Republic. But within months, that space was suffocated. Hitler understood that controlling the narrative was not a supplement to power, it was power. He and his Propaganda Minister, Joseph Goebbels, launched a total war against independent journalism with precision and speed.

The Reichstag Fire in February 1933 gave Hitler the pretext to pass the **Reichstag Fire Decree**, which suspended civil liberties and enabled the arrest of political opponents. This decree also allowed for the closure of newspapers deemed "subversive." Soon after, the **Editor's Law of 1933** was enacted, forcing all editors to pledge allegiance to Nazi ideology and effectively outlawing dissent.

The Ministry of Public Enlightenment and Propaganda took over all forms of communication, radio, film, publishing, and newspapers. Independent newspapers were shut down or absorbed by Nazi-friendly conglomerates.

By 1939, over two-thirds of the German press was under Nazi control. Hitler's regime did not simply silence journalists; it made examples of them. Editors were jailed, exiled, or executed. The SS and Gestapo infiltrated newsrooms, ensuring self-censorship through terror. The chilling effect was total.

Through state-run newspapers like "Völkischer Beobachter" and orchestrated events like the burning of "un-German books," the regime engineered a reality where only one truth existed: the Führer's. Dissenting voices were framed as "enemies of the people", a phrase that would echo into the 21st century.

The KGB Method: Putin's Quiet Coup Against the Free Press.

Vladimir Putin, a former KGB officer, came to power in a different age, but with a similar goal: the monopolization of truth. When he assumed the presidency in 2000, Russia had a vibrant if chaotic, media landscape born from the collapse of the Soviet Union. Within two decades, that pluralism was systematically erased.

One of Putin's first moves was to wrest control of Russia's major television networks. In 2001, NTV, the last independent national broadcaster, was seized by the state-controlled gas giant Gazprom. Critical journalists were dismissed or driven into exile. Once television, the primary news source for most Russians, was under state control, other platforms followed.

Through a mix of laws on "foreign agents," defamation, and extremism, Putin criminalized independent journalism. These laws were intentionally vague, giving authorities wide discretion to target any outlet or individual critical of the Kremlin. At the same time, the state weaponized advertising markets and tax authorities to bankrupt dissenting publications.

Just as Hitler ruled through fear, Putin's regime has cultivated a climate of terror for journalists. Since 2000, dozens of Russian journalists have been killed, most infamously Anna Politkovskaya in 2006. Rarely are these crimes solved, impunity is part of the message.

In the digital age, Putin expanded the battlefield. The state created a web of troll farms, surveillance tools, and censorship mechanisms to control online narratives. Social media platforms faced pressure to localize data and remove content deemed "anti-Russian." Independent news websites like Meduza and Dozhd have been labelled "foreign agents" or blocked outright.

Though the contexts of Nazi Germany and post-Soviet Russia differ, the underlying logic of their media repression is strikingly similar. Both regimes centralized media control under a state-run or oligarchic apparatus. Both regimes used legislation as a weapon to criminalize dissent and impose self-censorship.

Both regimes relied on psychological terror, either through arrests, assassinations, or the constant threat thereof. Both regimes manufactured consent by flooding the public sphere with propaganda, often cloaked as patriotic or anti-Western sentiment.

Yet their timelines diverged. Hitler acted with blitzkrieg speed, gutting the free press within months. Putin's approach was more glacial, allowing nominal pluralism to persist while hollowing out its substance. One used brute force; the other, bureaucratic attrition. Both arrived at the same destination: a landscape where truth is malleable, facts are fungible, and power is unaccountable.

The dismantling of the Fourth Estate is not merely a symptom of dictatorship; it is the engine of it. In Hitler's Germany, the silencing of the press enabled the rise of genocidal policies without domestic resistance. In Putin's Russia, the absence of media scrutiny allowed for the invasion of Ukraine, the poisoning of opponents, and the slow death of democratic institutions. When journalists are hunted, facts disappear into shadows. Without a mirror, a nation forgets its face.

The stories of Hitler and Putin serve as cautionary tales, reminders that a free press is never guaranteed, it must be defended. Today, the tools of suppression have evolved, but the aim remains the same: to replace truth with loyalty, inquiry with obedience. In a time when authoritarianism is once again on the march, the lessons of history are not just relevant, they are urgent. Because the moment the Fourth Estate falls silent is the moment democracy begins to die.

HISTORICAL TIMELINES: STEPS TO LIMIT THE PRESS AND FREE SPEECH. HITLER (NAZI GERMANY, 1933-1945).

1. Reichstag Fire Decree (1933) Legal foundation: Suspended civil liberties, including freedom of speech, freedom of the press, and the right to assembly. Enabled mass arrests of political opponents and silencing of dissent.

2. Ministry of Public Enlightenment and Propaganda: Headed by Joseph Goebbels, it centralized control over all media: newspapers, radio, film, literature, and the arts. Ensuring all messaging conformed to Nazi ideology.

3. Censorship of Independent Press: Non-Nazi papers were either banned or absorbed into Nazi-run media groups. By 1934, nearly all independent journalism was eliminated.

4. The Editor's Law (Schriftleitergesetz, 1933): Journalists had to be racially pure and politically loyal. Editors were legally responsible for content and could be punished for publishing anything deemed anti-state or un-German.

5. Book Burnings (May 1933): Symbolic and practical repression of intellectual freedom. Targeted books by Jews, Marxists, liberals, and other "undesirables."

6. Control of Radio (Volksempfänger): Cheap "people's receivers" were mass-produced to spread Nazi propaganda. Foreign broadcasts were banned and punishable by imprisonment or death.

7. Suppression of Dissent and Fear Tactics: Gestapo and SS enforced compliance and intimidated potential dissenters. Citizens were encouraged to report each other, creating a self-censoring society.

Putin (Russia, 2000–present): Steps to Limit the Press and Free Speech.

1. Centralization of TV Media (2000's). Took over or pressured independent TV networks like NTV and ORT. State-run or loyalist-owned stations became the main source of news for most Russians.

2. Control Through Oligarchs. Media ownership was concentrated among Kremlin-friendly oligarchs (e.g., Gazprom-Media). Business pressure was used to buy out or bankrupt dissenting outlets.

3. Legal Repression of Journalists. Journalists critical of the government faced harassment, arrests, or worse. Notable deaths include Anna Politkovskaya, a journalist murdered in 2006 after reporting on Chechnya.

4. "Foreign Agent" and "Undesirable Organizations" Laws. Label NGOs and media receiving foreign funding as "foreign agents." Used to discredit and shut down independent outlets (e.g., Meduza, Dozhd TV, Novaya Gazeta).

5. Internet and Social Media Censorship. Roskomnadzor (media watchdog) blocks access to dissenting websites. Invasive data storage laws force tech platforms to cooperate with the Kremlin.

6. Fake News and Extremism Laws (2019–present). Criminalize the spread of "fake news" and "disrespect toward the authorities." Laws are vague, enabling arbitrary enforcement against critics.

7. Wartime Censorship (2022–present). After invading Ukraine, Russia criminalized calling it a "war" punishable by up to 15 years in prison. Shut down independent outlets like TV Rain and Echo of Moscow. Social media platforms like Twitter and Facebook were restricted or banned.

8. State Propaganda. Promotes nationalist, pro-Kremlin narratives. Conflates patriotism with loyalty to Putin, vilifies opposition as Western puppets.

Trump (America, 2025–present): Steps to Limit the Press and Free Speech.

Karoline Leavitt is an American political aide and government official currently serving as the White House Press Secretary in President Donald Trump's administration since January 20, 2025. During college, Leavitt interned at Fox News, Rupert Murdoch's far-right news propaganda network, and at the White House Office of Presidential Correspondence.

In early 2025, White House Press Secretary Karoline Leavitt implemented significant changes to press access protocols, leading to the exclusion of certain journalists and media organizations from presidential events. What does this indicate? It indicates that Trump is "dipping his toes in Putin's bath water." It remains to be seen how long it will be before he fully immerses himself.

A Call to Reclaim the Fourth Estate through The Fifth Estate.

In every age, when the official voices drown in compromise and fear, the whisper of conscience returns. It echoes through those who will not bow to power, who will not trade silence for safety, who carry forward the defiant flame once lit by martyrs and truth-tellers long gone.

In Nazi Germany, that whisper took form in the "White Rose", a student-led resistance group that dared to speak out against the regime. At the centre stood Sophie Scholl, barely twenty-one years old, arrested and executed for distributing leaflets in a university courtyard. She did not beg for mercy. She did not recant. She said simply: "*Such a fine, sunny day, and I have to go. But what does my death matter, if through us thousands of people are awakened and stirred to action?*"

So where do we turn? We return to what Sophie Scholl knew: that truth is not an abstraction. It is a moral choice. It must be practiced, defended, and when necessary, spoken into silence. The Fourth Estate, if it is to survive, must become more than a profession. It must reclaim its role as "a moral institution", a defiant act of public service. Journalism must once again become a form of resistance, resistance to apathy, to manipulation, to oligarchic capture.

This does not mean a return to the past. It means building something new: Something independent, transparent, accountable not to shareholders, but to truth itself. Networked but grounded, and calmly fierce in the face of power. Like Katlin Collins from CNN at a White House Press conference.

Or like the Meidas Touch Network, a American progressive media organization known for its pro-democracy journalism and political commentary, founded in March 2020 by brothers Ben, Brett, and Jordy Meiselas. Ben is a prominent attorney and law professor, Brett is an Emmy-winning video editor, and Jordy has a background in advertising. Ron Filipkowski, a former Georgia prosecutor, serves as the editor-in-chief of the network.

You see when journalism cowers, democracy dies in confusion, but when it stands, even against impossible odds, it becomes a beacon.

Let the Fourth Estate rise again, not as an empire of content, but as a cathedral of courage, a relaunching of itself as The Fifth Estate. When the Fourth Estate falters, the Fifth begins to rise. Born not of institutions but of urgency, the Fifth Estate is the domain of citizen journalists, whistleblowers, hackers, truth-tellers, and dissidents, those who do not wait for permission to speak, who expose what was meant to be hidden, who record what others are paid to forget.

It is raw, imperfect, and often chaotic. It is also essential. Where legacy media hesitates, the Fifth Estate leaps. Where official narratives are smoothed into silence, the Fifth Estate shouts. It lives not in polished studios but on the street, the livestream, the leak, the data drop, the protest chant, the encrypted file sent at great personal risk.

Its prophets are not always saints, but its existence is a moral necessity in an age where the truth has been priced out of reach. As Sophie Scholl once said: "*Stand up for what you believe in, even if you are standing alone.*" The Fifth Estate is more than a digital phenomenon. It is the heartbeat of a larger movement: the Second Resistance, a new digital and verbal counterculture movement.

Sophie Scholl did not live to see the collapse of the Reich. But her resistance was not in vain. Her words crossed time, slipped through the cracks of history, and now arrive in ours, an echo and a warning. Because once again, the veil has dropped. Once again, the machinery of control is cloaked in law, wealth, and screens. And once again, a new resistance is needed, not in the shadows, but in the light of knowing.

A new Second Resistance, not a movement bound by geography or ideology, but by moral clarity. By the refusal to accept the normalization of lies. By the courage to speak even when the crowd chants silence. By the belief, still, that one voice can matter. The Fifth Estate gives us the tools. But the Second Resistance gives us the purpose.

It is every journalist or blogger or marcher who refuses to be bought. Every whistleblower who risks exile or prison to warn the world. Every protester who stands with a cardboard sign and shaking hands. Every teacher, coder, artist, and worker who dares to speak truth in a system built on performance and pretence. They are not saints. They are not perfect. But they are awake. And if you are reading this, if you still care, still question, still burn, then you, too, are a part of it.

When Donald Trump said, "I alone can fix it," Abraham Lincoln in contrast said, "The dogmas of the quiet past are inadequate to the stormy present. We must think anew, and act anew. We must disenthrall ourselves, and then we shall save our country."

When Donald Trump said, "We're going to have to see what happens" in response to a peaceful transfer of power, Abraham Lincoln in contrast said, "Elections belong to the people. It's their decision. If they decide to turn their back on the fire and burn their behinds, then they will just have to sit on their blisters."

13

GETTYSBURG'S GRACE VERSUS TWITTER TIRADES.

THE CONTRASTING GOVERNANCE STYLES OF ABRAHAM LINCOLN AND DONALD TRUMP.

Chapter Contents.

> "When Donald Trump said, "I could stand in the middle of Fifth Avenue and shoot somebody and I wouldn't lose voters," Abraham Lincoln in contrast said, "Nearly all men can stand adversity, but if you want to test a man's character, give him power." When Donald Trump said, "I'm a very stable genius," Abraham Lincoln in contrast said, "I do not think much of a man who is not wiser today than he was yesterday. "When Donald Trump said, "The press is the enemy of the people," Abraham Lincoln in contrast said, "The liberty of the press is essential to the security of freedom."

ABRAHAM LINCOLN AND DONALD TRUMP, THE CONTRAST.

The presidency of the United States demands more than authority; it calls for vision, restraint, and moral courage. Among the long roster of American presidents, Abraham Lincoln and Donald J. Trump stand as stark opposites in nearly every aspect of governance.

One led a fractured nation through its most existential crisis with humility, grace, and a reverence for democratic values. The other presided over and continues to preside over a period of hyper-polarization, wielding power in a way that often amplified division, personalized decision-making, and dismissed ethical norms.

In comparing their approaches to leadership, not just in terms of policy outcomes, but in their governance styles, team management, ethical frameworks, and decision-making processes, we gain a revealing lens into the health and soul of democratic institutions.

Abraham Lincoln governed through reflection, deliberation, and careful coalition-building. Though presiding over a nation engulfed in civil war, he consistently prioritized "unity over ego".

His decisions, even when politically risky, such as issuing the Emancipation Proclamation, were rooted in months of contemplation and input from a diverse cabinet of advisors. His famous Team of Rivals reflected his belief that "truth and wisdom emerge from tension and debate", not from blind loyalty.

Donald Trump, by contrast, in his first presidency, exhibited a governance style driven more by instinct and impulse than deliberation. Cabinet members were often selected for their loyalty rather than expertise, and dissent was frequently punished rather than engaged. Decision-making was highly centralized around his persona, often communicated via social media before formal consultation with staff or allies.

The abrupt withdrawal from northern Syria in 2019, announced via tweet without consulting national security advisors or allies, is emblematic of a governance style that privileged personal instinct and political theatre over institutional process and consequence.

Lincoln's approach to team governance reflected humility and moral confidence. He famously surrounded himself with political rivals such as William Seward, Salmon Chase, and Edwin Stanton, all men who had competed against him for the presidency and who often clashed with each other.

Rather than being threatened by disagreement, Lincoln saw value in it. He allowed open debate within his cabinet and often sat in silence as arguments unfolded, listening deeply before offering a unifying conclusion. His goal was not to dominate his team but to "orchestrate a collective wisdom" in service of the Union.

Trump, on the other hand, in his first presidency, fostered a White House environment often defined by volatility, turnover, and fear. According to multiple former aides and officials, his decision-making processes were erratic and opaque, with staff frequently kept in the dark until the last moment. This appears to be continuing in his second presidency.

A high rate of cabinet turnover, more than in any modern presidency, meant "institutional memory" was often sacrificed for loyalty. While Trump did at times bring in divergent voices (such as General Mattis and General Kelly), these figures were often sidelined or publicly humiliated once they voiced disagreement. Team governance under Trump was not collaborative but "hierarchical and transactional", a reflection of his background as a CEO who conflated governance with brand management.

Lincoln's moral imagination was expansive. While pragmatic in many of his decisions, he always tethered his governance to the idea of "a more perfect union" and the inherent dignity of every human being.

His understanding of power was stewardship-based, not self-serving. Even amid a brutal civil war, he resisted calls for vengeance. In his Second Inaugural Address, he famously called for "malice toward none, with charity for all," underscoring a deeply ethical view of leadership rooted in humility and reconciliation.

Trump's ethical framework, in contrast, centres more on transactional loyalty, personal vindication, and media optics. Rather than seeing the presidency as a temporary stewardship of public trust, Trump appears to view it as a personal stage upon which to assert dominance and punish enemies.

His attempts to overturn the 2020 election, culminating in the January 6 Capitol insurrection, represented a profound breach of the ethical covenant between a leader and the democratic system they are meant to uphold.

His administration was plagued by ethics violations, including the misuse of public office for private gain (e.g., the use of Trump-owned properties for government business), blatant nepotism, and a persistent undermining of democratic norms. This is now happening in his second presidency with his continual use of rooms for meetings at his Mar-a-Lago residence in Florida.

You see the mark of wise decision-making is the ability to balance short-term pressures with long-term consequences, and to place the interest of the whole above personal interest. Lincoln's leadership in the midst of civil war exemplified this. He carefully timed the Emancipation Proclamation to both weaken the Confederacy and solidify moral clarity in the Union cause.

He refused to accept easy compromises that would have preserved the Union at the cost of continuing slavery. His governance reflected strategic patience, a deep understanding of public sentiment, and the long arc of justice.

Trump, conversely, often placed personal gain and short-term political advantage above the national interest. His handling of the COVID-19 pandemic was emblematic: rather than embracing science-based strategies and modelling unity, he downplayed the crisis, contradicted his health advisors, and turned mask-wearing into a partisan issue.

Decisions were routinely filtered through a political and press lens, how they would play with his base, how they would affect his image, rather than what would serve the most Americans. Wise governance requires the courage to make unpopular decisions for the greater good. Trump rarely showed such restraint.

Two Different Presidencies, Two Legacies, and the Moral Judgment of History.

Abraham Lincoln is and will continue to be remembered not just as a skilled statesman, but as a moral visionary who saved the republic by remaining deeply grounded in principle. His legacy rests not only on the decisions he made but on how he made them, with empathy, consultation, and reverence for the democratic experiment.

Donald Trump's legacy is still being contested, but early historical assessments paint a troubling picture: a president who governed once and now continues to govern with a narrow, self-referential compass, who encourages division rather than unity, and who weakens democratic institutions through lies, intimidation, and the normalization of ethical transgressions. Where Lincoln sought to stitch the country together through shared ideals, Trump often pulls at the threads of the national fabric for personal gain.

The contrast between Lincoln and Trump is ultimately a contrast between two visions of leadership: one rooted in the slow, steady cultivation of trust, wisdom, and collective purpose; the other in the rapid, chaotic pursuit of loyalty, spectacle, and dominance. In Lincoln, America saw the power of ethical, inclusive, and patient leadership.

In Trump's first presidency, America was warned of what can happen when governance is stripped of ethics and shared truth. The presidency is more than a job, it is a trust, one that reveals not only the politics of an era but the moral character of those chosen to lead. The public was warned but did not heed the warning. And so we now are witnessing what a "Trump on steroids" presidency is like.

The presidency, at its best, serves as the moral compass of the nation. Abraham Lincoln understood this. Donald Trump sees it in a radically different way. One saw leadership as a burden of humility. The other, as a platform for dominance. To compare them is to compare two visions of American power: one unifying, the other polarizing. One rooted in service, the other in spectacle.

Abraham Lincoln approached governance as a methodical craft. He took time to consider diverse opinions before acting, often rereading letters, studying law, and debating quietly within himself. He once said: "Give me six hours to chop down a tree and I will spend the first four sharpening the axe."

Even in war, Lincoln resisted rash action. He delayed the Emancipation Proclamation until it could have both maximum moral impact and strategic advantage. Donald Trump on the other hand governed and is now continuing to govern like a media mogul, fast, loud, and reactive. One only has to look at his ever-changing tariff policies. And it really isn't about the "art of the deal" as he purports it to be.

As I touched on in Chapter 7, the image of Trump as some kind of master dealmaker is purely a gigantic myth. When Trump is involved in a contest of wills, for example in his current "tariff standoff" with President Xi of China, he is not manifesting unique negotiation skills, he is simply "the little boy at the dinner table continually refusing to eat his broccoli, hoping that his mother will eventually cave to his demands".

In his first presidency Trump often bypassed formal briefings and preferred "gut feelings" over detailed analysis, simply because his ego keeps reminding him that he is the smartest person in the room. He once said, quote, "I have a gut, and my gut tells me more sometimes than anybody else's brain can ever tell me." Complex policy decisions were often announced via Twitter (X), sidelining advisors and destabilizing institutions with abrupt pivots.

Rather than fear strong voices, Lincoln on the other hand welcomed them. His Cabinet included men who had openly opposed him politically. He saw tension not as threat, but as fertile ground for wisdom. He once said, "The dogmas of the quiet past are inadequate to the stormy present…we must think anew, and act anew." Cabinet debates were robust, but Lincoln's steady hand fostered unity even among ideological rivals.

Trump's first administration was marked by record turnover, driven in part by his demand for personal loyalty over public service. He once said, "I'm the only one that matters," on the subject as to who makes foreign policy decisions. Those who challenged him, from Rex Tillerson to James Mattis, were dismissed, marginalized, or publicly ridiculed.

For Lincoln governance was all about good stewardship, for Trump governance is all about grand spectacle. Lincoln's decisions were grounded in moral clarity, even when politically dangerous. His enduring commitment to justice defined his legacy. He once said, "If slavery is not wrong, then nothing is wrong." His leadership was ethical not because it was perfect, but because it was accountable, transparent, and humble.

Trump's ethics were shaped by personal loyalty and branding. He frequently blurred the lines between public duty and private interest. He once said, "When someone attacks me, I always attack back, except 100 times more." From using Trump-owned properties for state business to attempting to overturn a lawful election, Trump pushed the ethical boundaries of the office repeatedly.

Lincoln's strategic patience allowed him to balance public sentiment with moral purpose. His leadership during the Civil War, never impulsive, was always tethered to the broader vision of a united and just America. "The occasion is piled high with difficulty, and we must rise with the occasion", he once said in discussing the war, and even at the war's end, he chose reconciliation over revenge and retribution, he chose grace over grievance.

Even in victory, Lincoln sought to bind wounds and restore the American spirit. He said in reference to his post-war governance, "With malice toward none; with charity for all… to do all which may achieve and cherish a just and lasting peace among ourselves and with all nations." His legacy was not just a saved Union, but a reclaimed moral centre.

Trump's first presidency left a legacy of intensified division, weakened democratic norms, and the rise of "authoritarian flirtation". He said at his Republican National Convention, in 2016, "I alone can fix it". Rather than heal, Trump's first presidential leadership style exploited fracture. Rather than seek truth, he sowed doubt. Rather than empower, he ruled by grievance. And his second presidency is now in a far more consequential fashion doing the same.

Lincoln and Trump represent two archetypes of leadership. One views the presidency as a sacred trust, temporary, humbling, and morally bound. The other sees it as a throne to defend, a brand to protect, and a stage to dominate for as many terms as he wants.

In the long moral arc of history, the question is not just about what a president accomplishes, but how they do it, and at what moral cost. Abraham Lincoln's wisdom and ethical compass lifted a broken nation. Donald Trump's leadership in his first presidency, by contrast, strained democracy's foundations, leaving the nation more divided than he found it. And still the psychologically manipulatable many, voted him in for a second term.

THE MESSAGE AND THE MEDIUM: LINCOLN AND TRUMP IN THE ARENA OF PUBLIC RHETORIC.

In democracies, words matter. A president does not only govern by law but by language, by shaping the nation's imagination, its fears, its hopes, and its moral boundaries. Abraham Lincoln and Donald Trump each understood the power of the word, but they wielded it in radically different ways: Lincoln as a careful craftsman of national unity and moral resolve; Trump as a provocateur, performer, and disruptor. Their styles not only reflect their characters but shaped the emotional climate of the republic itself.

You see Lincoln understood the gravity of speech. His rhetoric sought to elevate, unify, and reflect timeless truths in accessible language. Whether addressing war or justice, his speeches were composed with care, delivered not to agitate but to reconcile. In his Gettysburg address he said: "A house divided against itself cannot stand. The world will little note, nor long remember what we say here, but it can never forget what we did here."

He rarely spoke spontaneously. He did not use a prompter. Lincoln's drafts reveal intense revisions, signifying that language was not just strategy but a form of spiritual labour. He was indeed the "commander in chief" in all his public and private rhetoric. Donald Trump on the other hand is "the showman in chief". His public and private rhetoric is spontaneous, combative, and performative.

Trump's communication style is inseparable from modern media culture. He breaks norms by tweeting unfiltered thoughts, using rallies as stand-up routines, and leaning into repetition, slogans, and emotional simplicity, with phrases such as, "Make America Great Again, I alone can fix it, it's a witch hunt, and it's fake news!"

He bypasses traditional press structures to speak directly to his base, often using inflammatory rhetoric to provoke reaction. Trump's communication style is not designed to unify but to divide and energize, to generate constant conflict and loyalty.

Lincoln's speeches belonged to a tradition of high republicanism, the Republican party rhetoric before MAGA took it over, where the office of the president was elevated through solemnity, reason, and universal moral appeal. Trump, in contrast, as the leader of the MAGA Republican Party lowered the rhetorical bar intentionally, leaning into spectacle and grievance to dominate the media cycle and to of course feed his own insatiable need for validation.

Where Lincoln sought to "speak for the nation's better angels", Trump often gave voice to its resentments. For Lincoln, speech was a bridge: between regions, races, and parties. For Trump, it was often a weapon, used to shame, distract, or threaten. Whilst Lincoln said, "We are not enemies, but friends. We must not be enemies," Trump said, "When the looting starts, the shooting starts." This divergence reflects not just different styles but opposing views of leadership itself: one restorative, the other performative.

Lincoln's legacy lives in the enduring power of his words, engraved in stone, taught in schools, recited at ceremonies. Trump's legacy may well reside only in the volume of his rhetoric, loud, prolific, and polarizing.

Presidents don't just guide history. They narrate it. They give language to the nation's conscience or its chaos. With Lincoln it was the former, with Trump it is the latter. Whilst Lincoln in his presidential rhetoric focused on truth, Trump in his presidential rhetoric focuses on falsity.

And no democracy can survive without a foundation of truth. The presidency, as the nation's highest office, carries the moral responsibility of speaking truthfully, even when it is uncomfortable or politically inconvenient. In the 21st century, where media ecosystems fragment reality into silos, this obligation is even more urgent.

The contrast between Abraham Lincoln and Donald Trump on truth is perhaps the starkest of all. Lincoln believed that truth was essential to governance and moral order. His honesty, even when politically difficult, earned him the enduring nickname "Honest Abe." His commitment to telling the hard truth, even when it cost him politically, was a cornerstone of his leadership.

Lincoln once said, "I am nothing, but truth is everything." Whether facing a nation divided or a battlefield in shambles, he did not sugarcoat reality. His addresses often acknowledged the pain of the moment while pointing to a higher ethical horizon.

Trump does not treat truth as sacred. Instead, he embraces a post-truth strategy: flood the zone with misinformation, discredit independent sources, and create alternative narratives to suit political needs. He said, "What you're seeing and what you're reading is not what's happening. I won the election by a lot."

As previously mentioned according to the Washington Post, Trump made over 30,000 false or misleading claims during his presidency. His ability to generate and sustain alternative realities through social media and partisan media ecosystems weakened the public's shared sense of reality. He force fed the public a "counterfeit Matrix red pill", which rather than enlightening them, enslaved them.

In "The Matrix", taking the "red pill" symbolizes awakening to "uncomfortable truths", a willingness to see through illusions, to face harsh realities, and to live authentically, no matter the cost. It is about "real enlightenment". However, in today's world, a "counterfeit red pill" has emerged: a simulacrum of awakening that actually misinforms and misleads.

Instead of offering genuine truth, it preys on people's desire for special knowledge, packaging conspiracy, resentment, and simplistic narratives as "secret wisdom." It's not about seeing reality; it's about reinforcing anger, fear, and tribal loyalty under the illusion of enlightenment. Now, consider this in light of Lincoln versus Trump rhetoric.

Lincoln's rhetoric called Americans to face hard, often painful truths, the sin of slavery, the need for unity through sacrifice, the demand for "the better angels of our nature." Like the true red pill, his words often humbled his audience, confronting them with their shared moral responsibility.

Trump's rhetoric, by contrast, mirrors the counterfeit red pill. He claims to reveal hidden truths ("the system is rigged," "they're coming for you") but often misleads, distorts, and inflames. His language feeds grievance, victimhood, and self-righteousness, offering the feeling of secret knowledge without the burden of critical self-examination or moral responsibility.

In short, Lincoln's "red pill" rhetoric revealed hard, humbling truths that aimed to elevate the nation. Trump's "red pill" rhetoric often reveals imagined or distorted enemies, aiming to divide and inflame. Thus, the true "red pill" liberates the soul toward greater responsibility and collective good, while the counterfeit red pill traps the soul in resentment and tribal delusion.

You see the "true red pill" is like stepping into the cold morning after a long dream, eyes aching, heart heavy, but finally awake. The "counterfeit red pill" is like stepping into a funhouse mirror maze, believing you've found secret passageways, but only circling endlessly in illusions crafted to flatter your fears.

Lincoln's "true red pill rhetoric" awakened people to hard reality, demanded moral responsibility, broke comforting narratives, and led to humility and unity. In contrast Trump's "counterfeit red pill rhetoric" awakens the people to flattering illusion, demands tribal loyalty, builds self-justifying myths, and leads to resentment and division.

Lincoln showed how truth can bind a fractured nation. Trump demonstrated how lies, repeated enough, can fracture it further. You see the presidency is not just a position of power, it is a position of moral influence. When that influence is used to distort truth, the consequences echo for generations. The republic can endure many crises, but not the death of shared reality. In the war for the American mind, truth must not be optional.

Every nation has a soul. It is not found in its wealth or weaponry, but in its ideals, its struggles, and the stories it tells itself about what kind of people it wants to be. And no single office reflects or shapes that soul more profoundly than the presidency of the United States of America.

The American presidency was designed not merely as an administrative role, but as a moral and symbolic one. Presidents are judged not only by what they do, but by how they make the nation feel, what they awaken in the people they govern, what they suppress, and what they leave behind in the long shadow of their leadership.

In moments of crisis, this role becomes existential. Do the leaders speak to our higher selves, or prey on our fears? Do they pursue truth, or manipulate it? Do they seek unity, or domination? In this crucible, the soul of the nation is either nourished or degraded.

If the American presidency were a TV series, Abraham Lincoln's season would be the intense, critically acclaimed drama that wins awards for its moral complexity. Donald Trump's first term? That was the surprise reality spin-off where the host of The Apprentice suddenly gets the nuclear codes. And now, in what can only be described as a glitch in the Matrix or a cosmic prank, we've entered Trump Season Two: The Re-Impeachment.

A Satirical Stroll Through Two Contrasting Presidencies.

Lincoln's presidency was the Civil War edition of "Extreme Makeover: National Identity Edition". He came into office with a country split in half, a haunted look in his eye, and a beard that said, "I read poetry at funerals."

Honest Abe took on slavery, rebellion, and a deeply divided nation, not with TikTok videos nor insult-laden pressers, nor late-night tweets, but with soul-wrenching speeches, handwritten letters, and an actual sense of guilt when suspending civil liberties.

Lincoln didn't yell. He ruminated, he read the Bible, not Infowars. His Twitter feed (had it existed) would have been 280-character elegies about the moral weight of governance, probably written in cursive, certainly not in bold caps. He ended slavery, preserved the Union, and got shot for it. He paid the ultimate price for leadership. Trump whined when a pre-Musk Twitter gave him a 12-hour timeout.

If Lincoln was America's tragic Shakespearean hero, Trump was the guy who showed up at the theatre, stole the spotlight, and demanded the actors wear red caps. Trump's first term was less "presidency" and more a "performance art piece about late-stage capitalism."

He turned the Oval Office into the world's most dramatic reality show set, complete with surprise cast firings, Twitter feuds with foreign leaders, and cabinet meetings that looked more like hostage videos.

Policies? Sure, some happened, often by accident or executive order, sometimes simply "sharpie signed without being read, between golf swings". But the real legacy of his first term was stylistic: insults as policy, scandals as entertainment, and a base so loyal they would storm a federal building dressed like Viking extras from a low-budget History Channel show. Trump in his first term governed the way a cat knocks things off a shelf, randomly, unapologetically, and mostly for attention.

Now, in a twist that feels like the world lost a bet with the universe, Trump is back, older, angrier, weirder, and somehow still convinced that the biggest threat to America isn't climate change or authoritarianism, but windmills and batteries in boats. His second term has all the subtlety of a monster truck rally and all the grace of a drunken conga line at a MAGA fundraiser at Mar-a-Lago.

The gloves are off, the ex-Project 2025 staffers are now Trump loyalists, firmly ensconced in his new administration, and the goal is clear: no more pretending this is about democracy. It's now autocracy Season1. It's about vengeance, ratings, and making sure history is rewritten with him as the misunderstood victim-genius.

Where Lincoln worried about the soul of the nation, Trump worries about his followers' loyalty on Truth Social. Where Lincoln mourned division, Trump monetizes it. Where Lincoln saved the republic, Trump seems determined to franchise it like a string of fast-food empires.

Lincoln gave the American people government for the people, Trump gives the American people government for the privileged. Lincoln led with empathy and egalitarianism, Trump leads with egregious intent and an out-of-control ego. Lincoln asked true Americans to rise up and be better angels. Trump asked the White Supremacist Proud Boys to "stand back and stand by."

When Donald Trump said, "You're fired!", turning leadership into a catchphrase, Abraham Lincoln in contrast said, "I don't like that man. I must get to know him better." When Donald Trump said, "I have absolute power, but I'm not going to use it," Abraham Lincoln in contrast said, "Any people anywhere, being inclined and having the power, have the right to rise up and shake off the existing government, such a right is a most sacred one."

From Lincoln to Trump, the evolution is staggering. America has gone from the "log cabin outhouse" to a "golden toilet" all with one stroke on the ballot. Lincoln read law books under a flickering candlelight. Trump reads his Truth Social posts under the illumination of a crystal chandelier hovering hesitantly over a Trump sized bed; while his St. Tropez Self Tan Classic Bronzing Mousse and his fairy floss hairpiece sit patiently on his bedside table waiting for the sun to rise on another day, another crypto dollar, and another crisis.

And as for Melania, the first lady, well she sleeps contentedly in a nearby bedroom, her prenup agreement tucked beneath her pillow, her constant written reassurance of a comfortable, extravagant, self-indulgent future.

THE FAULT LINE OF CONSCIENCE: FROM LINCOLN'S LIGHT TO TRUMP'S SHADOW.

SOPHIE SCHOLL: A SHINING LIGHT MIDST THE DARK SHADOW OF DESPAIR.

Leadership does not merely shape policy, it casts a moral shadow across the nation. In Abraham Lincoln, we saw a man who struggled in a nation's darkness to serve the light, whose sleepless nights were haunted not by ego, but by empathy, justice, and the fragile hope of reunion. Whose inner torment was tempered by a deep sense of duty to the Union, to justice, and to the better angels of our nature.

In Donald Trump, we witness a different portrait: governance fuelled by grievance, loyalty demanded over principle, and power wielded as personal armour rather than public trust. We see a man at ease in the theatre of conflict, one who governs not through reflection but reaction, a figure who does not wrestle with the moral weight of power but wears it like a crown made of chaos.

Each man ascended to the highest office in a moment of national fracture. Each became a mirror held to the soul of America. But the reflection each offered was strikingly different; one inviting us to rise above our worst instincts, the other inviting us to indulge them. Each man mirrored America back to itself. One reflected the enduring tension between moral aspiration and human frailty. The other, the seductive ease of abandoning that struggle altogether.

And so, as we step beyond the politics of office and the mechanics of governance, we enter a deeper terrain , not of policies, but of principles. Not of power, but of purpose. Beneath every law passed, every decree signed, every rally cry or inaugural pledge, there lies a more profound and enduring conflict: the war within the human soul.

Beyond the contrast in governance lies something more elemental, a battleground not of policy or partisanship, but of the soul. Beneath every decision made in the Oval Office, and every silence held in the hearts of citizens, runs an ancient and invisible war: the war between the Light Side and the Dark Side of the Soul.

It is a war as old as time, between the Light Side that seeks justice, empathy, and truth, and the Dark Side that seduces with fear, control, and lies. It is a war not only fought in the halls of government but in the silent chambers of every conscience. What happens to a nation when its leaders no longer wrestle with this war, but surrender to one side without question? And what happens to we, the people, when we cease to recognize the struggle within ourselves?

This war, Sophie Scholl understood with devastating clarity. As the world around her surrendered to darkness cloaked in legality, Sophie whispered truth through leaflets and martyrdom, reminding us that the soul must never be outsourced to the state, that conscience is the last line of defence when power turns tyrannical. Her words echo not in speeches, but in the quiet refusal to lie.

She was just twenty-one years old when she stood before the Nazi People's Court, accused of treason for distributing leaflets calling for resistance against Hitler's regime. Her name was Sophie Scholl. A university student. A sister. A thinker. A torchbearer of conscience in a time when silence was safer.

Alongside her brother Hans and their friends in the White Rose resistance, Sophie dared to speak the truth in a kingdom of lies; not with rifles or riots, but with paper, ink, and moral fire. Her final words before execution were simple and immortal: "Such a fine, sunny day, and I have to go. But what does my death matter, if through us thousands of people are awakened and stirred to action?"

Sophie Scholl is not just a historical figure. She is a whisper from the soul, a voice reminding us that true resistance is not merely political; it is spiritual. Her legacy endures not because she won, but because she refused to surrender her light.

And yet today, the war for the soul grows harder to recognize, because it no longer marches in jackboots or speaks in thunder. It lives instead in algorithms, illusions, and endless distractions. The Matrix is no longer science fiction. It is the ambient fog that tells us comfort is more important than truth, that apathy is safer than courage, and that freedom is just another filter on a screen.

In this system, this algorithm of ephemeral existence, the greatest rebellion is not political, but spiritual. It is the decision to wake up. To see clearly. To choose the light, even when the darkness offers more immediate rewards. For what is at stake is not merely who governs the world, but whether we can govern our inner beings, the self-governance of our individual and collective soul, that is what will truly decide the future of democratic governance around the world.

"The Light of the Soul reveals the beauty in every being, reminding us that we are all interconnected in our humanity. In the embrace of light, the soul finds clarity; it is in this illumination that compassion and understanding flourish. The light within us is a beacon of hope, guiding our actions toward kindness and empathy. When the soul is nourished by light, it radiates love, inspiring others to rise above their shadows. True strength lies in the light of the soul, where integrity and virtue illuminate the path of righteousness."

14

THE SELF-INTERESTED SURRENDER OF THE SOUL.

TRADING OUR INNER STRUGGLE FOR OUTER COMFORT.

Chapter Contents.

When darkness reigns in the soul, it clouds judgment and distorts the lens through which we view the world. In the depths of darkness, the soul may lose its way, wandering into the realms of apathy and moral decay. For as the darkness takes hold, the soul's light dims, and the once vibrant colours of compassion turn to pale shades of indifference. The battle between light and dark within us shapes our character; it is in our choices, that result from our individual battles, that we either elevate our soul or succumb to the shadows."

Holding the Line at the Edge of the Abyss.

There are rare figures in history whose lives act as moral hinges, souls upon which the direction of nations can turn. They do not rise because the world is ready for them, but precisely because it is not. They step forward when others retreat. They stand still while the storm howls. They remain human in moments when humanity itself seems to be fading.

Abraham Lincoln was such a figure. A man burdened by the impossible, preserving a fractured Union while confronting the moral cancer of slavery, he could have surrendered to cynicism, to pragmatism, to political expediency. But he didn't. He wrestled with doubt. He mourned deeply. Yet he held fast to the belief that a nation could have a soul, and that it was worth saving.

And Sophie Scholl, young, brilliant, unflinchingly principled, saw the seductive machinery of Nazi authoritarianism for what it was and said "no". Her voice was small, her resistance fragile. She knew the cost of defiance. But she chose it anyway, casting leaflets like seeds into the wind, believing they might bloom in a future she would never see. Her execution was meant to silence her, but it made her immortal.

Both Lincoln and Scholl understood that the battle outside is never separate from the battle within. The crisis of a nation is always, at its core, a crisis of conscience. They remind us of what it means to live in integrity. To struggle, not just against external injustice, but against the internal temptation to look away. To bend. To comply. They held the line, not with weapons, but with the quiet ferocity of an un-surrendered soul.

But what happens when that inner line of resistance is no longer held? When a society grows tired of the struggle? When it begins to abandon its internal discipline, its ethical bearings, its moral north?

For while history lifts up its heroes, the fate of nations is most often determined by the broader moral climate of the people themselves. And when that climate begins to change, when convenience outweighs conviction, when fear trumps freedom, when apathy overtakes empathy, then the soul of a society begins to erode.

This erosion is rarely loud. It does not always announce itself in the form of a dictator or a violent revolution. More often, it seeps in slowly. Through the language of distraction. Through the cult of personality. Through the elevation of wealth over wisdom, spectacle over substance, domination over dialogue. It happens in news cycles and social feeds, in boardrooms and classrooms, in the corners of conversations where no one speaks up anymore.

It happens when the individual ceases to see themselves as part of a greater moral struggle. When people become spectators in their own story, outsourcing their convictions to movements, influencers, or ideologies that promise simplicity in exchange for submission.

The surrender of the soul does not begin with a gun to the head. It begins when we stop asking questions. When we silence the still, small voice inside us. When we trade our inner struggle for outer comfort.

Abraham Lincoln once warned that "the dogmas of the quiet past are inadequate to the stormy present," and Sophie Scholl warned her fellow Germans that "somebody, after all, had to make a start." Both understood that moral clarity is not inherited. It must be fought for every generation anew.

We now live in a time when that fight has been deferred, delayed, and in some corners, denied altogether. This chapter is not just a critique of political decay. It is a lament for spiritual surrender. It is a map of the slow descent that follows when the soul of a people gives way, when the inner fire grows cold, and society forgets that democracy is not a system; it is a struggle. Primarily a moral one. And it never ends. Because when a society stops wrestling with itself, it does not find peace, it finds rot. And in that rot, the seeds of tyranny take root.

The Light of The Soul.

Wisdom in The Mind, Love in The Emotions, and Integrity in The Will.

The concept of the soul has long been a subject of philosophical, spiritual, and psychological inquiry for centuries, often regarded as the "essence of our being." It encapsulates what could be simply described as "the trifecta of our psychological being", our mind, our emotions, and our will.

It is Intellect, or **Mind,** where a person does their conscious thinking, it is **Emotion** where a person experiences their conscious feelings, and it is **Will** where a person gives attention, sets intention, and subsequently behaves consciously in accordance with what it is thinking (intellect), or feeling (emotion), the ever-changing moment-by-moment activities of our Mind and our Emotions.

Throughout history, great spiritual teachers, philosophers, and psychologists have sought to define the essence of human goodness, those aspects of the soul that enable individuals and societies to function in unity, peace, and prosperity.

This essence, which we may call the Light Side of the Soul, represents "the highest virtues" of the human being and as such the human Mind, Emotions, and Will as they manifest in alignment with timeless wisdom, the "advices of the essence in times long past." It is the force that fosters harmony, both within individuals and among nations, serving as the foundation for a just and flourishing society.

The Mind, when aligned with the Light Side of the Soul, seeks "truth, wisdom, and understanding". It is not clouded by "deception, ignorance, or selfish ambition", but is driven by a sincere quest for knowledge and enlightenment. Spiritual teachers like the Buddha and Jesus emphasized the importance of right thought and mindfulness, urging individuals to cultivate clarity and discernment. The apostle Paul said, "let your mind dwell on these things that are right, and just, and honourable."

A society in which the Mind operates under the Light Side of the Soul values education, critical thinking, and open discourse. It promotes intellectual honesty and fosters environments where people can seek and share truth without fear. When truth is cherished, policies and systems of government are created that serve the common good rather than the interests of the few, leading to relative societal peace.

The Emotions emanating from "a mind aligned" with the Light Side of The Soul, through "love, compassion, and empathy". These qualities transcend mere sentimentality; they form the core of ethical living and are central to the teachings of Jesus, Confucius, and other spiritual teachers such as the Dalai Lama. Love calls for selflessness, compassion for understanding, and empathy for the ability to see the world through another's eyes.

When individuals cultivate these emotions, society functions on the principles of kindness, generosity, and mutual support. Social policies prioritize care for the vulnerable, economic systems ensure dignity for all, and conflicts are resolved through dialogue rather than violence. A world governed by love and empathy naturally fosters peace, reducing division and hostility among individuals, nations and cultures.

The Will, when guided by the Light Side of the Soul, "exhibits integrity, courage, and a sense of higher purpose". It is the force that compels individuals to stand for justice, to resist corruption, and to act in alignment with ethical principles, even when facing adversity.

The Bhagavad Gita's teachings on righteous action, Kant's philosophy of moral duty, and the Holocaust survivor Viktor Frankl's insights on finding meaning, all emphasize the necessity of a strong and principled Will in achieving both personal fulfillment and societal progress. Jesus referenced the involvement of the will with the words, "not my will but thy will be done", prioritising divine integrity over personal agony. That is the story of the cross.

A society driven by integrity and courage stands resilient against oppression, corruption, and moral decay. Economic practices are rooted in fairness rather than exploitation, leadership is marked by accountability rather than self-interest, and social movements thrive on collective resolve for a better future. Such a society does not simply survive, it thrives.

But better still, when all three, the Mind, the Emotions, and the Will align with the Light Side of the Soul, individuals contribute to a collective reality where unity, peace, and prosperity become the natural order. Nations built on wisdom, compassion, and integrity create economies that value cooperation over competition, social structures that uplift rather than divide, and cultures that celebrate rather than fear diversity.

The great spiritual and philosophical traditions have always pointed toward this possibility, a world where human potential is fully realized in harmony with the greater whole. Thus, the Light Side of the Soul is not merely an abstract ideal, but a practical higher force that determines the destiny of individuals and civilizations alike.

By cultivating "wisdom in the Mind, love in the Emotions, and integrity in the Will", humanity can move toward a future where societies function as one, thriving in peace, social unity, and economic justice. It is not just a dream, it is not wishful thinking, it is a vision as ancient as it is urgent, calling upon each individual and every generation to live the Light within through their Mind, through their Emotions, and with their Will.

THE DARK SIDE OF THE SOUL.

Now on the opposite side of the light of life, so to speak, we see "the dark side of our Soul." Throughout human history, the concept of the "dark side of the soul" has been a subject of fascination and contemplation. This notion refers to the hidden, often repressed aspects of our psyche that emerge under stress, particularly during periods of emotional, financial, or even relationship distress. This trinity of distresses can manifest in various forms, including anxiety, depression, anger, frustration, and a sense of hopelessness.

These states can lead individuals to experience a profound internal struggle, where the pressures of their circumstances clash with their values and beliefs. For instance, financial hardship may compel a person to make decisions that contradict their moral principles, such as lying on a loan application or engaging in unethical business practices. Similarly, emotional turmoil can lead to feelings of resentment, anger, or despair, which may prompt individuals to act in ways that are inconsistent with their character.

When faced with adversity, the human psyche often resorts to defence mechanisms that can reveal its darker aspects. Fear and desperation can lead to a survival instinct that prioritizes self-preservation over ethical considerations. This phenomenon is evident in various psychological theories, including Sigmund Freud's concept of the id, which represents our primal desires and instincts.

In times of distress, the id may overpower the superego, which embodies our moral compass, leading to actions that are driven by immediate gratification rather than long-term ethical implications. Moreover, the social environment plays a crucial role in shaping our responses to distress. In a society that often equates success with financial stability, individuals may feel immense pressure to conform to certain standards.

This pressure can exacerbate feelings of inadequacy and lead to morally questionable behaviour as individuals seek to maintain their status or alleviate their suffering. The dark side of the soul, therefore, is not only a personal struggle but also a reflection of societal values that prioritize success over integrity.

The impact of distress on our moral compass can be profound and lasting. When individuals engage in unethical behaviour out of desperation, or sometimes purely through self-interest, it can create a cycle of moral disengagement. This cycle occurs when people cognitively rationalize their actions, convincing themselves that their circumstances justify their behaviour.

Over time, this rationalization can erode their ethical standards, leading to a gradual desensitization to wrongdoing. The once-clear boundaries of right and wrong become blurred, making it increasingly difficult to return to a state of moral clarity. Furthermore, the consequences of such actions can perpetuate a sense of guilt and shame, further complicating the individual's relationship with their moral compass.

The internal conflict between one's actions and beliefs can lead to a profound sense of disillusionment, resulting in a fractured identity. This struggle can manifest in various ways, including increased anxiety, depression, and a sense of alienation from oneself and others.

However in saying all that, the dark side of the soul is an intrinsic part of the human experience, particularly during times of emotional or financial distress. As individuals confront their vulnerabilities, the pressures of their circumstances can lead to a re-evaluation of their moral compass. The emergence of darker impulses, driven by fear and desperation, can result in actions that contradict one's ethical beliefs, creating a cycle of moral disengagement and internal conflict.

Understanding this phenomenon is crucial for fostering resilience and promoting ethical behaviour, as it highlights the importance of self-awareness and the need for supportive environments that encourage individuals to navigate their struggles without compromising their values. Ultimately, confronting the dark side of the soul is not only a personal journey but also a collective responsibility to cultivate a society that values integrity and compassion, even in the face of adversity.

THE SURRENDER OF THE SOUL: WHEN SOCIETY ABANDONS ITS INNER STRUGGLE.

Throughout history, the tension between the Light Side and the Dark Side of the Soul has been a defining force of human existence, a tug-of-war between higher ideals and base impulses, justice and tyranny, empathy and fear. This war plays out not only on the grand stage of government, politics, and culture but also within the quiet recesses of the individual conscience.

When societies are healthy, they wrestle with this conflict, acknowledging the complexity of human nature and the importance of balancing these opposing forces. However, when a society no longer engages in this internal struggle but surrenders to one side, usually the Dark Side, the consequences can be both profound and tragic.

When a society surrenders to the Dark Side without question, it often begins with the erosion of the collective conscience. Empathy, once the foundation of social cohesion, gives way to fear, and justice becomes a distant ideal, overshadowed by the allure of control. It is no longer a society that questions the morality of its actions or policies, but one that simply complies with the status quo. The internal struggle that forces individuals and groups to reflect on their values, to ask whether they are acting justly or out of self-interest, is suppressed.

In such a society, the concept of truth becomes malleable. Facts are no longer the guiding principles for action, but tools to be manipulated in service of those in power. Lies, propaganda, and misinformation become the weapons of choice for those who wish to maintain control. The individual, once capable of navigating the complexities of good and evil, now finds themselves overwhelmed by the certainty and simplicity of one-sided narratives.

A society that surrenders to the Dark Side becomes ripe for authoritarianism. Power is consolidated in the hands of those who exploit the fear and ignorance of the masses, stripping away the capacity for critical thinking.

The masses, seduced by promises of security or national greatness, abandon their moral compass, accepting control without resistance. Leaders who rise in such an environment are often those who promise to rid the world of complexity, offering clear-cut solutions that appeal to the basest instincts.

In this state of surrender, the ethical dimensions of governance dissolve. The power of the state shifts from a protector of rights to a force of oppression, manipulating laws and systems to serve its own interests. Dissent is criminalized, and those who challenge the established order are vilified as enemies of the state. The delicate balance of rights and responsibilities that underpins a functioning democracy is replaced by the tyrannical logic of might over right. And then comes the cost of that capitulation to the dark side, individually and collectively.

The surrender to the Dark Side has a deeply spiritual cost. When the individual or society forfeits the internal struggle between light and dark, the soul becomes dulled. The search for meaning, truth, and moral clarity is no longer pursued with the same intensity. Instead, convenience, security, and power take precedence. The individual's connection to their deeper, more spiritual self is severed, and the quest for personal growth and understanding is abandoned.

In such a state, there is a profound loss of hope. The soul becomes enslaved by the very forces it once sought to overcome. Human creativity, innovation, and compassion, qualities that emerge from a healthy inner struggle are stifled, and society stagnates. People begin to live not as active agents of their fate but as passive recipients of whatever the powers that be dictate. The very essence of what it means to be human is compromised when the war for the soul is no longer fought.

THE INEVITABLE COST TO SOCIETY, THE UNRAVELLING OF DEMOCRACY.

A society that no longer grapples with the war between the Light and Dark Side of the Soul faces an inevitable unravelling of its democratic structures.

Democracy thrives on the exchange of ideas, the rigorous questioning of authority, and the willingness of citizens to hold their leaders accountable. When a society surrenders to one side of the inner conflict, democracy becomes a hollow shell. The checks and balances that once kept power in check erode, and the governing class becomes a self-serving oligarchy.

Without the internal struggle for justice, empathy, and truth, the very foundation of democratic governance, public participation, civil discourse, and the rule of law, begins to disintegrate. Leaders emerge who claim to be above reproach, immune to the critical gaze of the populace, and their decisions are no longer subject to the scrutiny of a well-informed, morally engaged citizenry. The people, disillusioned and detached, no longer see themselves as stewards of their own democracy but as subjects under the rule of power.

If the world is to avoid the dangers of surrendering to the Dark Side, it is crucial that individuals and societies reignite the internal struggle between light and dark. This does not mean rejecting power altogether or denying the existence of complex challenges that demand decisive leadership. Rather, it means constantly questioning the path that power takes, holding leaders accountable for their actions, and never abandoning the pursuit of justice, truth, and empathy.

The war between the Light and Dark Side of the Soul is not one that can be won permanently. It is an ongoing battle that requires vigilance, self-reflection, and an unwavering commitment to the betterment of both the individual and society. When this struggle is abandoned, the consequences are grave: fear, control, and lies will triumph, and the soul of the nation will wither.

But when we embrace this war, confronting both our personal and collective darkness while striving to illuminate the path forward with truth and justice, the human spirit can once again rise to its fullest potential.

In the end, the war between the Light and Dark is not only a battle of ideas or political forces but a struggle within each of us. To surrender to one side without question is to surrender to the darkness within ourselves. But to wrestle, to question, and to seek the light, is to reaffirm the potential for growth, renewal, and moral clarity. This struggle is the heart of our humanity, and it is what will ultimately guide us toward a brighter future.

When the Ballot Box Becomes a Battle for the Soul, The Vote Becomes a Moral Act.

In every age, a society reaches moments of reckoning, when the decisions of the many shape the future for generations to come. These moments do not arrive with the fanfare of destiny but often in the quiet simplicity of a vote, a choice, a signature at the bottom of a ballot. Yet beneath this ordinary act lies something far more profound: the eternal war between the Light Side and the Dark Side of the Soul.

The 2024 presidential election was not just a contest between two candidates, Donald Trump and Kamala Harris, it was a referendum on the moral and spiritual trajectory of the United States. It was a test of whether the nation still wrestles with its inner tensions between empathy and fear, justice and control, truth and lies, or whether it has grown weary of that struggle and is now willing to surrender entirely to one side.

Voting has always been political, but it is also deeply moral. In casting a vote, we reveal not only our preferences but our values, what we are willing to tolerate, excuse, or even embrace in the pursuit of power. When citizens vote in alignment with the Light Side of the Soul, they vote with conscience, empathy, and a long view of justice. They seek leaders who may not be perfect, but who respect the democratic process, who strive to unify rather than divide, and who are accountable to truth rather than to their own ambition.

But when voters are guided by the Dark Side, elections become rituals of resentment. They are less about building a better society and more about punishing perceived enemies. In such a state, democracy is hollowed out from within, not by military coups or explicit dictatorships, but by the people themselves, who mistake domination for leadership and cruelty for strength.

THE CHOICES WERE OBVIOUS, TRUMP VERSUS HARRIS: A DEFINING CONTRAST.

In the 2024 presidential race, Donald Trump represented a return not merely to a previous presidency, but to an ethos rooted in fear and authoritarian instinct. His first term showed the country how democratic institutions could be weakened from within: the undermining of the free press, the corrosion of independent oversight, the vilification of dissent, and the transformation of public service into personal loyalty.

His second term, now being realized, was projected to be even more extreme. Harris expressed this with the words, "imagine Trump without guardrails". His second term, now stacked with loyalists, unbound by the need to seek re-election, and driven by a desire for retribution against political adversaries, is now marking a shift not just in policy, but in the very architecture of American democracy.

Kamala Harris, by contrast, represented the continuity of democratic norms, however imperfect, however flawed. Her candidacy may not have ignited revolutionary passion, but it signalled a belief in process, pluralism, and the rule of law.

A vote for Harris would not necessarily have been a vote for idealism, but it would have been a vote to preserve the space where idealism can still exist. It would have been a vote that kept the inner struggle alive, kept empathy and justice within reach of power, and prevented the machinery of government from being captured wholly by a will to dominate.

You see elections are not only about policy. They are about the direction of the collective soul. When a people stop struggling, when they no longer ask whether their leaders reflect their highest values but instead reward those who confirm their lowest instincts, they have, in essence, surrendered. They no longer engage in the vital tension between right and wrong, between the Light and Dark, but allow power to calcify in the hands of those who seek only to expand it.

The 2024 election was, in this way, a choice between two futures: one in which democracy remained an unfinished and flawed but still vibrant experiment, and one in which democracy is a shell, manipulated to serve the ego of a man who sees institutions not as sacred trusts but as obstacles to be crushed.

The most dangerous aspect of the Dark Side is not that it declares itself openly, but that it cloaks itself in patriotism, law and order, and tradition. It speaks in the language of "saving the country" or "restoring greatness," when in truth it seeks only obedience and submission. In 2024, this disguise was in full effect.

Many were tempted by the promise of simplicity in a world of chaos. But simplicity, in the hands of the power-hungry, is a trap. Complexity, moral, political, spiritual, is where the Light Side lives. It demands engagement. It demands humility. It demands struggle.

What the 2024 election ultimately asked the American people was this: "Are we still a people willing to wrestle with ourselves? Are we still willing to examine our fears, to confront our biases, to reject leaders who offer easy enemies instead of hard solutions? Or have we become so exhausted by the struggle that we are ready to hand the keys over to autocracy, simply because it asks nothing of us but obedience?

Democracy is not sustained by structures alone. It is sustained by the inner lives of its citizens, their capacity for self-reflection, their hunger for justice, their resistance to fear. If that inner life goes dark, then no constitution, no law, no institution can preserve freedom.

In 2024, every vote was more than a choice between Trump and Harris. It reflected whether the American public still believed in the Light Side of the Soul, the side that values truth, justice, and empathy, or whether a majority had given themselves over to the Dark Side, trading freedom for fury, and democracy for dominion. The 2024 election was not just about deciding who would lead the nation. It was about deciding what kind of nation America has become, and what kind of soul it will carry forward.

"When autocracy seizes the reins, it first hollows out the institutions that once held it in check, leaving behind empty shells draped in patriotic banners. The first sign of tyranny is not tanks in the streets, but the quiet evacuation of expertise from the heart of government. Dictators do not destroy governments overnight, they gut them from within, replacing public servants with loyalists and truth with obedience. For in the autocrat's playbook, talent is a threat, truth is a weapon, and governance is an obstacle to be reprogrammed for control. The agencies that once served the people now become instruments of power, staffed not by professionals, but by political puppets."

15

The Implementation of an Autocracy.

Puppets Installed, Expertise Purged, Power Centralized.

Chapter Contents.

From Reform to Ruin: DOGE and the Rise of Techno-Autocracy: Institutions as Living Memory: The Irreversibility of Systemic Collapse: The Trifecta of God, Gold, and Governance and its Inevitable But Predictable Fusion.

"The bureaucracy, sometimes dull but still vital, becomes dangerous when hollowed, because it is no longer a tool to resist tyranny, but rather a tool to transmit it. A republic does not necessarily die in battle, it can be bled, slowly, through the dismantling of its institutions. The machinery of state, once powered smoothly by public service, then begins to whir and vibrate erratically with a friction without end".

From Reform to Ruin.

The rhetoric of reform has long been a political tool in Washington. Politicians across the spectrum speak of cutting waste, reducing bureaucracy, and making government more efficient. But what is happening under the second Trump administration, fortified by the radical influence of Elon Musk and the DOGE initiative, is something far more sweeping and destructive. This is not reform. It is systematic ruination.

The DOGE effort, named both ironically and in an aspirational way after the decentralized meme-cryptocurrency Dogecoin, has become a vehicle for executing a deeper ideological purge of the federal state. Thousands of civil servants, from cybersecurity experts to public health officials, have been dismissed or driven to resign, stripping the federal bureaucracy of vital knowledge and expertise. What remains is a skeletal government apparatus, reshaped to serve the ideological whims of its leaders rather than the enduring needs of the republic.

Trump's second term marks a dramatic escalation over his first. No longer checked by inexperience, internal resistance, or lingering norms, free from prosecution, this administration is advancing a deliberate effort to neutralize the government's capacity to govern. The aim is not just to shrink government, it is to sever the state's connection to professionalism, science, and continuity.

Trump's 2025 administration is all about the dismantling of institutional knowledge, the rise of techno-authoritarianism, and the nearly impossible task of rebuilding what has been lost. We are living through a transformative moment, not just of policy shift, but of epistemic collapse. The consequences will not be measured in news cycles, but in generations.

This is not the chaotic attrition of a bloated bureaucracy, nor the random erosion caused by budgetary neglect. It is an orchestrated dismantling. Key agencies that once formed the backbone of American governance are being stripped of leadership, drained of talent, and reengineered to serve narrow political aims. At the heart of this effort lies a strategic understanding: control the mechanisms of enforcement, interpretation, and communication, and you control the state itself.

The Department of Justice has seen a significant turnover in senior prosecutors, many of whom were involved in investigations touching on presidential misconduct, corporate regulation, or white-collar crime. In their place are loyalists with mandates to shield allies and target opponents.

The Environmental Protection Agency has been gutted of career scientists and replaced with fossil-fuel friendly administrators whose chief task is to deregulate as swiftly as possible.

The State Department, once the jewel of American diplomacy, has been hollowed out to the point of near-irrelevance, with ambassadorial posts left unfilled and long-serving diplomats pushed out or muzzled.

Beyond the personnel shifts lies a deeper transformation: the repurposing of agencies to attack the very missions they once upheld. The Department of Education is tasked with undermining public schools; the Department of Homeland Security is weaponized for domestic political purposes; public health institutions are censored or ignored in times of crisis.

DOGE acts as the ideological and logistical engine behind much of this. Under Musk's influence, the vision of a decentralized, disruption-driven state has found fertile ground. Efficiency is redefined not as competence, but as compliance. Innovation means elimination. The bureaucratic state, designed to safeguard continuity and fairness, is seen as a drag on the swift exercise of executive power. The result is a gutted infrastructure that no longer operates for the collective benefit but as an extension of private will and presidential ambition.

What makes this moment especially perilous is not just the dismantling itself, but the speed and precision with which it is being carried out. Trump's first term was marked by trial and error, pushback from civil servants, and occasional court interventions. In his second term, those obstacles are being removed in real time. The administration is now armed with legal strategies, compliant judges, and a cadre of operatives who know exactly which levers to pull.

This is not the death of the administrative state, it is its repurposing. The machine still runs. But it no longer answers to the public.

DOGE AND THE RISE OF TECHNO-AUTOCRACY.

The DOGE initiative, under the stewardship of Elon Musk, is more than a bureaucratic project, it is the ideological crystallization of a techno-libertarian fantasy. At its core lies a belief that state functions can and should be reduced to algorithms, apps, and private command structures. This is governance by disruption: swift, personality-driven, and unconcerned with precedent or deliberation.

Musk's influence within this model cannot be overstated. His open contempt for regulators, his consolidation of media influence through platforms like X (formerly Twitter), and his affinity for authoritarian leaders around the world all point to a governing philosophy rooted in control without constraint. DOGE is the vehicle by which that vision is being imposed on the American administrative state.

Under DOGE, traditional checks on executive authority are bypassed through privatized systems of oversight and decision-making. Government IT systems, communications platforms, and contracting processes are increasingly run through Musk-linked entities or under his guidance. Instead of transparency, there is opacity. Instead of public deliberation, there is algorithmic decree.

The techno-autocracy being built does not seek to make government more responsive to the people, it seeks to make government more responsive to power, specifically the power of a narrow elite that sees itself as uniquely capable of solving complex problems. Yet what is lost in this shift is precisely what makes democratic governance durable: redundancy, accountability, and deliberation.

In this new model, speed is prioritized over wisdom. Loyalty is valued over competence. And scale, measured in media impact and disruption metrics, matters more than social consequence. This is not merely a change in tools; it is a transformation in the very logic of governance. It is government as startup: lean, fast, charismatic, and ultimately unsustainable.

In fusing Trumpism's authoritarian instincts with Musk's technological reach, DOGE represents a new form of power: one that strips the state of its public mission and reprograms it to serve a hybrid of corporate ambition and executive ego. It is not a glitch in the system. It is the system now.

INSTITUTIONS AS LIVING MEMORY.

Institutions are more than collections of rules and buildings, they are vessels of living memory. Within every agency, every bureau, every federal department, there resides an intergenerational lineage of knowledge, practice, and precedent. That lineage is not easily recreated. It is learned, transmitted, adapted. And when it is lost, it is not simply gone, it leaves behind a void. The problem is that many of the voting public of America don't understand this.

A recent New York Times survey (April 2025) revealed that a little more than a third, 36%, say that any significant changes Trump makes whilst in office will not have any long-term effects once he leaves office. They are wrong. The vessels of living memory within a government, once removed, can take decades to be rebuilt.

The mass departure of experienced civil servants is not just a labour issue. It is an epistemological crisis. In departments ranging from Treasury to Agriculture, career officials carry institutional memory that allows for nuanced decision-making, crisis response, and continuity between administrations. These officials are the ones who know how a system responded to a previous disaster, how a policy evolved over decades, how to navigate the arcane processes that make government function.

The loss of that memory cripples the state's ability to govern effectively. It creates vulnerabilities in cybersecurity, in emergency response, in foreign diplomacy. It turns regulatory agencies into hollow shells, unable to meaningfully enforce or interpret the laws they are charged with upholding. And it leaves behind a cadre of inexperienced replacements, often chosen for loyalty over competence, who lack the contextual understanding necessary for informed governance.

Rebuilding this institutional memory is not a matter of hiring. It is a matter of time. Expertise takes years to develop. Trust between departments, relationships with international partners, and fluency in bureaucratic languages do not materialize overnight. A future administration seeking to restore the integrity of the federal government would face an uphill battle, not just in staffing, but in reknitting the intellectual and operational fabric of the state.

Moreover, many of those who have left are unlikely to return. They have seen the fragility of the system, the ease with which years of service can be discarded for political expediency. The brain drain now underway is not only depleting the federal government of talent, but also deterring the next generation from entering public service altogether.

The institutional memory of a government is not something you can code, upload, or outsource. It is embedded in people, in their minds, their ethics, their accumulated experience. Once purged, it cannot be restored at the push of a button.

The Irreversibility of Systemic Collapse.

There is a moment in every system's decline when recovery becomes less a question of will and more a question of physics. That moment, in American governance, may have already passed. The damage being wrought by the Trump-Musk regime is not just about lost personnel or sabotaged policies, it is about eroded trust, frayed networks, and institutional rot that cannot be simply reversed with the stroke of a pen.

Once institutional legitimacy is lost, once people stop believing that agencies are acting in the public interest, restoring that faith becomes a herculean task. The public sees dysfunction, corruption, and chaos, and the idea of an impartial state begins to seem like a myth. In its place rises a cynical expectation: that government serves only the powerful, that rules are flexible, and that institutions are tools of private vengeance or profit. This cynicism is corrosive. It breeds disengagement, radicalism, and ultimately, authoritarianism.

The machinery of governance is delicate. It requires routine maintenance, cultural continuity, and sustained investment. None of these can be achieved in a political environment dominated by disruption for its own sake. DOGE thrives on collapse; it needs the chaos it helps create in order to justify its own necessity. This feedback loop, where dysfunction fuels further centralization of power, pushes the system toward a point where re-democratization is not just unlikely, but structurally impossible.

Future administrations may try to rebuild. They may appoint experts, re-staff agencies, rewrite rules. But without the institutional scaffolding of trust and memory, these efforts will be akin to rebuilding a cathedral with no blueprint, no stonemasons, and no public support. The edifice may stand, but it will be hollow.

This is the danger America now faces: not just that government is being destroyed, but that it is being reshaped in ways that make its former shape unrecoverable. We are not merely living through the decline of institutions. We are witnessing the emergence of something new and far more dangerous in their place.

The consequences of this hollowing out will stretch far beyond any one presidency. They will linger in the bones of the bureaucracy, in the public's distrust of government, and in the degraded expectations of what governance is meant to do. The legacy of this era will not be written in a single scandal or a sudden collapse, but in the slow and steady erosion of the state's capacity to function, to serve, to protect.

This is the great paradox: the more the government is stripped of its ability to help, the more it becomes a tool of harm. Agencies that once issued safety regulations or monitored environmental hazards now issue threats to political enemies or subsidies to favoured cronies. The very language of governance is inverted. Regulation becomes punishment. Deregulation becomes liberation. Public service becomes public spectacle.

In the long aftermath, a future administration will confront not just a gutted federal workforce and hollowed institutions, but a political culture poisoned by misinformation, by ideological capture, and by a performative cruelty that has become the norm. The challenge will not only be administrative, but it will also be cultural and psychological. How do you persuade a generation raised on chaos that structure is not oppression? That law is not inherently partisan. That expertise is not elitism.

This is the work of reconstruction. It will require not just policy, but pedagogy. Not just new appointments, but new imaginations. For those who believe in the promise of democratic governance, the path forward is long and uncertain. But to begin that journey, we must first understand the depth of the collapse we are witnessing. And we must tell the truth about it, not just for ourselves, but for those who may one day try to rebuild.

The Trifecta of God, Gold, and Governance and its Inevitable but Predictable Fusion.

History is littered with cautionary tales of what happens when faith, finances, and politics intertwine too deeply. Each on its own wields formidable influence, faith shapes hearts and minds, finance dictates economic realities, and politics governs the structure of society.

But when all three are fused into a singular force, the result is not balance, but domination; theocracy, plutocracy, and autocracy converging, to create a system where power justifies itself in divine terms, wealth secures its permanence, and governance becomes a mere tool for the elite.

The danger in such a union lies in its ability to manufacture legitimacy. When political power is cloaked in religious righteousness, dissent becomes heresy.

When economic power is justified as divine favour, inequality is reframed as moral order. When governance serves both faith and wealth, the interests of a few masquerade as the will of the people, or worse, the will of God. Such a system, whether in the form of medieval feudalism, imperial rule, or modern corporate-political alliances, inevitably leads to corruption, suppression, and stagnation.

Consider theocracies of the past, where rulers wielded religion to justify absolute power, ensuring obedience not just to laws but to doctrines they themselves controlled. Consider oligarchies, where economic barons dictate policy, turning governance into an extension of their financial empires.

Now, imagine these forces acting as one, a structure where faith demands loyalty, wealth purchases influence, and governance enforces the will of both. It is the ultimate consolidation of power, leaving no room for opposition, no avenue for reform, and no escape for those caught beneath its weight.

The PayPal Mafia that I spoke of, essentially privatized critical public functions, banking, surveillance, media, and political discourse Their rise reflects how modern oligarchy is no longer about controlling land or factories but about controlling information and digital finance, witnessing them linked in a type of God, Gold, and Governance control alliance.

They shape digital culture, narratives, and belief systems, (God-spiritual or ideological power), they control fintech and digital transactions, (Gold- economic power), and they influence government policy and elections (Governance -political power).

That unholy trinity of God, Gold, and Governance is the oldest empire the world has ever known, and the most enduring oppressor of men's souls. A ruler who claims divine authority, finances his power with stolen gold, and silences dissent with the law, is the most dangerous enemy of freedom. Faith should guide the soul, not the state. Gold should build society, not own it. Governance should serve the people, not the bishop, nor the bankers, nor the billionaires."

This is the peril of mixing God, Gold, and Governance. It is a trifecta that, rather than uplifting societies, shackles them. It distorts democracy into theocracy, free markets into monopolies, and leadership into rule by divine right. The question is not whether history will repeat itself, but whether we will recognize the pattern in time and be courageous enough to resist it.

The hollowing out of the state, now nearing completion, is more than an institutional crisis. It is a crisis of memory, of meaning, and of legitimacy. The institutions Americans once took for granted as imperfect but necessary guardians of public life are being erased or mutated beyond recognition. And when institutions die, so too do the possibilities they once protected.

The question now is not whether America can return to what was lost. It cannot. The world has changed too much. The question is whether the American people can build something new that learns from what has been destroyed, something more resilient, more inclusive, more democratic. That is the work ahead.

But first, the deniers and rationalisers and loyalists must stop pretending that this is temporary, or that it can be undone without sacrifice. The stakes are generational. The battle is epistemic. And the clock is running. What has been hollowed out can only be rebuilt by those who still believe in the soul of the republic, and who are willing to fight for it.

Chaos doesn't appear out of thin air. It builds slowly, steadily, in the silence between what was promised and what was delivered. It grows in the space where faith once lived. And when enough people feel betrayed for long enough, the storm breaks. We are living through one such moment now.

As protests swell across the nation in response to Donald Trump's second presidency, we're witnessing not just a political backlash, but a generational reckoning. The kind we've seen before. The kind that reminds us history is not a straight line, it's a circle, and we're right back where we've been.

The Sixties taught us this lesson first. Back then, hope was currency. The Civil Rights Movement rose with the voice of Martin Luther King Jr., a man who dared to believe that America could live up to its creed. But the dream he carried was met with dogs, batons, and bullets. Peaceful resistance was rewarded with state violence. Young people asked for answers and were handed a one-way ticket to Vietnam.

The government spoke of liberty while silencing its most courageous voices. King fell. Malcolm fell. Bobby and Jack followed. The dream didn't die in one moment, it died in pieces, scattered across Selma, Memphis, Chicago, and Saigon.

And then, as the music faded, Don McLean gave it a name. "I saw Satan laughing with delight / the day the music died." But what he captured wasn't just grief, it was the quiet horror of realizing the system you believed in was never going to save you. That realization, that betrayal is what gives birth to chaos. It's not madness. It's the natural consequence of gaslighted hope.

We're there again now. The signs are unmistakable. A government once more pretending not to hear, while the streets fill with voices it refuses to see. Chaos doesn't knock politely, it kicks the door in. And when the music dies, history doesn't mourn. It roars.

"This is the final hour when history waits for our answer; will we rise to the call of conscience or sink beneath the weight of our own indifference. In this decisive hour, the soul of a nation is not saved by words or wishes, but by the courage to act while there is still time. We are living through the hinge of history, and the door to the future swings only once, either we push it open, or it slams shut behind us. For the final hour demands that we become more than witnesses to history, we must become its authors."

CONCLUSION

"Between Twilight and the Final Hour"

> "The world is teetering at the edge of change, there is an urgency of the moment, that society must recognize, face up to, and deal with. This present moment is now the "final hour" of decision and action. The world is at a pivotal time, right on the cusp of a major shift, and the people in particular the American people, must decide if they will rise or let the moment pass."

In this present hour the American people find themselves at a critical crossroads in the moral and political evolution of their society, a place hauntingly familiar yet charged with even greater stakes. The echoes of the 1960's rumble all around: mass discontent, the fracture lines of culture wars, the disillusionment with government and media institutions.

But this time, it is chaos on steroids, turbocharged by the algorithms of manipulation, by a red-pill reality that promises awakening but often delivers deeper enslavement. The American experiment, once a beacon of democratic resilience, now teeters on the edge of an authoritarian precipice, its citizens increasingly numb to the erosion of freedoms they once thought unassailable.

The warning signs are everywhere. Truth is battered daily in the public square, repackaged into commodities for clicks and profit. Governance, once animated by spirited debate and common purpose, now staggers under the weight of cynicism, corruption, and oligarchic capture. The soul of the nation, and indeed, the future of free societies everywhere hangs precariously in the balance.

Yet history reminds us that moments of profound peril are also moments of profound possibility. We must recognize that what is needed now, not just in America but around the world is not just critique, but courageous creation: the rise of a true Fifth Estate, a new moral and informational vanguard built not on the shifting sands of profit-driven media, but rooted deeply in truth, in unflinching conscience, and in public action.

This new Fifth Estate must be more than passive information-sharing. It must march. It must sing. It must call. It must gather millions, peacefully but powerfully, to reclaim the public square. Just as Martin Luther King Jr. led the great Freedom Marches that stirred the conscience of a nation, so too must the American people, with the same passion, discipline, and hope, gather under banners of truth, justice, and the common good.

The American people must become the Pied Pipers of a new world awakening, leading their fellow citizens of the world away from the toxic brink of division, fear, and authoritarianism. If the great revolutions of history have taught us anything, it is that systems of oppression fall not simply because they are evil, but because ordinary people, moved by an extraordinary sense of purpose, refuse to be complicit.

In this spirit, we must all reject the apathy and despair that have become the currency of our age. We must declare, with our feet, our voices, and our hearts, that the future belongs not to the manipulators, not to the tyrants, but to those who still believe that democracy is worth fighting for. The hour is late, but it is not too late. The path forward is not without danger, but it is lit by the embers of every soul who has dared to dream of a better world and dared even more to make it so.

This is the American public's moment of truth. It needs to stand in a time that for many probably feels like the 1960's reborn, only wilder, harsher, and now fuelled by forces that move faster than their ancestors could have dreamed. The spirit of rebellion lives, but so does the threat of ruin.

The Matrix red pill that promised a Trump style economic awakening has now only delivered deeper illusions, leading the U.S.A. closer and closer to the cliffs of authoritarian rule. Every day, the world watches American democratic governance, once a standard bearer for all western nations, progressively bleed away under the twin knives of apathy and manipulation.

And yet, beneath the noise, there is I believe still a heartbeat. It is the heartbeat of history calling the American people to remember who they are. It is the spirit of "freedom marches" pounding again in the veins of ordinary people who know, deep in their bones, that democracy is not a spectator sport. It demands passion. It demands sacrifice. It demands that all rise together.

Now, more than ever, the world needs a Fifth Estate, not built on algorithms or clicks, but on truth, courage, and love for the fragile dream of human dignity. A living movement, not a dead media structure. A pulsing march of millions, peaceful and irresistible, led not by the loudest voices but by the clearest and cleanest hearts.

The ordinary citizens must become the Pied Pipers of a new freedom song, for the politicians through self-interest seem reluctant to take a stand, leading their brothers and sisters out of the maze of lies and fear, and back into the sunlight of civic hope. The citizens must carry signs and torches and the fierce beauty of knowing that "the arc of the moral universe still bends toward justice", but only if all in unison pull it there with their own hands.

The time for silent outrage is over. The time for mourning in private is over. Now is the time to march, physically and digitally. Today, as in another turbulent age, the soul of America, and as such the soul of the free world is being tested. The chaos of the 1960's has returned to America, amplified a thousandfold by technology, fear, and division. A red-pill reality, once a cry for awakening, has become for too many a descent into deeper delusion.

The institutions of democracy, worn down by years of mistrust and manipulation, now tremble under the shadow of rising authoritarianism. The American people stand, not on the precipice of renewal, but on the very edge of a great forgetting: forgetting who they are, what they believe, and what sacrifices were made to bring them here. But history is not yet finished. Destiny is not yet sealed. The American people are not yet defeated, unless they choose to be.

A new force must arise: a Fifth Estate, armed not with weapons of war but with the invincible power of truth. A moral movement greater than any algorithm, stronger than any lie. The people must seize the mantle of peaceful resistance, as Martin Luther King Jr. did in another perilous time, and summon the courage to march by the millions, into the streets, into the public square, into the digital space, and into the soul of the nation itself.

These marches must not be mere demonstrations. They must be living, breathing acts of reclamation. They must shout to the heavens and whisper to the heart: democracy lives only so long as the people are willing to defend it. I say to the American people, you must be the Pied Pipers of renewal, not leading your fellow citizens to ruin, but leading them back to the sacred idea that government derives its legitimacy from the consent of the governed, and that truth must never bow to fear.

The twilight of the republic is upon every American citizen . But in every twilight, there is a choice: to surrender to the gathering dark, or to become the torchbearers of a new dawn. There is only one choice. Let history say of the current American generation: they were the generation that did not bow, did not break, and did not lose faith. Let history say of them: they marched, they podcasted, they tweeted, and they saved the dream.

The current generation is a generation standing between two worlds. Behind lies a dream, battered but not broken, the dream of democracy, of dignity, of a people who govern themselves. Before looms a nightmare, vivid and real, a world where truth is bent into weapons, where fear marches faster than hope, and where the great American experiment edges closer to authoritarian rule.

This is not the first time the soul of this great nation of America has been tested. The chaos that tore through the 1960's now returns, faster, sharper, wired directly into the people's minds by forces that seek to divide and conquer. The Matrix red pill once offered awakening, now it is a tool of manipulation, pulling millions into deeper illusions, numbing them to the daily crumbling of the freedoms they once cherished. But history's greatest truth has not changed:

"*When ordinary people rise with extraordinary courage, tyrants fall, and dreams endure*".

The Trump-Musk era has given the world a glimpse into a disturbing future, one where governance is neither accountable nor coherent, where the state exists not as a collective instrument of democratic will, but as a sandbox for authoritarian ambition and corporate disruption and greed. What we are seeing is not just a power grab. It is a redefinition of government itself: what it is for, who it serves, and who gets to shape its future.

Today, the American people must call forth a new Fifth Estate, not one corrupted by clicks and cynicism, but one born of truth, duty, and love for all that freedom, only freedom makes possible. It is not enough to share the truth; they must embody it. It is not enough to know the danger; they must answer it.

They must march psychologically, digitally, and physically. Like the freedom marchers who crossed Selma's bridge with nothing but hope and stubborn faith, they must take to the streets in numbers too great for the politicians to ignore and take to Tik Tok and Twitter with passion and persistence. They must be the new Pied

Pipers of the people, not leading them into ruin, but leading millions back toward the light, back toward a government by the people, for the people, and of the people.

Let their marches be peaceful, but fierce. Let their songs be of sorrow, righteous rage, but also of unstoppable hope. Let their tweets and posts righteously engage and if necessarily righteously enrage. Let their banners and their posts tell a story: that they remembered that they cared, and that they stood. Let it be written that when democracy faltered, they did not. Let it be remembered that this generation of Americans marched in one step and of one mind, and that in their marching, they rose and reclaimed their democratic future.